Bunker Hill
to
Bastogne

Bunker Hill
to
Bastogne

ELITE FORCES AND
AMERICAN SOCIETY

BRITON COOPER BUSCH

POTOMAC BOOKS, INC.
WASHINGTON, D.C.

Library of Congress Cataloging-in-Publication Data

Busch, Briton Cooper.
    Bunker Hill to Bastogne : elite forces and American society / Briton
    C. Busch.
       p. cm.
    Includes bibliographical references and index.
    ISBN 1-57488-775-0 (alk. paper)
       1.   Guards troops—United States—History. 2. United States—
       History, Military. 3.
    Sociology, Military—United States. I. Title.

   UA25.B87 2006
   356'.160973—dc22

                                        2005054497

Potomac Books, Inc.
22841 Quicksilver Drive
Dulles, Virginia 20166

First Edition

10 9 8 7 6 5 4 3 2 1

Contents

Publisher's Note

Briton Cooper Busch died before this book went into production. Aside from some minor corrections, based on peer reviews that he did not have the opportunity to read, we have published the book as he wrote it.

Illustrations

Preface

Some men are more effective than others at making war. There is no commonly accepted formula to explain why this is so, and why—all else being equal—such men are more likely to emerge victorious over their opponents. Thomas Wentworth Higginson put it well; as colonel (1862–64) of the First South Carolina Volunteers (later the 33d U.S. Colored Troops), a worthy regiment formed of ex-slaves, he had an opportunity to judge men in battle, whatever their color. "In almost every regiment, black or white, there are a score or two of men who are naturally daring, who really hunger after dangerous adventures, and are happiest when allowed to seek them. Every commander gradually finds out who these men are, and habitually uses them; certainly I had such and I remember with delight their bearing, their coolness, and their dash. . . . These picked men varied in other respects too; some were neat and well-drilled soldiers, while others were slovenly, heedless fellows—the despair of their officers at inspections, their pride on a raid. They were the natural scouts and rangers of the regiment; they had the two-o'clock-in-the-morning courage, which Napoleon thought so rare."[1]

Some causal factors can be identified, including such variables as individual intelligence, physical conditioning, training in martial skills, unit cohesion by reason of shared experiences and traditions, and leadership. On the battlefield, when such factors are found concentrated in a particular group of men, the conditions exist for what may be termed an elite unit. Military elites may be defined in various ways as will be seen in the pages below, but in general, for the purpose of this book, an elite formation is one which believes itself to be superior, is so viewed by peer formations in its own army and likewise by that army's commanders, and above all, is perceived to be so by its opponents. The reasons why they are elite are not always easily identified, let alone assigned a rank order of significance. Similarly, isolating a clear self-image, or the image perceived by peers and enemies, may be equally difficult. Once won, however, a reputation of superiority, of elite status, may be a contributing factor on the battlefield. Few Greeks wished to do battle with Spartans, or Europeans of the Napoleonic era to face the Emperor's Old Guard.

But this book is about American history. In that context, a special problem arises, since America's citizens have traditionally distrusted even the concept of a standing army. Past experience in both Europe and the colonies taught that such an institution could be used to subvert rights or freedoms that had been won at great cost. Given this attitude, it was not likely that military elites would flourish, and in a general sense they have not, at least not before the twentieth century. From pre-revolutionary days through World War II, America's elected leaders have found perpetual difficulty in maintaining a standing army of a size adequate to complement the citizen militia which was expected to respond to any serious emergency. In every crisis sudden expansion was therefore essential—most notably during the Civil War—followed, when the emergency had passed, by rapid demobilization. Effective military elites are not made in a day, and America's mobilization patterns mitigated against their creation as much as her anti-army sentiment.

Yet to such dominant tides there are always eddies and counter currents. American independence was won only through the searing experience of a major war. Every generation through the end of the twentieth century has experienced a war; some, such as the Civil War, were of equally determining impact upon American society. As a consequence, many of America's heroes have been military men. George Washington, the greatest hero of all as "father of his country," has always stood as a metaphor for America's military history: the capable civilian rising to extreme military challenges when the time came, yet always resisting the temptation in a time of crisis to replace civilian with military authority. On the other hand, America's roster of heroic images has long included esteemed elites, variously defined, from Rogers's Rangers at Fort Ticonderoga to the paratroopers at Normandy and the Marines at Iwo Jima.

It is the goal of this book to identify elite units from colonial days through World War II and, where possible, to explain how and why that elite status was gained—and sometimes lost. An essential part of that story is the question of by what means, if any, elite status—whether of individuals or entire units—has been instilled, singled out, or rewarded. The task is most complex, which perhaps explains why it has not before been attempted, at least to the author's knowledge, in the same way. The thesis of this work, however, is simple. Even though American society on the whole has regarded its military establishment as little more than an unfortunate necessity required mainly for dealing with such problems as intractable Indians or urban disorder, elite formations have always been there, certainly in war and often in peace. They have regularly been supported in their continued existence by popular myths, but as will be seen, the myths have not always corresponded to reality. Above all, American military history has, for better or worse, cherished its favorite image: the legendary rifleman/ranger.

A few limitations must be stated. With the exception of the Marines (whose history is treated in Chapter 6), discussion is limited to selected land and air forces, with apologies to the valiant Americans who fought at sea. Nor has any attempt been made to draw comparisons among American formations at a divisional or higher level, except when they were deliberately created to be elites. Units whose main purpose was not directly combat itself have not been included, even though some were certainly combat-capable and indeed saw considerable action, such as the combat engineers, or "Seabees," intelligence teams from the Office of Strategic Services, and so on. On the other hand, as will be seen, it has been necessary to consider a few institutions, such as the United States Military Academy at West Point, whose very existence helped shape general American attitudes toward military elites. Sometimes the decision to include or omit may seem arbitrary, but then defining "elite" ultimately proves rather subjective. The author can only claim that the list is his own, and that the hunt for America's military elites has been a great challenge, and a great pleasure.

Another pleasure, as with any book, is to acknowledge those who have helped along the way. This book originally began as a part of a larger project on military elites around the world, and I am grateful to the Colgate University Research Council for a Senior Faculty Leave which gave me a year to explore the military aspects of numerous cultures from Apaches to Zulus. Discussions with fellow historians over many years have helped shape my views, and I owe a substantial debt to a number of Colgate faculty as well as colleagues in the Society for Military History and the Western Front Association (in the latter case, above all WFA president, Ambassador Len Shurtleff, a former Marine himself). Professor Michael Neiberg of the U.S. Air Force Academy was kind enough to read the manuscript and make a number of very valuable suggestions. I owe special thanks to my friend and fellow military historian Lt. Col. Ed Erickson, not only for many interesting discussions but also for taking time from his own books on Turkish military history to read and comment upon my remarks on American history. Neighbor, biologist, and fellow martial arts devotee Tim McCay listened patiently as I tried out various ideas on him; his friendship and support have been invaluable.

Just as the project was well underway, it came to a halt as a result of intestinal cancer. I mention this simply to record the fact that this book would not have been possible without the strong support of many people at Colgate University, my professional home for forty years. My very great thanks to Jane Pinchin, Jack Dovidio, and Ellen Kraly, respectively president, dean of faculty, and director of social sciences, for their understanding and friendship. Without the expertise of the surgery, oncology, radiation oncology, and interventional radiology departments of the Teaching Hospital of SUNY Upstate Medical University in Syracuse, New York, I would not have had the occasion to write these words. Many friends and colleagues helped in various ways: my thanks always to Tom Brackett, Ray Douglas, Graham Hodges, Marvin Labatte, Mike Leach, and David Robinson, as well as to family members Deborah, Peter, Terry, Mary Kelly, Shelly, Carey, Marge, and Duane.

I owe special thanks which are impossible to convey in words to my son Philip, my daughter Leslie, and my wife Jill Harsin for their constant support. Only Jill, however, has shared every day, with never a complaint though inevitably the course of many of those days interfered with her own full-time teaching and writing on French history. Last but by no means least, Gretchen and Lili were always there with their sympathetic concern—but then that is ever the way of German Shepherds.

1 The Colonial Tradition

From the beginnings of colonial American society, military men played a critical role. Indeed, conflict with the indigenous peoples was not long in coming. Wisely, the earliest ventures to the New World commonly included trained soldiers who, like Miles Standish, captain of Plymouth's pilgrim defense force, or Capt. John Smith of Jamestown, had acquired significant military experience in European wars. Military organization of settler communities soon required virtually every man from sixteen years to sixty to possess a weapon and to serve in the town companies or "trainbands" which each settlement established. Previous experience was invaluable, however, for as John Shy has remarked on the early days, "To make everyone a soldier when men were still concerned about starving was to ensure that no one would be much of a soldier," who had not been one already.[1]

In the seventeenth century, every colony save Pennsylvania had established a militia system based upon the trainbands, with muster and outfit regulations following English models. As the frontier receded into the interior, however, and the immediate dangers decreased, the trainbands no longer served as fighting units themselves, but rather functioned as training and recruiting resources from which were organized short-term fighting companies for special needs, such as expedi-

1

tionary forces or frontier guards.[2] Such a development was not surprising, since as the years passed not every militiaman was needed, let alone sufficiently healthy, motivated, or even trained. It was necessary, nevertheless, occasionally to pay bounties to entice the desired volunteers, and this too became part of the accepted system of military service.

Militia units came in many different varieties, by no means equal in skills or social background. Those men with sufficient interest and income might well join more expensive "volunteer" units, such as the Ancient and Honorable Artillery Company of Boston, chartered in 1638 on the model of London's similar company established a century earlier. When the colonies were in direct danger, the trainbands and volunteer companies were accepted as necessary but, in peacetime, the deeply entrenched suspicion of standing armies which was part of the British and continental heritage was likely to come into play. An organization which added social exclusivity and assumed elite pretensions faced even more problems. The Boston Artillery encountered the hostility of local magistrates who saw "how dangerous it might be to erect a standing authority of military men, which might easily, in time, overthrow the civil power." Approval was given only after the unit founders promised to obey civil leaders in all things.[3]

Volunteer units were often cavalry or artillery, requiring expensive uniforms and equipment, and accepting men only after nomination and election to membershi Massachusetts, for example, required a cavalryman, who would normally perform scouting duties, to possess at least £100 worth of property. But there were also elite foot companies of grenadiers, light infantry, or riflemen, usually urban and often devoted at least as much to social as to military purposes. But the wealthy could afford to pay the fines assessed for failure to appear at muster. As John Mahon has pointed out, "in this way much of the upper crust of society disassociated itself from the standing militia and either entered volunteer units or avoided service altogether."[4] More will be heard of volunteer formations. As will be seen, sometimes their social standing did actually translate into notable military prowess, particularly in the nineteenth century.

Overall, the record of colonial era volunteer companies was mixed. Massachusetts Bay, Plymouth, and Connecticut each fielded units that participated in the first major American conflict, the Pequot War of the 1630s. But coordination of disjointed and poorly trained elements proved less than satisfactory, though in the end the Pequots were broken and scattered in a most brutal conflict (why the training was inadequate will be discussed shortly). The danger of war against the Narragansetts in the next decade (brought about by Narragansett hostility to the Mohegan tribe, which was allied to the colonies), arguably led to the creation of the first American elite unit. By a regulation of 1645 promulgated by the joint colonial council of Massachusetts, Plymouth, Connecticut, and New Haven—a confederation known as the United Colonies of New England—each militia commander was "to appoint out and to make choice of thirty soldiers of their companies in ye hundred, who shall be ready at half an hour's warning upon any service they shall be put upon by their chief military officers."[5] Such men, fully outfitted and trained as a ready reaction force, with decentralized command and control and a supportive alarm system of signals and riders, were the origin of the minute man concept that would play an enormous role in American military history.

The final Narragansett conflict was postponed until the 1670s in what was known as "King Philip's War" (King Philip was leader of the Wampanoags, allies of the Narragansetts), by which time several new regulations affected the militias. That of 1653, for example, required one man out of every eight in each band to be "in a readiness to march in a day's warning should the Lord call us to war."[6] The war was bloody and vicious, with the colonists determined upon the annihilation of the Narragansetts. By the time the major fighting was concluded in 1676 and King Philip dead, the colonists had learned much about this method of warfare, including the need to maintain a system of alarm riders who would rouse the entire countryside in time of danger in addition to joining in battle or in tracking a retreating Indian enemy. As Douglas Leach explains, success over time came from a "blending of European order and discipline with Indian improvisation and individuality, and knowing when to emphasize each." As one colonist put it, "A few months actual service against the Indian enemy in Philip's war made better soldiers, than all their exercises at home had done in forty years."[7] The minutemen had proved an important basis for colonial forces, but their numbers were small, and in time of need leaders soon "called for volunteers to fill specific units or expeditions, then levied soldiers from the trainbands, and finally . . . simply gathered everyone in sight, both soldiers and townsfolk."[8]

In the second half of the seventeenth century British regulars arrived in the colonies. While they might have served as elite models because of their extensive training, under these circumstances it proved otherwise. Regulars were commonly intended for the suppression of internal colonial difficulties, such as the Virginian troubles of 1676–77 known as "Bacon's Rebellion," though in that case the one thousand–man force, some of which was drawn from the respected guards regiments, arrived too late to see action. The unpaid and tattered two hundred who remained to be disbanded in 1682—the others had died or been returned to England—had earned considerable hostility through their quartering on the local population. Difficulties in 1689 in Massachusetts and New York resulted in similar responses and similar tensions. In the case of New York, fighting occurred between regulars and militiamen led by Jacob Leisler, who suspected a Catholic conspiracy was afoot. Such clashes won no friends for the regulars, and when they actually came to be used in combat their record was less than awe-inspiring.[9]

But colonial conflicts were usually related to the great European struggles of the early modern era. In particular, the War of the League of Augsburg (1689–97), known to the colonies as King William's War, opened nearly a century of conflict between Britain and France for control of eastern North America. Queen Anne's War (War of Spanish Succession, 1702–13), King George's War (War of Austrian Succession, 1740–48), and the French and Indian War (Seven Years' War, 1756–63) were only the most concentrated periods of action. In addition to volunteers, levies from militia formations continued to be required. Despite tightened regulations for militia musters and penalties for malefactors, such recruiting methods were not notably successful, judging from the results of either formal campaigns or suppression of frontier marauders.

Such battles as were fought offered interesting lessons. Maj. Gen. Edward Braddock's campaign on the Monongahela in 1755, in particular, helped shape the American conception of the qualities needed by a capable, even elite, warrior. Braddock set out in June 1755 from Fort Cumberland, Maryland, to capture French-held Fort Duquesne (modern Pittsburgh). Braddock had only just arrived in America and knew little of local conditions, but he had with him a substantial force of perhaps 1,500 British and American soldiers of varying types, including a few volunteers, camp followers, teamsters, and the like. Two British regiments fresh from Ireland were included, the 44th and 48th Foot, each incorporating roughly two-fifths British regulars, one-quar-

ter British draftees, and another one-third new American recruits to
bring them up to strength, "the dregs of colonial society—seaboard
society, at that."[10]

Braddock was not above taking the suggestions of his various
advisers, including volunteer aide-de-camp George Washington, but
his small army approached Fort Duquesne in a lengthy column of march
spread out for half a mile or more. Braddock had only a half-dozen
friendly Indians to accompany him (contract negotiations had not gone
well), and they and such American scouts as he sent out proved incapable of providing advance warning. The column fell into an ambush
prepared by the French and their Indian allies who throughout the en-
suing battle never numbered more than nine hundred in all. Braddock
did have some "Rangers," perhaps one hundred men, including some
from the First Company of Virginian Rangers, but for reasons which remain unclear he had assigned these men to be the column's rear guard.[11]

The battle which ensued on the banks of the Monongahela River
remains clouded by the fog of war, but there is little question that the
British vanguard, under French and Indian pressure was pushed back
upon Braddock's main body, which in turn gave way in panic. Officers, so nicely distinguished by their uniforms, gorgets, and horses were
favored targets; the few who survived were able to provide little leadershi Only after several hours of fighting did the remnant of Braddock's
army manage to escape the battlefield. One third of the unit had been
killed or mortally wounded, including Braddock himself. Only the
Americans of the rear guard and a few others, probably not over two
hundred in all, had shown enough initiative to take up defensive positions behind trees and return fire, only to be shot from behind by confused British regulars. The regulars, "from what storys they had heard of
the Indians in regard to their scalping and Mawhawking [i.e., practicing the notoriously brutal methods of the much-feared Mohawks], were
so pannick struck that their Officers had little or no command over
them. . . . The greatest part of the Men who were behind trees were
either killed or wounded by our own people . . ."[12] Braddock, by one
account, grew furious at his men thus taking cover: "The General denied and stormed much, calling them Cowards, and even went so far as
to strike them with his own Sword for attempting the Trees."[13]

Individual heroism had certainly been demonstrated in the course
of this astonishing defeat, but more attention was paid to the search for
scapegoats, among whom the dead Braddock featured, and still fea-

tures, prominently. Washington, on the other hand, won a considerable reputation for valor in this battle. According to a widely believed report, Washington urged Braddock to allow him to organize and lead an Indian-style attack on the enemy, but was refused. Paul Kopperman in his detailed study of this battle stresses its major significance, including Washington's role, for American military tradition:

> Washington came to epitomize the new, pragmatic, American method of fighting, against the blind, stodgy, Continental tradition represented by Braddock. Washington was seen to speak for freedom and individual initiative, Braddock for regimentation. Washington, himself a volunteer, stood for that tradition of the amateur warrior so dear to his countrymen. Braddock and his regulars were the professionals, fighting for a livelihood, rather than for home and hearth. . . . The provincials who had fought for Braddock were quickly lionized, not only at home, but in Britain as well. Conversely, the regulars who had failed so dismally were universally execrated, along with their general. In the light of such stereotypes, it is scarcely surprising that some Americans began to wonder whether they might not be better off fighting on their own. The Battle of the Monongahela encouraged a self-reliant spirit that would one day turn smoothly into a desire for independence.[14]

British commanders, for the most part, only saw short-term colonial volunteers in action, and generally misjudged the colonists' true military potential. Fred Anderson explains: "Applying regular army notions of efficiency, organization, and discipline, redcoat officers saw the provincials as hopelessly disorganized, badly disciplined, and prone to desertion or mutiny. The reason for this, they concluded, was that the provincial soldier himself was a poor specimen." "Riff-raff . . . lowest dregs of the people, both officers and men . . . ," was how Maj. Gen. James Abercromby put it regarding the provincial forces of 1756, expressing a widely-shared opinion that would persist at least until the Revolution.[15]

At least as important as the set-piece battle, however, was the question of frontier raids and skirmishes. For these, various solutions were proposed. Massachusetts, for example, activated a plan to pay substantial bounties—up to £50 to volunteers without pay—for every Indian scal This offered new profit opportunities to men from outlying towns who were willing and able to take to the forest, particularly in wintertime, when the generally unguarded Indian villages were most vulnerable to attack by small patrols on snowshoes. As John Galvin notes, "The patrols grew in popularity and the 'snow shoe men,' as they came to be called, were the heroes of the day."[16] One long range patrol, headed by Capt. John Lovewell of Dunstable, netted £1,000 for ten scalps while operating in the Kennebeck area (the market price had doubled). But the profession was dangerous. In 1725, Lovewell was ambushed and killed along with many of his men. A further problem was that the loss of such men was likely to hit hardest at precisely the frontier settlements that were the most vulnerable to attack—one further reason explaining the need for strong financial incentives. But seasonal scalp hunters were not adequate substitutes for regular patrols, which explains why, when possible, colonial authorities preferred to pay regular wages. Unfortunately, rangers frequently demanded twice the pay of British redcoats.[17] Through the 1740s more than a dozen such bands guarded the frontier, providing enough security at least to permit muster of the substantial colonial expedition which in 1745 sailed off to besiege and capture the strategic fortress of Louisbourg on Cape Breton Island.[18]

These special elite companies were forerunners to the more famous rangers of the 1750s, the hardy, independent, skilled frontier riflemen who still dominate American military mythology. The image is important and persistent. It is no accident that at the start of the twenty-first century "Rangers" are among the United States Army's elite units, tracing their heritage to similarly-named colonial era scouts and frontier guards who "ranged" and watched along the wilderness tracks between settlements, protecting lines of march and supply. Some rangers served under militia terms and conditions, but most could be called professionals, hired on a contract basis. The Virginia House of Burgesses, for example, kept a standing force of "rangers" on regular frontier service during the 1690s.[19] Depending upon time and place, such bands might include slaves and Indians among their numbers, as did Col. John Barnwell's mercenary quasi-army of 1,100 men, which fought against the Yamasee Indians in the Carolinas in 1715.[20] It is often assumed that rangers of this sort were always elites. In a sense of course they were, for their skills of woodcraft and marksmanship were not easily learned, but as military units respected by peers and opponents alike, they did not always qualify.

The best known early force, in honor of which the World War II army named its own unit in 1942, were the Rangers of Robert Rogers of New Hampshire (1731–95). Rogers organized and trained several fifty to one hundred–man companies, first for New Hampshire and then for the Royal Government, which operated against the French and Indians in the Lake Champlain area beginning in the fall of 1756, when the general struggle had been reduced to a demoralizing stalemate. Though without formal military training himself, Rogers drilled his volunteers in such matters as terrain selection, security on the march and in camp, rapid mobility, and the application of surprise whenever possible, all according to his twenty-eight "general rules for the ranging service."

Rogers's rules were eminently practical and, while not exactly deathless principles, they certainly must have proved useful to aspirant rangers. Rogers wrote a brief manual in 1757 when the Earl of Loudoun, British commander in chief in America (1756–58), selected volunteers from his own regiments to form a company of light infantry which he placed under Rogers's immediate orders for training purposes. A sample: "3. If your march lies through marshes or soft grounds, change your position and march in line, to prevent the enemy from tracking you, till you are clear of such ground; then resume your files. March until quite dark before encamping; which do, on a piece of ground which will afford the sentinels an opportunity of seeing or hearing the enemy at a considerable distance."[21]

Discipline and obedience to orders were less easy to inculcate in Rogers's own men, but nevertheless he became famous for taking the initiative in seeking out the enemy in some fifty long-range patrols and several pitched battles. Though not always victorious, his exploits were notable. In one case, Rangers led a famous escape from encirclement in the Fort Ticonderoga area, though at a cost of a quarter of his hundred men and a serious wound to Rogers himself. Overall, his record of successes against the French *troupes de la marine* (colonial troops; the ministry of marine supervised French colonies) was mixed at best. To make matters worse, though the utility of his units was appreciated, the independent habits of his men were not. Over time, Rogers found himself with multiple critics and enemies. His conflicts with official bureaucracy ultimately caused this inspiring leader to serve on the British side in the Revolutionary War as the head of "Rogers's Queen's

Rangers." He went on to a tragic life of alcoholism, debtor's prison, and a lonely death in England, though the London publication (1765) of his French and Indian War *Journal* helped establish his permanent place in frontier legend.[22]

In early 1758, Loudoun authorized Rogers to recruit five additional companies (one to be composed of Indians) for one year's service, each composed of eight officers and NCOs and one hundred privates.[23] Four of these companies were sent to the garrison at Louisbourg, and it was there that Capt. John Knox recorded their appearance:

> A body of rangers, under the command of Captain Rogers . . . march out every day to scour the country; these light troops have, at present, no particular uniform, only they wear their cloaths short, and are armed with a firelock, tomahock or small hatchet, and a scalping knife; a bullock's horn full of powder hangs under their right arm, by a belt from the left shoulder; and a leathern, or seal's skin bag, buckled round their waist, which hangs down before, contains bullets and a smaller shot of the size of full-grown peas: six or seven of which, with a ball, they generally load; and their officers usually carry a small compass fixed in the bottoms of their powder-horns, by which to direct them when they happen to lose themselves in the woods.

Their enemies, however, were not above laying an ambush, and careless rangers could be taken by surprise, as was one party reported by Knox, which let itself be attacked while out cutting wood.[24]

Though Rogers's force was certainly the most famous ranger unit of the time, it was far from alone. While Rogers commanded five ranger columns, four additional independent ranger companies were also present on the Lake Champlain front in 1760. Indeed, before the war was over, Loudoun had ordered every colony to raise its own similar elite unit. The company of Capt. (as of 1757, Maj.) Israel Putnam, established well before this order, was particularly useful. Putnam's fifty five–man company was originally levied in from Connecticut in 1754. It is not clear whether they were known as "Rangers" from the start, but such was the function they performed in conjunction with Rogers's force. Indeed, Putnam is said to have saved Rogers's life while spying on British positions at Crown Point. Putnam's command was renewed in 1756, but he was taken prisoner in an ambush in July 1758 and his men routed until Rogers arrived to rally the unit. Putnam was later exchanged, and subsequently served in Cuba and the West Indies as a colonel—rising to major general in the Continental Army in the Revolutionary War until forced by bad health to retire in 1779.[25]

The rangers were exceptional men, not least for possessing necessary skills at hunting and woodcraft. The argument has been made, indeed, that relatively few men could claim such skills in late colonial America, which returns us to the question of why colonial militia were insufficiently trained for their struggles with their several Indian neighbors. In contrast to the situation in class-bound Europe, where possession of firearms was often restricted to socio-economic elites and draconian penalties were administered for crimes such as poaching, any free American could possess himself of a musket. This freedom, however, did not necessarily translate into proficiency.

Hunting for pleasure, which might have honed the skills of marksmanship, was not a popular pastime; farming and the raising of livestock consumed the lives of most early settlers. Game could indeed be an important source of both food and income, but as Daniel Justin Herman had noted, "colonists chose the cheapest and most efficient ways to hunt rather than the most sporting. Settlers snared birds and trapped beavers; netted pigeons, rabbits, and fish; set fire to woods to drive game into the open; and engaged in communal surrounds," in which entire communities gathered to kill whatever was trapped in an ever-smaller ring.[26] Randolph Roth has found ample evidence of the use of low-quality weapons for either fowling or vermin control, the latter being major assaults against squirrels, crows, and other competitors for grain crops.[27] But Herman's general conclusion seems fair enough: "New Englanders had never seen themselves as a hunting people. Far from being wilderness or genteel hunters, they were a people of the Bible, the plow, and the doctrines of moderation and industry."[28] Even Lee Newcomer, who is more confident than others about the role of hunting in creating military men, nevertheless concludes that "New Englanders were not marksmen; they lacked accurate rifles and powder for practice."[29] And Douglas Leach, while appreciative of the New England citizen-soldier, nevertheless notes that the colonists suffered a scarcity of arms and ammunition, and endured a lengthy series of defeats, until they learned to rely upon friendly Indian scouts and small skilled groups of rangers—such as, for example, Capt. Benjamin

Church's mixed force of about sixty colonists and some 140 friendly Indians, who managed to kill "King" Philip.[30] Some few colonists were hunter-marksmen; but far more, it would seem, had only occasionally used a fowling piece or squirrel rifle, and these experiences did not automatically translate into effectiveness in war.

Nor could all men easily lay their hands on good firearms, even if they wanted them. Harold Selesky, for example, found that more than half the Connecticut militia volunteers of 1747 lacked firearms—and this among what must have been the most eager recruits in a very troublesome year.[31] On the other hand, a militia man with a family might decide to leave his weapon at home for hunting and protection, hoping to be issued another at muster. The scarcity of guns, their high expense when available (many by necessity came from Europe), and the difficulty of maintaining and repairing them in a land of relatively few gunsmiths, made them into precious commodities.[32]

There is really no way to calculate the number of guns, particularly rifles, which were produced in the American colonies in the era 1760–90. However, it is possible to identify and catalog something under three hundred gun makers, many of whom were in business for only a short term, for all the colonies in that thirty-year period. Twelve of the thirteen colonies had only a handful. Massachusetts, for example, had twenty-four, Connecticut nineteen, Maryland sixteen, and each of the others a dozen or less, for a total of just over one hundred. It is a striking fact that nearly two-thirds of all colonial gun makers (172 to be precise) were to be found in Pennsylvania, and of these, eighty-one in the town of Lancaster and the surrounding county, with the bulk of the rest in adjoining counties and Philadelphia, which claimed forty-three (compared, for example, to just seven in Boston). This peculiar concentration is explained by the settlement of skilled artisans, particularly from Germany and Switzerland, in southeastern Pennsylvania.[33]

It is interesting to speculate that this concentration of gun makers was one motive, at least, for the British desire to control Philadelphia and its hinterland, just as it may have influenced Washington in his selection of Valley Forge for his winter quarters in 1777–78. In any case, there can be little question that British authorities tried to repatriate some skilled gunsmiths. Thomas Allen and John Woods, both of New York, returned to England in December 1775 after Gov. William Tyron gave each a paid passage, a bounty of twenty guineas, and the promise of employment in a government armory. However, Tyron had less bargaining power with German immigrants.[34]

One answer to the shortage of gun makers was for colonies to establish their own manufacturing armories. The Pennsylvania State Gun Factory was established in early 1776, but later in the year, as the British approached, it was moved to near Valley Forge, and in the fall of 1777 when the British came near again, to just east of Reading, using army wagons and guards for the purpose.[35] Virginia's Public Gun Factory was located in Fredericksburg, but it too was removed in 1784 to the "Point of Fork State Arsenal" at the junction of the Rivanna and James Rivers. Such dislocations and removals were commonplace as the scene of war shifted, and hardly helped solve the supply question. But these armories, as storehouses for weapons which the citizens themselves seemed not to possess, were important strategic targets.[36]

Most gun makers, finally, urban or rural, were not large-scale producers. Joel Ferree of Lancaster County, for example, was probably one of the larger producers in his area, furnishing thirty to forty rifles each week to the Committee of Safety during the Revolutionary War. Matthias Keeley of Philadelphia, on the other hand, produced one hundred "firelocks" for Pennsylvania over the course of a year from March 1776 to early 1777. All manufacturers, however, suffered from shortages and rising costs of raw materials while receiving low pay for their work, as demonstrated by a petition to the Committee of Safety dated November 1776, and signed by most of the gun makers of Philadelphia.[37]

Such data only underscores the perpetual shortage of weapons of any quality with which to conduct a war, and even more important for this study, a lack of both rifles and riflemen. It was not that the scarce marksman with woodland expertise was not sought out. Certainly after Braddock's defeat in 1755 it was clear that traditional European methods of linear warfare were inadequate in North America, and though the Rangers were regularly blamed for excesses, still the British commanders generally could not get enough of them. Lord Loudoun, known as a strict disciplinarian, put it to the Duke of Cumberland (captain general of the British army, 1745–57) in London in late 1756: "I am afraid, I shall be blamed for the *Ranging* Companies: but as realy [*sic*] in Effect we have no *Indians,* it is impossible for an Army to Act in this Country, without *Rangers;* and there ought to be a considerable body of them, and the breeding them up to that, will be a great advantage to the Country, for they will be able to deal with Indians in their own way . . ." Loudoun hoped for a "considerable body" indeed: "The number I propose to ask from the *four New England Governments,* is *four thousand,* all *Rangers,* without any of their Generals; but I would compound for *two thousand* . . ." (He would be lucky to have a few hundred.)[38]

Maj. Gen. Jeffrey Amherst, Loudoun's successor after a brief interlude under Gen. James Abercromby, faced the same problem and found it necessary to give special training to selected volunteers to bring their skills to something approximating an adequate level. Maj. John Hawks, on the Ticonderoga campaign of that year, set out some of the details:

> Eight of the Provential Battalion[s] gives 13 men each & two of the Provential Battalions 14 men each for the Ranging Service. The men to be told they will be paid the difference between theirs & that of the Rangers. Commanding officers of the Battalions to turn out all volunteers willing to serve in the Rangers. Tomorrow att [*sic*] one o'clock Major Rogers will attend & chuse [*sic*] the number that each Regt is to furnish out of such volunteers.[39]

Such emergency efforts leave some question of just how skillful these new rangers were likely to be, but necessity—and the scarcity of true rangers—left little choice.

The process of selecting the best men from colonial units, whether militia or otherwise, seems to have presented perpetual difficulties, and not just from the standpoint of manpower. An example is the 1757 effort by Massachusetts to form its own elite militia unit to be called the "Picket Guards." Pickets are outpost guards; the "picket guard" was the unit which was on duty at any given time in each garrison, ready to reinforce its pickets at short notice. The new unit in question was to include about one-fourth of the best men in existing militia companies—hopefully volunteers in the traditional fashion, but selected by careful draft if necessary, to a maximum of eight thousand men, a considerable number for the time. Each man would be furnished with the best available equipment, which he would be expected to maintain and have on hand for rapid deployment. The plan was voted down by a narrow margin in the Massachusetts House of Representatives.[40]

In any case, the tide was then turning in favor of the British in the war, and fighting would end in this part of the world after the surrender of Montréal in 1760. It is interesting to note, however, the special privileges which the men of this elite unit were to be given while in the service of the commonwealth and for an equal time after they left its ranks. As recorded by John Galvin: "Service under 'select and proper officers;' exemption from labor or taxes for highways (except bridges); excused from service in 'burthensome' public offices such as constable, tythingman, collector of taxes; free from 'impress,' or the drafting of men from the militia; free to resign from the Picket Guards on provision of an acceptable replacement; excused from bearing arms in the common militia."[41] Whether such concessions would have proved adequate to recruit to the desired strength must remain moot.

The British response to the ranger problem deserves particular attention. It has already been noted that both Loudoun and Amherst recognized the need for ranger-type scouts and irregular troops. For some time there seemed little alternative to hiring colonists with the necessary skills—or at least claim to them. In America, cavalry was not an important factor given the rugged terrain away from the settlements and the general lack of surplus horses. Indians were difficult to control and, in any case, were increasingly unwilling to serve as scouts. But rangers were expensive and not particularly amenable to British discipline either. Simply hiring more of them, as both generals had done, was a natural but ultimately unsatisfactory response. It was for this reason that Loudoun had sent junior officers along on ranger patrols in order to learn their methods, and, with luck, eventually become qualified to form special companies of ranger-like troops within his regular regiments.[42]

But such a process was bound to take time, and it is thus no surprise that the 1757 offer of Col. Thomas Gage to raise a regiment of irregulars at his own expense was eagerly accepted. The resulting regiment (the 80th) began with a draft of one hundred men from Loudoun's regulars, but soon emerged as a five-company regiment, the first such "light" regiment in the British army. While it was expected to take its place in the line of battle if necessary, its specially designed clothing and arms (altogether, about thirteen pounds lighter than the regular soldier's usual load) and forest training made the unit particularly useful in irregular warfare, and yet presumably avoided the common problem of indiscipline among the rangers. Loudoun was hopeful that this unit would not only save money, but would also provide "a Corps of Rangers that would be disciplined, and have Officers at their head on whom I could depend." Though certainly useful over the next six years in conflicts such as Louisbourg, where their marksmanship was particularly valuable, Gage's regiment was unable to avoid the results of attracting "a certain sort of soldier, more adventurous and independent," or as another officer put it, "the Jail birds of America."[43]

Yet another answer was to form a regular regiment and give it special training from the start, rather than recruit men with special skills. The experiment was made with the "Royal Americans" (the 62d Regiment, later renumbered the 60th), a regular regiment which after 1756 was recruited in the colonies, mainly among the German settlers of Pennsylvania. The regiment was trained in the standard formal marching and deployment routines, for any British regiment might well have to face in battle traditionally-trained French units. By Loudoun's order, the entire regiment was also given as much experience as possible in forest techniques: "They are then to fire at Marks, and in order to qualify them for the Service of the Woods, they are to be taught to load and fire, lyeing [*sic*] on the Ground and kneeling. They are to be taught to march in Order, slow and fast in all sortes [*sic*] of Ground. They are frequently to pitch & fold up their tents, and to be accustomed to pack up and carry their necessaries in the most commodious manner." In particular, on the command "Tree All", every man was expected to take cover and look out for himself.[44]

The light companies were disbanded after the Seven Years' War, only to be resurrected in the War of American Independence, during which the British found them indispensable. But as Richard Holmes remarks, they did not quite fit into the eighteenth-century model army. "There was a palpable tension between the light infantry ethos, with its emphasis on practical uniform, individual skills and relaxed discipline, and the older notion of unthinking obedience." As one disdainful British officer put it during that later conflict, the "light bobs" were 'for the most part young and insolent puppies, whose worthlessness was apparently their recommendation for a service which placed them in the post of danger, in the way of becoming food for powder, their most appropriate destination next to that of the gallows.'[45]

Soon enough all British regiments which served in eighteenth-century America were given at least some similar training. By the end of the French and Indian War, Loudoun's original goal of forming a light infantry company in each regiment was achieved. "We have chose out one hundred men from each regiment," reported one officer in 1759, "and pitched upon the officers to act this year as light infantry; they are cloathed [*sic*] and accoutred as light as possible, and in my opinion are a kind of troops that has been much wanted in this country. . . . They . . . have what ammunition they want, so I don't doubt they will be excellent marksmen."[46] Such light infantry companies were intended to complement the traditional elite grenadier formation of the majority of the men in each regiment (British infantry regiments now commonly included twelve companies of sixty men each, including one each of grenadiers and light troops). The light units certainly were intended to use forest tactics when necessary, but it was just as important that they retain their ability to maneuver as companies of the line and maintain the discipline expected of regulars entering combat with enemy regulars.[47]

As Stephen Brumwell has pointed out, contrary to long-lived stereotypes, the British Army had learned a great many lessons from the Seven Years' War in both America and the Caribbean. "Whatever colonial Americans may have thought of British soldiers and the government they represented in 1757, by 1763 the successes gained at Louisbourg, Quebec, Martinique, and Havana had done much to redeem the reputation of the King's troops and to enhance the prestige of the mother country. . . . There is evidence that the achievements of the 'American Army' evoked not only widespread recognition but also considerable shared pride amongst the colonial population. . . . It was the subsequent decision to tax the colonists, coupled with the employment of soldiers to uphold royal authority, that swiftly squandered the credit accumulated at such heavy cost: within a decade such policies had transformed the bold heroes of Quebec into the bloody butchers of Boston."[48]

By the third quarter of the eighteenth century, then, the American colonies had a considerable variety of military experience upon which to draw, including several different models of elite forces, from undisciplined but useful rangers to specially trained light companies of regulars. Overall, however, at least three certain truisms prevailed. First, standing armies were to be distrusted; the militia would provide adequate defenses, or at least recruits necessary for adequate defenses when the time came—"the militia myth," in Don Higginbotham's phrase.[49] Second, colonists who gave military service did so voluntarily (most of the time) by a contract subject to cancellation when it was breached or expired, and not simply at the will of the state.[50] Finally, above all a hallowed place was allotted to the citizen-musketmen and, of these, the respected elites were the frontier ranger riflemen.

Discussing Rogers's Rangers in a volume of his vast series, which he called his "history of the American forest," the famous historian Francis Parkman (1823–93) evoked the image with this romantic prose:

> The best of them were commonly employed on Lake George; and nothing can surpass the adventurous hardihood of their lives. Summer and winter, day and night, were alike to them. Embarked in whaleboats or birch-canoes, they glided under the silent moon or in the languid glare of a breathless August day . . . or in the bright October, when the jay screamed from the woods, squirrels gathered their winter hoard, and congregated blackbirds chattered farewell to their summer haunts. . . . Or, in the tomb-like silence of the winter forest, with breath frozen on his beard, the ranger strode on snow-shoes over the spotless drifts; and, like Dürer's knight, a ghastly death stalked ever at his side. There were those among them for whom this stern life had a fascination that made all other existence tame.[51]

In the War for Independence that followed, while rangers, and above all riflemen, would certainly have their place, combat would prove to resemble continental European linear patterns rather than the mixture of raids and sieges which had typified the mid-century American struggles. Accepted faith in the efficacy of the citizen militia and, indeed, in the principle of volunteerism, would be seriously challenged as well. But all this was before the first shots were fired by the Boston-area minutemen, never to be forgotten in America's collective military past as a nation-saving elite.

2 The Revolutionary War

The story of Lexington and Concord is as well known, in a general sense, as any epoch-making moment in American military history. The immediate cause was simple enough: as tensions increased between London and America, the colonial militia had undergone something of a renaissance. To prepare for a possible armed struggle, an arms depot had been established by the Continental Congress at Concord, some twenty miles from the Boston headquarters of Sir Thomas Gage, the former first commander of the 80th Regiment who had been promoted to lieutenant general and British commander in North America, as well as governor of Massachusetts. Concord itself had in the fall of 1774 organized two companies of men ready to 'stand at a minutes warning in Case of an alarm.' The men carried their weapons everywhere, and drilled twice weekly on the common. Of the 104 total members, mostly landowners and men of standing, fifteen had to borrow muskets from the town arsenal, meaning that in this village a fairly high percentage of men of property did possess weapons.[1]

To deal with this threat and provocation, in mid-April 1775 Gage dispatched approximately seven hundred troops under Lt. Col. Francis Smith (10th Foot). The force was composed of light and grenadier companies, the best Gage had. Unfortunately for Gage's plan, news of the

British movement was spread rapidly, by prearrangement. At Lexington, four miles short of Concord, Smith found 130 militiamen drawn up under Capt. John Parker, a forty-five-year-old veteran of Rogers's Rangers. After a brief fire-fight which cost the Americans eight dead and another ten wounded, and the British one man killed, the column moved on to Concord. At Concord, the minutemen were not swept aside so easily, for several thousand had assembled there. After a serious clash at the North Bridge, the British, unable to proceed further, retreated to Boston under fire for the entire route. British casualties amounted to seventy–three dead, 174 wounded, and twenty–six missing, in all an alarmingly high percentage of the force. Gage dug in to await reinforcements, while the militia under Gen. Artemas Ward laid siege to the town.

The next stage, equally famous, was brought about by the militia's establishment of an exposed position on the Charlestown Peninsula. Gage could not resist the opportunity thus presented, and ordered an attack on the fortifications at Breed's Hill and Bunker Hill. Maj. Gen. Sir William Howe was placed in command and chose to march his 2,100 elite grenadier and light troops in a direct linear uphill attack. Only on the third repetition, after Howe's force had absorbed 1,054 casualties, including many officers, and the Americans had run short of powder, did the colonists retreat from both positions. Technically the British had won the battle of "Charlestown" as it was then known, but the more than 40 percent killed, wounded, and missing was a catastrophic waste of British elite troops and a major psychological victory for the rebels. It was also an interesting demonstration of the point that in such a situation British elite companies were no more useful than regular line companies. If anything, the steadiness of the grenadiers, together with their height and size—exaggerated by their tall mitre headpieces—simply cost more lives, with some of these companies losing as many as 90 percent of their men. Howe later confessed, "the Light Infantry at the same time [as the grenadiers] being repulsed, there was a *moment that I never felt before*."[2]

Lexington, Concord, and Bunker Hill forever enshrined the minutemen in American military history. The credit for all three victories—for so they were regarded—not unnaturally went to the accurate shooting of the citizen-soldiers, "every soldier in our army having been intimate with his gun from his infancy," as Thomas Jefferson put it.[3] It was not quite that way, as subsequent events would demonstrate; that the Americans had defended fortified positions, including artillery, against an unprotected infantry assault uphill over open ground was forgotten by too many. Fortunately for the nation's future, it was not ignored by George Washington, who had already amassed considerable military experience on the frontier, including, as previously noted, at Braddock's defeat in 1757. The key to using amateur soldiers was always clear to him: "Place them behind a parapet, a breastwork, stone wall, or any thing that will afford them shelter, and from their knowledge of a firelock, they will give a good account of their enemy . . . arch boldly up to a work nor stand exposed in a plain. . . . I have never spared the spade and the pickaxe."[4]

Nevertheless, the early victories of the rebels were certainly surprising, and not just to British generals such as Howe and Gage. Charles Francis Adams put it well: "A more singular exhibition of apparently unconscious temerity on one side, and professional military incapacity on the other, it would be difficult to imagine."[5] Ironically, even in Concord the *rage militaire* passed soon enough. One Concord company took the brunt of the first assaults at Breed's Hill, and three new men were killed. Soon afterwards, like all the Massachusetts militia, these units were incorporated into the Continental Army. By 1777, when three-year enlistments were the rule, it was mostly the town poor and marginal men who enlisted. By 1780, only half of Concord's recruits had any known link with the town. "For Concord," Robert Gross concluded, "the Revolution was becoming a war by proxy."[6] Charlestown, or "Bunker Hill" as it became popularly known, was in June 1775. Nine months later, the British evacuated Boston and George Washington, who had arrived two weeks after Bunker Hill with an appointment from the Continental Congress to be "General and Commander in chief of the army of the United Colonies," could celebrate an important victory—but it would prove to be a very long war. As Washington wrote to Congress in September 1776, "When Men are irritated, and the Passions inflamed, they fly hastely and chearfully [*sic*] to Arms; but after the first emotions are over, to expect, among such People, as compose the bulk of an Army, that they are influenced by any other principles than those of Interest, is to look for what never did, and I fear never will happen; the Congress will deceive themselves therefore if they expect it."[7]

Washington's chief responsibility was to create an army that was something more than short-term militia units, responsible to their respective colonies which determined enlistment, selected officers, and

provided pay and equipment. Both militia units and the regiments created by the Continental Congress, hence "Continentals," had discipline and desertion problems, though units of both types proved loyal
and capable, overcoming hardships that, in the opinions of both the
Prussian veteran Baron von Steuben and the French Marquis de
Lafayette, a European army would not have withstood. Many loyal
citizen privates had little tolerance for their officers, often for good
reason, and were hostile to distinctions of rank in general. "Washington would have none of this 'leveling' tendency, which may have been
created, at least in part, by small-farm ownership and the peculiarities
of the New England political and religious organization. Washington
was accustomed to the use and observance of authority, as were so
many Southerners, perhaps because of the nature of the plantation system."[8] Willard Wallace in this remark perhaps exaggerates the difference between North and South, but it is an important theme in American historical writing and directly bears upon the issue of military
elites, as will be seen.

There is no question that Washington was a strong believer in
the importance of discipline, not least because the Americans were
fighting a regular, professional army. As he wrote to Congress in September 1776:

> To place any dependance upon Militia, is, assuredly, resting
> upon a broken staff. Men just dragged from the tender Scenes
> of domestick [*sic*] life; unaccustomed to the din of Arms; to-
> tally unacquainted with every kind of Military skill, which being
> followed by a want of confidence in themselves, when op-
> posed to Troops regularly train'd, disciplined, and appointed,
> superior in knowledge, and superior in Arms, makes them timid,
> and ready to fly from their own shadows. Besides, the sudden
> change in their manner of living, (particularly in the lodging)
> brings on sickness in many; impatience in all, and such an
> unconquerable desire of returning to their respective homes
> that it not only produces shameful, and scandalous Desertions
> among themselves, but infuses the like spirit in others. Again,
> Men accustomed to unbounded freedom, and no controul [*sic*],
> cannot brook the Restraint which is indispensably necessary
> to the good order and Government of an Army; without which,
> licentiousness, and every kind of disorder triumphantly reign.

To bring Men to a proper degree of Subordination, is not the work of a day, a Month or even a year. . . .[9]

Though in his "Sentiments on a Peace Establishment" of May 1783 Washington recognized that a militia system would have to undergird any future military establishment and support any small standing army which might remain, such a force must, in his view, be subject to common standards across the country.[10] But he had not really changed his view. As he had reflected in August 1781: "What glorious opportunities have been lost by us, and what almost ruinous advantages have been taken by the Enemy, in the times of our weakness, for want of a permanent force in the field; . . . we ought to have constantly such an Army as is sufficient to operate against the Enemy, and supersede the necessity of calling forth the Militia, except on the most extraordinary occasions."[11]

Washington's struggle for long-term enlistments and national control of all units lasted the length of the war. The Continentals were the best he would get, and certainly they became professional soldiers, but they suffered from serious difficulties which encouraged desertion just as much as those reasons listed by the general in 1776. The lack of uniforms (indeed, sometimes clothing of any kind), pay, food, and decent shelter; the demanding disciplinary measures; the need to help their families at home; the high enlistment bounties from state regiments: These were the main factors which took many men away from the lines, though some returned in due course. The numbers were high; for example, of the seven continental regiments from New York, more than 15 percent of the *officers* deserted, and at least one-third of the privates. Paradoxically, morale remained firm; "That men under these circumstances were held together," wrote Washington to his brother in 1780, "is hardly within the bounds of credibility, but is nevertheless true . . ."[12] The paradox is explained in part by Allen Bowman: "The independent spirit that defied regimentation was the very spirit which, when turned against the enemy, made for dogged resistance in a rebellion."[13]

While Washington could not solve the army's perpetual financial, manpower, and logistical problems, he could at least reward excellence among individuals, well aware of the morale-boosting effect of such a policy. The idea was long in generation. "I am led," he wrote in early 1778, ". . . to hint an idea, which may be improved and turned to no small advantage. This is the institution of honorary rewards, differing in degree, to be conferred on those, who signalize themselves, by any meritorious actions, in proportion to the magnitude and brilliancy of the achievement. These should be sacred to the purpose of their institution, and unattainable by loose recommendations, or vague, though arrogating pretensions; given only upon authentic vouchers of real dessert, from some proper board."[14] But it was not until August of 1782 that he ordered the establishment of a Badge of Military Merit: "Whenever any singularly meritorious action is performed, the author of it shall be permitted to wear on his facings over his left breast, the figure of a heart in purple cloth, or silk, edged with narrow lace or binding," the origin of the famous "Purple Heart." As a special privilege, "men who have won this badge will be suffered to pass all guards and sentinels which officers are permitted to do." Though intended to be a permanent institution, it soon fell into disuse (three men were awarded the honor in 1783, but there is no record of any others during the Revolution), not to be revived until 1932 on the 200th anniversary of Washington's birth.[15]

As another form of distinction, non-commissioned officers and privates who served with "bravery, fidelity, and good conduct" for more than three years could wear on their left sleeve an angular stripe of white cloth (soon changed to the color of uniform facings, which depended upon a man's branch of corps), with a second parallel stripe for a second three years—actually the origin of the good conduct medal rather than long service stripes. A board of officers was established to pass on the credentials of candidates for both conduct stripes and merit badges.[16] Though the Congressional Medal of Honor would have to await the Civil War, Generals Washington, Horatio Gates, and Henry "Light Horse Harry" Lee were all awarded special gold medals for their services during the Revolutionary War.

But the Continental Army was not composed solely of devoted, patriotic farmers and craftsmen defending their acres and shops. Often they were unemployed, a large category which ranged from younger sons to the dregs of urban settlements. They were often newly arrived from Europe; many Irish and Germans in particular fought in the American ranks, and Washington at least considered the idea of establishing a German legion. African Americans were to be found in the ranks, though not many in state militia elements. If a socio-economic bias was to be found, it lay in the fact that the state militia units tended to include more men of property than the Continentals.[17] That fact presented General Washington with something of a dilemma when he needed to form a commander in chief's guard company, but was reluctant to trust the assignment to any foreign group, considering that "in the Course of the Campaign, my Baggage, Papers, and other Matters of great public Import, may be committed to the Sole care of these men."[18]

The Guard, first established as a distinct unit in March 1776, came to number fifty rank and file, four sergeants, four corporals, and a fifer and drummer. Each regiment under Washington's command in the Boston area was to furnish four capable candidates from whom a final selection would be made. All were to be between 5'9" and 5'10" to insure uniformity of height, all volunteers, "Sober, Young, Active and well made . . . Men of good Character in the Regiment that possess the pride of appearing clean and Soldierlike."[19] The commander wanted his Guard to wear the same blue and buff uniform that he himself wore, if such clothing was to be had, though Capt. Caleb Gibbs, who was to command the unit and was instructed to provide the clothes, was enjoined to secrecy, "for though no extraordinary expense will attend it . . . yet the report of making a uniform . . . for the Guards creates an idea of expense which I would not wish should go forth."[20]

Washington did not want foreigners in his guard, as he made clear in writing to his colonels. "I am satisfied there can be no absolute security for the fidelity of this Class of people [i.e., rank and file soldiers], but yet I think it most likely to be found in those who have Family connections in the Country. You will therefore send me none but Natives, and Men of some property, if you have them. I must insist, that in making this Choice, you give no Intimation of my preference of Natives, as I do not want to create any invidious Distinction between them and the Foreigners."[21]

Even with careful selection (precisely who selected the final fifty from the original draft is not clear), not every Guardsman proved reliable. Thomas Hickey, an early member, became notable as the first man to be hanged in the Continental Army, before a crowd of twenty thousand people in New York in June 1776. His crime was treason, as part of a plot to assassinate Washington. Fortunately the bulk of the Guard proved more trustworthy. There was also a cavalry contingent of thirty–eight men, "the Cavalry of the Commander in Chief's Guard," which was called into use only when necessary to accompany Washington on the road. Technically, they were not permanently attached to the Guard, but kept on the rolls of the 3d Continental Dragoons. Colorfully outfitted (at least for this army) in black hat with foxtail, white coat, yellow trousers, and black boots, the cavalry, like the infantry Guard, fought at Brandywine, Germantown, and Monmouth.[22]

In April 1778, the Guard was completely reorganized since many of its members had served out their enlistments. It was then recruited entirely from Virginia elements encamped at Morristown. Washington, it seems, wanted fellow Virginians around him. Certainly they were close enough at Valley Forge, where they had their own quarters near those of the commander. In the following year, the number of privates was cut to forty, but then Steuben urged an increase of one hundred more "chosen" men (these were drafted from non-Virginia units in an attempt at balance), to be drilled by Steuben himself as a model unit that would both demonstrate European methods and encourage the direct involvement of officers in the training of their men.[23] This force too had its undesirables (three men were sentenced to be hanged in October 1778, though two of them escaped), but it seems to have been rather resplendent in new dark blue coats, red vests, buckskin breeches, and white cross belts. Its role as a model unit to be studied by the entire army was most significant. At the end of the war, sixty–four men remained to be discharged from Washington's Guard.

Some men certainly deserved their honorable guardsman status. Lewis Campbell, for example, from Woodbridge, New Jersey, had enlisted in July 1776 for five months, fought at Long Island and White Plains, and was discharged in December, only to re-enlist four days later in the 4th New Jersey, with whom he fought at Short Hills, Brandywine, and Germantown, before he transferred back to the Guard at Valley Forge in March 1778. Campbell went on to fight at Monmouth, Connecticut Farms, King's Bridge (where he was wounded), and Yorktown. He was finally discharged in November 1783 after more than seven years' honorable service—and there were many others like him.

Washington's was not the only special guard force for high-ranking officers. Maj. Gen. Benedict Arnold, when in command of the important garrison at West Point, had his own guard of one hundred picked men, drafting two men from each company in his command. Their assignments included guarding his house, running general errands, and manning an eight-oared bateau that he used for transport on the Hudson River, at least until he fled to the British in September 1780. Interestingly, Washington himself came to inspect the post shortly before Arnold's treachery, though Arnold, already planning to surrender the fort and garrison, was unable to provide that information to the enemy in time to be useful. Since Washington had with him at the time only a few top aides, including Knox, Alexander Hamilton, and Lafayette, and a small squad of nineteen of his own guards, they might all, guards and aides alike, have been asked to sacrifice their own lives in the commander in chief's defense. But as Washington rode up, surprised to find that no salute was fired, Arnold was being rowed downriver to a British ship and a most sorry end to an otherwise brilliant career. Arnold's treachery, like his grand lifestyle, was only another argument against allowing an American military aristocracy to flourish.[24]

The Guard, though an entirely separate select unit of Washington's army, did not total more than two hundred men. Within the context of the larger army, Washington had a clear appreciation for the rifleman who was capable of something more than linear warfare, which was the best that might be expected from many units (and not even that where some of the militia was concerned). The "rifles" generally were organized as independent companies in the ranger tradition, and Washington knew their value from his experiences in the French and Indian War. "More riffle [sic] Men," stressed the general in the notes for his first letter to Congress from his headquarters in Cambridge, though in fact he found it better wisdom to discuss the shortage of men altogether.[25] Not all riflemen, in any case, were all that they claimed, as the general soon discovered. In the Boston siege, as he wrote to his brother, they had little chance of showing their skills "or their ignorance, for some of them, especially from Pensylvania [sic], know no more of a Rifle than my horse, being new Imported Irish many of whom have deserted to the Enemy."[26] Later Washington would insist that in reporting numbers of riflemen in their returns, corps commanders were "to include none but such as are known to be perfectly skilled in the use of these guns, and who are known to be active and orderly in their behaviour. . ."[27]

Congress did authorize ten companies of "expert riflemen" in June 1775 to march to Boston from Pennsylvania, Maryland, and Virginia to join Washington's forces. They arrived with surprising alacrity in late July.[28] The intention was that they be light infantry, that is, generally deployed with more mobility and independence than regular troops. "Riflemen" were, of course, expected to carry rifled muzzle-

loading weapons which, while slower to load, had considerably more
accuracy and range than the smooth-bore ("Brown Bess") muskets with
which light infantry were normally equipped. There were other differences. Some light infantrymen might well be good marksmen and
qualify in that respect as riflemen; men of either group might or might
not be proficient in Indian fighting techniques, but normally such tactics were not yet expected of light infantry. Riflemen, on the other
hand, at least in the American context, were not asked to perform pa-
rade-ground movements which light infantry companies, as integral
parts of regular regiments, were expected to have mastered. Indeed,
riflemen were at a decided disadvantage in close combat with
musketmen, since muskets came equipped with bayonets and rifles did
not. 'I don't like Rifles,' declared Anthony Wayne, a soldier of considerable experience; "I would almost as soon face an Enemy with a good
Musket and Bayonet without Ammunition—as with Ammunition without a bayonet."[29]

Washington found the riflemen useful but undisciplined, and when
their officers attempted to impose order, some came perilously close to
mutiny. It was not simply an issue of their behavior when off duty.
Many saw their only mission in life as shooting at redcoats when and
where they found the chance. "They are such a boastful, bragging set
of people, and think none are men or can fight but themselves," wrote
one observer in 1781.[30] Nor could all riflemen be counted upon to be
expert marksmen, though that was their main claim to elite status. And
if their marksmanship faltered, so too would the respect in which the
enemy held them. Gen. Charles Lee made clear what the problem was:
"It is a certain truth, that the enemy entertain a most fortunate apprehension of American riflemen. It is equally certain, that nothing can
contribute to diminish this apprehension so infallibly, as a frequent
ineffectual fire." Ordering men under his command to fire at no more
than 150 yards when they had "almost a moral certainty" of hitting
their target, he made an important point about morale: "Distant firing
has a double bad effect; it encourages the enemy, and adds to the perni-
cious persuasion of the American soldiers, namely, that they are no match
for their antagonists at close fighting. To speak plainly, it is almost a sure
method of making them cowards."[31] It was probably with some relief
that Washington sent off three companies of these undisciplined riflemen under the command of Capt. Daniel Morgan on Col. Benedict Arnold's
abortive Quebec campaign of 1775–76. Among other interesting inci-

dents of the campaign was the riflemen's insistence, which Washington had to squelch with some determination, that they were subject to no commands but those issued directly by Morgan and Arnold.[32]

Such independence of mind, hopefully, would be less evident in a corps of Light Infantry under a brigadier, which Washington ordered created in August 1777 by drafting one hundred men with appropriate officers and sergeants from each of his brigades—about 450 men in all. By comparison, the entire force available to Washington at the time amounted to about eight thousand Continentals and three thousand Militia. By the following January, the commander recommended to a committee of Congress, meeting near his Valley Forge winter quarters, fairly wide-scale changes in Army organization, including the establishment of a light company of sixty–four officers and men from every regiment, the whole to be formed into brigades. "The body would compose the flying army; and, in conjunction with a body of horse would become extremely formidable and useful."[33] In August, the new corps, accompanied by a detachment of light dragoons, was sent into duty outside Washington's encampment to observe the enemy's lines at all times and insure against any surprise attack. Since the corps was to include hardy and active marksmen, commanded by capable officers, as John Wright notes, it soon "began to assume the character of a *corps d'élite.*"[34]

The following year more formal regulations for the corps were introduced by Baron Steuben, who was made inspector general of the Army of the United States, with the rank of major general, in the spring of 1778. For all their distrust of standing armies, the revolutionaries had—at least in the first years of the war—an exceptional fondness for foreign "experts" who came from such armies. Only a few, including Steuben and Lafayette, would remain in good standing.[35] The light infantry was organized in two brigades, each of four battalions and each battalion of four companies, formed of men 5'7"–5'9" in height, each of whom had been in service at least two years. In July 1779, under Brig. Anthony Wayne, the light corps of about 1,400 men (roughly 12 percent of Washington's total strength), performed a successful surprise assault on British positions at Stony Point on the Hudson River—a night attack performed with muskets unloaded and bayonets fixed, a difficult assignment for soldiers of any army, but managed very well by this elite unit which Washington himself had designated for the enterprise, spelling out in considerable detail how the attack was to be handled.[36] "Secrecy is so much more essential to these kind of enterprises than numbers," he wrote, "that I should not think it advisable to employ any other than the light Troops. If a surprize takes place, they are fully competent to the business, if it does not, numbers will avail little."[37] Wayne, who led the assault in person, announced that the first man to enter the defenses would receive $500, the second $400, and so on to the fifth man. Since morale was high in the unit as a whole, as demonstrated by the oversubscription to the call for volunteers for two twenty-man "forlorn hope" assault teams, such monetary rewards could only raise the men's spirits. As was customary, however, when the campaign ended the force was disbanded for the winter. Washington, for all his enthusiasm, had declined to permit a separate distinctive uniform for the light infantry, on the grounds that the men basically were detachments from the line and should continue to wear the uniforms of their original regiments: "The contrary would be a deviation from common practice and would not fail to create uneasinesses. . . ."[38]

In 1780, Steuben fought to put the corps on a more permanent basis, to serve as a model for the entire army.[39] The baron, who had been a Prussian staff officer, gave the unit his personal attention when it was reformed, and in particular focused upon bayonet training, a skill which had been less stressed in America than was usual in Europe. Steuben, who was given a free hand by Washington, continued to insist upon high physical standards and veteran credentials for all the unit's soldiers. By mid-1780, after much work and not a little angry shouting in English, French, and German, he wrote to Washington that "the corps will be the admiration of our allies as much as the terror of our enemies. There is hardly a man in it under twenty or over thirty years of age. They are all robust and well made and have a military appearance."[40]

At roughly the same time, the two brigades organized into a light division were given over to Lafayette's command to form an advance corps for the army. The marquis provided additional flags for the battalions, swords for the officers, and distinctive plumes for the men. Since the army had no grenadiers, this light force was the sole elite unit, and Lafayette in his correspondence clearly was proud of his command. As usual, the corps was dissolved in the winter, but reconstituted in the spring, with a draft of one company of thirty–four officers and men from each regiment. "The honor of every regiment," wrote the commander in chief, "is so much interested in the appearance and behavior of the Light troops which are a representation of the whole

Army that the General exhorts and expects the commanding officers of them will exert themselves to make a judicious choice for the formation of their respective companies."[41]

Soon enough Lafayette was ordered to Virginia with his corps, 1,850 strong including one hundred riflemen and three hundred cavalrymen. Clearly the process of selecting top companies from the New Hampshire, New York, Connecticut, Massachusetts, and Pennsylvania line regiments had gone well, despite the repeated disbandment. At least Lafayette was pleased; they were "the best troops that ever took the field," he bragged. He wished to provide each with a good uniform, but had to make do with an imported red and black feather for each man, swords, and other decorations for the officers, and a fine white horse for himself. At Yorktown in October, the light corps entered the trenches with envied elite status, and was assigned the honor position on the right of the line; once again, they attacked a redoubt with unloaded muskets and bayonets fixed. And once again, after the war, the unit was disbanded. The light corps disappeared, but it had established a unique place in history as "the first and only corps d'élite of the American army," as John Wright asserted in 1926. More elites were to come, but only later in the century.[42]

The independent rifle companies of the early war, however, deserve a share of fame. The most renowned was one of the two from Virginia, that captained by Daniel Morgan, an impressively large, barely literate, fiery-tempered frontier teamster and farmer with considerable militia experience. His Frederick County company of just under one hundred men was formed of carefully selected marksmen, most in their early twenties, outfitted, as many back country riflemen were, in Indian-style clothing. Though taken prisoner in the Quebec campaign of 1775–76, Morgan on his release was given command of a larger, provisional rifle corps of some five hundred marksmen skilled in woodcraft, drawn mainly from Pennsylvania and Virginia regiments, to serve as skirmishing light infantry. Interestingly, though the men were carefully chosen, not all had the necessary rifles, and Washington had to order his brigade commanders to exchange what state-owned rifles they had for Morgan's muskets, and to buy those that were private property.[43]

General Washington had an immediate use for Morgan's men. "The people in the Northern Army seem so intimidated by the Indians that I have determined to send up Col. Morgan's Corps of Rifle Men who will fight them in their own way," wrote Washington, who had some experience against Indians himself.[44] The commander in chief could have used these men elsewhere, but he was well aware of the psychological value of an elite force which would be respected by the enemy:

> These are all chosen Men Selected from the Army at large; well acquainted with the use of Rifles and with that mode of Fighting, which is Necessary to make them a good Counterpoise to the Indians, and have distinguished themselves on a variety of occasions Since the formation of the Corps, in Skirmishes with the Enemy. I expect the most eminent Services from them, and I shall be mistaken, if their presence does not go far towards producing a general Desertion among the Savages. I should think it would be well, even before their arrival to begin to circulate these Ideas, with proper Embellishments, throughout the Country, and the army to take pains to communicate them to the Enemy. It would not be amiss, among other Things, to magnify Numbers.[45]

Nor was Washington insensitive to the effect on his own forces of the presence of Morgan's corps, as he made clear to Maj. Gen. Horatio Gates, to whose command at Fort Ticonderoga the unit was sent. "This Corps I have great dependance on, and have no doubt but they will be exceedingly useful, as a check given to the Savages and keeping them within proper Bounds, will prevent Genl [sic] Burgoyne from getting Intelligence as formerly, and animate your other Troops from a sense of their being more an equality with the Enemy."[46] The unit did indeed prove most useful against Burgoyne's Indians in the Saratoga campaign which followed (1777), where the corps, augmented by another 250–300 selected light infantry musket men under Maj. Henry Dearborn of New Hampshire, played a pivotal role, not least in their night raids on the British pickets and their sniping at Burgoyne's officers and artillery men. Burgoyne himself complained about the "great numbers of marksmen, armed with rifle-barrel pieces; these, during an engagement, hovered upon the flanks in small detachments, and were very expert in securing themselves in high trees in the rear of their own line, and there was seldom a minute's interval of smoke, in any part of our line, without officers being taken off by a single shot."[47]

Morgan's men were valuable not only in such sharpshooter roles, but also proved essential in countering Burgoyne's advance force under Brig. Gen. Simon Fraser, which included grenadiers, light infantry, and a special corps of British marksmen drawn from every regiment (and quite probably diminishing the effectiveness of those regiments, though this conclusion is not easy to substantiate).[48] Indeed, Washington had the greatest difficulty in recovering Morgan's force from Gates. Surely, the general wrote to Washington, the commander "would not wish me to part with the Corps the Army of General Burgoyne are most afraid of."[49] Washington finally had to send a trusted aide to persuade Gates to release the unit. Thomas Frothingham, in his study of Washington as commander in chief, argues that Gates hoped to keep the skilled riflemen to enhance his own reputation for battlefield leadership and thus further his ambitions to replace Washington in the chief command.[50] In any case, Washington realized full well the value of Morgan's rifles, and after the war would recommend that in any American army, one man out of twenty should be a rifleman.[51]

After Saratoga, Morgan himself joined Washington's army near Philadelphia, but his men were dispersed to guard northern frontiers, and Morgan given command of a line regiment. What was left of the Rifle Corps was absorbed into the line as the Seventh Virginia Regiment. Not surprisingly, Morgan had aspirations to command the light corps when it was formed, but as has been seen it was given to Brigadier General Wayne, who outranked Colonel Morgan. Morgan did have another chance to show his abilities, however, for he was sent to the Carolinas with the rank of brigadier general to take command of an independent light corps, similar to that under Wayne, but considerably smaller (roughly four companies of infantry and one of cavalry), drawn from both Continental and militia sources.[52]

The Revolutionary War in the South is less well known than that of New England and New York. Not only have its battles acquired less permanent fame, but equally forgotten is its character as a vicious and brutal conflict, due in part to such factors as ethnic differences, lengthy British occupation, and a substantial pro-British Tory population. Here Morgan had the opportunity to confront the infamous "Tory Legion" of Lt. Col. Banastre Tarleton (16th and 17th Dragoons, combined with mounted Loyalist infantry and cavalry). Tarleton had won a reputation for ruthless and ultimately counter-productive brutality on his various raids. At the battle of Cowpens in South Carolina (1781), Morgan's

force, which included a majority of raw militia and was slightly outnumbered by Tarleton's well-trained 1,200 men, gained mastery over
Tarleton through skillful initial deployment and battlefield tactics.
Tarleton's losses were some nine hundred men dead, wounded, and
taken prisoner. The loss of this cavalry was a serious one to the larger
army of General Cornwallis, who had no alternative light reconnaissance force, and certainly contributed to his eventual abandonment of
South Carolina. Morgan went on to raise another force of riflemen in
Virginia, but ill-health forced the early retirement in 1781 of the very
capable leader. In Don Higginbotham's opinion, Morgan was "the outstanding battlefield commander in the Continental Army."[53]

Riflemen, however, remained a persistent need for American
forces, and even after the formation of the Light Corps, a few rifle
companies remained for detached service as a small "Rifle Corps."
Washington found these most useful, though as in the case of the Light
Corps it was customary to return such units to their regiments for the
winter—collecting their rifles for careful storage and issuing the men
with muskets in their stead. By the summer of 1781, however, there
simply were not enough such men available in the army's ranks, and
Washington wrote to Joseph Reed, president of Pennsylvania's supreme
executive council, to ask for three hundred "expert Rifle Men." These
men would be necessary in the siege-type warfare which the general
foresaw, in order "to fire into the embrazures and to drive the enemy
from their parapets when our approaches are carried very near their
Works," as well as to counter the expert fire of the elite light Hessian
Jägers.[54] Though the number of weapons gained was not large, Washington asked that the recruits bring their own rifles, for which they
would be paid; "if a considerable part of them should come unarmed
we shall be put to very great difficulties on that account, as we have
but very few Rifles belonging to the Continent[al Army]."[55]

It is clear that from the beginning of this war, whether as riflemen
or light infantry, men with marksman and skirmishing skills were considered elite, particularly when formed into special detached corps and
assigned priority tasks. Washington to the end of the war kept an eagle
eye on the performance of such men. After reviewing the First Massachusetts Brigade in June 1782, for example, while praising the unit as
a whole, he advised that "the Officers commanding the Light Infantry
should impress upon the men the necessity of taking deliberate Aim
whenever they fire and see that they do it when it is in their power. It is

the effect of the shot not the report of the Gun that can discomfort the Enemy and if a bad habit is acquired at exercise it will prevail in real Action and so vice versa," clearly a well-learned lesson of a long war.[56]

It must not be thought, however, that individual regiments were incapable of being seen as elite elements. One such was the 14th Continental Regiment, a colorful collection of sailors and fishermen from Essex County, Massachusetts, outfitted in white caps, blue coats, and tarred canvas breeches, and led by Marblehead businessman and sea captain John Glover. "Glover's Marblehead Regiment" fought through the latter half of 1775 and the whole of 1776 until it was disbanded (Glover became a brigadier general and finally retired from the army in 1782). The Marblehead men were Washington's "special boat unit" in effect, earning considerable fame for two striking contributions in addition to some early privateering forays at sea and their fair share of land battles. The first was to ferry the entire American Army from Long Island to Manhattan; the second was to carry the same army across the ice-choked Delaware river on Christmas Eve 1776. Though generations of Americans have obtained their image of this stirring event from Emanuel Leutze's massive (12' x 21'), but inaccurate, painting in New York's Metropolitan Museum of Art (the Rhine was his model; no sane man would stand erect during such a crossing on a small boat, and it is the wrong sort of boat anyway), few have bothered to remember the name of the unit responsible. They seem also to have held their own in camp as well, if one story of a ferocious brawl with Morgan's frontiersmen, which Washington himself had to quell, can be believed.[57]

Several American formations earned similar long-lived reputations, though the cause was more likely to have been the inspired leadership of their commanders, rather than any outstanding qualities of their men. For example, Col. Francis Marion, "a moody, introverted, semi-literate genius," in the words of one biographer, gained military experience in the Carolina Indian wars, and became commander of the 2d Regiment of South Carolina Continentals. When South Carolina was overrun by the British and his regiment broken up, he led a small band of survivors and other stray elements in a successful guerrilla campaign against British regulars. "Damned old fox," Tarleton called him, and the nickname "Swamp Fox" stuck. Marion yearned for the command of regulars again, but he was instead promoted to brigadier in 1780 and given command of South Carolina's cavalry, working in conjunction with Lt. Col. "Light Horse Harry" Lee, another famous

cavalry leader, and his legion of roughly 260 men in the campaign of
1780–81 which had its end at Cowpens with the eventual British withdrawal from South Carolina. The roles of Marion and Lee were important in this campaign, but it is hard to justify calling their commands
elite forces.[58]

Much the same conclusion must be drawn about Vermont's "Green
Mountain Boys" led by Ethan Allen, "that aggressive, loose-lipped Paul
Bunyan from the Green Mountains," in the words of Willard Wallace.[59]
Allen's force was a volunteer militia organized before the Revolution
with the purpose of keeping the area out of the control of New York
and thus defending their Vermont land titles. In the early 1770s, the
"boys" honed their expertise with raids and skirmishes, their order preserved as much by Allen's fists as anything else.[60] When the Revolution came, however, differences with the "Yorkers" were set aside for
the moment, and Colonel Commandant Allen led his band of "poorly
armed, undisciplined, rag-tail frontier farmers" in an astonishingly successful attack on Fort Ticonderoga.[61] The event was of great importance, though Allen's two hundred men (about fifty were veteran Massachusetts militia under Col. James Easton) had mastered a sleepy British garrison of less than half that number. Several score usable artillery
pieces were carried off by the Americans, whose artillery at that stage
was virtually non-existent. Soon afterwards, however, the Green Mountain Boys had enough of campaigning and virtually melted away; even
Benedict Arnold, another capable leader, could not keep them from
carrying off the plunder they had won at Ticonderoga. The best Arnold
could do was to insist, when he went off to capture Quebec, that his
army include no Green Mountain Boys.[62] Allen's story only proves that
legendary exploits are not sufficient for elite status.

One special volunteer unit which though short-lived was effective, however, was "Knowlton's Connecticut Rangers," formed on
Washington's orders in August 1776 after the Battle of Long Island, in
which the lack of effective scouts had led to American encirclement
and defeat. Lt. Col. Thomas Knowlton was known for his service with
Putnam's rangers in the French and Indian War, as well as his heroism
at Bunker Hill, and thus was a logical choice. (Putnam might have
been given this command, had he not now been a high-ranking general; Rogers now fought alongside the British.) His unit, roughly 140
men, chosen mainly from Connecticut regiments, was soon watching
for a British landing on Manhattan, and fought so tenaciously in the

subsequent battle of Harlem Heights that the hard-pressed Americans were given new heart as a combined force of Hessians and British light infantry and Highlanders were beaten back. Knowlton himself was killed in the fighting. Unfortunately, this Ranger organization was part of the garrison of Fort Washington which had to surrender on November 16, having been active only for some ten weeks. One officer of the unit, however, earned permanent fame. Yale graduate and New London schoolteacher Capt. Nathan Hale of the 7th Connecticut Regiment (19th Continental Regiment) was probably selected personally by Knowlton for his rangers, and recommended to Washington as a capable, active young man (he was twenty-one in 1776) who might be

ETHAN ALLEN, COLONEL COMMANDANT. ALLEN'S FORCE, THE GREEN MOUNTAIN BOYS OF VERMONT, WAS A VOLUNTEER MILITIA ORGANIZED BEFORE THE REVOLUTION WITH THE PURPOSE OF KEEPING THE AREA OUT OF THE CONTROL OF NEW YORK AND THUS DEFENDING THEIR VERMONT LAND TITLES. THE REVOLUTION BROUGHT THEM THEIR MOMENT OF GLORY WHEN THEY CAPTURED THE BRITISH GARRISON AT FORT TICONDEROGA. *ENGRAVING (ARTIST UNKNOWN) OF A STATUE OF ETHAN ALLEN BY SCULPTOR B. F. KINNE (VERMONT HISTORICAL SOCIETY).*

successful in spying out British dispositions on Long Island. Alas, Hale
was captured in disguise and subsequently executed on September 22
as a spy. He almost certainly did say "I only regret that I have but one
life to lose for my country," a famous wartime remark which like others that will be noted in this volume must be credited to the representa-
tive of an elite unit.[63]

It is probably due to the somewhat surprisingly conventional nature of the Revolutionary War that while riflemen and light infantry
were featured, little is heard of rangers in general aside from Knowlton's
unit. It is not that they disappeared, but rather that they were confined
to those frontier regions where guerrilla and anti-Indian operations were
the order of the day. Several ranger units were in fact organized for the
Continental Army, as opposed to the militia, but little seems to be known
of them. "Colonel Gist's Ranger Corps," for example, was authorized
by Washington in early 1777, and included several companies each
from Maryland and Virginia. Although it is known to have merged
with other regiments or part-regiments before it was disbanded in late
1780, it may not have been employed in traditional "ranger" duty at
all. The "New Hampshire Rangers," about seventy men, were created
by the New Hampshire government, but General Washington declined
their use. Reconstituted in 1778, they led a precarious existence with
minimal Congressional support until disbanded at the start of 1781.[64]

The historical record is weakest on this back country frontier aspect of the war. Numerous small companies of volunteers acted as "spies
and wood rangers" in the words of one veteran, in difficult conditions,
often receiving little in the way of pay, rations, or clothing. They were
as disdained by the regulars who held the forts as they in turn disdained the regulars "as a worthless set, not daring to set heads outside
the gates but under the protection of volunteers. . ." Their skills were
substantial, and there was often little means to tell them apart from the
Indians. George Roush, for example, a scout in the Fort Pitt area in the
company of Capt. Samuel Brady, was ordered "to tan his thighs and
legs with wild cherry and white oak bark and to equip himself after the
following manner, to wit, a breechcloth, leather leggins [sic], mocca-
sins, and a cap made out of a raccoon skin, with the feathers of a hawk,
painted red, fastened to the top of the cap." Their faces painted in red
and black war colors, in small groups, over the course of three years
(1777–80) Brady's men were the equal of the Indians they sought out.
Though little known, such rangers were the main security for the dis-

tant settlements, though many of them could not be defended.[65]

Historians have drawn a multitude of lessons from the Revolutionary War. To some, it was a case of a civilian people taking up arms to win and maintain their liberty, a process which could no doubt be repeated when required and thus obviate the need for a standing army. To others, it proved just the opposite: the war was nearly lost for the lack of a standing army. As has been noted above, it is an important question since elite military forces are seldom created on short notice. Yet, in a sense, that is exactly what the American Army did, at least in drafting a Light Corps from standing regiments and each winter disbanding it. It is not possible to pass judgment on whether that corps would have performed better had it remained intact, though it can be argued that there was a serious cost in unit cohesion as a result. But the make-up of the army changed constantly, in any case, through death, sickness, desertion, and enlistment expiration. It is also true that the army was relatively inactive in winter (training was possible, but survival was sometimes a higher priority as at Valley Forge in the winter of 1777–78 and at Morristown in that of 1779–80).

The Emperor Napoleon no doubt would have done things differently; a standing elite Guard in its several forms was always an important part of his military establishment. But Washington, and Congress, had no clearly demarcated social elite for which military jobs had to be found in the manner of European countries, nor did they have the vast armies the emperor manipulated at the height of his power and which, at least in his mind, required an elite force as a way of rewarding his grizzled veterans and providing a model for his line regiments to emulate. One of the most impressive points about George Washington is his general understanding of the limits of what Congress, and the colonial supporters of the revolution, would tolerate in the way of regular forces, and, within that army, of special elites. It would soon be proven that his successors did not necessarily share the same delicate sensibilities.

3 The Early Republic

In mid-1784, Congress, after a year of discussion, reduced the Continental Army to a token eighty men, because "standing armies in time of peace are inconsistent with the principles of republican governments, dangerous to the liberties of a free people, and generally converted into destructive engines for establishing despotism." Having slept on it for a night, the following day Congress raised the number to seven hundred men, to serve for one year: eight companies of infantry and two companies of artillery.[1] The number was a far cry from what even Washington, Steuben, and Henry Knox, all men who were well aware of Congressional political and financial sensitivity, recommended in the knowledge that there were still arsenals to be guarded and British, Spanish, and Indians to be watched.

In other words, the Continental Army was regarded as a quite temporary evil, its relatively long-term (three year) enlistments and federal control made necessary by the general unsuitability of short-term militia for dealing with British regulars or hired professional German mercenaries (the Hessians). Since fewer solid citizens were willing to volunteer each year, by the end of the war, the army was composed largely of substitutes, vagrants, unemployed, captured British and German soldiers, and even slaves. Soon enough however, as J. K.

Martin and M. E. Lender have put it, "selective memory returned the legendary citizen-soldier to the center stage of history, where myth has kept him in place ever since."[2]

But neither necessity nor the deference always paid by Washington to the superior authority of Congress had quelled fear of a standing army of professionals living under severe discipline and owing its primary allegiance to its officers, even if the object of that army, paradoxically, was to ensure the freedom of the people from arbitrary authority enforced by a standing army. Civilian leaders had reacted with understandable nervousness to demands from the army, even before the war was actually over, for the settlement of grievances regarding back pay, future pensions, and the like (the so-called "Newburgh conspiracy" of 1783).[3] Washington used Continental troops in Philadelphia to overawe some mutinous soldiers from the Maryland line, while Congress, in the meantime, deserted the city. Washington supported Congress, but would it always be so? Leading nationalists such as John Adams saw clearly the need for a strong army and navy to support a strong union, but the anti-federalists feared that while the army might not set out to make emperors, it might well be used to suppress the rights of states as well as of individuals. It was this basic disagreement which lent significance to the concept of perpetuating an officer corps, either by keeping its active members on a retainer of half-pay, in the fashion of Great Britain, or through a sort of fraternal, honorary, and suspiciously elitist order.

Though the Society of the Cincinnati does not fit our definition of a battlefield elite, its general elitist military character was sufficient to arouse considerable opposition at the time. The idea seems to have come mainly from Henry Knox (the society's first secretary general) with some help from others, perhaps including Steuben. Since 1776 Knox had cherished the idea of some sort of officers' organization that, through a badge or other symbol, would draw attention to the holder's contribution to the founding of the nation. As the war came to an end, Knox foresaw that with peace and the disbanding of the army, the officer corps would no longer have the means and influence to obtain the pay and pensions to which it was entitled. The precise meaning of the original "Order of Liberty" association may be argued; as Minor Myers, Jr., the historian of the society, explains, "some would see it as a pension fund, some as a political threat to the Articles [of Confederation], and some as nascent hereditary aristocracy, an attempt to establish an

American order of knighthood."[4] The name at least came easily enough: Cincinnatus was called out of his Roman poverty to lead his people in war (485 BCE), but after victory he willingly yielded up his dictatorial powers and returned to his plow—and to the poverty the American officers feared, particularly those who had found that officer status meant incurring substantial personal debts.

Knox and his associates began active planning in 1783, arguing that the society would speak not just for the officers, but for the army as a whole, and would be a far better solution than a general refusal of duty—i.e., mutiny—until arrears were paid. The organization outlined was to function at both national and state levels, since states were responsible for paying state units; membership would be hereditary. In June 1783, a considerable number of officers under Steuben's leadership met to choose a president general; it was no surprise that Washington was selected, thus adding his prestige to the society, though Steuben continued to serve as the group's actual presiding officer. Alexander Hamilton, like Knox a veteran officer and close associate of Washington, founded the New York branch and would succeed Washington as the society's second president.[5]

More controversial was Maj. Pierre L'Enfant's suggestion that the members would wear not a medal as originally proposed, but a badge or decoration, much as did members of elite European orders of knighthood—such as Steuben's badge and star of the "Order of Fidelity of Baden." L'Enfant, a capable military engineer who would gain fame as the designer of the city of Washington, under Washington's orders proceeded to Paris in 1783 to have the eagle badges manufactured according to his own drawings, returning the following year.

Meanwhile, however, while there had seemed to be little hostility to the purple heart badge and various gold and silver medals and presentation swords voted by Congress from time to time, the Society of the Cincinnati was another matter. "The clamour raised . . . was far more extensive than I expected," wrote Maj. Gen. Nathaniel Greene in August 1784. "I had no conception that it was so universal. I thought it had been confined to New England alone; but I found . . . all the Inhabitants in general throughout the United States were opposed to the order."[6]

In particular, Thomas Jefferson led the attack. To Jefferson, the institution was a dangerous haven for anti-democrats, "carving out for itself hereditary distinctions, lowering over our Constitution eternally, meeting together in all parts of the Union, periodically, with closed doors, accumulating a capital in their separate treasury, corresponding secretly & regularly. . . ."[7] Jefferson was not alone; John Jay, John Adams, and Samuel Adams all held similar views. Benjamin Franklin, minister to France, had no objection to a ribbon but many to a hereditary society, arguing that members should be content with a lifetime badge and ribbon, "and let the distinction die with those who have merited it."[8] Washington had feared just such a response from the start, and when in May 1784 the society's general meeting gathered in Philadelphia, he used his influence to remove all hereditary aspects. His real intent was to kill the society altogether, but this proved impossible in the face of officer grievances, the popularity of the idea of an organization, and the appeal of L'Enfant's badges.

The changes introduced in 1784 did not by any means quell suspicion of the society, not least because by mid-year the thirteen state societies had enrolled some 1,500 (2,160 would eventually belong) out of a potential total of about 5,800 eligible officers. Though ostensibly non-political, the Cincinnati was solidly behind a strong central government, and used its influence to that end as the only society (with the possible exception of the Masons) which reached throughout the new nation's elite socio-political strata. Indeed, the eventual foundation of the electoral college owes at least some of its origin to the Cincinnati, since delegates at the Constitutional Convention feared precisely the influence of such a society over the people in a popular election. As Knox's friend, Massachusetts Congressman Eldbridge Gerry, put it, his admiration for the various members of the society "could not blind him to the danger & impropriety of throwing such a power [of choosing the president] into their hands."[9]

The society in the end proved no threat to the Republic or even to the anti-federalists. Though in the post-war years the hereditary aspect of society membership was quietly restored (individual state organizations had never dropped it), the group entered a period of decline in the first half of the nineteenth century. After the Civil War, however, several societies flourished which commemorated ancestors from America's past and added social cachet to their members, such as the Sons of the Revolution (founded in 1876), the Daughters of the American Revolution (1890), and even the Daughters of the Cincinnati (1894). Though obviously not military elites as such, these organizations certainly did their best to preserve the memory of ancestors who, in some cases at least, deserved that title.

For the same reason that a hereditary society of military officers aroused opposition, so too did the idea of a permanent academy for the training of officers. As with the Cincinnati, Henry Knox was involved from the beginning. Knox was not only a close associate of Washington (and, at nearly three hundred pounds, one of the few men who was physically bigger), but before the Revolution he had studied things military, both as a member of the Boston Grenadier Corps and as the owner of "The London Book Store" in that city. Throughout the war Knox argued that America needed a military academy to impart intricacies of the science to its officers, but little was done until it was nearly over. Contact with the professionalism of men like Steuben, who entered American service, and the trained officers of America's ally France, helped prepare the ground for an academy, but even then the subject generated sharp debate between Knox and his supporters (including Washington and Jefferson), who argued that such tasks better fell to the individual states. In 1794, however, Congress approved a modest program for the training of cadets by the Corps of Artillerists and Engineers, the rather grandiose term used for the tiny handful of men stationed at West Point. Very slowly through the 1790s students and instructors were added, always facing the same fear of a body of trained officers which underlay public hostility to the Society of the Cincinnati.[10]

When Jefferson became president in 1802, however, he changed his attitude, primarily for educational reasons. It was time, he believed, for a national institution which taught modern sciences rather than the traditional classics. Such an academy—for sectionalists opposed a national university—would supply men trained in the skills of artillery and engineering which only the federal government was likely to require, though of course it would have to be kept under civilian control. With presidential support, classes could begin, with cadets ranging in age from ten to thirty-four, some of whom left after six months and some of whom stayed on for six years. But Jefferson had not managed to quell opposition from Southerners who wanted a school of their own, from politicians who wished to reserve for themselves the patronage power of granting commission in the army or militia, and from those diehards who continued to distrust the very idea of professional soldiers, let alone a self-contained officer aristocracy. Very slowly, the operations of the United States Military Academy were regularized, after its final establishment by Congress in 1802. After 1810, for example, cadets would be admitted only between the ages of fifteen and twenty. From 1817 to 1833 the Academy entered into something of a golden age under the superintendency of Sylvanus Thayer who did much to shape its curriculum, including its emphasis on mathematics and engineering, not only for the early nineteenth century, but right through to the twenty-first.

Even though the output of the school was small, it was still more than the army could use, and many of its graduates turned to rewarding civilian careers after short tours in an army in which there was little chance of rapid advance. The militia might have had a place for them, but the general attitude of professional officers toward the militia was disdain (though many graduates took up militia positions in both the Mexican and Civil Wars). Indeed the problem was serious enough for the academy, with the help of President Madison and Secretary of War Calhoun, to ward off an 1821 motion in Congress to abolish the entire institution. Even more dangerous attacks came when Andrew Jackson became president in 1829. Jacksonians looked at West Point and were angered by an institution that, in the words of Stephen Ambrose, was "obviously aristocratic, with its lily-fingered cadets in their fancy little uniforms who received money for their free education and became upon graduation snobbish officers in a caste-ridden army that was hostile to democracy or, worse, who resigned their commissions in order to cash in on the mathematical and engineering knowledge the government had given them." What saved the academy was the fact that the Jacksonians were empire-builders, and empires require the roads, harbors, canals, and railroads which only engineers can build. Until 1824, when Rensselaer Polytechnic Institute was established, only West Point trained such men. But survive it did, and its graduates would play commanding roles in every American war to follow.[11]

The resulting officer cadre certainly could not be called "aristocratic" in the sense of inherited privilege, but in the early nineteenth century it did become a distinct profession, sharing professional skills acquired by study rather than intuition, and absorbed in professional interests and concerns. And, as William Skelton comments, they did share a common background: "The vast majority of West Pointers were the sons of government officials, professional men, merchants, and landholding farmers and small planters, clearly middle or upper middle class in education and social status if less so in economic circumstances." In one sense, the Jacksonians were right: gradually "there emerged a distinct military subculture, sharing many characteristics of the larger society but containing its own configuration of values and traditions and commanding loyalty as an institution," often adding a feeling that this "devoted band of brothers" was under siege of a sort, "scorned and mistreated by petty politicians and an ungrateful public." Any monolithic elitist sentiment, as Skelton explains, was offset by intensive internal tensions between the several branches and departments, and indeed between individuals frustrated by an inflexible system of promotion by seniority.[12]

But such developments were in the future. In the aftermath of the Revolutionary War, the chief problem was that of inadequate military resources to meet substantial needs, an issue which would not be solved by either a society for veteran officers or a school for future ones. Growing Indian troubles in 1790 brought an increase of the army to 1,216 men serving three years, but the militia would still have to carry the burden of any substantial campaign. The dangers of this policy were demonstrated when Brig. Gen. Josiah Harmer, with a force mainly of militiamen, was badly cut up by Miami Indians in what is now Indiana. Congress added another regiment of 912 men in early 1791. In November, Maj. Gen. Arthur St. Clair, with another mixed force, took even more serious casualties in another defeat near Fort Wayne. Congress, now aroused, brought the army up to about five thousand men in 1792, formed them into a reorganized force known as the "Legion of the United States," and, in June, placed them under the command of Maj. Gen. Anthony Wayne. Wayne divided his men into four sub-legions (each with its own special headdress and flags) of mixed infantry, riflemen, dragoons, and artillery, instilled suitable discipline and, with a vengeance, drilled his men according to Steuben's *Regulations,* seeing to their proficiency with both rifle and bayonet. In August 1794, with about 2,600 men, Wayne's Legion was able to inflict a notable defeat on the Miami tribes at the Battle of Fallen Timbers. It was an important conflict, because it demonstrated to Britain that the new nation could not be ignored; that same month a treaty was negotiated for the withdrawal of British troops from the area.[13]

The Legion had proven a useful force, but given the momentarily peaceful situation on the frontier, the outbreak of a major war in Europe which was likely to keep the European powers occupied for some time, and the general prejudice against a standing army, it is not surprising that Congress once again steadily reduced the army's numbers. Enlistment dropped to 5,400 in the spring of 1800, and to 4,500 by the

end of 1801 (the Legion was abolished late in 1796). The Quasi-War
with France (1797–1800) and the War with Tripoli brought renewed
interest in America's naval strength, but the army was down to about
three thousand in the spring of 1802 and 2,600 in early 1805.[14]

Interestingly, 2,600 officers and men was the total figure which
Washington had recommended as a permanent force at the end of the
Revolutionary War, hoping that Congress would approve at least that
much of an army, inadequate though it might be. The president had
also outlined a select militia, which would be called up in time of war.
This force would be drawn from a uniform classification of young men
aged eighteen to twenty–five who would serve three to seven years,
and thus surely be an elite in the American context. At the same time,
he would merge Continental and state troops as far as possible, not
least as a means of consolidating the union. Alexander Hamilton wished
to go even further, supporting the creation of a special elite volunteer
element as a long-term reserve, at the same time putting all military
forces under Congressional control. None of these proposals had passed,
arousing as they did all the old issues of standing armies, taxation powers, and federal control over state militias. An awkward compromise
of 1787 divided control: the states organized their militias and appointed
officers, but Congress could use such forces in national service when
necessary. The Uniform Militia Act of 1792 required all adult white
males aged eighteen to forty–five to arm themselves and join a militia
unit, but no uniformity of organization or training was provided for,
meaning that such details were left to the local communities, with predictable results. One example will have to serve, in this case from
Cortland County in upstate New York (though undated, it comes from
the 1812 era; it might easily have come from a century earlier). As
Thurlow Weed recalled: "I attended one regimental review, or 'general
training,' as it was called. It was an eminently primitive one. Among
the officers were two chapeaux, to which Captain Carley, one of the
two, added a sword and sash; four feathers standing erect upon felt
hats; fifteen or twenty muskets; half a dozen rifles; two horse drums,
and as many 'spirit-stirring fifes.' Of rank and file, there were about
two hundred and fifty. In the way of refreshments, there were ginger-
bread, blackberry pies, and whisky. . . ." Assuming the rifles were all in
good repair, of a calibre large enough to be used for war, and carried by
men with the necessary skills to use them well (all questionable as-
sumptions), we are still left with only one rifle for each thirty–five or

forty men from what was then still a frontier area, who had come to do military training in generally troubled times.[15]

With the militia a complicated and uncertain structure upon which to rely, the tendency in a crisis was to bypass it and turn to the traditional response of organizing volunteer forces, as was done in both the Quasi-War and again in the War of 1812. In the latter case, as tension with Britain increased, Congress was willing to enlarge the standing army to ten thousand and if necessary to approve the service of up to thirty thousand volunteer troops organized by the several states. The actual strength of the army in 1809, however, was under three thousand men—not enough even to man the various forts and batteries spread across the country. When war arrived in 1812, the nominal ten thousand was increased by the sudden addition of ten regiments of infantry, two of artillery, and one of cavalry—all to be provided a bounty of sixteen dollars, three months' pay, and 160 acres of land. Militia and volunteers now came to a grand total of 185,000 on paper, but even on paper few were trained veterans of any kind.[16]

Overall, more than 525,000 men signed up in various categories for the war of 1812, according to an 1836 estimate by the adjutant general, but only a small percentage of this total was available at any one time to the federal government for such projects as the invasion of Canada. State authorities resisted the recruitment of men from the militia, while individual recruits found greater reward in being hired as legal substitutes for men seeking to avoid militia service. Since the army as a whole was short on uniforms and equipment in addition to all its other problems, it is a wonder that the Republic fared as well as it did in this war. As it was, J. C. A. Staggs explains, "most of the recruits received no training at all before being marched into action, and since the campaigns of 1812 brought only defeat, death, sickness, or capture to the American forces, the very structure of many of the regiments was almost completely shattered."[17] The situation was not much better in the next several years; overall, as Russell Weigley remarks, the United States fought "an inchoate, almost planless kind of war."[18] Fortunately for American history, the war at sea went rather better, but that is not part of our story.

It is not easy to locate elites in the 1812 conflict, but one candidate is Col. (and Congressman) Richard M. Johnson's volunteer regiment of mounted Kentucky riflemen, some one thousand men organized in 1813, wearing leather smocks and trousers and carrying long rifle, tomahawk, and scalping knife. Johnson trained them well, including considerable practice in charging into an opposing line of firing infantry—not a common American tactic, since the Republic had little cavalry. This was the only mounted unit to accompany Maj. Gen. William Henry Harrison's 1813 invasion of Canada, and at the Battle of the Thames, they rode through a British line of the 41st Foot and the Royal Newfoundland Regiment. As mounted riflemen, their method in general was to ride to a position, dismount, and continue to fight on foot—only on this occasion, they had first to ride through the enemy to establish their line behind them, and without the sabers or lances (or even short carbines) which cavalry was wont to use on such occasions. The battle was also notable for the death of the great Indian leader Tecumseh, whose loss was an important factor in breaking Indian military power in the Northwest. Johnson, who was severely wounded, was credited with personally killing Tecumseh, an achievement which carried him into the vice presidency in 1836. The British were badly outnumbered, poorly led, and inadequately supplied, but it was still a notable victory.[19]

At the end of the War of 1812, the Regular Army stood at over sixty-two thousand men, including four rifle regiments. The Revolutionary War precedent of a Light Corps, however, had not been adopted, and in the aftermath of the conflict, only one rifle regiment was allowed to remain intact, in conjunction with eight regiments of line infantry, and no cavalry at all. In 1821, further cutbacks reduced the Regular Army to about six thousand enlisted men, and resulted in the merger of the Rifle Regiment with the 6th Infantry. Skirmishers, of course, had been employed in the war, and were expected to be needed in any conflict, but no special elite or even rifle corps remained. Indeed, the army was in a sense lucky to remain at all, even in its reduced format. In addition to the longstanding distrust of a standing force and the usual budgetary pressures, the old mythology of the superiority of the backwoods rifleman had been reinforced by the success of General Jackson's Tennessee and Kentucky woodsmen, Baratarian smugglers, and other irregulars at the battle of New Orleans at the end of the war, a legend now added to those of Lexington, Concord, and Bunker Hill. That Jackson's artillery had been critical to the smashing defeat of British regulars was easily forgotten.[20]

Indeed, the years between the 1812 and Mexican Wars witnessed the flowering of the image of the idealized hunter-marksman, a man with ties as close to nature as any American Native: "a man whose character and conduct were products of his wilderness environment, a man whose tie to the land was more profound than that of any civilized individual." Daniel Boone (who died in 1820) or Davy Crockett, Tennessee and Texas politician from the backwoods (twice elected to the U.S. Congress), or even Natty Bumppo, who never lived at all (he was the hero of James Fenimore Cooper's Leatherstocking books) were all the rage, and as historian Daniel Herman has made clear, it was no accident that sport hunting began to come into its own.[21]

But the key event in perpetuating the rifleman-ranger image between 1815 and the Mexican War was the struggle at the Alamo in 1836. The Alamo was of course a seminal event in the formation of a special Texas identity, but its importance was hardly restricted to Texas. Put simply, the siege came about because Gen. Antonio López de Santa Anna was determined to destroy Texas's pretensions to independence. A mixed force of "regulars" from Texas's "Army of the People," under Col. William Barret Travis, and irregular backwoods volunteers under Jim Bowie (the two men rather uneasily shared command), some 180 men in all, occupied the derelict mission of San Antonio de Valero, known locally as the "Alamo," across the San Antonio River from the town of San Antonio de Béxar, doing their best to turn it into a defensible position. Unfortunately, their manpower was completely inadequate to defend the entire perimeter of their position, and when Santa Anna launched his forces in a surprise night attack (night conditions of course reducing the effectiveness of the Alamo's long rifles), he overwhelmed the garrison in a brief but bloody struggle. All of the Alamo's defenders were killed in battle or soon afterward, since Santa Anna had ordered "no quarter." Another Thermopylae, Texans and American alike believed: like the Spartans in the face of Xerxes Persian Army, they had all sacrificed themselves for a noble cause. (It was of course not quite so simple. For example, Mexico had abolished slavery, and Texas wished to keep it.)[22]

Travis, Bowie, and even Davy Crockett had died, left to live on in legend. Precisely how most of the defenders died will never be known. Only one woman, a child, and Travis's slave were allowed to live, but the men of the Alamo had died heroically and taken not a few of Santa Anna's men with them. The Alamo event perhaps needed no reinforcement, but it was easy to conflate with a struggle which occurred soon afterward at Goliad, where Mexican forces caught up with a badly-led column of Texans under Col. James W. Fannin. Fannin was caught in the open by Mexican cavalry and, after a hard struggle, surrendered. Though the surrender was accepted by the local Mexican commander, subsequently on Santa Anna's orders the prisoners, 342 in all, were exterminated: "342 martyrs to add to the Alamo's pantheon."[23] And quite a pantheon it was, one to be kept alive perpetually in story and song, becoming a permanent part of the rifleman/hunter/martyr image and helped along by such contributions as the hugely popular 1950s Disney television series *Davy Crockett* or John Wayne's 1960 saga, *The Alamo*.

To return to Jackson, the president himself, though always willing to praise the militia, appreciated the need for a standing army. Similarly, he realized the value of the military academy at West Point, and saw to its survival against considerable criticism from those who regarded this institution, above all, as the potential foundation of the sort of dangerous, militaristic professional elite that they most feared. In short, though President Jackson himself was a military hero, in his era military institutions in general were suspect as "the citizenry became increasingly wedded to military amateurism."[24]

Even the militia, in a general sense, decayed, but there always survived that strain of volunteer interest in the sort of unit which served social as well as military purposes. Some were very exclusive. The Chatham Artillery of Savannah, for example, required candidates to have two sponsors and win the votes of four-fifths of its members. The Washington Artillery of the nation's capital, begun in the 1790s, similarly required election; the Washington Artillery of New York City, founded in 1806, was yet another similar institution.[25] The Washington Artillery Company of New Orleans (it was a popular name) delighted in celebrating American traditions, in part out of rivalry with the Bataillon d'Artillerie d'Orléans, which drew on the French-speaking Creole elite. The Philadelphia Lancer Guard, founded in 1835, not only wore gaudy Napoleonic uniforms, but hired a Polish officer to train its men in lance and saber.[26]

The Light Infantry Blues of Richmond; the Philadelphia City Cavalry; the Washington Light Infantry of Charleston, South Carolina: typically such units took on a nomenclature and often the accoutrements—down to bearskins—of the sort of formation considered elite in the Napoleonic era. Politics might have played a role: the Worcester (Massachusetts) Light Infantry and the Worcester Artillery felt obliged to have separate Fourth of July parades in 1812—the former was Federalist, and the latter Republican. Some were immigrant companies, especially Irish or German (Jäger was a favorite nomenclature); it was not uncommon for individual families to have long associations with these institutions, though this was not the same as actual military experience. Often they faced considerable opposition from those who objected to their social exclusivity, their penchant for alcohol, their militarism in a time of peace—or simply their general apparent anachronistic character. Those that survived over time would find themselves on active duty, perhaps not in the Mexican War, but almost certainly in the Civil War.

Not all volunteer militia units were exclusive, and only a handful won lasting fame, but in peacetime all helped their communities celebrate festivals, holidays, and funerals with marches, balls, and banquets, helping out in emergencies, and often building an esprit de corps which established a basis for effective wartime service and even elite reputations. For those individuals who wished for a military education, military schools were available in both the North and South, though aside from West Point none had the elite reputation of the Virginia Military Institute (founded in 1839) or the Citadel in Charleston. Popular feeling might disdain professional military institutions, but these examples show that a "martial spirit" remained alive in America, and that it was one closely associated with social elites. It was not accidental that the favorite honorary title of the century was "colonel."

Rod Andrew, Jr., however, finds that the South was particularly distinguished for its militarism by the mid-nineteenth century. Without discussing the cause—a topic which will be raised in the next chapter—it remains the case, according to Bruce Allardice, that between 1827 and 1860 some ninety-six military schools—academies, colleges, universities—were opened in the slave states, compared to fifteen in the free states. While some have seen in this fact proof of a plot to break up the union, Andrew believes that sectional tension was less important as a causal factor than the general belief that Southern gentlemen were more likely to cooperate with authority in a system of military discipline than they were in a non-military, faculty-administered system. By the 1850s, however, political differences between North and South were a potent incentive for the military school craze.[27]

Meanwhile, the Regular Army was parceled out in small units on frontier duty, or assigned to arduous duty in the difficult struggle against the Seminoles (1836–41). Mostly the regulars were infantry. At least to mid-century, Congress seemed to have an inveterate distrust of cavalry elitism, though the mounted infantry known as dragoons proved too useful to forego. Two regiments existed in 1842, but in that year Congress ordered the 2d U.S. Dragoons dismounted and converted to a rifle regiment, leaving only one. The decision was reversed two years later, but the uncertain fate of such cavalry units shows both the distrust of cavalry elites and the desire to save money on the extra equipment these units required. When the Mexican War broke out in 1846, the Regular Army still had two regiments of dragoons, but combined with eight infantry regiments and four artillery, the entire Army numbered only 8,500 at the most. It soon more than doubled, increasing infantry companies to a strength of one hundred men each (from sixty– four in peacetime), and adding new regiments. Regular forces, however, remained small in comparison with those used in other American wars. Zachary Taylor had six thousand men at Monterrey and five thousand at Buena Vista; Winfield Scott had ten thousand at Vera Cruz, and only a few hundred more in his advance on Mexico City.[28]

One new unit created in 1846 was the United States Regiment of Mounted Rifles. Dragoons issued the Model 1841 rifle in addition to Colt revolvers, but no sabers, were essentially mounted infantry sharp-shooters. The regiment saw action in central Mexico as both infantry and light cavalry. The formation was not well received by the regular officers, since mounted rifle officers were appointed directly from civilian life; President Polk was determined to bypass the lock on officer appointments which West Point seemed to possess. In that sense, the unit "seemed a colossal snub to the army," and in particular to its officers, considered by many to be an undemocratic elite trained at public expense. It should be remembered that the Academy at the time was focused mainly on providing an engineering curriculum; the best graduates joined the exclusive engineer corps, with the others—in order of rank—becoming topographical engineers (map-makers), artillerymen, infantrymen, or, least prestigious of all, dragoon officers.[29]

The regulars also believed they had won the Mexican War. In fact, over the course of eighteen months of war, twelve pitched battles occurred; regulars fought the first two, but all others included at least some volunteers, though some militia units did serve on the Rio Grande with Taylor, who in particular relied upon several companies of Texas Rangers (discussed below) to help protect the Texas region from

Comanches as well as Mexicans. The volunteers were normally part of the militia as well, but the formality of volunteering for service, usually for the duration of the conflict, nicely avoided the serious legal problems of limited service time and the requirement that the unit only be called up for duty within its home state. It did not hurt, as well, that they normally were clothed at their own expense.[30]

On the other hand, as with the militia, volunteer officers were accountable to their men, a fact which could inhibit discipline. Volunteers from one state often found fault with those from another, and quarrels developed. Fights could even occur between units from the same state. The Jasper Greens, a mostly-Irish company from Savannah, Georgia, for example, was involved in a fight with the Kennesaw Rangers of northern Georgia, which left several dead and wounded (whiskey had contributed). Moreover, since the sort of militia unit eager to volunteer was commonly drawn from men of some property while the Regular Army found its recruits among the lower strata of society or new immigrants, serious rivalry between the two forms of military unit was not uncommon. Later, as in the Civil War, volunteers won the respect of Regulars, and recruitment sources were less exclusive, but in the short Mexican War, this did not happen. In the case of the militia as a whole, where all free, able-bodied men ages eighteen to forty–five might serve, the model of a people's army, in which even the lowest-ranking soldier had a chance of advancement, took precedence, in contrast to what was regarded as the European model in which the officers were a caste apart from their men, who lived under draconian discipline. This particular tension, however, was of little importance in the Mexican War, in which only 12 percent of the "common" state militia units were utilized.[31]

As in the War of 1812, elite units were not common. Some volunteer units earned a reputation for reliability, such as Col. Jefferson Davis's Mississippi Rifles, which did well at the siege of Monterrey and at Buena Vista. Davis (USMA 1828) had fought in the Black Hawk War, but had resigned in 1835, and taken up a career as a Mississippi planter. Turning to politics, Davis won election to Congress in 1845. When the Mexican War broke out, Congressman Davis, without leaving Washington, was elected to command the First Mississippi Regiment. Davis accepted on the condition that his men be armed with the percussion-cap .54 caliber United States rifle, model 1841, with a range in skilled hands of up to four hundred yards. Army Commander Winfield

Scott resisted, preferring his regiments to be equipped with the .69 caliber smoothbore musket to which a bayonet could be fixed; though not accurate at over fifty yards, it did better serve the accepted tactics of a close range volley followed by a bayonet charge. Davis prevailed, however, and one thousand rifles were purchased for his men, who were also authorized to carry an array of other weapons, including Bowie knives, artillery swords, and Colt five-shot revolvers. Davis trained his men with determination, and he was most proud of the end result, aware of the general army prejudice against volunteers. As he explained at a Vicksburg dinner honoring himself and the returned veterans whose enlistments had expired: "Through the whole of the fighting, and in all their movements, our men conducted themselves with the skill and courage of veterans, and have wholly silenced all doubts as to the efficiency of volunteers. . . ."[32]

Another unit deserving of mention is the Texas Rangers, short-term irregular frontier guardians who had been active from time to time in Texas since the 1820s, and in particular during the lifespan of the Republic of Texas (1835–46). Hard men, on the whole, they were said to "ride like a Mexican, trail like an Indian, shoot like a Tennessean, and fight like a devil."[33] Distinguished from both the regular army and the militia, the few companies of Rangers (about 150 men in 1835) were mainly responsible for watching the Indian frontier. Their particular attraction was the combination of their wilderness skills, their low cost overall when compared with militia or regular forces, their zeal in seeking revenge for such incidents as the Alamo, and the fact that they could be called out for short periods of three to six months as necessary. When the Mexican War began, three regiments of Rangers (some seven hundred men) were raised and did useful service as scouts and light cavalry for Gen. Zachary Taylor's advance on Monterrey. Their ferocity there in battle, above all in the assault on the "Bishop's Palace," was notable, and the Mexican forces rightly respected their effectiveness with the rifle and several sets of Colt revolvers which they favored: "The Mexicans are terribly afraid of them," recorded Maj. General Ethan Allen Hitchcock.[34] But they were equally famous for their indiscipline; Taylor found them "a lawless set," "licentious vandals," and was generally glad to see the last of them when their enlistments ran out and the bulk of the one thousand–man unit returned home. In addition, a re-enlisted and newly recruited regiment of about five hundred men accompanied Gen. Winfield Scott in the same campaign, assigned to keeping the road open between Vera Cruz and the advance American forces and, once the city was taken, to counterguerrilla activities and general terrorism, earning the nickname "los Diablos Tejanos."[35] As one officer put it: "The departure of the Rangers would have caused more regret than was generally felt, had it not been for the lawless and vindictive spirit some of them had displayed in the week that elapsed between the capitulation of the city [Monterrey] and their discharge. Gifted with the intelligence and courage of backwoods hunters, well-mounted and skilled in arms, they were excellent light troops. Had they remained and given their whole attention to the guerrillas, they might have been exceedingly useful. The commanding general [Taylor] took occasion to thank them for the efficient service they had rendered, and we saw them turn their faces toward the blood-bought State they represented, and with many good wishes and the hope that all honest Mexicans were at a safe distance from their path."[36] After this war the Rangers returned to their frontier and police functions in their home state, but as Robert Utley remarks, "The Mexican War nationalized the Texas Ranger tradition and earned it an enduring place in the imagination of Americans."[37] The Rangers played no notable role in the Civil War, since most members were drawn off to the regular armies.

The most famous Mexican War volunteer unit at the time, however, was probably Brig. Gen. Alexander William Doniphan's 1st Missouri Mounted Volunteers. Doniphan, 6'4" and some 250 pounds, recruited a company of hardened and well-mounted riflemen, and then was elected commander of the entire regiment of eight hundred generally undisciplined men. His seven companies marched from Fort Leavenworth, Kansas, to New Mexico and on from Santa Fe deep into Mexico as far as Saltillo (Coahuila) to join Taylor's army, "in what was probably the most difficult trek in a war which saw several American units make long, arduous marches."[38] His variously uniformed men did well, making their journey of some 3,500 miles without supplies, pay, or even orders, and several times as at El Brazito and Sacramento routed substantially larger Mexican forces on the way. Doniphan "became *the* hero to the citizen-soldiers," and received a great reception on his return, once again gilding the reputation of the hardy volunteer rifleman.[39]

Despite the proliferation of rifle companies in the Mexican War, the musket remained much more common than the rifle, which was considered a weapon for special uses. The regulation tactical manual assumed that only one of the ten companies in a regiment would be armed with rifles. These companies might be detached to create a rifle battalion, as was done in Brig. Gen. Joseph Lane's Indiana Brigade at Buena Vista. There were also ten new regiments created by congressional legislation of February 1847, one of which was the "Regiment of Voltigeurs and Foot Riflemen." This unit's performance does not seem to have been particularly remarkable, though it did good service at Chapultepec.[40] In general, riflemen were used to cover the flanks of a larger formation, or to skirmish; muskets and bayonets were expected to decide the battle. The rifleman in this war was not necessarily the most capable soldier on the field, and certainly he had a reputation for indiscipline—or at least a reluctance to give automatic obedience to orders. In the Civil War, the situation would change dramatically, for by the end of the conflict most combat infantrymen were equipped with rifled muskets.[41]

Riflemen were not the only troops who might be detached, however. General Hitchcock recalled in an 1847 diary entry that in the conquest of Mexico City, Brig. Gen. William J. Worth, whose division was ordered to assault a heavily defended group of stone buildings and bastioned earth works known as El Molino del Rey (or the "foundry," rumored to be in use as a factory for casting cannon), ordered an assaulting column of five companies of selected veterans (five hundred men in all), to be chosen from the six regiments of his division. "The effect," commented Hitchcock, "was to separate officers from their men, to bring into the same conflict, side by side, men who did not know each other, and, above all, to separate men from their colors—a very serious matter, for every regiment has its own name and its own glory under its own flag. Now it is remarkable that this assaulting column of veterans was broken in its charge upon the enemy and about 150 men absolutely ran about 100 yards before they could be rallied. But the remnants of the same regiments charged the hacienda [the Casa Mata], equally well or better defended, without any break at all." This "picked command" under Maj. George Wright was assigned to assault the western front of the buildings while another column attacked on Wright's left; since Wright was attacking emplaced artillery with little in the way of artillery support of his own, his unit was demolished. In other words, it may be that the attempt to create an instant elite made little difference on the day. It would still appear reasonable to agree with Hitchcock in concluding that Worth's was not the best of plans.[42]

Once the Mexican War was concluded, the volunteers were sent home and disbanded along with most of the regular formations, though the Regiment of Mounted Rifles remained in service. The regulars were ultimately cut to a total force of just under ten thousand. The motive was not simply to reduce expenses; as tensions increased over slavery and states' rights, Southern representatives were unwilling to support a substantial institution which might become an instrument of repression. But once again, demands upon the army proved nearly overwhelming, and the number was increased, slowly at first (to about 13,000 in 1850; 13,800 in 1853). Four new regiments—two each of infantry and cavalry—in 1855 brought the total to about 17,800 by 1855, a number which had increased by only a few hundred when the Civil War began.[43] Basically, the army's mission remained what it had been before the Mexican War, though the geographical framework had been much enlarged by the annexation of Texas and Oregon and the conquest of California and New Mexico.

Over the next thirteen years until the Civil War, little seemed changed in the regular round of army life. The basic combat army was formed of mounted dragoons, riflemen, and regular cavalry, tasked to patrol the often moving Indian frontier as well as that with Mexico. Scattered about the frontier, small units operated from fixed stations. As Durwood Hall points out, while regiments "bore different names and practiced eccentric regimental traditions," little difference was to be found between them in the way of operational or tactical principles.[44] Duties varied, however, for not all assignments involved Indian fighting. San Francisco's problems, for example, were more than a handful for the tiny army garrisons at Benicia and the Presidio in the wake of gold rush–era vigilante justice and the organization from that port of filibustering expeditions to Mexico and beyond. The Mormons in Utah, the British in the San Juan Islands off Washington, and various partisans in "Bleeding Kansas" all involved the army in one way or another.

It is not really possible in the context of the history of what was basically a police force to trace particular elite units. That being said, it is nevertheless clear that some elements, and commanders, developed skilled "scouts" of mounted men to hunt down and destroy Indian raiding parties or—a generally more effective, if brutal, policy—Indian camps or settlements. A devoted officer such as Lt. William W. Averell of Company F, Mounted Rifle Regiment, constantly drilled his men on horseback and on foot, evolving his own "special drill for Indian fighting," which involved rapid deployment of his company from a column of twos into a front of one hundred yards in any direction. But time for such exercises was rarely adequate, nor was the zeal always present among either officers or enlisted men. Indeed, the former were just as likely to turn out the latter to work as general carpenters, laborers, and even farmers as each small garrison was often left to fend for itself.[45]

Occasionally, there were suggestions to develop a special sort of unit for Indian chasing. For example, in New Mexico territory the army was often stymied by the inability of cavalry horses, unlike Indian ponies, to sustain themselves on the spare grass which was often all that could be found for feed. Lt. Col. Edwin V. Sumner, for example, suggested the withdrawal of most cavalry from New Mexico, moving instead with well trained infantry to which were attached small units of *"very select horse"*, which would be led on long marches and mounted only at the last critical moment to ride down the Indians. "A small body of this kind would be worth ten times their number of ordinary men on broken down horses," advised Sumner, in putting forth a plan which interestingly had close parallels to the methods used by Arabian and North African raiders, who rode to war on camels but used horses for battle. As usual, however, the demands of time, space, and manpower meant that no such units were ever formed. On the other hand, the odds were always with the army in the long run. As Ball summarizes, "Constantly deploying company-sized and seasonal brigade-sized expeditions, the army chipped away at the edges of American Indian societies until they crumbled by century's end."[46] It was this Indian-fighting, peace-keeping small army, therefore, which would have to face the extreme challenge of the Civil War.

In the antebellum era, however, the militia tradition persisted, and, in some circles, participation in elite organizations remained quite popular. Interest only increased as the possibility of civil war became a probability. The most notable units included the better-known and most prosperous men of their communities. One such group was the Richmond Howitzers, founded in 1858 by G. W. Randolph, later secretary of war for the Confederacy. The three batteries of one hundred men each spent considerable time at their drill, a necessary diversion if they were to be effective as a unit of horse artillery. They would prove very reliable in the war, their losses generally made up with volunteers of the same sort from Richmond—and the unit remained extant through the end of the century.[47]

In the 1850s, however, the popular rage was for Zouaves rather than the hussars and lancers of the previous generation.[48] The Zouaves of the French army had their origin in the creation of a new French army elite in 1838, the *Chasseurs à pied*. The concept was to establish a new light infantry, highly mobile, trained at a special school at Vincennes in a variety of skills, including field craft, gymnastics, bayonet drill, and musketry, and capable of independent and decentralized operations with the esprit de corps to be expected of elite forces. One experimental battalion formed in 1838 grew into ten battalions in a general expansion in 1840, and in them were found many of France's best officers. The attention of Paris, and of international observers, was aroused at the triumphal entry into the capital of the Chasseurs, moving at their special *pas gymnastique*, a high-stepping trot of more than 150 paces per minute, which could cover ground nearly as fast as cavalry. This innovation was not simply for mobility nor a demonstration of conditioning, but was an attempt to find a solution to the problem of attacking an enemy equipped with the new and more efficient infantry rifles available since the Napoleonic Wars. Speed, *élan*, and the "furia francese," were seen as the answer to a terrible tactical dilemma.

The *Chasseurs à pied* were the infantry elite of France's Metropolitan army. In the separately constituted *Armée d'Afrique*, created for the conquest of Algeria, the Zouaves were trained in the same weaponry and tactics, were held to the same standards, saw at least as much action, and were equally ranked as elites. In origin, the force of about seven hundred officers and men was formed soon after the conquest of Algiers in 1830 of native infantry recruited from the Berbers of northern Algeria, and particularly from among the sedentary Kabylia tribes. The latter included the Zouaoua of the Jurjura mountains, roughly one hundred kilometers southeast of Algiers, who lent their name to the new unit. By the early 1840s, a single battalion had grown into a regiment of three. Though a few Algerians remained, the units were recruited now mainly from Frenchmen, particularly Parisians who had participated in the revolution of 1830 and now were given an opportunity to enlist by a government which found them an embarrassment at home. Over time, volunteers continued to be attracted to the Zouaves by the greater degree of freedom than that found in line regiments and the prospect of considerable action, to say nothing of the colorful uniforms. Zouaves wore loose, baggy trousers, short, open jackets, and a turban or a fez—all considerably freer and more comfortable than traditional tight, fitting high-collared regular uniforms.

In 1852, the regime of Louis Napoleon created three Zouave regiments, with one battalion of the old regiment forming the nucleus of each. There was no lack of veterans to fill the new ranks of a force which totalled ten thousand men and was intended for accumulating more North African glory. In 1854, however, the Zouaves were sent off to the Crimea, where they took a leading role at the battle of the Alma and in the siege of Sebastopol. Distributed among three French divisions, they took high casualties, but their reputation was enhanced by the conflict as well as by subsequent service in the War of Italian Unification and France's "Mexican adventure" of 1863.

Select Zouave officers and men among the survivors of Crimea went on to serve in the Zouaves of the Guard, newly formed in 1855, a unit as admired as the finer guards regiments had been in the days of Napoleon I. Capt. George B. McClellan of eventual American Civil War fame was a member of the U.S. Military Commission in Europe in 1855–56. After intense study of all European forces he concluded that the Zouaves were "the most reckless, self-reliant, and complete infantry that Europe can produce. . . . Of all the troops that I have ever seen, I should esteem it the greatest honor to assist in defeating the zouaves."[49] It is no wonder, then, that numerous American Zouave and pseudo-Zouave formations were to be found in the Civil War era, though their actual training in French *chasseur* methods usually left much to be desired. The power of fads in military fashion was demonstrated across the country. The long-established Boston Light Infantry discarded its traditional bearskin-topped guard uniforms for bright Zouave plumage in 1861; the socially exclusive Cleveland Grays adopted the new quick-paced drill style, but voted against discarding their handsome (and expensive) bearskin caps which they had begun to wear in 1856.[50]

The first such creation to attract considerable popular attention, however, was formed in 1859 by Elmer E. Ellsworth, a young man inspired by Crimean accounts, who led the "United States Zouave Cadets," a well-disciplined company of the 60th Regiment, Illinois State Militia.[51] Their brilliant uniforms, intricate drill, and complex gymnastics caught the public eye, and their twenty-city tour of the northern states in 1860 aroused much interest, including that of the West Point cadets and staff before whom they performed. Ellsworth soon left Chicago for New York City, where, after Fort Sumter, with President Lincoln's permission, he raised a regiment from the tough men of the New York Fire Department, with himself as "colonel." The 11th New

York Volunteer Infantry, or "Ellsworth's Fire Zouaves," rather lost their direction, however, after Ellsworth was killed in May 1861 by a secessionist tavern keeper in Alexandria, Virginia. Ellsworth's grieving unit fought in the first battle of Bull Run in July, but never again saw significant action. The passion for Zouaves lasted well into the Civil War, but that is a topic best left for the following chapter.

All in all, it may be said that on the verge of the Civil War, America, in general, had a strong sense of tradition where her military heritage was concerned, but, right or wrong (and often as not, wrong), it was primarily temporary, militia-type units that were seen as the great exemplar of the triumphant citizen soldier. Rangers, minutemen, and the myriad of volunteers of 1812 or the Mexican War had been enough, and, it was felt, so they would be again if the need arose. That there was also a heritage of intensely-trained special purpose units such as the Revolutionary War's Light Infantry was a fact known to few. The Civil War, of course, would be a war of mass armies in which the militia tradition, rather than that of the regular army, not surprisingly would take precedence. Nevertheless, within that context, the search for elites remains rewarding.

4 The Civil War

In the traditional sense of the word, there were no elites in the Civil War, on either side. Neither the Union nor Confederate armies had special guard regiments in the Napoleonic tradition. Nor did either follow the continental model of light and grenadier companies selected from each regiment and, when necessary, formed into battalions for special purposes. Though the first and tenth companies of a regiment were still termed "flank companies," they were no longer specially selected light troops and grenadiers, and in this war there were really no practical differences between these companies and the other eight.[1] When given a choice, men might prefer some colorful garb (at least until experience showed the danger of over visibility), but no Civil War units were issued the vast helmets, bearskin bonnets, shiny breastplates, or hussar jackets that still distinguished elite European formations.

There were good reasons for this change from the continental model. The age of mass armies had arrived in the nineteenth century, and though in the Napoleonic era guard formations still suited the desired imperial image, they had definitely not typified the American or French revolutionary impulses. Like the French and American Revolutionary Wars, the Civil War was a citizen's conflict in which the typical soldier who fought through the war and survived, though he may have been a professional at the end of the conflict, was not likely to have been one when he began it. Secondly, the American tradition, as has been seen, worked against any sizable standing army. Though the existing officer corps was divided enough to serve both Union and Confederacy, the bulk of the Regular Army's rank and file remained with the North, but it was numerically modest even after substantial increases had been authorized by Congress, and part remained on the western frontier until relieved by militia units. Both sides would find it difficult to find fresh manpower to feed into existing formations or to create new ones, though the problem was substantially greater for the South, which had a smaller white male population (Certainly throughout the war the use of black troops was unthinkable in the Confederacy). The removal of the most experienced veterans into guard-type regiments, even if politically acceptable, would certainly have made the seasoning of fresh recruits even more difficult than it was, and it is doubtful that they would have performed any better than line regiments. Over time, pride in guardsman status might have over-come loyalty to a man's original regiment; that certainly was the case in Napoleon's army. As it was, however, the hometown and kinship ties of regiments for officers and men alike, at least in the war's early days, were powerful links in many of the units to be considered below. Any selection and separation of the most skilled survivors would only have undercut morale in that context.

Many letters home make the significance of those links painfully clear. One example must suffice, as Confederate Capt. Ujanirtus Allen wrote home to his wife from Richmond in July 1862, after the battle of Gaine's Mill, with the toll of friends and relatives: "John Anderson died June 29th from a ball that entered the brain . . . Tom Wilkes and Wm Philips are both shot through the back of the neck . . . Corpr Joe Horsley through the flesh part of the right leg . . . and Tip Horsley through the muscle of the arm . . . Cousin Robt in the groin by a spent ball. . . ."[2] It is no wonder that units commonly resisted with anger when reduced numbers prompted amalgamation: "Regimental pride has always run very high with us," wrote Charles Haydon in November 1862, at the news that his 2d Michigan might be thus treated. "We have labored & fought for the glory of the 2d & to see it made anything save 2d. Mich. Inf. was to make an end of all desire to excel & to destroy what we deem the best reward, next to the final success of our cause, which can be given. It would entirely break the spirit and hopes of both men & officers."[3]

The Civil War was one of horrendous losses on the battlefield, not least because time and again the defensive power of massed rifles and artillery, particularly when coupled with entrenchments, prevailed against the traditional infantry attack in line, a method much more suited for the age of shorter-range muskets. On this point, admittedly, there is considerable debate. Paddy Griffith is particularly outspoken in challenging the generally accepted view, noting that "the arrival of the rifle musket actually made very little practical difference—whatever may have been its theoretical potential to revolutionise the battlefield. . . . The widespread psychological fear of attacking fortifications later in the war had nothing to do with some new prowess of riflemen firing at long range, but everything to do with a combination of exaggerated fears, doctrinal orthodoxy, and war-weariness."[4] Whatever one's opinion on that question, it would seem that the difficulties of replacing losses on the battlefield, of simply keeping enough men on the line, argued against the luxury of elite creation.

But every war has heroes, not the leaders who inspired admiration—the Lees or Jacksons, Grants or Shermans were rare enough in any case—but rather those units which commanded special respect. Before considering individual cases, however, it is necessary to examine the question of whether the Confederacy as a whole had a special military heritage which should qualify some or all of its soldiers as a "national elite." Few Civil War questions have aroused so much debate, and certainly as a subjective evaluation no definitive answer is possible.

The sense of a special Southern heritage is an old one, and has never quite died out. In part it is one of a gentlemanly aristocracy, early familiarity with the use of weapons and with horsemanship (the question of cavalry will be considered below), and a quickness to defend one's honor by a fight or a duel. But the tradition includes an equal measure of the self-sufficient yeoman—rifleman, fighter, roughneck perhaps, and framed by the same peculiar social and economic institutions of the South, including slavery and an underdeveloped political system. William R. Russell of the London *Times* found such a mix in 1861. No doubt absorbing the self-image of his informants, he believed he had found a "modern Sparta," ruled by "an aristocracy resting on a helotry, and with nothing else to rest upon," except perhaps its honor.[5]

British Coldstream Guards Col. James Fremantle added yet another explanation after his tour of both sides. Many Northerners he met would, he believed, make good soldiers in other circumstances, but "they did not show any disposition to *fight themselves* in this cause," since that cause was not so much suppression of an insurrection but "a war of aggression, ambition, and conquest" of a "gallant race."[6] In short, it was as easy for foreign observers as it was for Americans to find those special character differences.

Nearly a century later, this interpretation was given more scholarly form by the eminent historian John Hope Franklin, in his influential book *The Militant South, 1800–1861* (1956), who found a reputation for fighting to be "identified as an important ingredient of Southern civilization," replicated in the life of its social elite, its militia units, its "West Points of the South." Other scholars have followed the same course, pointing out that the South had a higher share of West Point cadets, for example, than the North (the figure was roughly forty percent of graduates, under half, of course, but the South had only 30 percent of the white population of the country), and that it contributed a higher percentage of volunteers (three-fifths) in the Mexican War.[7] This argument has had its critics, as one might expect. Marcus Cunliffe, for example, has pointed out the existence of an equally strong military spirit in the North, with just as much violence to be expected on the western frontier or in an urban mob.[8] But the point is less the accuracy of comparative numbers, than the apparent belief—on both sides of the war—that such a special Southern heritage existed. Dudley Cornish, in his respected work on blacks in the Union army, explains:

> The South had also the advantage of an aristocratic respect for officer class and a tradition for hierarchical social gradations infused with a clannish willingness to follow the man on horseback, the *beau sabreur*. The South maintained a romantic myth of warfare in the spirit of Sir Walter Scott's novels, while the more mechanically and pragmatically inclined North rather quickly came to look on war as an interruption of normal business pursuits and at length as an unpleasant business to be organized and planned along practical lines in order to get it over with as soon as possible.[9]

If such a characterization is too sweeping—and many would say it is—perhaps the answer is to confine the image to the patricians of

Virginia, or at least to the men of the army that above all stood for the South: Lee's Army of Northern Virginia. Richard McMurry, in his study comparing this army with the Army of Tennessee, which had a much less successful battlefield record, outlines the "Lee Tradition," which worked to mythologize the Army of Northern Virginia "as a group of cavaliers whose gallantry, chivalry, education, heritage, wealth, background, knightly manners, courage, and 'breeding' set them apart from and a notch or two above other Americans and even other Southerners." Interestingly, McMurry speculates, without making a definite conclusion, on the potential negative effect on other Southern formations from the pessimistic belief that they were not as good, simply, as Lee's army. An even greater effect resulted, it can be argued, when Lee surrendered. As Gary Gallagher remarks: "The death of the Army of Northern Virginia removed the Confederate people's cherished rallying point and effectively marked the demise of their nation."[10]

These images, it should be added, were not merely carved on a large scale, but extended to individual contacts. John Beatty, an officer in the 3d Ohio Infantry, had occasion to negotiate an exchange of prisoners with a Confederate major who happened to be Robert E. Lee's son. "Major Lee is near my own age, a heavy set but well-proportioned man, somewhat inclined to boast, not overly profound, and thoroughly impregnated with the idea that he is a Virginian and a Lee withal. As I shook hands at parting with this scion of an illustrious house, he complimented me by saying that he hoped soon to have the honor of meeting me on the battlefield. I assured him that it would afford me pleasure, and I should make all reasonable efforts to gratify him in this regard. I did not desire to fight, of course, but I was bound not to be excelled in the matter of knightly courtesy."[11]

The question of whether the South can be said to have had a national identity—and Gallagher insists that it did—is one that may be avoided here, but one last general dispute requires mention: the strategy pursued by Lee and his army in carrying the war into the North, against what was clearly a more powerful enemy in terms of potential resources if not immediate military strength. Was that strategy initiated at least in part in response to a general belief held by the South's military leaders of the superiority of Southerners, man for man? Conversely, was the North defeated in the war's early battles in part because it accepted the South's self-image of superiority? Once again, one can only raise these questions, for no definitive answer is possible.

The South's offensive strategy brought critically important victories—above all the first Battle of Bull Run—but it also bled the South to death over time.

Any study of the massive literature on the Civil War will indicate the arguments. On the one side is found the view that the South should have husbanded its resources, forcing the North to come to it, wearing down the North's willingness to fight a difficult and costly guerrilla war in enemy territory. On the other side, however, it can be argued with some persuasiveness that the South could not maintain its spirit of resistance without victories, and major victories were not to be won in a guerrilla war—nor were the foreign recognition and aid hoped for by the South to be gained that way. And, finally, the South was fighting for many things, but one of them was slavery—and slavery, like the South's social system as a whole, was not likely to have survived a long-running guerrilla war. Lee no doubt recognized this at the time of his surrender when he rejected the concept of continuing the struggle in that manner. Reid Mitchell has argued "that the North had a will to make war superior to the South's when the war placed a lighter burden on its society than it did on Southern society. Perhaps all one can conclude is that the North had a superior will to fight the war it had to fight than the South had to fight its war." It is a very arguable conclusion. The evidence would seem to indicate, rather, that the South went to war with a very good will indeed, but that over the course of the war that energy, that will, dissipated; as Gallagher puts it, lack of will is rather different from loss of will.[12]

The issue of elitist images, self and otherwise, is interesting. When one believes that one has an "edge," a special advantage—the favor of the gods, better weaponry, or a special tradition—it may help, even prove decisive, in battle. In the American Civil War, such a belief may have helped the South in the first half of the struggle, in which it generally did well. In the second half, however, the energy was gone, the better leaders often dead, and the armies of both sides, even if they really had been different at the start, had become very much alike, a point highlighted in Bell Wiley's well-known studies of "Billy Yank" and "Johnny Reb."[13] The Union army was always more literate, more politically aware, more differentiated by ethnic, religious, or linguistic categories, while that of the Confederacy was more religious, more rural, and more homogeneous. But at the end of the struggle, leaving aside key issues of manpower and supply, the forces of both sides seemed much the same. John M. Schofield, who finished the war a Union lieutenant-general and a successful commander in Sherman's Atlanta campaign, put it thirty years after the war: "I doubt if any soldiers in the world ever needed so much cumulative evidence to convince them that they were beaten. 'Brave boys were they!' If they had been fighting in a cause that commanded the sympathy and support of the public conscience of the world, they could never have been beaten; it is not necessary to search for any other cause of the failure of the Confederate States."[14]

It is within these contexts of both differences and similarities that more specific elites must be sought. Certainly at the start of the war, the opportunity existed for substantial distinctions between various units. Aside from the few Regulars, units were formed from the expansion of existing militia units or the creation of entirely new regiments under the auspices of civilian commanders commissioned from the War Department of their state—and most, indeed, retained their state designations throughout the war. Training of the state units depended entirely upon the energy and skills of their officers, and most officers lacked both attributes. As Russell Weigley points out, the fact that regiments routinely took 50 percent losses, and sometimes much greater, was due not simply to technological changes but also to the general result of sending inadequately trained raw recruits into battle.[15]

But some officers were conscientious, and even with only their militia training behind them—if that—they did their best to prepare their men for battle. When opportunity permitted, competitions in drill and marksmanship improved both skills and unit cohesion. In the Army of the Tennessee, for example, each brigade entered its best regiment to contest a highly coveted palm ornament for its flag, for superiority in skill (artillery had similar competitions of their own). The 13th Tennessee, in the same army, was sufficiently skilled at target practice with the .58 Springfield or .577 Enfield rifled muskets to hit the mark approximately 50 percent of the time at four hundred yards, generally regarded as the maximum effective range of such weapons though they could kill at up to one thousand yards.[16] Even by the end of 1862, when many men had been equipped with and trained in the use of rifled muskets, they were still being ordered to apply tactics more suitable to the age of shorter range smoothbore muskets. Terrain, of course, was an important factor: Numerous Civil War battles were fought in rugged, densely wooded areas where by necessity fighting was at close range. Nor was artillery the answer. Though well-placed artillery was most dangerous to attacking infantry, as was horse artillery if brought in close enough to be effective with man-killing grape or canister, at that range artillerymen were likely to be victims of the same rifle fire. Weigley puts it well: "The rifled fire power of a defending army well entrenched brought battle to an impasse."[17]

At such moments of impasse, when rival armies faced each other across defended lines—a status which particularly typified the latter stages of the war—the specially selected, or self-selected, sharpshooter, who might compile a considerable tally of victims from a concealed rifle pit or forest position came into his own. Armed with telescopic sights, an expert could "pick off a man at the distance of nearly a mile," as one North Carolina officer put it, "and the enemy are thinning our ranks with comparative impunity—our men being compelled simply to suffer and endure—a moral effect is being produced which may prove very detrimental to our future success." The Confederates, with less ammunition at their command late in the war, were at a disadvantage in sharpshooter duels, and had to husband their resources. "The Yankee sharpshooters are so good on a man's head that I am afraid to raise my head above the ditches, &c.," explained W. Casey of the 34th Virginia.[18] Such experts were hardly beloved. "[T]he regular sharpshooter often seemed to me little better than a human tiger lying in wait for blood," wrote artilleryman Robert Stiles.[19] Little mercy was shown to enemy marksmen, not to be confused with skirmishers, who were used to harass the enemy, scout their positions, and probe for weaknesses—a task which any veteran unit might be told to perform.

Frank Wilkeson, a light artillery private in the Army of the Potomac, probably spoke for a majority of men on both sides: ". . . as a campaign cannot be decided by killing a few hundred enlisted men— killing them most unfairly and when they were of necessity exposed,— it did seem as though the sharpshooting pests should have been surpressed [sic]. Our sharpshooters were as bad as the Confederates, and neither of them were of any account as far as decisive results were obtained. They could sneak around trees or lurk behind stumps, or cower in wells or in cellars, and from the safety of their lairs murder a few men. Put the sharpshooters in battle-line and they were no better, no more effective, than the infantry of the line, and they were not half as decent. There was an unwritten code of honor among the infantry that forbade the shooting of men while attending to the imperative calls of nature, and these sharpshooting brutes were constantly violating that rule. I hated sharpshooters, both Confederate and Union, in those days, and I was always glad to see them killed."[20]

Yet the assignment always had individual appeal. "I would like above all things to belong to the sharpshooters," wrote Charles Haydon. "I am sometimes almost tempted to throw up my commission for the sake of joining them. I know that with a good gun I could shoot on the average of a half dozen men per day during this siege [of Yorktown, Virginia, by the Army of the Potomac in 1862]. Three good sharpshooters will often render a line more unsteady than a battery of artillery."[21] South Carolinian William Rhadamanthus Montgomery, part of a sharpshooter battalion in General Wofford's Confederate brigade, clearly took pride in his status in writing to his mother: "Perhaps you don't know what our duty is. Well, I will tell you. We are always in front of the Brigade, about 300 to 400 yds., to clear out the way & I tell you we done it too, to perfection. You ought to hear Gen Wofford praise us. . . ."[22]

Even for men who were not sharpshooters, in some situations their presence simply dominated life. Near Corinth, Mississippi in 1862, for example, Edwin Fay, sergeant in a Louisiana cavalry unit, reported that a fusillade continued all day at long range from both Yankees and Confederates; in his case, he used the opportunity to play a most dangerous game. "I could see the villains across an old field some 8 or 900 yds. and I would step out in plain sight and draw their fire and then get behind a tree before their balls came and then proved Philosophy at fault, for sound travels faster than a bullet at 600 yds. distance. I could see the flash, hear the report and the bullet would not come along till after a second or more. One of Capt. Fuller's horses was shot through the thigh at least 400 yds. behind our sharp shooters and full 3/4 of a mile, and a Tennessee trooper had his horse killed outright fully 400 yds further, nearly a mile distant."[23] Occasionally the sharpshooters themselves would arrange a local truce for an hour or longer. For example, it was agreed not to shoot in the broad daylight hours during the 1864 siege of Petersburg. "This is a very agreeable arrangement," wrote John Walters of the Norfolk Light Artillery Blues, "as it enables us to move about with considerable freedom, though it does not pay to be too exposed as both sides have a sly way of throwing an occasional bullet over which hurts where it hits. These shots are always fired from the main lines; the pickets preserve the purity of the white flag."[24]

Though any unit might produce its own expert shots, in the Union army the idea was soon in circulation to recruit a special regiment of sharpshooters. Whatever the origins of the scheme, its success owed to the energy of Col. Hiram Berdan, a successful inventor and business-man, and also a noted marksman with a target rifle. Berdan's plan was to recruit the top marksmen of every Northern state—selected by prov-ing their ability to put ten shots in a fifty-inch string (meaning that all ten shots must average under 5" from the target's center) at two hun-dred yards without telescopic sights but with a rest (and 150 yards offhand), no impossibility for the experienced deer hunter or target marksman with a quality weapon. Since his proposed unit would be federal rather than state in origin, Berdan found it necessary to go to Washington to win approval, starting at the top with President Lincoln.[25]

HIRAM BERDAN, WHO COMMANDED THE 1ST REGIMENT OF U. S. SHARPSHOOTERS, BETTER KNOWN AS BERDAN'S SHARPSHOOTERS. MUSTERED IN 1861, THIS UNIT WAS COMPOSED OF THE BEST MARKSMEN IN EACH STATE OF THE NORTH. *PHOTO BY MATHEW BRADY, 1862. U.S. NATIONAL ARCHIVES AND RECORDS ADMINISTRATION*

Nothing if not persistent, Berdan soon received permission to form a mounted regiment (the idea of horses was soon dropped, however), and in mid-1861 he set off to recruit an infantry unit which, according to the *New York Post*, "will be used not in the midst of battle, but on the outskirts, where, beyond the smoke and fury of the engagement, they will act independently, choose their objects, and make every shot tell. . . . They will confine their attention to the officers, and by picking these off, will bring confusion into the enemy's line." Since Berdan (or at least his agents) appears to have promised that his men would not have to fight in the line of battle, would never have picket (guard) duties to perform, and would be equipped with the best available Sharps breach-loading target rifles (and no bayonets), he was soon swamped with volunteers, above all from Michigan, his home state, and New York where he was a resident. Ten companies were formed (including four from New York and three from Michigan) into what was officially called the 1st Regiment of Sharpshooters, United States Volunteers (USSS); the overflow made up another eight companies of the 2d Regiment. Berdan at first was in command of the 1st but not the 2d Regiment, but both were generally known as "Berdan's Sharpshooters."[26]

Though Berdan's idea appeared to make sense, implementing the concept was not easy. The recruits were undoubtedly marksmen, but many were also individualists with little conception of discipline, and since the men came from many different areas, the sense of community was missing from the start. The Sharps rifles failed to appear, and it took some time for the men to be equipped with a five-shot Colt repeating rifle (1855 model) which was regarded as less than reliable (though Confederates who captured them found them most useful). Many men continued to carry their own weapons, at least in the early days, but target weapons of .44 to .50 caliber could weigh fifteen to thirty pounds, sometimes considerably more. (A "bench" rifle, fired from a supporting rest or bench, with its carrying box and various tools might weigh thirty-five to fifty pounds and was generally carried in a wagon until needed.)[27]

A variety of caliber made the supply of ammunition a nightmare, though some men had powder horns and cast their own bullets, until, eventually, in June 1863 the men were given their Sharps rifles. The 1859 model of this weapon could fire ten shots a minute, had a double trigger to aid accuracy, and could be used very effectively from a prone position since it loaded from the rear. Some of the heavy long range weapons with telescopes were still kept, however; Wyman S. White, who served in the 2d USSS, noted in his memoirs that such weapons were given to the best men in turn. As his editor explains, "The giving of these telescopic rifles, but a few of which were now carried at this period of service, was in the nature of a mark of honor, as the sharp-shooter thus armed was considered an independent character, used only for special services, with the privilege of going to any part of the line where in his own judgement he could do the most good." A large muzzle-loading weapon of this sort used four ounces of powder as a charge and a bullet weighing more than an ounce; it could shoot more than a mile and outranged the Sharps rifle.[28]

Berdan trained his men at a "camp of instruction" a mile or so north of Washington, and here they not only went through rigorous drill, but much target practice, including at man-sized targets set at six hundred yards. Visitors, including Lincoln and army commander McClellan, were frequently present to see such marvels in their green rifleman uniforms (Berdan also ordered grey overcoats for fall/winter conditions, but this proved a most unwise choice, since men thus out-fitted looked like Confederates). But Berdan had absolutely no mili-tary experience, and soon proved a controversial commander. Indeed, once his sharpshooters went into action Berdan would be court-martialed (and acquitted) for conduct unbecoming an officer—meaning he usually found a way to be somewhere else when the fighting was hot. His men hated him, burning him in effigy; his officers quarreled with him and moved on to other units: the Sharpshooters seemed off to a bad start.[29]

In fact, the 1st and 2d USSS amassed an exceptional record. At-tached first to the 3d Corps (later to the 5th, a unit which was known as "high toned" since it contained most of the regiments originally from the Regular Army), the USSS were generally used in small detach-ments, sent out as skirmishers or snipers, often deployed in two to four company strength stretched across a broad front, a usage which cost steady casualties. "In almost all of our minor engagements somebody was killed, and usually we lost heavier, comparatively speaking, in these affairs, than in general engagements," recalled one veteran after the war.[30]

The USSS fought at Malvern Hill, dueling there with the elite Richmond Howitzers, who made the cardinal error of riding up on their grey horses to unlimber within range of four companies of the USSS; unable to fire a single round, the survivors were driven into the woods.

At the second Battle of Bull Run, the 1st USSS lost 65 out of 290 men present; at Antietam, the 2d USSS lost a quarter of its strength. Chancellorsville, Gettysburg (especially at Little Round Top), Mine Run; the USSS saw much serious combat, and was steadily reduced in numbers. In march 1863, only 723 could be counted in both regiments, and the losses continued. In 1864, when it was mustered out of service, Company A of the 1st USSS—a German and Swiss unit mainly from Michigan—had 12 men left of its original 106.[31]

Their reputation, however, was secure. Lt. Col. Fox, in his remarkable compendium of "three hundred fighting regiments" of the Union forces noted that "Berdan's United States Sharpshooters were the best known of any regiments in the Army." A Confederate officer at Gettysburg recorded the enemy's view: "The Sharpshooters were the worst men we have to contend with," and he was not referring to their lack of discipline.[32] Those who ignored the danger of sharpshooters did so at their peril, as testified to by the experience of Union Maj. Gen. John Sedgwick, commanding the 6th Corps at Spotsylvania, who was killed within his own lines by an enemy rifleman only seconds after assuring nearby soldiers that "the Rebels couldn't hit an elephant at this distance."[33]

Unfortunately, many men, especially in the 1st USSS, declined to re-enlist once their three-year term of duty expired. In late 1864, two regiments could no longer be sustained, and the 1st was amalgamated into the 2d USSS, which in its turn was discontinued in early 1865. Whether or not "Berdan's Sharpshooters" should be seen as the original prototype for the modern Green Berets is best left to historians of that force; at a minimum, however, the Sharpshooters had proved a success in their mission, though they had not always been put to the best use by some commanders of higher units who did not understand their special training and capabilities. Nevertheless, Paddy Griffith perhaps goes too far in his conclusion: "The dread of snipers was quick to spread throughout the armies of the Civil War to an extent which was quite disproportionate to their actual numbers and effectiveness."[34]

The South was slower to form specialized sharpshooter units, though no doubt individual men were assigned such duties very early on. Only in the early months of 1864 did Gen. Robert E. Lee order the formation of special sharpshooter battalions in each of his brigades before the beginning of the new campaigning season. These battalions were composed of from two to four companies, or 125 to 200 men each. Since Lee's Army of Northern Virginia included some thirty-six brigades in its three corps (nine divisions in all), the force thus recruited was substantial—substantial enough, indeed, to be formed into a separate "light division" of something over five thousand men, though records of its service appear to be scant, according to Capt. William S. Dunlop, who commanded a battalion, in Gregg's (later McGowan's) South Carolina brigade, and later wrote its history.[35]

For Dunlop's battalion, each of the five regiments in his brigade contributed about three dozen men at the rate of three or four from each company, forming, in all, three companies of about sixty men each with three non-commissioned officers in addition to Dunlop himself. The selection process had chosen the best men, those possessed of "intelligence, sound judgment, accuracy of marksmanship, fidelity to the Southern cause, and unfaltering courage in that trying ordeal of battle." The men were then specially trained according to a "unique and concise system of tactics . . . prepared and compiled from the American skirmish and French zouave drills," featuring such skills as "estimating distance, target practice, movements and dispositions against cavalry, bayonet exercises, etc."[36] Those who failed in the training were replaced by others, as the skills of all were honed—in marksmanship, for example, moving from a man-sized target with a five-inch diameter bull's eye at one hundred yards, to a 6' x 6' foot target at nine hundred yards. Another sharpshooter officer attested to seeing one of his top men pick off a Union sharpshooter, outlined on a ridge, at more than one thousand yards: ". . . the best shot I witnessed during the war."[37] By the summer of 1864, the new battalions were ready to be used on picket duty when the army was in camp, or as skirmishers in advance or retreat, often with considerably more freedom to take initiative than men in the regular line units.

Dunlop's account makes clear that the sharpshooter battalions were henceforth constantly used as a light infantry force for such responsibilities from which, indeed, they were seldom relieved. A sharpshooter's circumstances were particularly hard; he often lived several hundred yards in front of his own lines, dueling with similar keen-eyed marksmen from the other side. At Ream's Station, Virginia, for example, Dunlop's men by his calculations kept up a continuous fire on the Federal Works for some five hours, while a relay of couriers brought up ammunition for the men, each of whom fired 160 rounds, roughly one shot every two minutes, to keep the Union troops pinned down. At Jarrett's Station, Virginia, in a night attack on the Weldon railroad, the van was formed from four battalions of sharpshooters in the ad hoc "light division," and for the final assault, eight men "of superior courage and activity" were selected to lead. At McIlwaine Hill (Fort Steadman) in March 1865, the light division was again chosen as a forlorn hope to assault a most difficult position. The commander promised, with the assent of General Lee, that if the attack were successful, every survivor would be rewarded with a thirty-day leave. The attackers were discovered thirty yards from the Federal position, and the carnage began; the hill was taken and defended for an entire day against numerous counter assaults, until the sharpshooters were relieved.

Capt. Robert F. Ward of the 42d Mississippi adds an account of how his sharpshooter company of the same battalion was formed: he was simply ordered by his colonel to take one man from every ten in the regiment. These men "were relieved from all camp duty, guard duty and fatigue service of any kind; and to be drilled six hours a day in skirmish drill and in estimation of distances until the opening of the approaching [spring, 1864] campaign."[38] Relief from the more tedious camp duties proved appealing, and of the 240 men present for duty in his regiment, ninety volunteered, from which the twenty-four were chosen. How many of them had actually foreseen the added dangers of their new duties is unknown. Once trained, the men on the march remained with their respective companies in the line until called out for special duty, at which point the sharpshooter battalion formed up on the regiment's right wing.

Elite sharpshooter units aside, if the rifle altered the nature of infantry battle, as it certainly did to some extent, it similarly modified the status of cavalry. In the Civil War, cavalry of course played an important role, but it was secondary to that of infantry. Even the most famous long-range raids and intelligence-gathering forays, such as Jeb Stuart's circumnavigation of McClellan's entire Army of the Potomac, while they might result in a commander's change of plan, were not likely to alter the course of the large-scale infantry and artillery battles which typified this war. Events such as the 1865 capture of Selma, Alabama by 1,700 cavalrymen under Maj. Gen. James H. Wilson from 7,000 defenders under the well-known Maj. Gen. Nathan Bedford Forrest were rare indeed, but even that victory came in the course of a massive *chevauchée* or raid, as Paddy Griffith points out, "a reversion to the fourteenth-century methods of the Black Prince rather than a step forward to the twentieth-century *blitzkrieg*."[39]

Most commentators agree that in the first two years, the Confederate cavalry "literally ran rings around their opponents." The North was slower to grasp the tactical utility of cavalry, especially in grouping cavalry regiments into brigades and corps for raiding purposes, but substantial cavalry forces were seldom available in any case. Certainly it was true that few men drawn from the cities and the towns of the North had the necessary skills without extensive training, to say nothing of the added expense of their mounts and equipment. As William Woods Averell, a ten-year cavalry veteran, explained, there was nothing simple about teaching a man about a horse, "how to saddle him and ride him at all gaits, over all kinds of country, to perform properly all the multifarious duties of caring for his horse and his equipment, arms and ammunition, and finally to use his saber, revolver or carbine against the enemy with confidence and skill. . . ."[40]

As the war progressed, the Union adapted and developed capable cavalry which could effectively screen the movements of its armies, though it never used cavalry in close support of the infantry in any significant way. As with infantry, the problem was the rifle: cavalry might have some success, however costly, against infantry armed with ordinary muskets. Riflemen, however, were another matter. While the rifle, if anything, was slower to load than the musket, in the right conditions the rifleman could begin firing at cavalry at a much longer range, making the latter's swords fairly useless. (The lances of earlier militia units were a thing of the past, save for the occasional unhappy experiment, such as the 7th Pennsylvania Cavalry.)[41] Civil War cavalry could and did dismount to take an infantry role, but the lighter carbines with which they were generally equipped were not a match for rifles in veteran hands. When not raiding or scouting, the cavalry of both sides could find themselves used as "file closers," guarding against desertion, rounding up stragglers, protecting supply wagon columns, or detached for picket or headquarters guard duty. Since they still possessed the traditional attributes of cavalry such as foraging and quicker escape from a losing battle, yet seldom appeared on the infantry battlefield itself, cavalry in general was not held in the highest regard by infantry foot soldiers: "mere vampyres hanging on the infantry—doing but little fighting but first in for the spoils," wrote an Iowan fighting in the West.[42] Though commanders such as Jeb Stuart won lasting fame, the same cannot really be said of Civil War cavalry as such; that infantry of both sides seldom if ever bothered to practice forming squares, the traditional defensive formation against cavalry attack, indicates the general low tactical regard which infantry had for its peers on horseback.

Leading cavalry commanders like Stuart and Forrest at least were respectable soldiers. Some cavalry leaders, however—particularly Southern raiders such as Virginia lawyer John Singleton Mosby, the failed Kansas farmer and schoolteacher William Clarke Quantrill (actually not a Southerner at all), or the Kentucky merchant John Hunt Morgan, attracted much attention at the time, whether they were regarded as cutthroat bushwhackers (Quantrill in particular) or admired as aggressive partisans taking the war to the enemy. Missouri and Kansas witnessed a brutal form of guerrilla warfare that tarnished entire units, for example the 7th Kansas Volunteer Cavalry, "Jennison's Jayhawkers," with "Jayhawking" meaning to rob and kill soldiers and civilians alike, whatever their political allegiance. Such units engendered official military responses from the enemy they harassed, but none made a particularly notable contribution to the progress of the war. Often the chosen refuge of deserters and marauders, they were not commonly regarded as elites by either side, though they certainly were successful in terrorizing civilian populations.[43]

Even Robert E. Lee was reluctant to make official such bands, which ostensibly fought for the Confederacy, and urged their disbandment, with the exception of Mosby's unit, which he considered to be of a somewhat higher level. On the Union side, the same distinction should probably be made for the organization of "Independent Scouts" which was established in the fall of 1863 to counter Mosby, generally known as "Blazer's Scouts" from the name of one of the early organizers and eventual leader. Most of Blazer's men came from the Appalachian foothills of Ohio and West Virginia, often refugees from border districts whose main allegiance was to the Confederacy. Volunteers, these hundred men (plus officers and NCOs) were known as "the best shots, best woodsmen, best marchers and the most dashing fellows that could be found in the three old regiments," which provided most of the volunteers (9th West Virginia Volunteer Infantry and 12th and 91st Ohio Volunteer Infantry). Well-mounted and outfitted with Spencer rifles and multiple pistols, Blazer's men contested control of the Shenandoah Valley until, in November 1864, they were largely destroyed in battle by Mosby's band at Kabletown, West Virginia.[44]

Marksmen or cavalry units are not the only candidates for elite status among Civil War units, however; such status might also be

claimed by units formed on the basis of social connections or racial or
ethnic identity. Not surprisingly, some of the socially prominent militia organizations of the post-1815 era survived to take part in the Civil
War. The Washington Artillery of New Orleans was certainly one of
the most famous, but even it had fallen on hard times after the Mexican
War—most likely because of the unpopularity of actual drill rather
than its requirements of social connections, election to membership,
and annual dues—and could muster no more than a dozen men by 1857.
But three years later, it had grown again, and when the War came, four
companies went off to fight in Virginia. A fifth company was organized later, and saw four years of hard and highly-regarded service
with the Army of Tennessee. The bulk of the Washington Artillery served
in the Army of Northern Virginia through every major campaign, all
the while doing their best to keep appearances up to a standard which
Napoleon might have expected from his Guard artillery. Rice Bull, a
soldier of the 123d New York Volunteer Infantry, saw them unlimber
near where he lay wounded on the field at Chancellorsville—and remembered them not only for their appearance and discipline, but also
for their consideration for the Union wounded lying in their path.[45]

The Washington Artillery was certainly not the only socially
prominent militia unit on either side to earn honors in the war, though
most of those which had existed before the conflict and served in it
were absorbed into larger formations. Many from the South lived on:
the Richmond Howitzers already mentioned, the Oglethorpe Light Infantry of Savannah, the Norfolk Light Artillery Blues, the Richmond
Blues (Southern units named for the blue uniforms, like Northerners in
gray, often found it wise to change colors for obvious reasons), the
Crescent Regiment of New Orleans, known as the "Kid Glove Regiment" for the number of city blue bloods it included, and so on. One of
the most famous was the "Hampton Legion," founded by Wade Hampton III of South Carolina, a man rich enough (his family owned three
thousand slaves it was said) to outfit his mixed force of one thousand
infantry, cavalry, and even artillery with rifled cannon from England.
The Legion, interestingly, included the Edgefield Hussars and the
Watson Guards, two earlier, smaller prestige formations: elite elements
in some circumstances tended to pyramid in this fashion.[46]

Not every exclusive militia organization could maintain its identity throughout the war, however. The Cleveland Grays may serve as
an interesting example. In April 1861 the unit responded to President

Lincoln's call for volunteers. Since the state mandated that serving volunteer units contain at least seventy-five men, the Grays opened enlistment for the first time to the "general public," meaning trades-men, railroad workers, and the like, untrained men who suddenly made up half the company. As part of the 1st Regiment Ohio Volunteer In-fantry, the Grays saw action at the first Battle of Bull Run, but, having volunteered for ninety days only, they were mustered out and were back home in Cleveland by August. Some of the men then joined new elements of the reformed 1st OVI—a three-year regiment—while oth-ers were absorbed into a variety of Ohio units. The Grays continued to survive at home in Cleveland as part of the Ohio National Guard, as the unit's historian puts it, "carefully venturing from time to time into the backwaters of the war as a hundred days' regiment."[47]

Bell Wiley surmised that the urban origins of such socially elite formations meant that they were composed of men better used to adapt-ing to changing circumstances and new psychological pressures, and it was that background which provided a tangible basis for higher mo-rale: urban people were simply better at taking care of themselves.[48] Perhaps this was the case, though certainly urban people had little ex-perience with such useful campaign survival skills as lighting a fire in the rain. Urban life, however, probably did give its veterans more pro-tection against adult-killing childhood diseases such as measles and smallpox, though townsmen were just as likely to succumb to camp illnesses such as dysentery, diarrhea, and malaria. One point which is certain is that units which had more educated members (and survivors) were likely to play a larger part in subsequent histories for the simple reason that literate, educated men were more inclined to write their memoirs.[49]

Ethnicity was another basis for uniqueness among Civil War regi-ments, but far more so among Federal units than Confederate, since the vast majority of new immigrants went to those states which re-mained in the Union, if only because the South offered few opportuni-ties for unskilled non-slave laborers. William Burton, in his useful study, defines ethnic regiments as those in which all of the men were either foreign-born or the sons of foreign-born fathers and were deliberately recruited on the basis of ethnic affinity; who regarded their regiment as an ethnic organization; and who were similarly regarded as such by society in general.[50] Such identification was perfectly natural in a na-tion of immigrants, serving like social or charitable or sports clubs to make the men feel more at home. Certainly many ethnic units were based on a small geographical area—part of a county, an urban neighborhood, an electoral district—just as non-ethnic units were, though in the former case one national flavor would predominate. Each had some particular distinction. Many Germans gave orders and kept accounts in German; the Irish wanted Catholic priests for their chaplains and whiskey as their beverage of choice: stereotypical definitions, perhaps, but they represent Civil War realities, as Burton demonstrates. It should be added that no ethnic element won the respect of its peers simply by virtue of having an ethnic identity—there was no residual fear of Hessians or British Grenadiers. Indeed, there was not even much place for trained foreign veterans if they expected automatic elite status—no Steubens, no Lafayettes. The prominent German immigrant Carl Schurz recounted the delightful story of a Prussian with a long pedigree whom he introduced to Lincoln, and who began to regale the president with his distinguished lineage. "'Well,' said Mr. Lincoln, interrupting him, 'that need not trouble you. That will not be in your way, if you behave yourself as a soldier.' The poor count looked puzzled, and when the audience was over, he asked what in the world the President could have meant by so strange a remark."[51]

On the whole, ethnic units were considerably more in evidence at the start of the war than at the end. Attrition dampened the ardor of new recruits, and three-year enlistments proved much harder to find than the eager ninety-day volunteers of 1861, even where old regiments were replenished rather than new ones formed u The war itself proved a melting pot in the sense that when a member of an ethnic unit died it became increasingly unlikely that he would be replaced by a countryman. Indeed, as regiments disappeared in the smoke of battle, their ethnicity went with them: "Perhaps the most significant element of commonality is the gradual loss of ethnic identity for the regiments as the war progressed."[52]

A few regiments were Scots; of these the most famous was the 79th New York Infantry, or "Cameron Highlanders." Many of its members were born in Scotland and, on appropriate occasions (and assuming the baggage train had caught up), the regiment wore kilts or trews (tartan trousers), though rarely in battle.[53] Other regiments were Scandinavian, or multi-ethnic but non-English speaking, most notably the 39th New York, the "Garibaldi Guards," which included single companies of Frenchmen, Italians, Hungarians, Swiss, and Spanish, and, most notably, five companies of Germans. They were certainly colorful in their distinctive uniforms with chasseur-zouave-jäger elements, though at first they proved troublesome, with a record that included a mutiny prior to First Bull Run in protest over the poor quality weapons they felt they had been issued. After a checkered career, including the court-martial of its first commandant for corruption, the unit claimed some redemption at Gettysburg.[54]

Zouaves, as has previously been noted, were not necessarily associated with any particular ethnic element, though few were as assorted as the three companies of "New Orleans Avengo Zouaves" (part of the 13th Louisiana Regiment), resplendent in red cap, baggy red trousers, and gold braided blue shirts, which one commentator recorded

ELMER ELLSWORTH ORGANIZED THE ZOUAVE CADETS IN CHICAGO IN 1859–60. ELLSWORTH IS SHOWN ON THIS SONG SHEET COVER SECOND FROM THE RIGHT. THE CADETS' BRILLIANT UNIFORMS, INTRICATE DRILL, AND COMPLEX GYMNASTICS CAUGHT THE PUBLIC EYE, AND THEIR 20-CITY TOUR OF THE NORTHERN STATES IN 1860 AROUSED MUCH INTEREST. *SAM DE VINCENT COLLECTION OF ILLUSTRATED AMERICAN SHEET MUSIC, ARCHIVES CENTER, NATIONAL MUSEUM OF AMERICAN HISTORY, SMITHSONIAN INSTITUTION, BEHRING CENTER.*

as a "hard-looking set composed of Irish, Dutch, Negroes, Spaniards, Mexicans and Italians with few or no Americans."[55] Some fifty Zouave regiments were raised in the war, with most, but not all, raised in the North. Indeed, Ellsworth's unit was not the first accepted for Federal service. That honor went to the 1st New York Zouave Regiment, formally the 9th New York Volunteer Infantry, or "Hawkin's Zouaves;" mustered into the Army in April 1861, the regiment was virtually annihilated at Antietam. That both sides had regiments with similar uniforms made for dangerous confusion at times, particularly in the early going. At First Bull Run, for example, both the 11th New York Zouaves and the 14th New York (not a Zouave regiment, but nevertheless outfitted with red trousers) resembled Wheat's Tigers from Louisiana. Combatants could do little better than try to observe the flags of each.[56]

Many Zouave regiments saw significant service, some with distinction. One of the best was that organized by Col. Abram Duryee, a wealthy timber merchant who in 1861 formed the 5th New York Volunteer Infantry, or "Duryee's Zouaves," recruited mostly from Manhattan, also known as the "Red Devils" from the color of their trousers (and the "Zoo-Zoos" to the press of the day). In the opinion of one regular soldier who served next to them, this regiment had been brought by its commander, Lt. Col. G. K. Warren (USMA 1850), "to a state of discipline, efficiency and drill that was not equalled by any other volunteer regiment in the Army of the Potomac." (Duryee himself had been promoted to brigadier general but resigned in 1863 for health reasons.) Duryee's Zouaves took enormous casualties—326, at least 124 killed or mortally wounded, out of 550 men—in a single day at Second Bull Run: "the highest number of fatalities suffered by a Federal infantry regiment during a single battle for the entire war." The 5th New York had certainly won the respect of its peers when at the expiration of its two-year enlistment the regiment was dissolved in 1863 (its three-year men were incorporated into other units).[57]

Probably the Zouave unit best known to history, however, was the 114th Pennsylvania Volunteer Regiment ("Collis's Zouaves," also known as the "Zouaves d'Afrique"), raised in the spring of 1861. Seriously cut up at both Fredericksburg and Gettysburg (the Peach Orchard), in 1864, as an honor for its service, General Meade selected the regiment to serve as the Provost Guard for the Army of the Potomac, a role in which it became a frequent subject for the photographer Alexander Gardner. This was a distinction unavailable to most regiments, but one which it could claim to have earned in battle.[58]

Zouaves were present in every major Civil War battle; by the war's end in 1865, the Army of the Potomac still contained "at least seven regiments which were distinctly dressed and prided themselves in being Zouaves," according to Michael McAfee.[59] No doubt that pride contributed to regimental esprit de corps. While it cannot be claimed that all Zouave formations were considered by their peers or opponents to be elites, some certainly were. It is a striking fact that in 1863–64, three Union regiments which had *not* been Zouaves—the 140th New York, the 146th New York, and the 155th Pennsylvania— were issued Zouave uniforms "as a reward for their proficiency at drill and to maintain the proud Zouave legacy." All three were assigned to Brig. Gen. Romeyn B. Ayer's brigade, which participated in the bloody Wilderness campaign.[60] There is no way of calculating the number of times individual regiments were promised such Zouave and/or rifle-man status. For example, an ineffective colonel of the 3d Ohio Infantry in the process of being removed from his position attempted just such a ploy: "The colonel's friends tell the boys that if he were to remain he would obtain leave for the regiment to go back to Camp Dennison to recruit, that he was about to obtain rifles and Zouave uniforms for them, and that there is a conspiracy among the officers to crush him." (The maneuver was not successful, though enough troublemakers listened to create a temporarily mutinous situation.)[61]

It should not be thought, however, that Zouaves were for everybody. It did not escape notice, for example, that the most colorful uniforms simply "made a fine mark for our rifle men," as one southerner noted. When the 5th New York (Duryee's Zouaves, now reorganized) was merged with the 12th New York, a veteran but non-Zouave regiment, the men of the 12th were not pleased, as Robert Tilney wrote home: ". . . we fear we may be compelled to adopt its uniform, which consists of crimson zouave pants, buff leather gaiters, light blue jacket with scarlet braids sprawling fantastically over it, a variegated waistband wound round half a dozen times, and horror on horrors, a crimson skull cap with a yellow tassel, or else a crimson or white turban."[62]

Most legitimately ethnic units were German or Irish. Some were brigaded with other similar regiments, but only the Germans had an ethnic division in the war. Some won permanent fame: By the end of the war the 32nd Indiana carried the names of sixty-one battles on its flag. At one point, its commander had faced down Gen. William Sherman to demand that the regiment receive its regular supply of five kegs of beer each day or its morale would suffer. Of the five hundred men in the mainly German 9th Ohio, half died at Chickamauga, and this story was not unique.[63]

Among Irish units, the 69th New York was certainly the most famous, receiving its baptism as a ninety-day regiment at First Bull Run, and then mustering back into service with the same unit number as a three-year regiment. One of its founders, Thomas Francis Meagher, an Irish nationalist who had been banished to Tasmania but escaped to America, commissioned a Zouave company of the "Fighting 69th." With the 63d New York, another Irish regiment, the 69th took 60 percent casualties at Antietam's Bloody Lane. Both continued to fight in the Irish Brigade, but at Fredericksburg, of the brigade's 1,300 men present, 545 were killed, wounded, or missing in action. The brigade never recovered; over the course of the war, its units, the 63d, 69th, and 88th New York, 28th Massachusetts, and 116th Pennsylvania, began with about five thousand men, enlisted two thousand more in subsequent years, but ended with only about seven hundred.[64]

Meagher himself did what he could to perpetuate a feeling of Irish identity, commonly leading his men into battle with green Irish flags and a green sprig for each man, symbols which, according to William McCarter, color sergeant of the 28th Massachusetts, "the Rebels had frequently admitted was a terror to them because they well knew the dogged, stubborn fighting qualities of the men who bore them." Meagher paid particular attention to this ritual before the brigade assaulted Marye's Heights at Fredericksburg, with disastrous results. As William McCleland from the same regiment explained: "We all looked gay and felt in high spirits, little dreaming, though we expected a heavy battle, that in so short a time after so many of our poor fellows would have been sent to their doom. After the evergreen had been inserted in our caps, the General came along the line and said a few words to each regiment. . . ."[65]

Not every Irish regiment was quite so Irish; the 116th Pennsylvania, for example, was only about 30 percent Irish in its original composition, and never carried green flags, though it was part of the Irish Brigade.[66] But most Irishmen who served in the Civil War on either side did so in non-ethnic regiments, and the same conclusion holds for every major ethnic grou Some ethnic regiments were excellent as judged by battlefield performance, but the reasons for their success were precisely the same reasons for success by non-ethnic regiments: their training, their leadership, and their luck, with ethnicity a useful but not a decisive cohesion-making factor.

To turn from ethnicity to "race" (in the Civil War era, the terms were far more interchangeable), when the war began, neither side was interested in using black soldiers in combat. By the time it was over, the Union had formed numerous black regiments (nearly 180,000 black soldiers served in the Union Army, and more than 33,000 died from various causes) and tested at least some in battle. By the last days of the war the Confederacy, desperate for manpower, reached the point of considering the unacceptable: the recruitment of black regiments. But the war effort crumbled before any such units could be formed. There is no need to repeat here a story which has been considered at length by others. Suffice it to say that African American soldiers had some notable disadvantages working against them resulting from racial prejudice on both sides of the war. The North, for far too long, refused to give black soldiers pay equal to that of whites, while the South had a particular animosity towards black Northern soldiers captured in battle.[67] Some African American units were superior, others less so. The most famous, unquestionably, was the 54th Massachusetts Infantry, which was a model for other African American units. Its moment of glory came when it stormed Charleston's Fort Wagner with its bayonets against artillery and rifles, losing nearly 250 officers and men killed, wounded, missing, or taken prisoner in the action.[68] It was an epic and subsequently popular story, but many fine regiments suffered a similar fate, a fact which can only arouse astonished admiration, but which is not sufficient cause to qualify them as elite.

We are left with only one category of elite to consider in the Civil War: the hardened veteran unit, which if not well-trained at the start learned maximum survival techniques from experience in battle, on the march, and in cam Even the best units, of course, could be destroyed by being launched at impossible objectives, and knowledgeable troops sometimes resisted orders in such situations, but more commonly did what they were told, sometimes fatalistically pinning a bit of paper with their name and other particulars on their clothing or placing it in their pocket so that their bodies might be identified, as happened at Fredericksburg, Cold Harbor, and elsewhere, "a precaution not uncommon," wrote Private Goss, "when going into desperate battle."[69] Such men, indeed, seemed more inclined to accept the necessity of both training and discipline, and were contemptuous of those who disdained either.

In this war, with the exception of some of the militia formations previously mentioned, volunteer regiments had not existed prior to the commencement of hostilities, and had to learn survival the hard way. There were, of course, the regiments of the regular army: five cavalry, four artillery, and ten infantry (raised in 1861, respectively, to six, five, and fifteen).[70] Once the war began, a critical decision had to be made by general in chief Winfield Scott on whether to break up these regiments and use them as a training cadre, or keep them together, in which case they might serve as model units for the quickly forming militia. To Scott, there was no choice at all. All his previous career experience had led him to distrust volunteer soldiers; moreover, he feared that if the regular army were broken up it might well never be reconstituted. His plan was to enlarge the small regular force of some 16,300 men through substantial enlistment and then train the new recruits up to the standards of the regulars, using volunteers only as auxiliaries when and where necessary. C. W. Elliott, a Scott biographer, notes the problem with this policy: "The folly of supposing that the embattled nation, Federals and Confederates alike, would fold hands and wait until so puissant a weapon had been forged, seems to have been overlooked in his calculations. Even after the discouraging defeats of the [first] summer, he stuck obstinately to his dogma." But Lincoln had not disagreed, foreseeing a short war in which it was politically useful to appoint new commanders to lead volunteers—and in any case, the regulars were needed on the frontier.[71]

Scott was soon replaced, but his decision to keep the regular units intact had numerous ramifications, not least of which was to block the promotion of West Point officers who might otherwise have been expected to provide leadership throughout the army—unless, that is, they resigned their commissions. As it turned out, the Union army made use of 754 West Point graduates to the Confederacy's 283 in both regular and volunteer formations. Since the Union created 3,559 separate formations (to the Confederacy's 1,526), the percentage of men under the direct command of a West Point graduate was quite small in both armies.[72] While it could be said that the regular regiments served as models for those units which served with them, again, from a purely numerical standpoint, few state regiments actually had that experience. "I wish we had more regulars to tie to," complained William Tecumseh Sherman (USMA 1840) shortly after First Bull Run, but it was not going to happen.[73]

The largest single grouping of U.S. regulars was in Maj. Gen. George Sykes's Division (5th Corps) of the Army of the Potomac, which included the 2d, 3d, 4th, 6th, 10th, 11th, 12th, 14th, and 17th Infantry Regiments divided into two brigades supplemented by other volunteer units. The division fought heroically and took terrible losses at Gaines's Mill and Gettysburg, and though it is fair to say it was the best officered division of this army since its leaders were regulars rather than untrained civilians, this fact did not save its regiments from terrible casualties, most notably for the 14th Infantry. The remnants of these excellent, but ultimately decimated units, were withdrawn from field service in 1865.

The other major concentration of regulars was in King's or the "Regular" Brigade of Rosseau's Division, 14th Corps, which included the 15th, 16th, 18th, and 19th Infantry together with a battery of the 5th (regular) Artillery. This division saw serious action in Kentucky, Tennessee, and Georgia. At Stone's River in Tennessee, the 18th U.S. Infantry took 603 officers and men into the fight, and emerged with 48 percent killed and wounded—the highest percentage of losses suffered by a regular army unit.[74] The few remaining regiments were scattered about; one, the 9th Infantry, remained on the West Coast throughout the war. Fine troops they no doubt were, but their numbers were insufficient to make any major impact on a war in which 2,800,000 men were mustered into Federal service from the spring of 1861 to the end of 1864.[75] Perhaps had Scott's decision been otherwise and a few experienced men assigned to each new regiment, the early conduct of the war might have gone differently, but such a conclusion would be pure speculation. In any case, the term "regular" is misleading in the sense that the standing army at any one time was composed of a high percentage of raw recruits owing to turnover resulting from sickness, desertion, and low reenlistment rates.

Nevertheless, the regulars remained the ideal in many respects, and this attitude was perpetuated by the many West Point graduates who either resigned their army commissions or returned to service from civilian life to lead volunteer regiments. A solid dose of effective training could persuade a thinking man that the regulars had much to emulate. "How I used to pity the regulars when I first came down here," wrote Charles Haydon in late 1861. "Poor fellows I used to think you are laced up in a straight jacket & imprisoned without hope of relief for the next 5 years. After all I could not help noticing that they did not

seem to feel very bad about it & that they looked a vast deal better than
we. Times & thoughts have so far changed that nothing pleases men or
officers more than the thought of being made into regulars."[76] Abner
Small of the 16th Maine had a rather different view as a result of his
training at Meridian Hill outside Washington, where "we were developed into parade soldiery of the regulation pattern by a lieutenant fresh
from West Point, who appeared to take an exquisitely painful pleasure
in the development. In his eyes we were a different species of verte-
brate from that evolved at the Academy; an inferior species, not capable of standing fully erect; a species grown all awry and possessing
neither comeliness nor sense. It didn't seem to occur to him that his
laced figure, his crammed education, and all his other military attributes
were the product and property of the government, which lent him for
our use. He put us through our paces with a competence only equaled
by his contempt for us. He might easily have won our esteem; but as it
was, we soon cared less for him than for the indifferent bread and bacon that were dealt out to us as rations."[77]

Whatever their sense of superiority, however, West Point graduates could not be everywhere, any more than the regular regiments
themselves. If only by default, the most famous regiments of both sides
were volunteers. (Few pre-war regulars aside from officers joined the
Confederacy; the few "regular" regiments formed in the Confederacy
were not successful.)[78] Over time, hardened volunteer units developed
that would have paid little deference to regular units on the battlefield.
One example of such a force is the army which Sherman took on his
"March to the Sea." As Joseph Glatthaar points out, three of Sherman's
four corps (14th, 15th, and 17th) had extensive experience through
years of campaigning, mostly in the west, and were well familiar with
long marches and short supplies. The fourth, the 20th Corps from the
Army of the Potomac, was better-dressed and better-disciplined, but
required some time to prove itself to the westerners, which it certainly
had done by the end of the campaign. When Sherman had culled the
sick and extraneous, and selected "the best men from the best infantry
corps and cavalry units in the west," often including regiments that
had remaining only a few hundred professional survivors, the result
was an army which certainly considered itself elite. Confederates shared
this view, however they hated the results of Sherman's march: Gen.
Joseph E. Johnston, one of Sherman's adversaries, remarked after the
war that "there had been no such army since the days of Julius Caesar."[79]

Yet Sherman's army in this campaign was not forced to fight the set-piece type of battle for which the war is remembered. Only in such struggles was it possible to make the sort of permanent reputation like those of the South's Stonewall Brigade and the North's Iron Brigade.[80] These two units may be said to stand as the premier examples of fighting elites in this war. Aside from the obvious difference in loyalties, these brigades were not quite comparable; Union brigades, for example, tended to include three or four regiments, while Confederate brigades with five or six were larger, at least if the regiments were at full strength. In addition, while the Stonewall Brigade set a splendid example for the Confederacy in the first year of the war, the Iron Brigade was not really involved until the following year, when it arguably became the best unit in the Army of the Potomac.

The Stonewall Brigade included the 2d, 4th, 5th, 27th, and 33d Virginia Regiments and the Rockbridge Artillery (named for Rockbridge County), basically all from the Shenandoah Valley. Most of the soldiers were farmers and farm laborers; few were slave holders, but a significant number had received higher education at schools like Washington College, the University of Virginia, or the Virginia Military Institute (VMI). Many recruits found friends and relatives in their regiments. "Few, if any, Confederate brigades reflected such commonality of place, heritage, and kinship," Jeffry Wert has explained in his comparative study of the common soldiers of both the Stonewall and Iron Brigades.[81] Indeed, one of the striking points about both brigades was the fact that over time the loyalty of soldiers in both units was as strong to their brigade as to their regiment, which was not generally the case in the rest of the army.

Both units also benefited greatly from having capable commanders from their inception. Col. Thomas J. Jackson, West Point graduate, Mexican War veteran, and former instructor at VMI, was hard-working, disciplined, and pious, and began at once to shape his Virginia brigade, appointing nineteen VMI cadets to instruct in drill. While he could, Jackson drilled his 2,300 men for six hours a day: "Drills and marches and work was the order of the day under our new commander," complained a brigade member. The discipline and spirit which Jackson instilled proved vital, for his command was soon badly cut up at the first Battle of Bull Run (known as First Manassas in the South). Jackson's men, however, had stood firm, and as he wrote to a friend, ". . . the First Brigade was to our army what the Imperial Guard was to the

First Napoleon—that, through the blessing of God, it met the thus far victorious enemy and turned the fortunes of the day."[82] At this battle, the Virginians earned the sobriquet of "Stonewall" for themselves and their commander, though it was not given official recognition until a special order of May 1863 was signed by Confederate President Jefferson Davis.[83] Jackson soon went on to higher command, though his brigade remained under his authority. In his farewell address to the brigade in October 1861, he made clear his admiration of their conduct: "You have already gained a brilliant and deservedly high reputation throughout the army of the whole Confederacy. . . ."[84]

It seems beyond question that Jackson himself was a major contributing factor to the morale of the Confederate army, and not just the brigade, despite his penchant for hard discipline, including the use of capital punishment more often than any other Confederate officer.[85] "O my dear, I wish you could just see him," wrote Capt. Ujanirtus Allen of the 21st Georgia in July 1862 (Allen died of wounds received at Chancellorsville nine months later). "See him before or after a battle as he passes the boys. They will run two hundred yards to see him and yell like wildcats. He invariably, when they cheer him, uncovers his head and dashes along at a rapid pace glancing his proud eagle eye from side to side."[86] And from a Rockbridge gunner: "Cheering began far behind us, so far away that we scarcely heard it, increasing until in tremendous volume it swept by us with Stonewall bareheaded on Little Sorrel [a pacing horse of well-known accomplishments] at his best speed, the staff strung out away behind, doing their level best to keep up, until gradually the cheering died away in the distance far ahead." And when, in September 1862, his battery was reassigned to another command: ". . . our whole battery was proud to be known as an integral part of that immortal brigade. To me the separation was sad and weighed on my spirits for months."[87] Not every Confederate agreed, of course. "I have read with interest the heroic actions of the *Stonewall Brigade*," wrote one soldier from the lines at Fredericksburg in early 1863 to *The Southern Illustrated News,* "and I see no reason why the Army of [Northern Virginia], except the *Stonewall Brigade*, should not be disbanded and sent home, and leave that *Immortal Brigade* which has done all the fighting to crown themselves with immortality, by ending the war alone."[88]

Indeed the Stonewall Brigade went on to more glory, and not simply on the battlefield. These veterans, for example, performed one of the war's most famous marches, some fifty-four miles in thirty-six hours. But once again the brigade was badly bloodied at the Second Bull Run, on Culp's Hill at Gettysburg, and yet again at the "East Angle" of the Mule Shoe, where Grant attacked Lee's center in the battle of Spotsylvania Court House.[89] The brigade's 2,600 men at the start of the war were probably augmented by a like number to replace losses and desertions (at least one thousand brigade members deserted in 1862 alone, but often simply to visit their homes for a shorter time, only to return on their own in due course), to a total of five thousand. After Spotsylvania, only two hundred remained to answer the roll call.[90] The Stonewall Brigade had been destroyed in a few minutes of savage fighting at close range. "Our old division has lost all of its past renown," lamented an officer of the 21st Virginia. "My shattered nerves will not allow of my writing more. . . ."[91]

The North's Iron Brigade survived only a month longer into the war. This brigade was composed of "westerners" in the usage of the day—the 2d, 6th, and 7th Wisconsin and the 19th Indiana, each raised in its own state. The 2d Wisconsin was first into battle, at First Bull Run, and until the other regiments were "blooded" tended to take on airs. Like the Stonewall Brigade, the Iron Brigade was recruited by a most capable commander, in this case Brig. Gen. John Gibbon.[92] Gibbon, like Jackson, was a West Point graduate, and a veteran of both Mexico and the Seminole Wars, though he had not had much actual battle experience. He was also a former assistant instructor of artillery at the Point. Though born in Philadelphia, Gibbon grew up in the South; three of his brothers and two brothers-in-law served the Confederacy. Like Jackson, Gibbon went to work on his brigade, "trying to knock the *kinks* out of it!," as he wrote to his wife, "and indoctrinate the officers and men into the ways of the regulars." Within a short time he had them maneuvering "with clock-like regularity, until finally I began to perform them at the double quick."[93] "There were early morning drills, afternoon drills, evening and night drills, besides guard mounting and dress parades," wrote one veteran—but there were also rewards, for example a twenty-four-hour pass for the smartest man at guard mounting.[94] Gibbon in his later memoirs was clear on the basic issue: "The mere efficiency in drill was not by any means the most important point gained in this month of instruction. The *habit* of obedience and subjection to the will of another, so difficult to instill into the minds of free and independent men became marked characteristics in the command. A great deal of the prejudice against me as a regular officer was removed when the men came to compare their own soldierly appearance and way of doing duty with other commands, and although there were still malcontents who chafed under the restraints of a wholesome discipline and would have chafed under any, these were gradually reduced in number and influence."[95]

But Gibbon did more than train his brigade; he also altered their uniforms. Within a short time he had issued his regiments the blue frock coats and trousers worn by regulars, and most notably the "Hardee" hat, made of stiff black felt with high crown and a broad brim tacked up on the right side (so as not to interfere with the maneuver known as "shoulder-arms"), ornamented with blue hat cord and tassles, brass bugle, regiment number, and company letter. "An absurd change," as an old soldier recalled the original introduction of this headgear, done on the recommendation of Maj. William J. Hardee. The hat was at first used only by cavalry, but in 1858 ordered for the regular army as a whole with the Kepi, the standard headgear for volunteer units in the Civil War. "A single black feather or plume was fastened on the left side of the hat, which few of the soldiers knew how, or cared to keep curled neatly. In damp weather it looked like a drenched rooster's tail-feathers."[96] But the brigade appeared to welcome the changes—except for the white leggings, impossible to keep clean—which went with the uniform, and gloried in appearing exactly like regulars, differing in this regard from nearly all other volunteer state regiments at this stage of the war. When, after Antietam, the brigade was so reduced in numbers to require the addition of another regiment, the newcomers, the 24th Michigan, were not given their black hats until May 1863 after they had earned them at Fredericksburg and Fitzhugh's Crossing.[97] But the brigade's regiments each had their own characteristics, as explained by one 2d Wisconsin soldier: "The 2d is probably the hardest set of boys, but good natured and easy to get along with. They wear an air of fearless carelessness wherever found. The 6th is more stately, and distant, and march to slower music than we do. The 7th puts on the least style and crow the least; it is now the largest regiment in the brigade, and is well drilled. It is the truest friend the 2d ever found. The 19th Indiana is an indifferent, don't care regiment. They pride themselves on their fighting pluck—which is undoubtedly good—more than their drill. As a brigade we get along finely together."[98]

Gibbon had trained his men well, for in their great test at Turner's

Gap, South Mountain, Maryland, (the opening stage of the bloody struggle of Antietam Creek, September 1862) the brigade stood without breaking though it took some 1,600 casualties. Within days it had earned the nickname of the "Iron Brigade," though it has never been clear just who originated the term. Gibbon made up his losses with the addition of the Michigan regiment, and for nearly all of the next year the Iron Brigade "with their famous black hats were arguably the best combat infantrymen in the army."[99] But at Gettysburg, of nearly 1,900 men who began the battle, more than 1,200 were killed, wounded, captured, or missing. The brigade was still in existence, but its core element was gone. At the Wilderness, the unit took another one-third casualties, and broke in battle: it no longer had the same combat discipline, or the same willingness to go into the fray. Gibbon was no longer in command, having been promoted to division command in November of 1862. "I hated to leave the old Brig. but could not refuse a higher command & have just finished my farewell order to the Black Hatted Brigade *almost* with tears in my eyes. I would rather take them into action than any Division I know of but cannot expect to keep them always...."[100]

The lesson of these two brigades is certainly clear: even the finest of military units cannot withstand annihilation. The two formations had directly faced each other once, at the Brawner Farm on the Warrenton Turnpike, in August 1862, as part of the second Battle of Bull Run. In one of the most intense of the war's small actions, both sides took heavy casualties; the 430 officers and men of the 2d Wisconsin, the "Ragged Ass Second," in particular, for some minutes alone held off a determined Confederate attack from Stonewall's brigade, most of the time at no more than seventy-five yards distance, until other units came up in support. Brig. Gen. Edward S. Bragg (himself once of the 6th Wisconsin) summed up: "... there it was that Jackson's stubborn fighters learned that iron was as enduring and immovable as stone."[101]

That the Civil War was an enormously costly conflict hardly needs repeating. In its course, many fine units of veteran soldiers were created only to disappear in the carnage. The Stonewall and Iron Brigades were simply the most famous, and the most studied after the war. They must therefore stand in lieu of those regiments and brigades (divisions, corps, and armies may be assigned unique characteristics, but loyalties were seldom very entrenched at that level) which compiled equal records of valor but were survived by no special nickname. One of the most capable was A. Hill's brigade of Virginia regiments. Hill, West Point class of 1847, resigned from the army to become a brigadier general of volunteers, and his brigade, which he led from the front garbed in his famous red shirt, earned an enviable reputation. Promoted to divisional commander in 1862, Hill called his unit the "Light Division" (an exception to the general rule that divisions and corps were called by the name of their commander), perhaps out of admiration for British light infantry units (Hill was a reader of history), perhaps because he wanted a distinguishing slogan or cachet denoting hard and fast marching. With nearly thirty regiments and batteries, Hill's division was prominent at some major battles, including Mechanicsville, Gaines's Mill, Second Bull Run, and Antietam—until Jackson was mortally wounded at Chancellorsville and Hill took over command, soon moving on to become a corps commander.[102]

That the stories of Hill's and other similarly distinguished units must be left to Civil War historians is in no way to denigrate their status. In another time and place, many would have been their era's guardsmen. But in the Civil War, it bears repeating, such units emerged essentially by accident: little attempt was made to concentrate the most experienced veteran formations as a special attack or reserve force, but rather they were left scattered about in both armies.

Within a man's unit, however, what chance was there for special recognition? Some men enlisted on the very promise of elite status guaranteed by unscrupulous recruiters, such as the several hundred Philadelphians who were told they were destined "for a body guard and special service at the headquarters of Maj. Gen. D. C. Buell, then commanding the Army of the Ohio," and that they could expect duties of "scouting, secret expeditions, guards . . . [and in general] service of a daring and dashing character." When none of this proved true, the result was a mutiny which had to be suppressed, and the reorganization of those men who remained as the 60th Pennsylvania Infantry.[103]

Once a man found himself on the battlefield, there might be an opportunity to win distinction. Particularly in siege warfare, there was often a call for volunteers to lead a "forlorn hope" assault in the best European tradition. Vicksburg, Petersburg, Port Hudson: at the latter, in 1863, one thousand volunteers were called for with the promise of medals and promotions. Since several efforts of this sort had already failed, volunteers were conspicuous for their absence. A bit of pressure was applied until the number was made up; "a curious medley as to character, some of them being our best and bravest men, while others were mere rapscallions, whose sole object was, probably, to get the whiskey ration issued to the forlorn hope." As it turned out, Port Hudson surrendered before an all-out assault was necessary; defense of the town was no longer tenable once Vicksburg had surrendered. But the "Volunteer Thousand Storming Party," many of whom were officers, had pride of place when the Union troops entered the captured town.[104]

Of course a man might be promoted to non-commissioned officer, as many were, but responsibilities came with the honor. Particularly honorable—and dangerous—was the position of color sergeant, for carrying the regimental flags into battle was to make oneself a target. John Beatty explained after Murfreesboro in October 1862: ". . . I have only time to mention the fact that our colors change hands several times during the engagement. Six of our color-bearers were either killed or wounded, and as the sixth man was falling, a soldier of Company C . . . sprang forward, caught the falling flag, then, stepping out in front of the regiment, waved it triumphantly and carried it to the end of the battle."[105] "There is no such thing as taking shure [sic] aim in the battle field the smoke of powder the noise of firearms and cannon and the excittement [sic] of the battle field makes it impossible," wrote Peter Welsh to his wife in March 1863, trying to explain away the dangers of his new position as color sergeant of the 28th Massachusetts Infantry, "so that if the colors are fired at those on either side of the colors for the lenght [sic] of a company are more likely to get struck then [sic] the color bearer. . . ."[106]

Medals of any kind were rare indeed, particularly in the Confederacy, where the striking of actual medals would simply have increased the burden on an already inadequate metal industry. The Confederate Congress in 1862 authorized President Davis to issue medals and badges as awards, but Davis showed little interest in exercising this power. It was a strange conceit, on both sides, for it seems safe to conclude that such honors, legitimately bestowed, would have had a positive effect far beyond the effort involved, as evidenced by the popularity of both rumors of pending medals and of such distinctions as were actually introduced. "A list of names for rewards & another for promotions has been made," wrote Charles Haydon in July 1862. "Tis said that medals of some kind are to be given & a sort of Legion of Honor formed. Nine commissioned & 4 non-comd. officers have been recommended for promotion and rewards, six officers & 169 men for reward (i.e. medals). . . . As in all such things there will be some unfairness & injustice. . . ."[107]

The Union's Medal of Honor, on the other hand, was intended to redress the lack of means for recognizing outstanding bravery and to supersede the growing tendency of various lesser commanders to award some sort of medal within their own commands. Established first by the Senate for the navy in 1861, the honor was extended the following year to the army; officers were not at first eligible, but were made so in 1863, retroactive to the start of the war. Though intended for outstanding bravery, as it happened, not all its awards were made for that reason. In one notorious case just before Gettysburg, President Lincoln and Secretary of War Edwin A. Stanton authorized its presentation to all members of the 17th Maine who reenlisted at a moment when it seemed that their presence was desperately needed for the defense of Washington. Some 300 men did stay on briefly until Gettysburg was over, but in error the medal was awarded to all 864 men in the unit, though the regiment had yet to be tested in battle.[108] In many cases, on the other hand, the actual award was long delayed. Some sixty-six medals were eventually awarded for the Gettysburg campaign, for example, but only eighteen were presented during the war itself, the rest coming in later ceremonies. C. W. Reed received his for saving the life of a wounded officer at Trostle's Farm—but was informed of the honor, to his complete astonishment, only in 1895! The award was certainly haphazard, but could nevertheless be most effective, as was the public presentation by Maj. Gen. G. Meade in September 1864 to three individuals, each of whom had captured unit flags from the Confederates.[109]

One effective designation was that of "veteran volunteer" awarded to those Northern regiments in which the men collectively reenlisted in 1863–64, and were thus distinguished from the general run of conscripts and bounty soldiers which was then coming into the army. Sometimes a relatively simple step such as this made a definite contribution to morale and esprit de corps. In 1862 Maj. Gen. Philip Kearny ordered a red patch for the caps of the officers of his Third Corps; after he was killed in September of that year, one of his veteran regiments, the 2d Michigan, adopted a medal of their own with a raised likeness of the general, ". . . a seven point gold Star, two inches across the extreme points, on each of which is engraved the name of one of the seven battles we fought under him."[110]

When, in 1863, Gen. Joseph Hooker took command of the Army of the Potomac, following Kearny's example, he ordered the officers and men of each corps and division to wear a distinctive two-inch identifying badge on their caps, as well as marking it on wagon covers, headquarters flags, and the like. The badges were quite noticeable: a red disc for the 1st Corps, a white trefoil for the 2d, a blue lozenge for the 3d, and so on. Equally important, he did much to improve conditions in camps and hospitals in such matters as sanitation and food; to keep the men busy with drills, reviews, and other duties; and to regularize the granting of leaves and furloughs to well-disciplined regiments. Though "Fighting Joe" did not prove a resounding success as a battlefield commander and eventually requested his own replacement, his methods helped restore his army's battered pride, as Kearny had similarly inspired his Third Corps.[111]

For officers, battlefield promotion to regular rank was notably rare. Neither Lee nor President Davis permitted promotions for valor; on the other side, General Grant is known to have only twice granted this honor. Instead, recognition on both sides came mainly in the form of "brevet" (honorary) rank; so common was brevet rank in the Union army, at any rate, that mules were sarcastically known as "brevet horses." Brevet rank made for many complications, since assignments to command could be made on the basis of an officer's brevet rank, and he would commonly wear the uniform, but not the rank insignia, of that rank. (Congress at least ended that practice by ordering several years after the war that officers would wear only the uniform of their regular rank.) Further confusion was added by the rule that a man with a brevet commission was addressed by that title rather than that of his substantive rank. In the North, a proposal of 1864 that brevet rank be conferred for administrative expertise as well as battlefield performance was quashed by generals such as Gibbon, Hancock, and Meade, but the end of the war brought a flood of brevet promotions, not a few politically inspired. Gibbon, ranked as major general but technically only a regular captain at the end of the struggle, refused to accept brevet promotions in the regular army to major, lieutenant-colonel, colonel, and brigadier general out of protest at the practice, though he did accept that of major general in 1866—at a moment when his actual command responsibility was as colonel of the new regular 36th Infantry Regiment posted to the western frontier.[112]

Failing all else, an army commander could always issue a general order remarking on the actions of a particular individual or unit. Jeb Stuart, a cavalry division commander in 1863, felt that J. S. Mosby had received insufficient recognition from Lee for a raid which had resulted in the capture of a Union brigadier general, taken from his own bed in the midst of a garrisoned village at Fairfax Court House. As a result, Stuart distributed a general order praising Mosby's exploit, but he could only circulate it among his own command.[113] In general, it appears that both sides in this war gave little attention to the establishment of a credible system of rewarding valor. That such a system might have encouraged greater reenlistment is certainly an insupportable conclusion, but the generally subjective evidence would seem to indicate that equitable systems of rewards encourage the belief among soldiers, particularly veterans, that they are valued as soldiers. On the other side of the coin, ferocious discipline was not generally a feature of Civil War units; the democratic principles of non-professionals on both sides would not allow that. But punishment there was, particularly for persistent deserters and bounty-jumpers; the Union army executed 267 of its men during the war (147 for desertion).[114] A Roman centurion would have understood the utility of a counter-balancing reward system.

Who then were the true elites of the Civil War? The answer must be the unit which had some significant training before plunging into battle, capable leadership, and above all, luck—a factor of great importance in war in general, but perhaps even more so in war of such high attrition. Luck was essential for the unit to have the time to "simmer down" as the expression of the day had it, to lose its sick and its weak men who could not last, to experience battle but not to be so crushed as to be either demoralized or destroyed as a unit. It is estimated that there were perhaps ten thousand Civil War battles and skirmishes—fifty to one hundred of significant scale. Some soldiers fighting in Virginia were under fire one hundred times. As Griffith remarks, "Such men can be accounted veterans indeed. . . . Only the strongest of men could survive this way of life for long, and those who did must of necessity have become expert in the art of minimising the rigours of their ordeal." Over time, hardness, wisdom, and esprit de corps shaped the regiments and brigades that were most admired and respected. It was no accident that when Lee surrendered and his Army of Northern Virginia marched with its colors in its last parade; Gordon's Corps came first, and at the Corps' head, in turn, "marched the proudest unit of the army, a tiny fragment of the Stonewall Brigade."[115]

5 From The Civil War to World War II

When the Civil War ended, no one was able to predict that it would be three quarters of a century before American soldiers would again be involved in a war of the same duration. War would come with Spain at the end of the century, but in the framework of world military history it was a small affair. World War I would require enormous efforts on behalf of the United States and its armed forces to put two million men in France. Nevertheless, American soldiers and marines occupied front line positions only from January 1918 until the fighting stopped on November 11. For America, the war was far shorter and less costly in blood than it was to any major European state. For most of the years between Lee's surrender and Pearl Harbor, to put it somewhat differently, there were neither incentives nor resources for the creation of military elites.

In the long peace which followed the Civil War, the Regular Army was significantly reduced several times, cut to about fifty–seven thousand officers and men in 1866, and then to some twenty–five thousand from 1874 until the Spanish-American War. These were in fact official maximum figures, seldom met in practice. Of those who did serve, a substantial number were spread along the Texas-New Mexico border to deal with the plains Indians and Apaches. In addition to the desire to

save money on public services, there were other reasons for army re-
ductions, including public hostility to the use of military forces during
the railroad strikes of 1877 and 1894. Basically the army in these years
was "little more than an Indian constabulary," some twenty-five infantry, ten cavalry, and five artillery regiments (two infantry and two cavalry were restricted to African Americans) spread over 255 separate
posts in the 1860s, reduced to ninety-three as the century came to a
close. Pay was low ($16 per month, cut to $13 in 1871), food and
housing miserable, and desertion high, most notably during general
economic up-cycles. At least until the mid-1870s, half of the new recruits were foreign born; even of those who were not, many enlisted
only for an opportunity to reach the west before deserting. Discipline
was erratic and often severe, while the opportunity for training at the
regimental level was minimal. The army was hardly a desirable or respectable profession; until the late 1870s, it was virtually impossible for
an enlisted man to reach officer status. It is little wonder that few men
wished to stay on for the full five years of their voluntary enlistments (no
pensions were available to soldiers until 1885), but the figures are still
astounding: in 1871, 8,800 men deserted, nearly one-third of the total force.[1]

Certainly there was no room for complacency among thinking
officers, who found in the lessons of the Civil War much food for
thought. William Tecumseh Sherman, for example, had a fairly clear
vision of what the future of warfare held. He appreciated the efforts of
volunteers, but the power of the defensive as demonstrated on the battlefield meant that success would require dispersal, movement, adapta-
tion—in other words, trained, disciplined intelligence as well as raw
courage: "The more we improve the fire-arm the more will be the necessity for good organization, good discipline, and intelligence on the
part of the individual soldier and officer." This was not really a new
argument; it had been made, at least in the call for a well-trained, aggressive officer corps, by Dennis Hart Mahan in his lectures and book
produced at West Point in the 1830s and 1840s, not surprisingly using
Napoleonic France as his model. The reality was, however, that the
diminished and widely-dispersed army was most difficult to mold in
Sherman's model.[2]

The real "prophet of professionalism," however, was Emory
Upton.[3] Upton, West Point class of 1861, had a remarkable career in
the Civil War, rising from first lieutenant to brevet major general in
command of a regular cavalry division (at age twenty-five, certainly

one of the youngest divisional commanders in either army). Self-confident, stern in discipline, ambitious—insufferably pompous, some said—and studious, Upton had little doubt of what the model army should look like, and when he was made commandant of cadets at West Point in 1870 (second in authority only to the superintendent) and thus responsible for training, he had his chance for the next five years to express his views. To Upton, as to a number of officers before him, the army ought to have been more than just a small, disparate force to police Indians. Indeed, in his time, the Indian wars were nearing an end. While a large army might be desirable in theory, Upton knew this was not possible in the American context. The army which was possible therefore would best serve as a nucleus for a big army, a permanent cadre of professionals which in time of need could train the necessary conscript recruits—a function which had generally been denied the regulars in the Civil War. Upton did not object to militia in theory, but militia units controlled by the states rather than the national government were little more than a recipe for military failure, at least in the short run. Upton himself was never particularly optimistic regarding the future, a conclusion reinforced by his own suicide in 1881. His views were fairly influential among some officers, circulating in a manuscript entitled *Elements of Military Art and Science*, but the volume was little known to the public, even after it was published as a government document in 1904.

Nor was Upton's the only view available. John A. Logan in 1887 published a massive answer to Upton's views (though Upton had yet to write his major work), *The Volunteer Soldier of America*. Logan was a senator from Illinois, and Republican candidate for vice-president in 1884; he was also a successful major general during the Civil War, rising to command of the XV Army Corps in the Army of the Tennessee. He believed command of that army had been kept from him solely because he was not a graduate of West Point. Logan had less faith, to begin with, in the elite professionalism of the Academy; after all, its cadets received their appointments as plum awards in the American political system, and as the officer defections early in the Civil War proved, their allegiance was first to party and section, not to the military institution. Even if loyal to their country, they were not necessarily men with the talent or inclination for war: "Throughout the war," as Michael Neiberg remarks, "West Pointers drew a great deal more scorn than praise," as their academy training proved less than adequate. Lo-

gan, like many others, had little faith in Upton's reliance on the elite
Academy's graduates. How widely that view was shared is demonstrated by the Morrill Act of July 1862, proposed by Vermont Congressman Justin Morrill, which basically established the land grant
college system for every state—on the condition that such colleges
teach military tactics as well as other subjects.[4]

Logan himself had no real plan for the future, but it was clear to
him that the nation in its emergencies would continue to rely on the
soldiers of the militia, however organized and controlled. True enough,
they had often failed, but just as often they had become proficient officers and men, even though they lacked the cachet of Academy credentials.[5] In one sense, at least, Logan was right and Upton wrong: in a
serious national war, whatever their training and professional standards,
the regular force which the country was willing to pay for in peacetime
would be swamped. This would prove to be the case in World War I.
There was, of course, a larger issue which always underlay the con-
flicting principles of professional army and civilian militia. Maj. Gen.
John Pope, himself a professional officer (but not an "Uptonist"), put
it well in an 1873 speech quoted by Russell Weigley in his study of
nineteenth-century American military thought:

> So long as the soldier remains one of the people; so long as he
> shares their interests, takes part in their progress, and feels a
> common sympathy with them in their hopes and aspirations,
> so long will the Army be held in honorable esteem and regard,
> and so long will the close ties which now bind together the
> soldier and the citizen be perpetuated among us. When he
> ceases to do this; when officers and soldiers cease to be citi-
> zens in the highest and truest sense, the Army will deserve to
> lose, as it will surely lose, its place in the affections of the
> people, and properly and naturally become an object of suspi-
> cion and dislike.[6]

Despite such warnings, to a considerable extent the army ossi-
fied between the Civil and Spanish-American Wars, remote from the
bulk of American society both socially and physically, and preserving
its own nearly unbridgeable gap between officers and men. Andrew
Carnegie was only reflecting popular opinion when he remarked in
1881, that "the real glory of America lay in the fact that she had no

army worth the name."[7] On the other hand, the Regulars had a well-deserved reputation for toughness from their Indian fighting experience (nearly one thousand engagements were catalogued from 1865 to 1898). The argument is sometimes made that the few black regiments—10 percent of the army and 20 percent of the cavalry after 1860—were of elite quality, a judgment based mainly on their high reenlistment and low desertion rates, but outside the South, black deserters were too visible, and desirable civilian job opportunities few. William Dobak and Thomas Phillips lay this impression to rest: "There were some statistical differences in behavior between black soldiers and white, but on the whole neither group was much better, or much worse, than the other." West Point graduates certainly did not see service with black troops as desirable, except perhaps the few who were eager for action in an army which now generally saw little. On the other hand, since they did the same duty as white soldiers, and had to be given the same supplies, equipment, and pay, they were not elites. But neither were they second-class soldiers. It should be added that while the Comanche may have called them "Buffalo Soldiers," a term made popular by the writings and paintings of Frederick Remington in the late 1880s, they called themselves "black regulars" and resented "buffalo" as an insult.[8]

In the same era, however, some positive changes were introduced in the conditions of service for the army as a whole, and an attempt made to attract a better quality of recruit.[9] Some hallowed traditions were even discarded in the process. In 1889, for example, the mandatory weekly inspections were changed from Sunday to Saturday, leaving Saturday afternoon and Sunday for various forms of recreation, at least in theory. Regimental banks, schools, and libraries become public responsibilities, with funding no longer deducted from the soldiers' pay. Many of the infamous sutlers' stores which sold supplies and drink at a profit were replaced by regimental canteens (later known as post exchanges).[10]

Particularly important was the issue of education, and here another military educator and reformer, Arthur L. Wagner, had important influence. Wagner (USMA 1875) began his career as a convinced Uptonian, but soon realized the need to impose some practical American limitations on some of Upton's goals, particularly conscription. In a prizewinning 1884 article, he made it clear that while he had little enthusiasm for the militia, there was no practical alternative given the American suspicion of standing armies. More pragmatic than Upton,

Wagner focused upon the improvement of education, within and without the army, for officers and men alike. The goal was an army which would not only be more effective but also serve as a guide and model for militia units—hopefully with more federal control placed over them. Wagner was not the only officer with this conviction; post schools were created, for example, in 1866, and by 1891, basic abilities in reading, writing, and understanding English were made mandatory.[11]

But Wagner had a definite contribution to make when in 1886 he was transferred to Fort Leavenworth and assumed teaching responsibilities at the Infantry and Cavalry School which had been there since 1881. The school had not been notably successful, largely because its mission was unclear, and many commanding officers in the Army, assuming the School was essentially for remedial purposes, sent their worst officers to the "Kindergarten," as it was known for some years. Now, with the assistance of the school's new commander, Col. Alexander McCook, the curriculum was completely overhauled to stress advanced studies. It thus began to approach the sort of "war college" Wagner had in mind. Wagner was particularly concerned to modify the over-enthusiasm for anything Prussian in the wake of the wars of 1866 and 1870–71. More use of American Civil War lessons was one concern, but more important for the question of elites was Wagner's realization that Upton's tactics were increasingly obsolete.

Upton had quite naturally based his tactics upon the battle line of the Civil War, but even in that war technology was making that reliance more costly. In the latter decades of the century, breech-loading magazine rifles and massed, accurate field artillery made dispersal a necessity. But how could control be maintained over a dispersed army in such a way that it could retain cohesiveness and deliver a shock attack to the enemy? Europe offered two models. The first was the French stress on the aggressive attack with the bayonet from compressed, not dispersed, lines of battle. Continental strategists Baron Henri de Jomini (1779–1869) and Charles Ardant du Picq (1831–70) believed that spirit, élan, and the will to conquer, not fire superiority, were the key. The Germans had a different view, stressing dispersal. Each focus, however, required a different kind of training, and that is why the entire question is of vital importance to the study of elites. The Germans certainly counted on the spirit of the offensive, but they also believed in the role of firepower, and, most importantly, the "extended" (i.e., dispersed) order which gave considerable autonomy to leaders in the field from company commanders down to non-commissioned officers at the squad level. The American tendency, certainly as advocated by Wagner, was toward the German model, "with a healthy dose of French audacity."[12] With the help of Wagner's teaching and writings, a "Board of Revision" in 1890 brought out a new tactical manual, which for the first time adopted German extended order and the squad as a unit in the chain of command.

Not all officers were happy at the change, particularly those who could not bring themselves to believe, as T. R. Brereton explains, "that an average soldier had the wherewithal to control himself under fire, much less direct the movement of others. The very idea that mere soldiers were now expected to do what officers did was considered an insult to the officer corps."[13] Nevertheless, the reforms went through, guided by Wagner's important books on tactics which were required Leavenworth texts from their appearance in the early 1890s until shortly before World War I (Wagner himself died in 1905 after rising to the rank of brigadier general, which he had ardently coveted). The meaning for elites is not difficult to comprehend: while courage would always be important in the making of a good soldier, it was now the courage to act independently and take the initiative, rather than the willingness to march in close order, bayonets fixed, into the very real prospect of death. In due course, German storm troopers or British commandos would be the model to emulate, not Napoleon's Old Guard.

For Wagner, interestingly, one important model, at least for scouting and intelligence-gathering, was the American Indian, especially the Apaches and the Sioux. When "acting as *small infantry patrols*" nothing escaped their notice. "It is not because of his courage, expertness with firearms, or celerity of movement that the Indian is a formidable foe—indeed, in the first two qualities he is greatly surpassed by our troops. He is formidable because his thorough knowledge of all the essential details of the science of security and information generally enables him to give battle when he chooses, and to avoid conflict when he sees fit. As a scout he is a model; and it may be said that the scouting methods prescribed by the best European authorities are valuable in proportion [only] to the degree of their approach to those of the North American Indians."[14] Though not entirely accurate (Indians were not always competent at camp security, for example, nor were they less courageous), nevertheless this was a standard which would be difficult to attain, and in the end it would be necessary for the army to employ Apaches themselves to catch Apaches.

There were other changes in the army at the century's end. At the higher levels of command, a postgraduate school system was completed in 1901 with the creation of the Army War College, and a general staff system established the same year in emulation of Germany's proven success, though not without arousing congressional fears of the creation of a dangerous elite in the general staff corps, to say nothing of the opposition of the powerful entrenched bureau chiefs (the new system became law in 1906). A most important role in this key reform, which did much to reduce the power of those virtually independent bureau chiefs, was played by New York lawyer Elihu Root, President McKinley's choice as secretary of war, 1899–1904. When World War I arrived, however, the general staff's effectiveness was handicapped by the old fears; Congress had limited the General Staff Corps to only fifty-five officers, and only twenty-nine of these could work in Washington at any one time. Not only the civilians distrusted the staff: "Resented, if not hated, by many line officers, the Leavenworth men symbolized a break with the past," as Edward Coffman explains.[15] As far as the militia was concerned, finally, the Uptonians were at least partially successful, when various legislative acts culminating in the National Defense Act of 1916 established federal control over the state militias in wartime in what henceforth would be called the "National Guard," a force that would be ordered into federal service before any call for volunteers would be issued. By this time, of course, the United States had experienced the success—and confusion—of the war with Spain.

The Army in 1898, despite its small numbers, was not unready for combat. The problem was that it was not of a size sufficient to control the west and at the same time take on a power even of Spain's limited might. Once again, the Regular Army had to be supplemented by volunteers joining as individuals or as entire militia units which were re-enrolled, while at the same time states raised new units in the hope that they would find a place in the Army. Once again, the army was swamped, as its numbers exploded from about 25,000 to 250,000 amidst a great deal of mismanaged confusion. "The command system," as Clarence Clendennen puts it, "did not so much fail as simply cease to exist."[16] Medical arrangements, intelligence, transport, supplies of food and appropriate clothing: in many ways, the conduct of this war was a disaster.

But there was glory to be won. An act of Congress of 1898 had allowed the secretary of war to form volunteer units with "special qualifications" from the nation at large, though not to exceed a total of three thousand men. These proved to be the 1st, 2d, and 3d Regiments of United States Volunteer Cavalry, of which only the 1st, the "Rough Riders" of Col. Leonard Wood, with Theodore Roosevelt as its lieutenant-colonel, won special fame. The expeditionary force which actually embarked for Cuba, however, totaling nearly 17,000 men, included fewer than 2,500 volunteers: the Rough Riders and two National Guard regiments, the 71st New York and the 2d Massachusetts.[17]

Perhaps the Rough Riders should occupy a category of their own, as a "propaganda elite," but to deny them any elite status on the basis of the publicity they received, largely due to Roosevelt's energy (and contacts), would perhaps be unfair. The unit, some one thousand men divided into three squadrons, each of four troops, was organized as cavalry, but was not permitted to take its horses (except for those of the officers) to Cuba. When Wood was given command of the Regular cavalry, Roosevelt took over the regiment, and indeed he had been responsible for much of its recruitment. Media attention had brought some twenty thousand applications for one thousand places, and "Teddy" had a very mixed unit. Though Roosevelt rightly claimed that most were Westerners ("three-fourths of our men have at one time or

LIEUTENANT COLONEL ROOSEVELT AND HIS MEN OF THE 1ST REGIMENT OF UNITED STATES VOLUNTEER CAVALRY, KNOWN AS THE "ROUGH RIDERS," ON THE HEIGHTS OVERLOOKING SANTIAGO, CUBA. *LIBRARY OF CONGRESS*

another been cowboys or else as small stockmen") including some of
the famous Texas Rangers, it also included some fifty Easterners, "Fifth
Avenue Boys," the equivalent of Kipling's "gentlemen rankers," drawn
from the best clubs and universities of the east. But whatever their origins,
Teddy was serious about seeing to their training on the way to the war.[18]

In actual combat, the Rough Riders certainly fought bravely
enough in attacking Kettle Hill (not, as often thought, San Juan Hill,
though both were part of the battle of San Juan). Attrition had reduced
the regiment to fewer than five hundred men, but they followed
Roosevelt against the Spanish defenses, losing, according to official figures, some 15 percent in casualties. Roosevelt later claimed that his unit
took the highest losses of any American regiment in the campaign, but
such was not the case. The 6th, 13th, and 16th Regiments all suffered
higher losses but, like so many details, these figures were obscured in
the search for heroes. The Rough Riders fought elsewhere in Cuba
before returning home, an experience which confirmed that the Spanish could fight with tenacity, but the war was a short one. For Roosevelt,
the image of the Rough Riders, and of his leadership, helped him along
the road to the White House.[19] For John J. Pershing, whose African American 10th Cavalry also went up Kettle and San Juan Hills, and whose
men became thoroughly entangled with Roosevelt's, the exaggerated
publicity long given the Rough Riders rankled for years, and was revealed in his draft autobiography: "It is safe to say that in the history of
the country no man ever got so much reward for so little service."[20]

For Pershing, as for the Regular Army as a whole, the Rough
Riders had only enhanced a general distaste for volunteers, as would
be demonstrated in 1917. For the country, however, the image of
Roosevelt's Rough Riders tended instead to perpetuate the by-now traditional image of the frontier hero. That image, however, had undergone a transformation since the Civil War and, while it certainly included a leavening of heroic Civil War commanders, had in a general
sense shifted westward. It is not that Daniel Boone and Davy Crockett
had been displaced, but rather that they were joined by such figures as
Buffalo Bill Cody and Wild Bill Hickok, not to mention George
Armstrong Custer, above all after his "Last Stand" at Little Big Horn
in 1876. Cody, a legitimate frontier warrior as well as a capable show-
man, had himself borne the message of the deaths of Custer and 215
Seventh Cavalry troopers to his own Fifth Cavalry near the Red Cloud
Agency in Nebraska—but by that year he already spent his winters

living out his adventures on stage for delighted audiences. In the ensu-
ing years Cody and his friends in an important sense invented a wild
west of their own, complete with buffalo, Indians, and even Annie
Oakley.

Joy Kasson in her study of Buffalo Bill's career makes the valuable point that, at least in part, Cody's performances evoked memories
of the Civil War, and in particular "resonated with Southern preoccu-
pations. Hard riding, marksmanship, individual heroism, the battle between 'civilization' and 'savagery' were all familiar themes in the
South." As she herself notes, however, the appreciation of the individual was an important American theme in general in "an increasingly urban, industrial, and corporate society," as Cody's career reached
its later stages (he died in 1917). But it seems equally safe to see this
development somewhat differently, that is, as paying homage yet again
to the intrepid rifleman-hunter-frontiersman, the "ranger."[21]

It is interesting to note how both Teddy Roosevelt and Buffalo
Bill each made use of the other's image. Cody's Wild West program
included trick riding displays by his "Congress of the Rough Riders of
the World," made up of cowboys and Indians as well as cavalrymen
recruited by Cody on his European tours (1887–1892). Roosevelt
adopted the name for his unit, while meanwhile Cody replaced "Custer's
Last Fight" with the "Battle of San Juan Hill" in his 1899 program,
which included sixteen of Roosevelt's recent veterans. The exchange
was not without a bit of acrimony, however, since Cody claimed the
name "Rough Riders" was his, while Roosevelt responded that the usage was spontaneous; "hardly credible," historian Richard Slotkin comments, since Roosevelt had certainly seen the show, and, in any case,
some of Cody's cowboys and Indians had enlisted in his cavalry regiment when the war had begun (Cody's show had been playing in New
York at the time). Since Roosevelt was willing to proclaim his pride in
sharing the name with the "free fearless equestrians, now marshalled
under the leadership of the greatest horseman of all," the dispute did
not amount to much: The pantheon of elites had room for both.[22]

The truth was, of course, that the intrepid horseman had begun a
long, slow decline since the Civil War: it was an indication of war to
come that Roosevelt's riders had not ridden up San Juan Hill at all. The
application of the industrial age to warfare was thus providing a serious challenge to the meaning of "military elite" well before the end of
the nineteenth century. If the point had not yet been made, World War

I would certainly do so. But World War I lay some years off, and after the Spanish War the army shrunk to an authorized strength of sixty–five thousand men. This number almost immediately proved insufficient to deal with an unanticipated conflict in the Philippines, not against the Spanish, but rather to quell the Philippine independence movement, which America preferred to term an "insurrection." For the Philippine troubles, Congress authorized another thirty–five thousand men for two years. Since the struggle lasted well beyond the two-year limit, the volunteers were replaced by regulars in 1901.[23]

In consideration of military elites in the last half of the century, however, it is necessary to go beyond regular units and volunteer forces in order briefly to note some unique formations which emerged in the course of American imperial expansion. Because the growth of that empire was—with the exception of a few Pacific Ocean islands—limited to the North American continent until the Spanish-American War at the end of the nineteenth century, it is sometimes overlooked just how many diverse enemies the nation faced from its earliest colonial days. Aside from the obvious European rivals—Britain, France, Spain—the number and varying characteristics of indigenous societies, lumped together under the unsatisfactory but still useful term "Indians," is quite striking.

Many of these nations were relatively small and weak, and often were under considerable pressure from their own indigenous enemies. But some were impressive societies and dangerous foes in the military sense, even great empire-builders in their own right, from the Iroquois confederacy of the eastern forests to the Sioux, Cheyenne, and Comanche of the plains and the Apache of the southwestern desert/mountain frontier. It is often overlooked, as well, that American military history displayed a tradition of making use of indigenous peoples as scouts and auxiliaries. It is useful here to borrow Thomas Dunlay's distinction of scouts as those whose duties were mainly in the area of intelligence, such as finding and following the enemy's trail, and auxiliaries as those who were expected to engage in combat alongside, or instead of, regular troops, though Dunlay himself admits the distinction was often blurred in practice.[24]

It was one of the great weaknesses of American Indian resistance that, with few exceptions, each society acted for itself, as willing to play out old scores as to deal with new enemies. It was not lost on white society that manipulating such internal divisions had both the short-term effect of redirecting hostile energies onto other Indian groups, and the long-term effect of destabilizing Indian societies in general. The tale is certainly familiar, an example shown in James Fenimore Cooper's *The Last of the Mohicans* (1826). Gen. Anthony Wayne had Choctaw and Chickasaw scouts in the Northwest Territory; the Choctaws and Cherokees supported Andrew Jackson against the Creeks at Horseshoe Bend (Tohopeka, eastern Alabama) in 1814; and a Choctaw force guarded Jackson's left flank at the Battle of New Orleans. By the end of the century, young Lt. John J. Pershing, serving with the 6th Cavalry at the Pine Ridge Indian Agency in South Dakota in 1891, found himself suddenly appointed to command one of four companies of newly enlisted Sioux Scouts, signed up for six months to help preserve order among less cooperative tribal brothers (their contracts were not renewed). In such fashion, various tribal elements from the Warm Springs reservation in the Pacific Northwest cooperated against the "Snakes" (Shoshones and Paiutes), Winnebagoes worked against the Sioux in the Dakotas, Arapahoes against the same enemy in Colorado, and so on.[25]

The regularized use of such allies has long been known and practiced by historic imperial structures such as Rome and Byzantium, and continues into the twenty-first century through Britain's employment of professional Gurkha soldiers from Nepal. For whatever reasons, however, the United States was unwilling to give Indian auxiliaries any regular status until after the Civil War. In July 1866, Congress approved the formal enlistment—for periods of three months to a year—of not more than one thousand Indian scouts. Congress was seldom eager to increase military spending, but Indians accepted lower pay than regulars. One reason for the legislation, indeed, was to limit the number of Indians fighting alongside the regulars, for the one thousand would have to be spread over the several Indian territories and frontier districts.[26] While Indians from many nations continued to be used by the army, three such elements in particular played significant roles. Pawnee Scouts were used against the Sioux in the 1860s and 70s. Seminole Negro Scouts were employed not in the Seminole Wars of 1817–18 and 1835–42 in Florida (a third, small struggle of the 1850s is sometimes called the Third Seminole War) in which the Seminoles proved determined adversaries of American forces, but rather were formed in the 1870s, after the remaining Seminoles were removed from Florida, for service against the Apaches along the Mexican border. Finally, in the 1870s and 80s only by using Apache Scouts against Apaches could the last Apache strongholds of the southwest be conquered. The detailed treatment which each of these groups deserves, however, will have to await a further volume.

One obstacle which complicated dealings with the Apaches was their easy access to Mexico. Indeed, since the Mexican War that frontier had absorbed a considerable share of America's military might. It was in that sense appropriate that the last American conflict before the United States entered the Great War involved the expedition sent into Mexican territory in pursuit of Francisco (Pancho) Villa, who in March 1916 raided Columbus, New Mexico. The raid was costly to Villa, who lost more than one hundred men, but more important to President Woodrow Wilson, eighteen Americans were dead. The border was in a state of general insecurity, and had been since revolutionary troubles broke out in Mexico in 1910. Mexican President Venustiano Carranza had not managed to assert control of the state of Chihuahua, where Villa was in control. Wilson, floundering to find an effective policy towards Mexico, authorized an invasion of Chihuahua, according to a press release written by himself, "with the single objective of capturing him [Villa] and putting a stop to his forays." John J. Pershing, by then promoted to brigadier, was selected to command the force. His orders, however, read rather differently, for Wilson, realizing that Villa might lead the general on a merry chase—to Guatemala, for example—told Pershing that his objective was to break up Villa's band or bands.[27]

Washington, and Pershing, had every hope that Carranza, who was no friend to Villa, would not only welcome the American incursion, but would make Mexican supplies, and the railroads on which to move them, available to the Americans. It was soon evident that Carranza had no such intention—national pride took first priority— and thus American plans were thrown into disarray almost at once. Still, Pershing moved off with the 7th, 10th, 11th, and 13th Cavalry; 6th and 16th Infantry; and two batteries of the 6th Field Artillery, more than five thousand men, all regular army units (roughly 20 percent of the entire United States Army). He had commanded the 10th—an African American unit of considerable reputation for its work in various Indian actions, and in the Spanish-American War once before, in 1895— for which reason "Black Jack" seems to have earned his nickname.[28]

There is no need to consider the hunt for Villa in any detail. The campaign was rigorous, the terrain unknown to the Americans, the inhabitants generally hostile, the logistical problems nightmarish, and their erstwhile enemies difficult to bring to battle. Pershing's small "1st Aero Squadron" was of little help, fruitlessly attempting with their handful of unstable Curtis JN-2's "to get over 12,000 foot mountains with 10,000 foot airplanes," while his ad hoc truck transport too often broke down or was mired in thick dust or mud, trying to make roads where none existed. In search of intelligence on Villa's whereabouts, the general found it necessary to form fast-moving "provisional squadrons," small units of picked men, drawn from all the troops of the cavalry regiments, to roam ahead or on the flanks of his columns. Pershing was criticized for thus breaking up the normal units and removing the best soldiers, but given the state of his men, horses, and equipment after a long march into Mexico there probably was little choice. In one case, such a squadron from the 11th Cavalry, about 265 men, covered almost seven hundred miles in twenty-two days on half rations. "I have been in three wars, and for unmitigated hardship, the Punitive Expedition was the worst of all," recalled one veteran. Pershing himself said, "I do not believe that the cavalry in all its experience has done as hard work as the cavalry with this expedition."[29]

While Villa's bands were dispersed and some of his leading lieutenants killed, Villa himself was never hunted down, and since in the public eye that had indeed been the objective, the campaign was popularly held to have been anticlimactic at best and a failure at worst. The reputation of the "Colored" 10th Cavalry in particular suffered. Although Villa's men had been defeated in every shooting clash, the troops of the 10th came up against Carranza's Mexican national forces, angered by the unauthorized U.S. invasion, at the small town of Carrizal, and retreated in disarray after taking heavy casualties. What matters is that there were many questions regarding what had gone wrong, but Carrizal was the only American defeat in this campaign, and it served mainly to reinforce existing racial prejudice in the army.[30]

Combat with Carranza's forces, nearly produced another Mexican-American War. In May 1916 President Wilson called up more than one hundred thousand generally unprepared National Guard soldiers from across the country and moved them to the border, the first arriving only twelve days after they were called.[31] Fortunately, some restraint on both sides prevented war, though unrest on the border was hardly ended; Villa himself lived on until his assassination in 1923. The Punitive Expedition had the positive effect of revealing a good many weaknesses in American methods, and some lessons were applied when the United States declared war against Germany one year later. Pershing, too, had gained experience, helping to ensure his selection as commander of the American Expeditionary Force sent to France. The United States could hardly be said to have been ready for the sort of war it would find in Europe in 1917, but at least it had worked through the varied campaigns of Cuba, the Philippines, and Mexico, in which many of her World War commanders and NCOs experienced combat and earned their spurs. Though small, the American Army in 1917 could not be written off as unprofessional.

Nevertheless, on America's entrance into World War I, it was immediately obvious that existing military formations, whether regular army or National Guard, would be completely inadequate to meet coming needs. President Wilson from the start was a believer in universal service liability in the cause of liberty. Soon after the declaration of war, Congress rushed a conscription bill through. Not surprisingly, there was considerable opposition, and not just from those who put their faith in volunteerism or recalled the questionable success of the draft in the Civil War. Neither the Navy nor the Marines were willing to accept anything but volunteers, which were still permitted. Wilson accepted this point, but politely refused to allow arch-rival Teddy Roosevelt to organize and lead a volunteer division. On May 13, 1917, the Selective Service Act became law. The recruits thus gained were expected to form units of the new "National Army," at least until the government concluded that draftees would also have to be assigned to the regular army and National Guard. Nearly seven hundred thousand men aged twenty-one to thirty were called up by local draft boards in the first round, and the army was swamped. Over the course of the year, more than twenty-four million males registered, of whom just under three million were actually inducted; they provided some 77 percent of the four million officers and men who served through the years 1917–20 (10 percent came from the National Guard, and 13 percent from the pre-war army). America did not lack manpower for its "doughboys" (it is not clear where the nickname came from, though it dates at least to the mid-nineteenth century), but it did lack experience and all the accoutrements of going to war.[32]

Once again, America faced tough choices in training the new influx. The regulars would be required as soon as possible in France; though many NCOs were kept behind for training of new recruits or were newly promoted to commissioned rank, no serious attempt was made to divide existing formations among the new units. But officers were another matter, and the small existing officer force of about six thousand was "scattered so widely through the new Army as leaven that half of them never did reach France."[33] But the existing cadre was not enough, and some twenty–six thousand fresh company-grade officers (captains and lieutenants) were trained in newly created camps, winnowed out from about forty thousand volunteers—"the educated, athletic, and bold . . . Ivy League men, professionals, and business people . . ."—in other words, the upper classes would lead the newly created army into battle.[34]

By mid-summer 1917, the "1st Division" (newly created as well, since the American Army in peacetime did not organize tactical "divisions") had arrived in France. The "Big Red One," as it would be called after the large red numeral one which was its insignia, was composed of "regulars" from the 16th, 18th, 26th, and 28th regiments together with field artillery elements. In fact only about 20 percent were soldiers with campaign experience, the remainder being recent recruits. The pre-war regiments numbered about seven hundred men on average, and half of these had been removed to train others, while the regiments were built up to two thousand men with raw recruits.[35] The 5th Marine Regiment, as will be explained, was part of the first contingent as well.

THE NEWLY CREATED 1ST DIVISION ARRIVED IN FRANCE IN MID-SUMMER 1917. THE "BIG RED ONE," AS IT WOULD BE CALLED AFTER THE LARGE RED NUMERAL ONE WHICH WAS ITS INSIGNIA, WAS COMPOSED OF "REGULARS" FROM THE 16TH, 18TH, 26TH, AND 28TH REGIMENTS TOGETHER WITH FIELD ARTILLERY ELEMENTS. HERE, THE 18TH INFANTRY REGIMENT, 1ST DIVISION, CROSSES THE MOSELLE RIVER INTO MUHL, GERMANY, DECEMBER 1, 1918. ARMY WAR COLLEGE.

The American commander was Maj. Gen. John Joseph Pershing. Determined, capable, aloof, self-conscious, stubborn, discreet when necessary, and loyal to the policies of President Wilson's administration, Pershing earned many enemies through "his rigid insistence on military punctilio." No American general then serving, including Pershing, had ever commanded a division or corps, but now the American commander would have to negotiate directly with allied commanders and political leaders who had entire armies in their charge. His difficult mission was to insist that Americans form not only independent divisions, but an American army with its own sector of the front line. Pershing soon realized that more than a million men would be needed in the short run, and in the future, at least three times that number, totaling perhaps as many as five million. Eventually more than two million Americans sailed to France to go to war; 50,475 would be killed in battle, and another 193,611 wounded—terrible figures in the absolute, but only a small percentage of the cost to any of the main European participants.[36]

Of that two million, about ten percent were African American. Of these, however, about 150,000 were labor troops, used only on the lines of communication. The pre-war regular army had included four black regiments, the 9th and 10th Cavalry and the 24th and 25th Infantry, but none of these was permitted to go to France. The 9th served in the Philippines, and the rest in the United States, mostly along the Mexican border. The 24th Infantry found its battalions divided, and its 3d Battalion, stationed in Houston, Texas, became involved in a historic racial clash with townsmen, brought about by the soldiers' refusal to adhere to rigid local Jim Crow laws, in an incident which certainly did not further the cause of integration in the military.[37]

Given the army's attitude toward black soldiers in general, it seems odd that an African American Guard unit was mobilized a month before America declared war to provide guards for federal buildings in Washington, D.C., including the White House and the Capitol, together with key bridges and water supply facilities. The "First Separate Battalion (Colored)," some 950 men and 55 officers from the Washington area, took considerable pride in this assignment as a reward for their loyal service. In actuality, aside from the fact that the battalion was ready at hand, it seems that it "was chosen for this sensitive mission because of army confidence that a German agent could not possibly conceal himself in a black unit . . ." Complaints from a racist Kentucky congressman to the White House, however, brought their removal and incorporation in the 372d Infantry Regiment, eventually going on to service in France.[38]

Despite this setback, when the war came, considerable pressure upon Wilson's administration caused the 93d Division's four black infantry regiments, all drawn from the National Guard, to see action (369th, 370th, 371st, 372d), but in the French sector under French army command, wearing French helmets, using French equipment, and eating French rations—except that they were denied the standard French issue of one quart of wine per man per day. All fought well, and the French made it clear they would be happy to absorb all such units they could get. The 369th in particular, formerly the 15th New York, spent 191 days at the front; it and the 371st and 372d were awarded the French Croix de Guerre unit citation.[39]

On the other hand, the other black division, the 92d, was considered throughout the army to have compiled a dismal record in the Argonne. Its 368th Infantry Regiment was believed to have disintegrated and, with the exception of a few men, turned and ran from the Germans. What actually happened has never been entirely clear; it is possible that the regiment was in fact ordered to withdraw, but that was not apparent at the time, and the incident acted only to reinforce existing prejudices, while the excellent record of black troops fighting with the French was ignored. That the raw 92d was badly trained and poorly led was similarly forgotten. The division recovered its confidence, and fought on to the end of the war, but those who wished to found in the Argonne the evidence they wanted to support the widespread conviction that black troops could not be trained to an adequate degree, a conviction that extended downward from the highest level, including Pershing. Certainly black troops had little chance in this war to prove their worth, let alone become elites.[40]

Pershing's American Expeditionary Force (AEF) was sent to Lorraine, not least because the British insisted on guarding the approaches to the Channel and the French the roads to Paris. Lorraine was generally regarded as a quiet sector, but one in which the Americans had before them an interesting challenge: the German salient around the town of St. Mihiel, roughly twenty miles southeast of Verdun, which not only was a tempting bulge some two hundred miles square into the Allied lines, but also included important rail communications serving much of Germany's Western Front.[41]

At first Pershing had only the 1st Division, which soon went into detailed training with the elite French 47th Division, the Chasseurs Alpins or "Blue Devils" from the color of their uniforms. All did not go smoothly, since the Americans stressed the rifle and at once set up shooting ranges. The French "began to talk to us about the use of the hand grenade and the digging of trenches and accustoming ourselves to the use of the gas mask, asserting in substance that there was little use in warfare for the individual rifle or pistol; that the artillery would do all the shooting for the infantry; the infantryman would advance with his gun slung over his shoulder and use grenades against ma-chine-gun nests," recalled Maj. Gen. Robert Bullard in his later mem-oirs. "Without gainsaying our very agreeable and tactful instructors, we adhered to our individual rifle shooting and learned all their gre-nade-throwing and gas work also. This had to be done very tactfully."[42]

Meanwhile, Pershing was busily establishing important training programs to provide useful trench experience over a three-month cycle for all newly arriving divisions. Indeed, schools of every sort were opened to train the needed specialists in everything from artillery to poison gas, and a number of skills which the American Army had never been called upon to provide, such as mining or railroad engineering. Of particular importance was an intensified staff officer training pro-gram, to replicate the Fort Leavenworth system, without which the planned massive American force could have expected serious manage-ment and supply difficulties, to put it mildly.[43]

By early summer 1918, there were 650,000 Americans in the AEF. But at the end of 1917, the AEF numbered only some 10,000 officers and 165,000 men in four divisions. They would in due course dub them-selves the "'old reliables,' the divisions destined to be used in the most difficult situations," in other words, the American Army's elite forma-tions in that war. These were the 1st and 2d composed of "regulars," and in the latter case, Marines as well, and the 26th and 42d from the National Guard. Both the latter divisions included some units with ex-perience on the Mexican border in 1916. The 42d in particular was a showcase unit of sorts, known as the "Rainbow Division" since men from every state had deliberately been included. Only in January of 1918 did the French and the Americans jointly agree that the AEF's 1st Division was ready to be given a divisional sector of the line, on the south side of the St. Mihiel bulge. Here it remained, learning the tech-niques of trench warfare. As it turned out, the American units were trained by roughly equal numbers of French and British instructors (something fewer than three hundred key men in each case); their contribution was most important.[44]

In early April, the 1st Division was reassigned, its place taken by the 26th "Yankee" Division, a New England National Guard formation with little experience, but a good many sons of New England's social elite. Within three weeks, the 26th division was humiliated by a swift, damaging attack by Germany's 259th Infantry reinforced by a special raiding component known as "Hindenburg's Traveling Circus." Ludendorff, hoping to break through the 1st Division to teach the Americans a lesson, but found the 26th in their place. The Germans proceeded to slash into the American positions for nearly a mile, capturing the town of Seicheprey before retreating, as planned, to their own lines. The 26th suffered 669 casualties (eighty–one dead), and 187 missing or captured. The incident is important, as Meirion and Susie Harries explain: ". . . it allowed the Allies to be openly skeptical about the fighting efficiency of American troops under American leadershi Somehow [Pershing] had to prove them wrong."[45] In fact, the Americans had not really done that badly, considering that about six hundred New Englanders had been attacked by roughly 3,200 Germans and still managed to counterattack the next day, but that was not what the Germans claimed or how it was viewed at Chaumont, Pershing's headquarters.[46]

Pershing's response was to order the capture of Cantigny, a ruined village which formed a German strong point. The task was assigned to the 1st Division's 28th Infantry Regiment, commanded by a tough regular colonel named Hanson Ely, with elements of the 16th and 18th, together with supporting machine guns, artillery, engineers, and a dozen French tanks (Cantigny was in the French sector). The attack was carefully planned and well executed on May 28; the German 82d Reserve Division, a third-class outfit, was thoroughly battered by the opening Allied artillery barrage. Despite serious counterattacks, the position remained in American hands; by May 30, the Germans had lost eight hundred dead, five hundred wounded, and 255 prisoners, compared to American casualties of just over one thousand men dead, wounded, and missing. Cantigny—in Laurence Stalling's memorable phrase, "a mere wart on the hide of the God of War"— admittedly was not worth the cost except in shoring up American pride (since the Germans were busily attacking in the direction of Paris, the larger propaganda value of Cantigny was lost in the tide), but it certainly demonstrated Pershing's inflexible determination.[47]

That determination included a conviction about tactics which ran counter to the lessons the French and British had learned on the Western Front and tried to instill in the Americans. Pershing refused to let his growing army become trench-minded. "Trench warfare naturally gives prominence to the defensive," he wrote. "To guard against this the basis of instruction should be essentially the offensive in spirit and practice. The defensive is accepted only to prepare for future offensive. The rifle and the bayonet are the principle weapons of the infantry soldier. . . . An aggressive spirit must be developed until the soldier feels himself, as a bayonet fighter, invincible in battle."[48] Allan Millett and Peter Maslowski summarize the difference: "Pershing wanted his men to practice large-unit assaults with principle emphasis on rifle fire and artillery support, while the Allies stressed small-unit raiding with emphasis on grenades, mortars, and automatic weapons."[49]

Nor had Pershing altered this view after the war: "The infantry soldier, well-trained in stealthy approach and in the art of taking cover, makes a small target, and if he is an expert rifleman there is nothing that can take his place on the battlefield."[50] For too long, Pershing refused to recognize the terribly effective killing power of the machine gun as he ordered repeated offensives, and his refusal would prove costly. In the higher ranks, wrote Maj. Lloyd D. Ross of the 42d Division, there persisted "an ever present tendency to rush troops forward and keep pushing them against enemy machine guns without adequate support from machine guns, howitzers and artillery. . . . Finally it dawned upon the General Officers they were sacrificing their infantry . . ."[51] As Maj. Gen. Hunter Liggett put it ten years after the war, "The French preferred to take a position in half a day at small cost, where the impatient young men from afar carried it in fifteen minutes and paid the price."[52]

The basic explanation was nothing new. As Robert Zieger has pointed out, the "unspoken national self-image depicted U.S. citizen-soldiers as sturdy individualists, rangy and resourceful descendants of the pioneers. Underlying official U.S. Army tactical doctrine was the notion that the typical American male was somehow a born rifleman, eager to practice his marksmanship against the enemy." The planners knew that machine guns were increasingly important, but they believed that the rifleman would overcome. "Hardened by the frontier, eagle-eyed and rugged, army doctrine held that he would soon seize the initiative and restore movement to the trench-ridden European battlefields."[53] We have met this enduring American image before, based as it was upon the colonial era rifleman/ranger, reinforced not only by subsequent historical experience (or at least the popular understanding of that experience), but also by the theoretical writings of de Jomini and Ardant du Picq, much favored in the pre-war discussions at West Point and Fort Leavenworth, which stressed the individual soldier's role.[54] In the case of World War I, the image, and the resulting training methods, would prove surprisingly effective, but at terrible relative cost to a fresh and as yet unbloodied army. One may surmise that had the war extended into and through 1919, attitudes might have changed.

But in the summer of that year, still more effort was necessary to push the Germans back, and French plans for June included an attack by the 2d Division on Hill 142 and Belleau Wood, "an insignificant piece of woodland in the middle of France."[55] Belleau Wood (June 6–26) won fame for Marine courage, but the struggle was much more costly than it should have been. American intelligence was totally inadequate; the wood was considered lightly held, but was in fact heavily entrenched. Orders to infiltrate the area were disregarded or simply not understood; the Marines attacked in dressed lines of men, perfect targets for well-sited German machine guns. The men of the 5th Marines here "became the first to demonstrate the chilling marine theory that the only sure way to overcome machine-gun positions of this kind was to rush them."[56] After the Second Battle of the Marne, a captured German pocket memorandum demonstrated the Germans' incredulity at what they saw: "Witnessed the attack of 16 Americans—two squads—on a machine-gun position. Ten were knocked down, killed or wounded. The remaining six took the gun and killed the crew. We could not expect our troops to do this."[57] Or as another German letter put it, "The Americans are here. We can kill them but we can't stop them."[58] Over the course of June 6, the division lost 1,087 men, including 222 killed in action.[59]

But Belleau Wood's sacrifices proved an important point, and not just that Marine marksmanship was superb. Ludendorff had ordered that the Americans be hit as hard as possible, both to test their resolve and to make the formation of an American Army all the more difficult. Both sides were ordered to hold at all costs, for psychological reasons at least as much as military need. As a result, "Belleau Wood itself was taking on an exaggerated significance in Germany and among the troops in the field in terms of its propaganda value," as the struggle stretched on for two weeks of fighting.[60] A general order of June 8 to the German 28th Division from its commander made this very clear: "It is not a question of the possession or nonpossession of this or that village or woods, insignificant in itself; it is a question whether the Anglo-American claim that the American Army is equal or even the superior of the German Army is to be made good."[61]

The Germans now ranked the 2d "as a very good division, perhaps even as assault troops," which carried out its attacks "with dash and recklessness."[62] On the other hand, at least one German intelligence summary reported that "The American Infantry is very unskilled in the attack. . . . [T]he American troops are not a dangerous adversary when their method of fighting is known beforehand."[63] In 1927, Ludendorff reflected on this stage of the war: "It was assuredly the Americans who bore the heaviest brunt of the fighting on the whole battle front during the last few months of the war. The German field army found them much more aggressive in attack than either the English or the French. . . . their attacks were undoubtedly brave and often reckless. They lacked sufficient dexterity or experience in availing themselves of topographical cover or protection. They came right on in open field and attacked in units much too closely formed. Their lack of actual field experience accounts for some extraordinarily heavy losses."[64]

Elite status, however, can be noted by allies as often as by enemies. The French were not far behind in recognizing the heroism of the soldiers and marines who fought in this battle, ranking the 1st and 2d Divisions as *soldats de la première classe pour le combat*.[65] Grateful indeed for such a morale-sustaining effort, the French high command issued orders renaming the wood the "Bois de la Brigade de Marine." Pierre Teilhard de Chardin, later a distinguished philosopher, served in the French lines next to Americans. "Everyone says the same," he wrote; "they're first-rate troops, fighting with intense *individual* passion (concentrated on the enemy) and wonderful courage. The only complaint one would make about them is that they don't take sufficient care; they're too apt to get themselves killed."[66] Praise was always welcome. As Norman Summers of the 167th Infantry, 42nd Division, recorded in his diary in July, "The French were very proud of the way we stood up under fire and a French General said we were as good as any of his storm troops. They were using the 'Blue Devils' as storm troops and when they heard that the 42d Division were backing them up they cheered. After the battle the French would put their arms around our men and say 'Bon camarades'."[67]

The 1st Division had paid a high price for its elite reputation, but there was more fighting to be done. In July, the division was ordered to attack toward the high ground overlooking Soissons. Gen. Charles Summerall, "perhaps the most remorselessly determined of all Pershing's generals . . . was perfectly prepared for his division to die in the attempt." It nearly did. Four days of fighting near Soissons cost the division 60 percent of its officers, and 50 percent of the rank and file: 8,365 men in all, 1,252 killed.[68]

By late August, the Allies sensed that victory was possible; one massive push, all along the Western Front, would overwhelm German defenses. The American role was simply stated, but extraordinarily demanding. In order to prevent his army from being broken into sections as Allied commander Foch requested, Pershing agreed to close out the St. Mihiel salient (an operation which Pershing had been planning for some time), and then shift his six hundred thousand men and 2,700 guns as quickly as possible by three roads roughly sixty miles to the north-west in order to attack the Hindenburg Line between the Meuse River and the Argonne Forest. The latter assignment in particular was daunting, not least since no American planners had expected—or planned for—action in this notoriously difficult sector, for which Pershing's staff had exactly three weeks to prepare.[69] Subsequent critics have not spared Pershing for this plan, using raw, largely untrained divisions in difficult terrain against serious defenses: "Pershing was asking the impossible and in so doing revealed himself to be neither a great man nor a great general."[70]

The first stage at St. Mihiel went well; in this first major operation which was commanded by American generals, the Germans were pushed back some fifteen miles. On the other hand, the massed attack by twelve American divisions (with six more in reserve) across a front of roughly fifteen miles, from the scrub and underbrush of Argonne Forest to the Meuse River against well-prepared German defenses, was another matter. The "Kriemhilde" line (the "Hindenburg Line" to the Allies) in particular was a challenging "elongated honeycomb of entrenchments, a stretched-out maze that forced the attacker to cross multiple trenches in order to penetrate it," and which moreover was a series of strong points, the fall of one of which did not necessarily mean the fall of its neighbors. In an impossibly ambitious plan, justified, if at all, by the conviction that the German sector was lightly manned, the American attacks were supposed to penetrate this line, ten miles from their jump-off positions, on the first day of the attack. In actuality, over four days in late September, the First Army took forty–five thousand casualties before Pershing suspended the operation, unable to fulfill his promises to the Allied leaders.[71]

In the depths of the Argonne, however, the orders were not received, or not received in time. One famous result was the fate of the 1st Battalion, 308th Infantry Regiment, 77th ("Liberty") Division, commanded by Maj. Charles W. Whittlesey (he also had elements of the 306th and 307th regiments among his 500–700 men). Whittlesey had led his men in a successful advance, but units on his flanks had not done as well. German forces managed as a result to surround him, and pressed home numerous attacks on his position. When finally relieved a week later on October 8, Whittlesey's "lost battalion" (it was never "lost," but it proved impossible to reach) had run out of food, water, and ammunition, and was using weapons taken from dead Germans to defend themselves. Figures vary, but only around two hundred of his original force were able to walk out.[72] "The hour we were relieved there was less than an average of fifteen rounds of ammunition to each living man. The Germans were preparing to lay down a liquid fire attack that night and they probably would have succeeded in burning alive the remaining survivors had not succor come just when it did," recorded Lt. Maurice V. Griffin, who was there.[73] "[Y]et another tale of valiant doughboy heroism," note the Harries, "the myth once more helping to disguise the reality of serious incompetence" in the management of the overall struggle. True, no doubt, but Whittlesey deserved his promotion to lieutenant-colonel and the Congressional Medal of Honor he was awarded.[74]

The Argonne provided another legend: that of Acting Cpl. Alvin York. York was a skilled hunter from the hills of Tennessee, who was also a pacifistic church elder (he had at first registered as a conscientious objector). He was fighting in the 328th Infantry (82d Division) when his battalion's attack on a heavily defended ridge was brought to a halt. York virtually single-handedly picked off more than twenty machine-gunners, taking some thirty-five of the machine guns out of action before rounding up 132 prisoners, using his Colt .45 to persuade a German major to assist in the surrender process. York was promoted to sergeant and awarded the Distinguished Service Cross and the Medal of Honor, receiving the latter direct from General Pershing. York was the preeminent American hero of the war, once again conforming to the long-standing image of the hardy civilian with his rifle winning America's wars. It is also worth noting that neither the Lost Battalion nor Sergeant York belonged to a division which was considered "elite."[75] Indeed, while it is clear that a few divisions emerged at the end of the war with outstanding reputations, there were many other tough fighting units, just as in the Civil War. To give only one example, the 107th Regiment, part of the 27th Division which was one of two American divisions that fought under British command throughout the war, in its attack on the St. Quentin Tunnel (late September 1918), lost roughly one thousand men, half its assault troops, in Edward M. Coffman's view, "the most casualties suffered on a single day by an American regiment during the war." The division as a whole was awarded twelve Medals of Honor, more than any other American division in World War I.[76]

Note should be taken of those dozen Medals of Honor, because far fewer such awards were made in World War I than in the Civil War. To be precise, ninty–five Medals of Honor were approved for World War I, compared to 1,200 for the Civil War, 416 for Indian Campaigns between 1861 and 1898, thirty for the War with Spain, and seventy for the "Philippine Insurrection;" adding four for the Boxer Rebellion and one for the Mexican Campaign, the total is 2,116 medals between 1861 and 1917 (another 292 would be awarded during World War II).[77] One reason why the Medal of Honor could be reserved for very special cases involving conspicuous gallantry at risk of life and beyond the call of duty, such as Sergeant York, was that by a Presidential Order of January 1918 and an act of Congress in July, a "pyramid of honor" was constructed by establishing the Distinguished Service Cross to single out "extraordinary heroism against an armed enemy," the Distinguished Service Medal for "exceptionally meritorious service to the Government in a duty of great responsibility," and an Army Silver Star Citation to recognize a citation for gallantry in conjunction with a service ribbon (the Silver Star was made a formal medal in 1932; the Bronze Star was added in 1944), in declining order of precedence after the Medal of Honor.[78]

Nothing is ever quite so simple, however, and in World War I one controversy concerned the award of war service chevrons. The French army gave its men a badge for six months of war zone service, but the AEF, in adopting the concept, objected that the French War Zone reached fifty miles behind the front. The AEF preferred a more narrowly defined "Zone of the Advance," which would honor dangerous combat rather than simply honorable overseas service. Objections were raised, most notably that some units saw hard combat, but were rotated behind the lines for recovery and thus did not meet the six months' requirement. As a consequence, in July 1918 Pershing's headquarters altered the rules to give a gold service chevron for service in the "Theater of Operations," meaning all units under Pershing's command, therefore including supply line non-combatants. A silver chevron, on the other hand, was awarded for honorable service at home, and thus was something of a "badge of shame," particularly to those who did not see that valuable non-combatant service at home was as worthy of reward as non-combatant service abroad.[79]

Whatever the medals and chevrons, however, losses such as those sustained by the 27th division had an effect not very different from what happened to top units in the Civil War. As trained men were killed or wounded, raw replacements who had too little training filled their places. After the war, Donald Drake Kyler (private, then sergeant, in the 16th Infantry, 1st Division) was clear in his own mind on what had happened:

> Whatever success in fighting in that war that our army may have had, was the result of its willingness to go forward to engage the enemy, regardless of its ineptness, and in spite of its losses. Many writers of the history of that war state that the battle experience of the veteran divisions made for increased efficiency and fighting ability in the lower units. That is not true. However, it is true that regiment, brigade, and division officers may have become more efficient. The officers commanding them had gained the know-how to use them. But in the infantry battalions, companies and platoons of our division (the most veteran one among them), the truth is somewhat different. We reached the peak of lower unit tactical efficiency about April, 1918. We then still had about half of our strength as trained Regular Army men of long standing. All of us were volunteers. About a third of our officers were professional career officers. At that time our lower units were more battle effective than any except a few picked units of the French and British Armies. In June and July, our severe battle losses began. Those of us who remained could not bring up the standard and efficiency and training that our units formerly had.[80]

It was fortunate indeed that the war did not last into 1919 and beyond as some had predicted.

The well-regarded fighting unit, like the 1st Division or the Marine regiments (discussed below) or the individual fighting hero, like Sergeant York, were nothing new to history, but in this war the hero emerged in a new element: the air above. Certainly if any small unit of Americans fighting on the Western Front earned undying fame, it was the pilots of the Lafayette Escadrille.

The Escadrille's origins lay in the handful of Americans who, when World War I broke out in Europe, enlisted in the French Foreign Legion, the *Légion Étrangère*, which was the only branch of the French armed forces legally empowered to accept non-citizens. Such volunteers promised only to serve faithfully and honorably, and were not required to swear an oath of allegiance to France and thus forswear their previous citizenshi In the first wave of enthusiasm, forty-three Americans signed up as Legion privates for the magnificent pay of about thirty cents per month.[81]

As the war unfolded, however, and it became clear that it would not be over in a matter of weeks, a handful of American legionnaires managed to display sufficient motivation and potential to transfer to the *Service Aeronautique* and receive pilot training; some had learned how to fly before the war, but others had not. The legal problem was dealt with by keeping the men on Legion rolls, but officially on loan to French air units. With the help of some wealthy and well-connected Americans in Paris, in 1915 a movement was begun to concentrate the seventeen Americans then either in training or flying in French squadrons into a squadron of their own. Though the bureaucratic process moved slowly, there were enough men in France's higher command to appreciate the propaganda value such a squadron might bring. In February 1916, the Germans began their attack on Verdun, and the need to excite American support for the Allied war effort became all the greater. In late April, *l'Escadrille Americaine*, officially squadron N. 124, was formed. Its commander was French Capt. Georges Thenault, an eager St. Cyr graduate, trained pilot, and experienced squadron leader who had helped to get the squadron started for his American friends.[82]

The squadron embarked on a brief but glorious career in a variety of fighter aircraft, from the small and maneuverable Nieuport 11 ("Bébé" to its pilots, because of its diminutive size; the "N" in the squadron number stood for Nieuport) to the heavier but faster Spad S-VII. Over its relatively short life, the unit flew out of a dozen separate bases in six different sectors of the front, including the cauldron of Verdun. For a brief few days, the squadron even did battle with the scarlet-nosed Fokker planes of Jagdgeschwader 1, better known as the "Richthofen Circus," after its leader, German ace Manfred von Richthofen, who when the two units dueled over Courtrai already had fifty-seven confirmed victories.

For political reasons, Thenault was told to handle the unit with maximum leniency and was denied ordinary disciplinary powers over his men, a fact that they not surprisingly took advantage of on the ground and in the air, following orders only when they felt like it, and adopting virtually any variety of uniform which pleased them. Two live lion cubs (named "Whiskey" and "Soda") who served as unit mascots were a particularly notable feature. The squadron was a focus of media attention in any case, not least because the favorite off-duty hangout for the squadron in Paris, the Hotel Chatham, where they could relax over "excellent Martinis, prepared by the expert hand of Santo," was also a favorite for journalists. A combination of victories in the air and idiosyncratic behavior made them a source of endless copy in both France and the United States.[83]

The squadron's numbers remained small, beginning with only seven pilots, and never numbering more than eighteen or twenty pilots at one time. Over the course of the unit's career until it was dissolved in February, 1918, a total of forty-three pilots served in its ranks (over one hundred more Americans served in other French flying units). In late 1916, a major change was introduced when the squadron was attached to a larger command, Groupe de Combat 13, which included four other squadrons (Since the Escadrille was the only active American squadron in France, there was no question of forming a separate American Groupe). Groupe 13 was stationed at Cachy in the Somme Valley, at an uncomfortable aerodrome which it shared with Groupe de Combat 12, the famous "Storks" ("Cigognes") whose three squadrons contained France's leading aces, including the legendary Georges Guynemer, already, at age twenty-two, with eighteen victories to his credit.[84] At Cachy they lost many of their special privileges; the pets, too, were gone after "Whiskey," no longer a cub, knocked down the commander of Groupe 13.[85]

At Cachy, N. 124 converted from the obsolescent Nieuports to Spads and was renumbered as SPA. 124. Also at Cachy, the Escadrille gained a distinctive unit insignia to replace the American flags formerly painted on their aircraft. Perhaps at Thenault's suggestion, the squadron adopted the head of a Seminole Indian, borrowing the image from the side of an American-made ammunition box, though the design was eventually altered into a rather ferocious Sioux brave in full war regalia by an artist in the unit.[86] They also gained a new name, since the U.S. government, as yet still neutral, found German complaints rather embarrassing, and asked France to drop "Escadrille Americaine." After a difficult three weeks as "Escadrille des Volontaires" the Ministry of War wisely approved the popular name "Escadrille Lafayette," apparently suggested by the French ambassador in Washington, and so it remained.[87]

When the United States entered the war, as an embarrassing display of ineffective air power in the Mexican troubles of 1916 demonstrated, it was absurdly behind all the European powers in the development of an air force of any sort, and quite naturally the Escadrille was seen as a most useful source of instructors. In the army's defense, however, it must be said that the problems it faced were many, including the Signal Corps' determination to maintain control of all aircraft activity, and a paralyzing legal lockhold by the Wright Brothers over most American patents for the essential workings of airplanes. Throughout the war, the growing American Army Air Service would, for the most part, have to use borrowed British or French planes.

In the end, the ultimate exchange from French to American service was handled very badly, mostly by men with absolutely no experience with airplanes—or pilots—at all. After much red tape, filling in of forms, and considerable ill will, the squadron became the "103d Pursuit Squadron" of the U.S. Army Air Service, though most of its remaining veterans were dispersed to become squadron commanders and flight leaders. The Escadrille had served just under twenty-two months with the French. Over that time, the unit was credited with thirty-nine confirmed German aircraft shot down; of the sixteen pilots with "kills," Maj. Raoul Lufbery was the squadron's only high-scoring ace, with seventeen to his credit alone. On the other hand, six pilots had been killed in combat, one by antiaircraft fire, and two in accidents; another five were badly wounded. The name of the Escadrille Lafayette was not lost to history, however, for the French Armée de l'Air carried on the name in various units of the interwar and World War II eras.[88]

Certainly the Escadrille was regarded as a group of heroes during its era, but a group of heroes does not necessarily constitute an elite force. Philip Flammer, in his study of the unit, is convinced that it was elite, and that "the combat record of this elite group further softened the French attitude and thus helped make the formation of the Escadrille Americaine a reality." Many other air units did just as well, or better, on both sides of the front; but the Escadrille Lafayette no doubt generated more publicity, and as Flammer points out, "The French were much impressed that such men would volunteer their services."[89]

What were called "elite" air units in this war, in reality, were simply those with the most pilots who had the physical talents and learned the skills of aerial combat quickly enough to survive and prevail. The best were "aces," and while they may have patrolled in groups, sometimes of considerable size, in most combat situations from 1917 onwards, even in the mass dog fights which typified the later stages of the war they were dueling individual pilots from the other side for at least a few seconds, which of course was a strong part of their appeal. The Escadrille had its heroes, or at least one hero in "Luf," who was technically American but who was raised in France. But the top American ace was not Lufbery, who was killed in June 1918, but Capt. Edward Rickenbacker. "Eddie" was Pershing's former chauffeur, and for ten years had been a race car driver; he flew with the 94th "Hat in the Ring" squadron. Rickenbacker's total was twenty-six; four were tethered observation balloons shot down. There should be no misconception about balloons, which were very dangerous targets, not least because they tended to be surrounded by anti-aircraft guns; the Germans, at least, counted two balloons destroyed by their pilots as the equivalent of three aircraft shot down.[90]

The air aces were enormously popular in the public eye—"a new breed of heroes," as Lee Kennett comments—individualists who "ached" to earn the Iron Cross or the Victoria Cross ("Kreuzschmerzen," the Germans called it). Such men, above all the fighter pilot, the hero in the *avion de chasse*, in some sense made war again individualized and thus at least partially fathomable, as opposed to the unimaginable mass horrors of the land war. They were surely important in the war, but this fact did not necessarily make their units "elite" in the sense used in this book.[91]

There was no real "type" which could be selected for fighter squadrons. True, the aces were mostly young (and thus had the necessary physical reflexes), though there were exceptions. But whatever their age, pilots needed not only to learn to fly in combat, but also to shoot. It could be months before they developed the "nice combination of geometry and experience," as Denis Winter terms it, which might permit a man to score five kills and thus become an "ace"—but during those months they could easily be killed (the British calculated that the likelihood of reaching "ace" status was roughly 1:20 of pilots entering the service).[92] The soldiers on the ground might indeed have hated the pilots who strafed their trenches, and at the same time admired their skills and their lifestyles, but the extensive literature on the first great air war is conspicuous for the absence of one factor: one finds no sense of moral superiority felt by one nation's pilots over those of another. They surely distinguished themselves from other branches of their armies, but once in the air, they were all taking equal chances, and they knew it only too well, even in the famous Lafayette Escadrille. Rickenbacker explained in his 1919 memoirs: ". . . I have yet to find one single individual who has attained conspicuous success in bringing down enemy aeroplanes who can be said to be spoiled either by his successes or by the generous congratulations of his comrades. If he were capable of being spoiled he would not have had the character to have won continuous victories, for the smallest amount of vanity is fatal in aeroplane fighting. Self-distrust rather is the quality to which many a pilot owes his protracted existence." He might also have added ambition, for the best pilots sought out the enemy and did their best to see to it that their kills were confirmed. To be the "Ace of Aces" was to hold an admired championship, but also, as Rickenbacker noted, it brought "a haunting superstition that did not leave my mind until the very end of the war," the doom, in other words, that each previous holder had met. "I wanted it and yet I feared to learn that it was mine! In later days I began to feel that this superstition was almost the heaviest burden that I carried with me into the air. Perhaps it served to redouble my caution and sharpened my fighting senses. But never was I able to forget that the life of a title-holder is short."[93]

With the conclusion of the Great War and the return home of the Doughboys—except for those needed for Rhineland occupation duties, America's brief and confused adventure in Murmansk-Archangel and Siberia (the latter involving the 27th and 31st Infantry Regiments from the Philippine garrison of regulars, augmented by reinforcements sent on from San Francisco), or elsewhere in the world, roughly twenty

–five thousand in all—the old question once again resurfaced: What sort of army did the United States require now? It certainly would not be the army of 1918, with its more than 3,700,000 men; "By the end of June 1919 more than 2,700,000 soldiers had picked up their discharge papers, a uniform, a pair of shoes, a coat, and the $60 bonus," along with a helmet and a gas mask if they had served overseas.[94]

The practical choices basically were the same as they had been at the start of the century: Emory Upton's standing army of professionals which would be expanded in time of war by the addition of either volunteers or conscripts, or John A. Logan's much smaller regular force which would be strengthened in time of need by a mass of trained reserves. Both proposals, unfortunately for their prospects, required the continuation of conscription; the difference rather lay in whether the country would put its faith in Upton's expandable professional force or Logan's citizen army. In either case, it was clear as rapid demobilization proceeded in 1919 that Congress was unlikely to pay for more than the barest minimum, and perhaps considerably less than that.[95]

The support of General Pershing for Logan's principles proved critical, and the National Defense Act of 1920 established an "Army of the United States," which included three essential parts, beginning with a small regular army of 17,000 officers and 280,000 men in nine divisions, ready for action anywhere, and not simply the officer-heavy skeleton Upton had envisaged. In support would stand a National Guard of 435,000 men; regular army men would supervise its training, and though the units would be under state control in peacetime, the Guard would come under federal control in wartime. Finally, the Organized Reserves under federal control would include officers and enlisted men organized by geographical district in skeleton units which could be expanded, if needed, by conscription.

But, at least for now, there would be no conscription because Congress had omitted this essential element of Logan's plan from the 1920 act. The act, therefore, while perfectly logical in theory, providing a regular force for immediately predictable needs and a format for potential expansion, was considerably reduced in effectiveness from the beginning. Since the army was seriously underfunded, without enough money to maintain even half the strength authorized by the 1920 act, it was forced to make another choice altogether: use its limited resources to keep intact as much of the three hundred thousand-man regular force as possible, or spread its resources among a skeleton, Upton-like army, and proceed with its mission to train the National Guard. To do both was simply not possible. In choosing the latter, the army simply declared that in the long run, the greater danger which the country faced was another conflict with one or more major powers, not brushfire, border, or Indian wars.[96]

These issues are of importance in studying elites, since it was fairly clear in the inter-war era that little, if any, funding was likely to be available either for innovations or for training any skeleton formations of regulars up to elite standards. Another relevant point in that regard, however, is the matter of doctrine. William Odom's study of the key army training manual, the *Field Service Regulations 1923*, which governed training and practice until replaced by a slightly revised volume in 1939 and a much more altered version in 1941, demonstrates that the army had not really changed its attitude toward what tactics would win on the battlefield.

After much study, including the work of over twenty separate boards, the outcome was one which no doubt much pleased Pershing, for the stress was very much on the offensive, the counterattack in defense, and the rifleman with his bayonet as the key—not artillery, or trench weapons, or even the machine gun, though the importance of all was recognized. Rather the stress was on what were seen to be innate American qualities of "aggressive, self-reliant infantrymen." Morale, ultimately, was everything: "All training should, therefore, aim to develop positive qualities of character rather than to encourage negative traits." The Allied forces had taken refuge in a defensive mentality; this was why, by 1918, the Americans in France had assumed control of virtually all their own training of the AEF. As Odom comments, criticisms of Allied methods "were both naive and ill-founded. All combatants had turned to open warfare when the opportunity presented itself."[97]

Unfortunately for American tactical development, while the importance of the machine gun was recognized in theory, the stress on the individual rifleman (and his bayonet) came also at the cost of maximizing the new weapons' firepower. The inter-war Infantry School at Fort Benning, for example, discouraged the formation of special combat teams built around automatic weapons, as the Germans had done with their *Sturmtruppen* or "Stormtroop" elements over the course of the war. The *Field Service Regulations 1923* actually did introduce "the concept of a combined arms approach to tactics," including automatic rifles, machine guns, and the like, but the idea did not harmonize well with what was taught in practice. Maj. Gen. Stephen O. Fuqua, chief of the Infantry Branch, typified the lack of understanding of the changes which had taken place by insisting (in 1930), that any light machine gun "be capable of aimed shots from the shoulder and of not much greater weight than the present automatic rifle." It was an impossible criterion. In any case the necessary new weaponry was not developed, and in the hard times of the 1930s even the training, including target practice, was reduced to dangerously ineffective levels. In 1939, Maj. Gen. George A. Lynch, Fuqua's successor since 1937, was still making the same point about the rifleman: "We have rejected the European conception that a platoon consists of so many automatic rifles—that every man in the front line exists only for the purposes of the automatic rifle, either to serve it, carry ammunition for it, or protect it. We believe we shall have a much higher morale when the soldier feels that he is a combatant in his own right than when he views himself as the adjunct of a piece operated by another man."[98]

The combination of the stress on infantrymen and low budget allocations meant that potential special forces, each of which certainly had its advocates, generally were impossible to establish, even had a consensus been reached in their favor. There would be no special Machine Gun Corps, for example, such as the British established, and the Tank Corps, which had been established early in the war, just barely managed to preserve its existence with two light, and one heavy, battalions, and its own doctrine of tying light tanks to the infantry divisions (an understandable if erroneous conclusion based on the record of tanks in the war).[99] Similarly, artillery received insufficient development, most particularly in the area of anti-tank elements: the U.S. Army would not replace the inadequate 37mm gun until the middle of World War II. Two divisions of cavalry, on the other hand, lived on, despite the fact that of the army's seventeen wartime cavalry regiments, only one had actually been sent to France, and that saw very little action. Though mechanization did impinge on the cavalry's collective consciousness, most notably in the establishment of a very experimental mechanized brigade of light tanks in 1933–1937, still the horse was the preferred all-terrain mode of transport. In the cavalry's defense, effective cross-country vehicles had not yet been developed, and a persuasive argument could be made that if the army was going to be needed again in Mexico, as Millett and Maslowski point out, "the two divisions of horse cavalry and horse artillery would be more useful than all the tanks in Europe."[100] Nevertheless, the result was to sustain a world in which horse-handling, polo, and endurance rides predominated, in other words a cavalry "long on *blitz* and short on *krieg*."[101] Only the airmen began to come into their own, and a separate Air Service ("Air Corps" as of 1926) was written into the 1920 act. As will be seen, there would be an American response to the challenges of special forces which appeared early in World War II, such as paratroops and commandos, but this would only come rather late in the day. (Such units will be considered in the following chapters.)

Through the 1920s and early 1930s, economy was the watchword, though it was also reinforced by a general feeling that the United States faced no serious threats at a time when the world seemed to be turning in a more peaceful direction, if such indicators as the reduction in naval strengths agreed to in the Washington Conference of 1921, the Locarno Treaties of 1925, or the Kellogg-Briand Pact of 1928 were accepted. It was thus easy to adopt a viewpoint similar to that of Sen. John Williams of Mississippi, who believed that a substantial army was ". . . a form of insanity, if not idiocy. . . . In some of the finest years of our history the United States progressed most satisfactorily with an army of 25,000 men."[102]

In 1921, Congress cut the army's authorized strength in half to 150,000; by 1922, it was down to 12,000 officers and 125,000 men. The effect was not simply to cut men from the rolls. Since the number of men in each grade was limited, those who stayed on faced demotion in rank and pay cuts of 15–20 percent—as did 1,600 NCOs in 1921.[103] Even at that, assuming the ranks were kept up to strength (by no means the regular case), the actual available military force was much smaller. Since more than 25 percent served in overseas garrisons, and another twenty thousand along the Mexican border, once instructors serving with the Guard and others on detached service were subtracted, the army had fewer than thirty–five thousand men for serious training or the development of new weapons and tactics. It is little wonder that this residue "could hardly attain proficiency in much beyond small unit tactics, marching, and marksmanship."[104] The latter was especially important in the hard depression years. A private's pay was $21 per month, cut to $17.85 in 1933 (and men were unlikely to make private first class until their second three-year enlistment, corporal in their third); a PFC $30; a corporal twice what a private made, while a second lieutenant started at $125. Qualification on the rifle range as an expert rifleman paid an extra $5 per month for a year, until the next qualification tests, and five dollars "bought a lot of beer and Bull Durham tobacco."[105] It thus paid a man to learn to control his excellent but hard-kicking Springfield 30.06 rifle, introduced in the mid-1930s and replaced by the more tractable but poorly balanced semiautomatic Garand M-1 only when the war came. On pay day, at least, the experts were the elites in the beer halls and crap games of the "old army."[106]

There were few success stories in those lean years, with the possible exception of the thirty or so special service schools along with the key Army War College, Army Industrial College, and General Staff School, which at least passed all officers through their branch schools. "The goal was to ensure that every officer was minimally competent, not to maximize brilliance," a goal which Odom believes was fully met.[107] As for the men, in the early 1920s privates and privates first class who were designated "specialists" in a trade (and the army schools were helpful in that regard), could receive "specialty pay" to a maximum total pay of $60 per month. Since skilled laborers in the civilian work force might make $40–50 per week, it is not surprising that the army had difficulty in retaining such men. That particular problem was short-lived, however, for budget cuts soon eliminated the educational and vocational training which had seen such a promising development immediately after the war. Even food was a problem: the army allocated thirty cents a day to feed each man in the mid-1920s, when costs were at least thirty–six cents. The allocation was raised in 1927 to fifty cents, and only then did Army food levels equal those of the Navy and Marine Corps which had long been able to spend more on this necessity. Given such developments, it is not hard to understand the difficulties in the way of preserving an effective army nucleus, let alone developing any designated elites. Indeed, the only relieving factor was actually the Depression, which produced volunteers in plenty and allowed the army to be fairly selective in choosing quality enlisted men.[108]

The general slide continued into the 1930s. In 1935 the army was allocated its smallest budget in the era 1920–40, just over $277 million; it would rise to $742 million in 1940, but it was rather late in the day to get started with the substantial overhaul and development program which was needed in all areas, with the possible exception of the favored Air Corps.[109] It was by no means the case that Army leaders were satisfied with this situation, but it was necessary to take what they could get, and meanwhile criticism of government policy, at least in any public forum, was ruthlessly suppressed; for example, both Dwight D. Eisenhower and George S. Patton, Jr., were issued warnings for advocating independent tank missions that were not necessarily tied to infantry. As it turned out, the first tank units were not organized until 1940, at which time a mechanized cavalry brigade and an armored infantry regiment were established respectively at Fort Knox and Fort Benning, but the cavalrymen, at least until 1942, still had their horses.[110]

The simple fact was that America had emerged victorious in the Great War, feared the attack of no world power, and possessed a vast surplus of World War I equipment that many assumed would be adequate in case of need. For World War II, the French 75mm gun or the Stokes 3" mortar were going to be as inadequate as the horsed cavalry. It is true that some improvements were made after 1936, but it remained the case "that in 1939 the United States still lacked an army capable of taking the field against a modern military power."[111]

At least the manpower situation was addressed before America actually entered the war. In 1937, Congress approved expansion to 158,000 men; in July 1939, 210,000; in September, President Roosevelt authorized 227,000; in May, 1940, alarmed by the events in western Europe, Congress approved 255,000, and 375,000 in June. In the fall, National Guardsmen began to be called up for a year's training, and in September the Selective Service and Training Act introduced the nation's first peacetime draft and began to bring in large numbers of raw recruits. The rush to build the citizen army was on. By the summer of 1941, the "Army of the United States" included 1.2 million men, strengthened, no doubt, in numbers, but at the serious cost of dilution of experienced soldiers by training assignments, to say nothing of basic equipment shortages.[112] A beginning had been made, but much would have to be done while in the midst of a world war against powerful enemies, including the formation of special elites as considered necessary.

6 The United States Marine Corps

No consideration of American military elites in World War I would be complete without discussion of the United States Marine Corps, certainly at the start of the twenty-first century universally recognized as an elite force.[1] But that recognition was long in coming; though their existence is of very long standing the Marines really cannot be counted as elite until the twentieth century. Still, well before the founding of the new nation, marines were a standard element in naval vessels of all major western fleets, used as musket marksmen, substitute gun crews, and shipboard police. By the end of the Napoleonic War, for example, Britain had some nineteen thousand Marines in her service.

In the case of the American Marines, their real foundation came in an act of Congress of late 1775 to raise two battalions of marines for an expedition against Nova Scotia. The battalions were never actually formed, owing to George Washington's objection to the units being drawn from his own army (and he was presumably well satisfied with the work of his own Marblehead militia). The date November 10, 1775, however, is still celebrated by the Corps as its birthday. But in that same month Congress began the formation of a Continental marine force on a smaller scale to serve aboard the warships it was building. The Marines thus established served through the Revolutionary War

with credit, but they were perhaps most useful in deterring or even
suppressing mutiny aboard American vessels, even John Paul Jones's
own *Bonhomme Richard*.[2] Jones, a defender of Marines and their discipline, advocated a regiment based at Boston from which guards could
be drawn for all naval vessels, but the proposal came to nothing; by the
mid-1780s, the Continental Marines, like the Continental Navy, had
ceased to exist. As Allan Millett makes clear in his standard history,
the Marines really "had little opportunity to establish themselves as an
elite force" in the Revolution or the War of 1812.[3] Meanwhile, eight of
the united colonies had their own Marines to support their own state
navies, none of which earned special notice. Indeed, Benedict Arnold
summed up the situation in his characterization of the Massachusetts
Marines serving under his command on Lake Champlain as "the refuse
of every regiment."[4]

In June 1798, as a result of the Quasi-War with France, Congress
finally organized the Marines as a formal corps, though for more than
three decades it would still be unclear if this force of well under one
thousand men was part of the Army or the Navy. Pay was low; privates
received $4 per month, for example, 40 percent less than seamen, a
clear indication of their relative status. Though several subsequent attempts were made to abolish the Marines, their primary function—to
protect the officers and the vessels from their own crews—meant that
they were always necessary at least in small numbers. Since they also
were useful in guarding naval yards ashore, manning the heavy guns
of warships at sea, and occasionally landing expeditions in remote
foreign places, the force remained in existence through the century.
Such glory as it accumulated was due in part to luck, for example the
squad of Marines, aided by a motley force of several hundred Greek
mercenaries and Arab auxiliaries, that marched six hundred miles over-
land across North Africa to the walls of Derna in 1805 ("To the Shores
of Tripoli"), and in part to the perseverance of some of its commanders, most notably Archibald Henderson, commandant 1820–48, who
saw to it that the Marines were involved in the Mexican War and thus
contested "the halls of Montezuma." Some Marines earned considerable honors in the unsuccessful defense of the city of Washington and
the more successful battle of New Orleans, both in 1814, as well as the
Mexican War's siege of Vera Cruz and the assault on Chapultepec
(1847), but, in general, in the early Republic it is difficult to regard the
"Leathernecks" (a term derived from the leather stock or neck piece
which the Marines wore) as particularly elite.[5]

To the contrary, it is clear that some American leaders regarded the Marines as expendable. President Andrew Jackson, in particular, recommended in late 1829 that the Marines be merged into the army or artillery. His reasons included the anomaly of administering a separate small corps subject both to Army and Navy regulations (the Army ruled on land, the Navy at sea). The senior Navy captains who served as Navy Commissioners thought that the Marines, if they were needed at all, should be nothing more than small detachments entirely under the command of ship and shore station commanders. Congress debated the abolition of the Corps in 1830, but Henderson was able to mobilize sufficient support to kill the proposal in the Naval Affairs Committee—but it was by no means the last such attempt. At least part of the problem was resolved in 1834 when Congress decreed that the Marine Corps would be part of the naval establishment whether ashore or afloat, though it would not be merged totally with the Navy proper, thus establishing the basic relationship between the services which would last into the twenty-first century.

As was to be expected, the Marines, who numbered just over two thousand in 1859, fought in the Civil War—on both sides (there was a Confederate Marine Corps as well as a Federal Corps). Fighting for the Union, a Marine battalion suffered severely at First Bull Run where, like other Federal units, it gave way under pressure. (The best that could be said of the marines, said a later Marine General, was that "Surely they were among the last to run.") Seventeen Marines received the new Medal of Honor—admittedly given more readily in those days—in that war, the vast majority serving as gun captains and gun division commanders aboard larger warships. A total of 148 Marines were killed in action, 1861–65.[6]

After the war, the Marine Corps remained extant, for it was a regular force, but its size remained fixed at about two thousand officers and men. Though its officers (after 1882, appointed from the Naval Academy rather than civilian life)[7] might have enjoyed the Washington social whirl and the Marine band earned justified fame under the leadership of John Philip Sousa (band master, 1880–1892, and author of the Corps' official march, "Semper Fidelis," the Corps' motto as of 1883), the Corps had still not earned elite status by the end of the century, though it had certainly seen a variety of service worldwide. This included "China (1866, 1894, 1985), Formosa (1867), Japan (1867, 1868), Nicaragua (1867, 1894, 1896, 1898), Uruguay (1968), Mexico

(1870, 1876), Korea (1871, 1888, 1894), Panama (1873, 1885), Hawaii (1874, 1889, 1893), Egypt (1882), Haiti (1888, 1891), Samoa (1888), Argentina (1890), Chile (1891), and Columbia (1895),"[8] as well as occasions on which they were called out within the United States to assist civilian law enforcement agencies, most notably during the violent railroad strike of 1877. In the process, the force had to overcome another serious challenge to its existence led by a group of naval officers determined to force the Marines off their ships and into the Army, or preferably oblivion.

In 1889 a special board examining shipboard organization in the Navy recommended that Marines not be carried aboard warships. The argument was that the recruitment of a better class of men for the Navy was blocked by the discipline system in effect aboard vessels carrying Marines, little more than "room-takers and idlers," as police.[9] The attempt was warded off, and fortunately for the Corps, the Spanish-American War interceded to provide a chance for the Corps to improve its image. The Marines, as of 1898 numbering 119 officers and 4,713 enlisted men, fought a difficult campaign in the seizure and defense of Guantanamo Bay, in the larger picture "a minor skirmish of no consequence to the course of the war," but one which, in Millett's words, "took on incalculable importance for the Marine Corps."[10]

In the wake of its successful conduct in this war, the Corps grew steadily in the years before World War I: 6,200 in 1899, nearly 10,000 in 1908. It badly needed such manpower for its land operations in the new century: the Philippines, the Boxer Rebellion in China, Honduras, Cuba, Nicaragua, the Dominican Republic, Korea, Morocco, even Syria and Ethiopia.[11] Rather surprisingly for its record of usefulness, however, the Corps suffered one more attack in 1908–9, this time spearheaded by President Theodore Roosevelt and his secretary of war and successor, William Howard Taft. Roosevelt by Executive Order 969— long to be remembered by the Corps—removed all Marines from Navy warships. As Roosevelt explained to an aide, the downfall of the Corps was their own fault. "They have augmented to themselves such importance, and their influence . . . has given them such an abnormal position for the size of their corps that they have simply invited their own destruction. I do not hesitate to say they should be absorbed into the Army, *and no vestige of their organization should be allowed to remain.*"[12] Both Roosevelt and Taft, however, found that the Marines had enough friends in Congress and the public as a whole to defeat not only the order but also to overcome a powerful alliance of two presidents, a number of congressmen, and the bulk of the top Navy leadershi Millett's interesting conclusion applies to more than one elite unit studied in this volume: "When a military service can defend itself on grounds other than its present and future utility, it has clearly reached a point of high institutional autonomy and stability."[13]

Part of the story of the survival of the Corps was the increasing level of skills which it demonstrated, most notably in marksmanshi As of 1906, a Marine received an extra $1 per month by qualifying as a marksman, $2 as a sharpshooter, and $3 as an "expert rifleman." Such "beer money" acted as a considerable incentive: "Within three years, more than a third of all officers and men were qualified as marksman or higher."[14] On a larger level, in 1910 a Marine Corps Advance Base School was founded at New London, Connecticut, to train officers and men in the formation and utilization of "advance bases," meaning landing forces as necessary around the world, by now a Marine Corps speciality. Corps abilities in this regard were certainly demonstrated in their generally successful interventions in the Caribbean area (including Vera Cruz in 1914) in the last years before America entered World War I (one special contribution was the formation and leadership of the Gendarmerie d'Haiti). In 1916, the Corps was increased to 596 officers and 14,981 enlisted Marines, with a standby capacity to augment numbers to 17,400. Since 1912 they had been outfitted in the well-known forest or rifle green uniforms long typical of Europe's historic rifle or Jäger regiments. As Edwin Simmons points out, however, the original marines were not riflemen, and green seems to have been chosen only because it was what was available at the time.[15]

At the outset of World War I, therefore, as a result of its recent enlargement and far-flung adventures, the Corps in the words of Robert Heinl "was larger, better trained and organized, more combat experienced, and better led, than at any time in its previous 142 years' service."[16] Old rivalries, however, were not forgotten when it came time to make use of the Marines "over there." The 5th Marine Regiment, which arrived in the first American convoy to France thanks to some string-pulling by the Commandant, Maj. Gen. George Barnett, found itself, at Pershing's orders, spread throughout France in support of the Army's 1st Infantry Division as military police and line-of-communication troops, though in fact many of its men had pre-war service and thus could be counted as veterans. In a sense, Pershing's decision to use the Marines as guards, couriers, and police could be taken as a compliment upon the Marines' discipline and reliability, which he did indeed admire, but that interpretation hardly satisfied the Marines consigned to menial work alongside prisoners and African American army units:

> So here we are at Saint-Nazaire
> Our guns have rusty bores
> We are working side by side with Huns
> And nigger stevedores
> But if the Army and the Navy
> Ever gaze on Heaven's scenes
> They will find the roads are graded
> By United States Marines![17]

Only when the 6th Marines, composed of old-line officers and newly recruited enlisted volunteers, arrived together with an additional machine gun battalion could a complete Marine brigade be organized ("4th Marine Brigade"); only then was the Corps permitted to field a fighting unit, though never an entire Marine division. After training with the Chasseurs Alpins—who as always stressed the bayonet over marksmanship—the brigade, just under ten thousand officers and men now outfitted in Army olive drab and British-style flat helmets (but retaining red-trimmed chevrons and USMC buttons and hat and collar insignias), was incorporated into the American 2d Infantry Division. Soon enough the unit was considered by the Germans to be of first-class, even elite "storm trooper" quality. "The Marines are considered a sort of elite Corps, designed to go into action outside the United States. The high percentage of Marksmen, Sharpshooters, and Expert Riflemen, as perceived among our prisoners, allows a conclusion to be drawn as to the quality of the training in rifle marksmanship that the Marines receive. The prisoners are mostly members of the better class, and they consider their membership in the Marine Corps to be something of an honor. They proudly resent any attempts to place their regiments on a par with other infantry regiments."[18]

The German comment had some justification beyond personal observation. The Marines passed some sixty–one thousand volunteer enlistees through their ranks before the war ended, most of which were trained to a high standard at the Parris Island, South Carolina, recruit depot in an experience that no recruit forgot: "The first day I was at camp I was afraid I was going [to] die. The next two weeks my sole fear was that I wasn't going to die. And after that I knew I'd never die because I'd become so hard that nothing could kill me." In particular, The Corps continued to stress marksmanship standards. As Millett summarizes, "The rigor and standardization of Marine recruit training at the depot assured the Corps of better-trained enlisted men than the Army could provide for the American Expeditionary Forces."[19] Marine zeal could not be questioned, but the Corps had much to learn, most notably in tactics, above all the use of machine gun and artillery support, and in communications generally. Still, as Simmons points out, the Corps expanded from about fifteen thousand to seventy–five thousand, while the Army grew from 130,000 to some four million, meaning that in the Corps the dilution of officers and NCOs was never quite so great.[20]

The brigade saw minor action in the spring of 1918, but it was only in June that the American 2d and 3d Divisions had a chance to demonstrate their own determination in holding up the German advance near Chateau-Thierry on the Marne, fifty miles east of Paris. As they were moving up, the 2d Division's Marine Brigade (5th and 6th Marine Regiments) had to pass through French lines to get there, and the retreating French suggested that the Marines might find it advisable to pull back as they themselves were doing. Marine Capt. Lloyd Williams (6th Marines) uttered one of those famous remarks which are scattered through American military history: "Retreat, hell. We just got here."[21]

It was not until Belleau Wood, June 6–26, however, that the Marines could begin to earn general respect as a unit capable of more than "small actions or expeditions against native or informally trained enemies" which had characterized their previous history.[22] In the tough fighting at Belleau Wood the 5th and 6th Marines, led by Brig. Gen. James G. Harbord (an Army man, not a Marine; a favorite of Pershing's, he had been the latter's chief-of-staff) took heavy casualties (1,500 men) from well-entrenched German veterans, thus learning Western Front techniques in a great hurry. In particular, the 4th Marine Brigade's attack on June 6, in the words of John Eisenhower, "had been a tragedy, a useless slaughter of valiant, dedicated men for minimal gains. But that was not the impression the outside world received of the action."[23]

To the contrary, the colorful reports sent home about Belleau Wood by Chicago *Tribune* correspondent Floyd Gibbons (himself wounded three times in the battle) gained considerable new attention for the

Corps. Contrary to general censorship regulations, Gibbons was permitted to mention the Corps by name: "U.S. MARINES SMASH HUNS . . .," screamed the headlines. Not surprisingly, the other services "afterward went through life convinced that the Marines were a corps of publicity hounds." Assistant Secretary of the Navy Franklin Roosevelt was so impressed, while reviewing the brigade in August, that he directed that enlisted Marines be allowed to wear the Corps emblem on their collars (only officers had held this privilege before).[24] Corps lore, meanwhile, was forever reinforced by the legendary leadership of Gunnery Sgt. Dan Daly, already twice winner of the Medal of Honor, who drove his men on with memorable words of encouragement: "Come on, you sons of bitches. Do you want to live forever?"[25]

In actuality, though the Corps itself had not been directly responsible for all the attention, it certainly did have a well-developed sense of the value of positive publicity. As early as 1907 a USMC publicity bureau had been established in Chicago, and four years later this was expanded into a general "Recruiting Publicity Bureau." The Marines had proved enormously successful in their wartime recruiting efforts, not least by appealing to all those young men eager for quick action: the slogan "First to Fight" was used before World War I, but it was that war which made it famous. This slogan was dropped after the war, but not forgotten, and the Corps continued to make its presence known through advertising, home town press releases, and the services of professional journalists and combat correspondents. A motion picture section was established in 1926 in the Marine Corps Recruiting Bureau in Philadelphia, and it lent support to such inter-war films as *The Fighting Marine*, featuring former Marine and famous prize fighter Gene Tunney; *Tell It to the Marines*, with Lon Chaney; *What Price Glory?*, with Victor McLaglen and Dolores Del Rio; and *Devil Dogs of the Air*, with James Cagney and Pat O'Brien as rival Marine pilots.[26]

After Belleau Wood, the 1st and 2d American Infantry Divisions were attached to the French XX Corps, joining those units of the French army—Moroccans, Senegalese, and the Foreign Legion—considered to be their elite shock forces. The Marines again did very well in the fighting at Soissons in July, but again took heavy casualties—1,972 men by the time the 2d Division was withdrawn from the lines. In September came the relatively easy battle of St. Mihiel (706 casualties) and in October the tough struggle of Mont Blanc Ridge, a Marine assault which cost 2,538 Marines killed and wounded and won for the

Marines their third French unit citation, an honor which entitled the units concerned (in this case, the 5th and 6th Marines and the 6th Machine Gun Battalion) to stream the Croix de Guerre on their colors and individual members to wear the green and red *fourragère* ("pogey ropes" to other Marines) on their shoulders. There is little question that the 4th Marine Brigade, despite the achievement of other units, remained the Corps' "centerpiece."[27]

Over the course of the war, the Marines rose to nearly eighty thousand men, some thirty–two thousand of which served in France, taking 11,366 casualties (2,459 killed or missing), more than had been suffered in the entire history of the Corps to that point. The meaning of such figures to an individual soldier's unit is perhaps grasped more easily by considering Warren Jackson's experience. His 6th Marine Regiment company contained 250 men when it was organized in Quantico, Virginia, in August of 1917; when the war was over, the company had added three hundred replacements for killed and wounded, and only four of the original complement were left.[28] For the whole of the Corps, over the course of the war only twenty-five Marines had been taken prisoner, itself an interesting commentary on their attitude. Their record was outstanding, but nevertheless the experience had its frustrations, including the refusal of the Army commanders to permit the establishment of a separate Marine division. It can be argued that the refusal meant that the Marines were able to reinforce their front line forces with well-trained men, since their replacement system was not swamped in a way comparable to the Army's. Still, some Marine leaders at the time were firmly of the belief that the Army discriminated against the Marine Corps, and such is the view of historian (and USMC colonel) Heinl: "In reviewing Marine Corps attempts to go to war in France, it is difficult to escape the conclusion that, from the outset of the war, there existed a deliberate Army policy to minimize, if not prevent, Marine participation in the AEF." If a rationale needed to be provided, it was that the Marines had been trained for landing parties and operations in backward countries, their officers inadequately prepared for larger-scale Army operations, but this is an argument difficult to substantiate.[29]

Before moving on to post-war developments, it should be noted that Marine Corps units were not immune to a tendency to create internal elites for special purposes. For example, the 6th Marine Regiment's 1st Battalion in 1918 combed through its ranks to form a special group of fifteen scouts and ten observers, technically called the "intelligence

section" but better known in the regiment as the "suicide squad." The
lieutenant chosen to lead was trained in one of Pershing's special AEF
schools for terrain analysis and photograph interpretation, while the
men went through special training in map reading and similar skills.
The unit was used in various patrols toward enemy lines through the
spring, but in May was disbanded by a new battalion commander who
seems to have concluded that these skilled men were of more use in
their original platoons.[30] The problem of special Marine elites would
emerge again in the next war.

The Marine Corps was quickly reduced in size at the conclusion
of the war, down to 17,400—too small, it soon proved, and Congress
in 1920 authorized a force of about 28,500 officers and men, but provided the funds for only 20,000. The Marines were needed, however,
for a return to their pre-war interventionist role. It must have seemed in
a sense that the size and function of the Corps during the war had been
some sort of aberration, as the Marines found themselves again on
active duty in Cuba, Haiti, and Santo Domingo in the immediate post-
war era. It was fortunate for the Corps that its new commandant as of
June, 1920, Maj. Gen. John A. Lejeune, was a popular and capable
field commander who realized that the Marines needed a mission over
and above the traditional one of "colonial infantry" whose era was fast
passing (the Corps' thirteenth commandant, Lejeune would serve until
1929). Lejeune was not only a proven commander in World War I, but
he also had a knack both for understanding Washington's bureaucratic
politics and for influencing public opinion by developing a systematic
program for that very purpose.

Lejeune's answer was based upon pre-war studies of the problems associated with quick-response action in the creation of expeditionary forces or the advance bases needed for them or even larger
operations. Such a function was all the more necessary since the United
States really did not have a standing army once demobilization was
complete. Lejeune and his staff focused upon Marine Corps *readiness*,
meaning "the ability to project expeditions overseas to seize and secure advance bases."[31] This concept in turn meant substantial amphibious capability, again a goal towards which the Corps had been working, albeit slowly, before World War I. The Corps certainly had not
abandoned its shipboard role, nor its willingness to fight as land forces
in Europe or elsewhere, but such functions were not the primary mission as defined at the Marine Corps Schools at Quantico which honed

the professional skills of Corps officers (as did such institutions as the Army's Command and General Staff School and the Navy's Naval War College, to which Marine Corps officers were also sent).

Lejeune explained in his 1930 memoirs: ". . . while Marines are not necessary as a police force on board ship, yet their service afloat is necessary in order to provide the Navy with an efficient expeditionary force habituated to ship life, accustomed to being governed by Navy laws and regulations, and officered by a personnel whose members have been closely associated with the officers of the Navy. . . . Duty on board the combat ships of the fleet is not only the best, but is practically the only means by which these eminently desirable results can be attained." Above all, the Marines were necessary for shore operations which could complete a successful naval campaign. "The operations of such an expeditionary force are extraordinarily difficult and hazardous and require unusually skillful and resolute leadership, and troops which are especially trained for the accomplishment of their mission." And that objective, finally, could only be obtained by the officers of the Corps, in whose hands the future of the institution thus rested.[32]

Despite this redefinition, however—and the addition of Marine air power to its capabilities—through the 1920s and on into 1933, the Marines found themselves mainly engaged in yet another "banana war" in Nicaragua, with other units long active in watching over American interests in China, most notably the fourteen years spent by the 4th Marines guarding Shanghai's International Settlement.[33] When it could, however, the Corps practiced amphibious landings, with a particular eye, as the years passed, for a potential conflict against Japan. Despite Depression-motivated personnel cuts (to 15,355 enlisted men), and the need to parcel out various shipboard and base-protection detachments, in the interwar years through a process of trial and error the Corps evolved the "Fleet Marine Force," which would play a critical role in the evolution of the Pacific Ocean campaigns of World War II.

It is not proposed here to review in any detail the astonishing story of the growth of the Marine Corps to nearly five hundred thousand officers and men in order to fight the Japanese in the Pacific War (Aside from a brief, early war role for the 6th Marines in Iceland, Marines did not serve in the Atlantic except from shipboard detachments). Beginning with the struggle for Bataan and Corregidor in the Philippines, marines on land and in the air learned on the job the skills necessary for victory in four different environments, each demanding in different ways, as pointed out by Allan R. Millett: "the jungle warfare of the south Pacific, the atoll warfare of the Gilberts and Marshalls, the mobile warfare of the Marianas, and the cave warfare of Peleliu, Iwo Jima, and Okinawa."[34] In each case the Marines adjusted by altering training regimes; increasing firepower with tanks, flame throwers, and artillery; and evolving an effective doctrine which integrated naval and artillery fire and close air support.

The substantial growth of the Corps did not come without troubles, not least the difficulty of finding enough qualified volunteers. In April 1942, the Corps lowered its entrance standards, and soon raised the upper age limit to thirty–six from thirty–three. At the end of the year volunteering was ended as all American men aged eighteen to thirty–six came under Selective Service jurisdiction (in June, for the first time the Corps was opened to African-Americans; seventeen thousand served over the course of the war, twelve thousand overseas, but almost entirely in depot companies, beach parties, and support roles).[35] The Marine Corps then faced the challenge of inculcating an elitist volunteer image in draftees. As far as possible, this was done by identifying draftees who wished to serve in the Corps and encouraging them to alter their status to regular or reserve Marines, a policy which was successful in all but about 70,000 of the more than 224,000 draft-

MARINES RAISING THE FLAG ON MOUNT SURIBACHI DURING THE BATTLE OF IWO JIMA, FEBRUARY 23, 1945. *JOE ROSENTHAL, COURTESY OF THE NATIONAL ARCHIVES AND RECORDS ADMINISTRATION.*

ees who became Marines. When coupled with yet another successful public relations campaign in this war, enhanced by the new policy of training newspapermen and photographers as combat Marines who were sent into battle to cover the campaigns, it is no surprise that the elite Marine image was maintained. Certainly there can be little question that it was well-deserved when such battles as Guadalcanal, Tarawa, Betio, Saipan, Peleliu, Iwo Jima, and Okinawa were over, but there was frequent controversy with an Army which tended to stress more methodical attacks than did the Marine Corps, which put a stress on unremitting assault and on pushing forward whenever possible. Such differences in tactical concepts were inevitably exacerbated by different approaches to command, logistics, and fire support, though the Marines and Army frequently fought side by side. The Marines had no monopoly on island warfare, but the Corps suffered, losing nearly twenty thousand killed and sixty–seven thousand wounded. Though the Marines included less than 5 percent of America's armed forces, they had taken nearly 10 percent of all casualties suffered on the battlefield, a statistic caused mainly by the fact that 98 percent of Marine officers and 89 percent of enlisted men served in the Pacific, while all American armed forces together sent only 73 percent of man (and woman) power overseas.[36]

THE 6TH MARINE DIVISION SEES FRONT LINE ACTION ON A RIDGE NORTH OF THE CITY OF NAHA ON OKINAWA, MAY 4, 1945. THEY BATTLED STRONG JAPANESE FORCES FOR FORTY-EIGHT HOURS BEFORE CAPTURING THE POSITION, IN PREPARATION FOR THE DRIVE INTO THE CITY. *U.S. MARINE CORPS.*

Though clearly an elite corps overall, the Marines also found them-selves creating internal elite units, such as raiders and paratroopers, which also need consideration. The power of military fads has already been demonstrated in this volume, and the Marines were in no way immune from the influence of developments in foreign military estab-lishments. Though Marine planners had discussed special reconnais-sance patrol units before World War II broke out, the example of Brit-ish commando raids on Axis targets in Europe and Africa early in the war was too persuasive to resist. Shortly after Pearl Harbor, the president's son, Capt. James Roosevelt (USMC Reserve) wrote to the Corps Commandant advocating the utility of commando-style units for the Pacific War to come. The general reaction was hardly total en-thusiasm, since many Marine officers believed that Marines who were ready for action with the amphibious force were capable of any tasks which might be assigned to such special elite raider units; in other words, the Marines were already raiders. As a further issue, such spe-cial units were likely to drain off the most experienced officers and NCOs in a Corps already short of such men in a time of vast expansion.[37]

Nevertheless, the orders came down from the highest levels—meaning President Roosevelt and Secretary of the Navy Frank Knox—that the Marines would form two separate battalions (one on each coast, though that based at Quantico was soon moved to San Diego) of four companies each. Marine lieutenant colonels Merritt A. Edson and Evans F. Carlson, both with considerable experience during the Sino-Japa-nese conflict in China, were assigned respectively to the 1st and 2d Raider Battalions (James Roosevelt, now a major, was Carlson's ex-ecutive officer).[38] Existing Marine units were combed for suitable of-ficers and men, particularly those who had served in three pre-Pearl Harbor Provisional Rubber Boat Companies, to the considerable an-noyance of frustrated commanders. "Edson's levy against our division," later wrote Gen. A. Vandergrift, "coming at such a critical time, annoyed the devil out of me but there wasn't one earthly thing I could do about it."[39] There was no appeal: America would have its commando force.

The Raiders were carefully selected. "The type of man chosen for this job had to be tough," recalled Gen. Holland M. Smith. "Our four battalions of Marine Raiders, eventually incorporated into the 4th Marines, were the elite of toughness. A 20-mile march with a hundred pounds of equipment on their backs, followed by hand-to-hand combat with a knife, was sometimes their role. They were taught all the tricks of undercover combat, they could out-read a jungle-tracker and out-swim a fish." But there was a cost: "By the very nature of their organization, the Raiders were highly expendable."[40]

The Raider battalions had been organized in February 1942; in August, they were in action, the 1st Battalion in a diversionary raid on Makin Island in the Gilberts, transported by submarines. Evaluation of these actions—particularly that at Makin—was mixed, a result which only increased the controversy over the Raiders.[41] A new proposal, this time from Rear Adm. Richmond K. Turner, who commanded the Amphibious Force, South Pacific, that every Marine regiment include a Ranger battalion for similar such actions, only aroused more opposition, not only from the Commandant of the Marine Corps, Maj. Gen. Thomas Holcomb, but also Adm. Chester Nimitz, commander in chief, Pacific, on the grounds that results were questionable so far, and had been conducted at the cost of taking some of the best leaders from existing units. In the end, two new Raider battalions were formed, but they were constructed in the manner of the first two, that is, as separate, permanent units rather than integral elements of existing regiments. In March of 1943, the Raiders were themselves amalgamated organizationally into the 1st Raider Regiment, and in this form continued to see action on Guadalcanal and elsewhere in the Solomons. By early 1944, however, the need for such units had apparently passed, and the Marine Corps high command accomplished its objective of merging the Raiders into regular Marine units, in particular the resurrected 4th Marines, a regiment which had been lost in the Philippines in 1942. The Marines had always objected to the creation of internal elites, believing, as a memo of December 1943 put it, "any operation so far carried out by raiders could have been performed equally well by a standard organization specially trained for that specific operation." Or as Vandergrift put it, "Luxuries had to go."[42]

Marine Parachute battalions had a similar origin in 1940, beginning with a small force (one battalion of infantry) that could be used to reconnoiter, raid, spearhead an attack, or operate as an independent force behind enemy lines in a guerrilla role. Inspired by reports of European parachute actions, in October Commandant Holcomb ordered that each Marine regiment would train one battalion as "air troops" which could be moved by air, and each such battalion would include a company trained in parachute use, thus providing, in all, a force of some 750 parachutists for the whole Corps.[43]

The idea of parachutists seemed to generate little if any opposition, in comparison to the Raiders; it was relatively self-evident both that parachute capability might be useful and that it would not be available without special training. The parachutists were volunteers from existing units, and qualifications were stiff, including above-average intelligence and physical conditioning. Parachute officers received $100 extra per month, and enlisted men $50, but the official history of the unit is no doubt accurate in noting that to most men "the aura of adventure surrounding the parachutists and the promise of action seemed more important . . ."[44] Only some 60 percent of those attempting the course completed it.

Eventually four Marine parachute battalions were formed and grouped into the 1st Parachute Regiment. Unquestionably this was a fine unit, and its various elements amassed an excellent record fighting at Bougainville and elsewhere in the Pacific, often alongside the Marine Raiders. But always they fought as infantry; no combat jumps (as opposed to training jumps) were made by Marines in World War II. This fact was due to a combination of causes, including lack of airlift capacity, but above all to the unsuitability of either large densely jungled or small, heavily defended islands to their use. In the end, the Marine paratroopers were judged a rather expensive luxury (including the extra pay), and at the end of 1943, the Commandant ordered that all Marine parachute forces be disbanded. On the whole, while their record was excellent, the Marine special units had not made a notable impact on either the Pacific War or the Corps itself. As Marine Corps historian Charles Updegraph concludes, in the sort of war the Marines fought, "it was apparent that the specialized units were, at best, no better suited to the task than were regular Marine infantry forces."[45]

Despite numerous, sometimes quite serious challenges to its very existence, the Marine Corps had not only survived, but emerged as a recognized elite force, more Navy than Army, inevitably, but always with its own individuality. Considering the Corps' early history, this result might have been difficult to predict. The Corps had, after all, suffered from the hostility of both the Army and the Navy at different periods; as Holland Smith put it in the mid-twentieth century, "Looking back in this period from the vantage of years and distance, I sometimes wonder if we didn't have two enemies: the Japanese and certain brass hats in the Army and Navy."[46] The only relieving factor, it might be argued, was the fact that since the Corps was drawn from the civilian population, neither of the other services could complain that their best men were drawn off for the Corps (indeed, those Annapolis graduates who went to the Marines were long regarded as less than the cream of the crop). But Marine leadership was tenacious in defending its role and in maintaining the standards which made the successful performance of that role possible. The result was the creation of an elite corps despite the prevailing anti-elite military tradition in the society at large. On the other hand—and not too surprisingly—the Corps resisted the creation of internal elites in the Raiders and paratroopers, and, at least through the end of World War II, won that battle as well.

7 World War II: The Early Formations

Roger Beaumont, in his 1974 study *Military Elites*, entitles his chapter on World War II units, "Mobs for Jobs." It is a British term, meaning "the gangster-warrior elites" who "ran about the rear areas of the enemy, destroying, confusing and avoiding a fair fight whenever possible. . . . Private armies. Not soldiers, really. Nor civilians. Wore what they liked; developed their own vehicles and tactics. Drove higher commanders and the MPs wild. And their leaders usually had enough influence to keep them free of control by higher command. Like the airborne, they played against the second-string. . . . They were guerrillas in uniform . . . scalpels to be wielded against enemy lines of communication and critical points. But there was a difference. The storm troops and tanks opened up the enemy for conventional forces following. The 'mobs for jobs' operated as harassers."[1]

There is considerable food for thought in this characterization, which well fits Britain's Commandos, Chindits, and Long Range Desert Grou Certainly some American units, such as the Army's Rangers, the Marines' Raiders, or Merrill's Marauders, appear to fit the definition, at least in some respects, as will be seen in the discussion that follows. But the brush strokes are far too broad. Merrill's men, for example, came up against top Japanese units in Burma, while a similar experi-

161

ence awaited the special units which fought at Salerno, or Anzio, or Normandy. Some special formations, such as the Navy's Underwater Demolition Teams, were hardly harassers, and did indeed "open up" the enemy, as had also been the intended mission of a number of other units. Nor should it be forgotten that the largest of America's elite forces, the division-sized formations of Marines and paratroopers, were used more often than not as conventional infantry in demanding situations.

Beaumont's characterization goes further, adding that the twentieth-century elite forces he studies (for he considers no unit before 1900) were normally voluntary, and were assigned elite status *before* they were assembled. "Usually, this meant that physical and mental standards for admission were high. They had distinctive uniforms or insignia and traditions and customs—frequently highly synthetic—which formed rapidly. The new elite forces also were relatively free from ordinary administration and discipline. Entrance to these units was often through the surviving of an ordeal, a 'rite of passage,' requiring tolerance of pain or danger and subsequent dedication to a hazardous role." In many cases, units of this type have been mirror images of similar enemy formations. In fact, as will be seen below, at least as often the American elites were mirror images of *Allied* units.[2]

There is always a cost, of course. Beaumont makes the important point that corps d'elite, raised to solve particular challenges, often raise as many problems themselves. "Their special access to status and resources produced inter-organizational tensions, a kind of military class war. . . . With tiresome and tragic regularity, forces raised to cope with a specific problem often found the original challenge gone by the time they were ready for action. This led to their being used—and misused—for other purposes."[3] All this is quite true, but as will be seen, the capabilities of such elite units were such that non-elite commanders, once they gained temporary control of them, despite their own predictable disdain for elitist units, were inclined to maintain that control as long as possible, whether a more appropriate form of utilization was feasible or not (Mark Clark, Omar Bradley, and Bernard Montgomery are all cases in point).

Finally, Beaumont also treats a larger issue: the function of corps d'elite as "a symbol of aggressiveness" in modern societies, offering an outlet for would-be (or actual) gangsters by providing society-authorized "gang" membership once the selection and initiation processes were complete. Now given a group membership and the symbols (and sometimes the pay) of special status, members of such groups relished their achievements and sense of importance: only paratroopers may wear paratrooper boots. "They felt tough, heedless of death, favored by fate, and sure that they were many cuts above the average man," always assuming, of course, they survived.[4] Such attitudes were not always there, but when they were, elite formations of World War II would have found much in common with Sparta's hoplites or Napoleon's Old Guard. To claim that "most modern corps d'elite were expected to behave more like gangsters than soldiers,"[5] goes too far, however, at least where America's elite combat units in World War II were concerned.

But there is another way of defining elites, one closer to the Revolutionary and Civil War traditions: the hard core, experienced, combat soldiers, marines, and sailors, who formed the "sharp end" of America's military effort. John Ellis estimates that of the approximately 7.5 million men used by the Army and Marines in World War II, almost five million saw overseas service, but only about 35 percent overall ever experienced combat (the figures were higher for the Marines than the Army, and so were the casualties, respectively 8.7 and 4.6 percent killed or wounded). Mere survival brought "a fierce sense of pride among front-line soldiers about their ability to hang on in conditions inconceivable to those further back. Out of this pride there arose a sense of exclusivity, of apartness, that in turn blossomed into a deep compassion for and loyalty towards other members of the same elite brotherhood. Pride was a shared emotion, in which *mutual* esteem, a sense of common suffering, dominated over any tendency to selfish individualism." For Ellis, clearly, the war's elites were only incidentally the specific units which are discussed below. Indeed, only the Marauders and the paratroopers receive the briefest of references in Ellis's study. Instead, like the soldiers of the Iron and Stonewall Brigades, Ellis's elites are those men of whatever formation who survived and prevailed at the "sharp end."[6]

World War I veteran and military historian S. L. A. Marshall, in a well-known 1947 study, went considerably further, arguing that, "In an average experienced infantry company in an average stern day's action, the number engaging with any and all weapons was approximately 15 percent of total strength," and even in the most "aggressive" companies, "the figure rarely rose above 25 percent of total strength from the opening to the close of action." If Marshall's figures are accepted, in an important sense the war was fought by just over 5 percent—at the most, 10 percent—of the total of American forces. Marshall's figures were criticized by many when they appeared, and have only diminished in credibility over time. Yet his book is still reprinted—and read—as a valuable study of training and command issues. Marshall himself claimed that in the Korean War, the 15 percent rose to over 50 percent, due mainly to a very striking change in training methods, again, assuming his figures are accepted.[7]

Specific numbers aside, Marshall was at least right in noting that some of the men at Ellis's "sharp end" will be better trained, or natural leaders, or both, and perhaps they are the true elites of World War II. Much, clearly, depends upon definition. With that caveat in mind, we will proceed to consider those elites which more closely approximate Beaumont's usage, proceeding roughly in the chronological order of their creation.

Certainly the American Army's paratroop forces must be considered elite, though their heritage—compared to the Marines, for example—spans relatively few years. Parachutes were in fact quite common in World War I as safety gear for pilots and virtually defenseless balloonists. Plans existed for the use of parachute infantry, but no serious experiments were made until the inter-war era, and then primarily in Europe. The Soviets in the 1930s proved the most innovative pioneers in using paratroopers as advance shock troops and in "airlifting" larger units to reinforce smaller advance forces. Many problems remained though, whatever the army, including the availability of suitable planes and pilots and the obvious vulnerability of such operations. Such soldiers required the necessary qualifications of excellent physical condition and the courage to jump into enemy territory with little in the way of covering fire, communications, and other supporting factors normally considered essential for successful military operations. As always, the cost of subtracting substantial numbers of such men from other units was likely to cause a significant decline in leadership or readiness, or both.[8]

Nevertheless, the successful use by Germany of paratroopers, glider-borne infantry, and air-transportable infantry in the early stages of World War II impressed the leaders of every major army. The occupation of Norway, the seizure in the spring of 1940 of the bridges over the Maas and Waal Rivers in Holland, the striking capture of Belgium's Fort Eben Emael, and finally the airborne assault on Crete in May of

1941 dictated that every army organize its own such forces, and think about the defenses against them. That German losses on Crete were great enough to persuade Hitler not to use his airborne forces again in such a campaign was a result yet unknown to Western generals.

Already in the late 1930s, Army Chief of Staff Gen. George C. Marshall had commissioned Chief of Infantry Maj. Gen. George Lynch to study the feasibility of a unit of "air infantry." The general idea was to train it to seize an airfield for a follow-up landing, or perhaps to send small elements to seize a bridgehead or key installation. Marshall passed the report to Maj. Gen. H. H. "Hap" Arnold, the Army's Air Chief of Staff, but Arnold's staff had mixed opinions. While the Air Corps Tactical School Commandant saw the value of such a force—naturally, within the Air Corps—as a sort of "Marines," to be called "Air Grenadiers" or "Air Corps Grenadiers," others worried about a shortage of transport aircraft. For the moment the idea was shelved, until the Russians used paratroops against Finland in late 1939. The following February, the infantry urged that an experimental volunteer unit be formed. The role of German *Fallschirmjäger* in the invasion of the Low Countries in the spring of 1940 was not overlooked, and the pace accelerated.[9]

By June of 1940, the United States had a Parachute Test Platoon of one lieutenant and forty–eight enlisted men (thirty-nine would form the unit; the rest were reserves in case of injury) training at Fort Benning, Georgia. The men had all volunteered from the Infantry School's 29th Infantry "Demonstration" Regiment, thus setting an important principle of accepting volunteers only; because of the anticipated dangers, no married men were permitted to join. As William Yarborough, a pioneer with the 509th Parachute Infantry Battalion (he designed the "jump wings," and later went on to command the Special Forces), put it: "In those days, damn few people rode in airplanes, let alone jumping out of them. We felt, 'Boy, we are in the forward edge of something that is really something big and important."[10]

In July, the first eight-week course was begun at Fort Benning (the "Frying Pan"), including much physical training as well as parachuting and small unit tactics, in the process establishing many practices and traditions which would become standard with American paratroopers, including the yell of "Geronimo!" when jumping from aircraft. Their final practice jump went well, an important moment since Generals Lynch and Marshall and Henry Stimson, the secretary of war, along with other notables, were all on hand to judge its success or failure.

The battalion now became the cadre for the parachute training school at Fort Benning. In September, the first Parachute Battalion (the 501st) was established, with the 502d, 503d, and 504th soon to follow, using men from the 501st as cadres. The Air Corps had lost its battle to control the new force; Marshall had ruled in favor of the infantry. Early in 1942, these first battalions in turn were utilized as the nucleus of an expansion to six parachute regiments, each composed of three parachute battalions. The final step was to establish two airborne divisions (eventually five would be created by the end of the war), though considerable debate developed over the most desirable form for the new arm. The eventual decision was for each airborne division to include about 8,300 men (roughly half a normal infantry division's sixteen thousand), divided into one parachute regiment (two thousand men), for which the six already authorized would form the logical source, and two two-battalion glider regiments (1,600 each), drawn from regular infantry, together with supporting artillery and other elements. The glider troops would be ordinary infantry, and their function would be to land in support of an "airhead" already seized by the paratroops.[11]

Not all volunteers were acceptable. A special physical had to be passed; recruits had to have scored 110 or above on the general intelligence test (AGCT), the same score required as a minimum for officer training, and possess a clean police record in their home town. (There was no practical way at the time to check anywhere else.) Paratrooper training was demanding, and the accomplishment of their unique skills gave them a special élan. Kurt Gabel, who fought in Europe as a battalion scout with the 513th Parachute Infantry Regiment, put his experience of basic training in historical perspective.

> Many years later, during the Korean War, when I was an officer, I watched troops going through their twelve-week cycle of infantry basic and I saw them again during the Viet Nam era. But never have I seen or experienced the likes of parachute basic, as never again have I seen the product of such training, given within a line regiment and administered by the officers and NCOs who would lead the same men in advanced training, in maneuvers, and in combat.
> Every minute was accounted for; field application followed ev-

ery classroom presentation. "Everything was done with extreme care and on the double at the same time," with the stated intention of disqualifying any man who did not do it right, and forcing the weak to sign "quit slips." A willingness to take the initiative, knowledge of multiple weapons systems, physical stamina: all were important qualifications. The end result was "a spirit that would evolve and grow, as other, more somber events enveloped us throughout the life and much of the physical death of our regiment, into an esprit de corps of enduring magnitude."[12]

Paratrooper élan was only enhanced by the distinctive uniforms they wore, copied from those of Hitler's *Fallschirmjäger*. The uniform was designed by 501st Lt. William Yarborough (as a brigadier general, in the 1960s he would help the Special Forces obtain permission to wear the green beret).[13] As early veteran Lou Varrone put it: "Due to our distinctive deportment, jump boots, and bloused trousers, we were considered to be swaggering, cocky, overbearing, and arrogant. But these views were grossly mistaken, for the qualities of self-esteem, a strong sense of destiny, supreme confidence, arduous training, a mystical camaraderie, and the pioneering spirit of a challenging new frontier, were what we were all about. How were super-elite troops supposed to act—like we had an inferiority complex?"[14] Gabel again: "Having once worn that parachute patch and the jump suit with boots, nobody could have endured going back to units that were not airborne."[15] Maj. Gen. Lesley J. McNair, commander of Army Ground Forces, put it somewhat differently: "They . . . are our *problem children*. They make a lot of money [i.e., $50 per month jump pay], and they know they're good. This makes them a little temperamental, but they're great soldiers."[16]

The first division selected for airborne duty was the 82d; the second was the newly created 101st. Each would incorporate a trained paratroop regiment, with the 504th assigned to the 82d and the 502d to the 101st, while the 82d's infantry would be divided between the two divisions. The 82d had a distinguished pedigree from World War I, having spent considerable time in the front lines in that conflict, taking over 7,400 casualties, and noting among its alumni Medal of Honor winner Sgt. Alvin C. York. Deactivated after World War I, the "All-American" division was recalled to duty and recreated from scratch with sixteen thousand draftees formed into three infantry regiments of three battalions each, together with divisional artillery. The 82nd did well in its training schedule, and in July 1942, with Brig. Gen. Matthew Ridgway in command, it was selected to be a "motorized" division, equipped with trucks for action in conjunction with armored forces. No sooner had this decision been made, however, than it was altered: the 82d would be an airborne division.[17]

From all sides there were concerns about the new orders. Officers of the 82d were surely pleased to be chosen for the honor of this new experimental role, but the division would now be divided in two, thus inevitably sacrificing hard-won cohesion. Merger of draftee infantry with the elite volunteer paratroopers created doubts, and the decision to put the 82d's infantry into gliders was decidedly unpopular. After all, the gliders were vulnerable and dangerous, the men had not volunteered for such duty, and there was understandable resentment at the fact that glider-borne infantry did not receive the extra pay given to parachute officers and men until mid-1944.[18] Nevertheless, the divisions were organized, trained for battle, and given their first combat airborne assignment: Operation Husky, the invasion of Sicily.

For the airborne paratrooper elements (504th and 505th regiments), Sicily proved a disaster, with the men dropped—at night—up to sixty-five miles away from their designated drop zones. Though the disorganized paratroop elements certainly caused confusion in the German-Italian ranks, and in some cases established useful blocking positions, it was clear that much rethinking had to be done about large-scale airborne operations. Some 5,300 82d Division paratroopers had left North Africa for the drop; the casualty rate was a very discouraging 27 percent, leading some higher commanders to conclude that future missions for paratroopers should be in units no larger than self-contained regimental combat teams, that is, a single regiment supported by the necessary artillery and special services—or even smaller, perhaps no greater than battalion level.[19]

Decisions on this question had not really been made when Allied forces crossed into Italy and began to creep up the peninsula. First designated for a drop on Rome, the 82d was next used to parachute into the American perimeter in the poorly conceived Salerno operation. Their contribution was real enough; Col. James Gavin, commander of the three-battalion 505th Regiment which did the drop believed that their presence changed the tide of the battle in favor of the Americans, a conclusion which soon became an airborne article of faith. Certainly the drop, of about two thousand men, was thoroughly successful, giving new heart to the airborne forces in general, but it had not been made behind enemy lines. On the other hand, the 509th Airborne Battalion (already used on a drop behind German lines in North Africa), was, rather inexplicably, dropped at Avellino, far behind the Germans; this operation could only be regarded as a failure, causing the Germans little inconvenience but losing 120 of the 640 men who dropped. The verdict, in other words, was still out on the efficacy of airborne operations as the Allies shifted their attention to planning for Overlord, the cross-channel attack set for June of 1944.

The process of planning for the use of airborne forces in the D-Day invasion went through numerous stages, which need not be followed here. In the end, both the 101st and 82d were committed to Neptune (the assault phase of Overlord), to be dropped behind German positions. Over 13,000 American paratroopers were dropped in the American sector (and another 4,800 British paratroopers in their own area). Once again, the operation could not be termed a success when judged by how many (or few) men landed where they were intended to go, the high rate of casualties, and the general disorganization found among the units once on the ground, much of which, as Clair Blair concludes, could be attributed to "lack of vigorous training in the American troop-carrier command,"[20] to say nothing of the fact that the drop was made at night.

Once regrouped and in action, the paratroopers not surprisingly lived up to their fighting reputation, despite the lack of transport, heavy artillery, or armor. If anything, they were too successful. Doctrine—according to Ridgway at least—called for airborne units to be withdrawn once they had done their job and the "heavy" regular divisions had reached their lines. The difficulty was that ground commanders found paratroop infantry too good to relinquish, a fact which had already become evident in Sicily and Italy; in this case, the 82d was used to push American positions across the Cotentin Peninsula after having suffered severely in holding off considerably larger German forces at Ste. Mère-Eglise. When it was finally relieved on July 8 after thirty-three days in action, the 82d, in Blair's words, was regarded as "the toughest, most resourceful and bloodthirsty infantry in the ETO [European Theater of Operations]."[21] Of the 12,000 men committed in Normandy, just over 6,500 were eventually embarked on landing craft for England from Utah Beach: 46 percent had been killed, wounded, or reported missing (the 101st suffered 4,670 casualties). These fine divisions were now to be rested and refitted, and linked with a new 17th Airborne Division into an American Airborne Corps (XVIII Airborne Corps) under Ridgway's command.

Just how these elite divisions would be used again was the substance of much discussion over some months, just as basic Allied strategy was the subject of debate once the virtual stalemate in Normandy was broken. At least a half-dozen plans were drawn up for airborne operations, but most were canceled. Some nine thousand British and American paratroopers and gliderists were utilized in support of Operation Dragoon, the controversial landing in southern France in mid-August 1944. Once again, the operation did not go particularly well, due less to German resistance, which was light, than to unfavorable flying weather. Some 60 percent of the Americans, and 40 percent of the British, were dropped too far from their designated drop zones to have any useful effect, though estimates at the time reported a far more favorable result, supported by the fact that casualties had been very slight.[22]

Much more famous was the Market-Garden affair, the attempt to seize a bridgehead across the Rhine at Arnhem (Market was the air assault; Garden was the complementary supporting British ground attack). The scope of the enterprise was vast: some twenty thousand parachutists, fifteen thousand gliderists, and ten thousand airlanded regular infantry were involved in the original plan. Again, there is no need here to recapitulate a story which has received intense historical attention. While it may be said that the mission of the American 82d and 101st Airborne Divisions was successfully completed, the operation as a whole was a defeat when the British 1st Airborne Division was unable to hold Arnhem and take the "one bridge too far."[23]

After Arnhem, American airborne units fought on the ground, earning further fame in the Battle of the Bulge. The 101st Division, in particular, would evermore be known for its heroic stand at Bastogne; Brig. Gen. A. C. McAuliffe's famous one-word reply ("NUTS!") to a German demand to surrender became permanently enshrined in the pantheon of great American military moments. The 82d received less publicity for its similar defense of St. Vith for six days, but that operation, which seriously delayed the German offensive, was perhaps even more significant; in that action, for example, the 509th Parachute Infantry Battalion (attached to the 82d Airborne) went into battle with about seven hundred men, but emerged with only fifty–five, and was simply disbanded as a result, its survivors sent to other units.[24]

In the Battle of the Bulge, three American Airborne divisions (the

17th had joined in the last stages) together suffered some ten thousand killed, wounded, and missing (and another five thousnd to illness), but once again they were too valuable in combat to be pulled out for special operations training. One more combat drop was made in Europe, Operation Varsity, in which the 17th Airborne and British 6th Airborne were dropped to support Montgomery's crossing of the lower Rhine River. About 9,800 Americans were dropped or towed into Varsity, which despite some problems was a general success, though it cost two thousand casualties in what some commanders at the time and subsequent historians have concluded was an unnecessary example of Montgomery's penchant for overkill.

Fine as they were, however, the paratroop regiments were not what they once had been. Casualties had been heavy, and now replacements went into the line fresh from basic training and a month of jump-school. David Webster, a squad leader in the 82d, explained: "It was the first time we had ever received replacements on line, and none of us liked it, because it meant that we would stay in combat much longer than usual. . . . Previously it had been the custom to receive replacements in base camp and work them into the regiment there, so that they could

ON DECEMBER 31, 1944, TROOPS OF THE 101ST AIRBORNE DIVISION DEPART BASTOGNE, WHERE THE DIVISION WITHSTOOD TEN DAYS OF ATTACK AND WAS FOR A TIME ENCIRCLED, TO CLEAR THE SURROUNDING DISTRICT OF GERMAN FORCES. *U.S. CENTER FOR MILITARY HISTORY.*

get to know the other men before they went into action. Now they just
threw them in and let them take their chances. I did not envy them."[25]

By the end of the fighting in Europe, Ridgway (featured on the
cover of *Time* magazine on April 2, 1945) and his XVIII Airborne Corps
were definitely among America's heroes of the European Theater of
Operations—now designated for forthcoming operations against Japan's
home islands, though that campaign was never required.[26] It should be
added that paratroopers of the U.S. Army were used in the Pacific Theater, but only sparingly. Both the 11th Airborne Division and the separate 503d Parachute Regimental Combat Team saw action, mostly in
non-parachute ground operations. The 503d, however, did drop in New
Guinea, on Corregidor, and near Aparri, Luzon on Camalaniugan Airfield during the reconquest of the Philippines.[27]

One other American paratroop unit deserves to be mentioned as
an elite force, though it saw no combat in World War II. The 555th
Parachute Infantry Battalion, the "Triple Nickles," was an all-black
formation, trained to the highest paratroop standards at Fort Benning
in the winter of 1943–44. If anything, the 555th had to meet higher
standards than the average volunteer paratroop unit, since it was an
important social experiment: a black elite combat unit in an army in
which, while blacks certainly served, they often did so in non-combat,
often menial roles. Such exceptions as there were, for example the all-
black 332d Fighter Group (the "Tuskegee Airmen"), or the 758th Light
Tank Battalion, faced discrimination even in the attempt to get into
combat. Though the 555th was entirely black, including its officers,
the intention was to integrate it as all new parachute battalions were
commonly integrated into an existing (all-white) parachute division.
The 555th was built into a unit too late for European combat (it surely
would have served in Japan had that been necessary), but it was called
upon in 1945 for hazardous duty as "smoke jumpers," paratroop
firefighters used to fight forest fires in the Pacific Northwest, some of
which, at least, had been caused by Japanese balloon-borne fire bombs.
Ironically, in early 1946, the 555th was attached for administrative
purposes to the 82d Airborne Division, and when that division was
given a hero's welcome parading down Fifth Avenue in New York on
January 14, 1946, the 555th, 350-strong, marched with them, wearing
both the red and green Belgian fourragère and the orange lanyard for
the Netherlands which had been bestowed on the 82d for, respectively,
the Battle of the Bulge and Market-Garden, though not a man of the

555th had reached Europe. The divisional commander, James Gavin (by then a Maj. Gen.), had ordered that all in the division would wear those symbols. The 555th would go on to be fully integrated in the 82d, but that post-war story falls beyond our chronological limits.[28]

Whatever the issues regarding their contributions to various campaigns, there can at least be no question that paratrooper units were elites, and intended to be so from the first. Their spirit was undeniable, and it was something not to be forgotten. As Webster, still a corporal (acting sergeant) after three years in the 506th Parachute Infantry Regiment, put it: "The paratroops were life itself, life and death and the thrill of conquering yourself by jumping from an airplane. I would miss the din and clamor, the foul-mouthed good humor, the sound of marching men, the wild excitement as I went out the door and fell a hundred feet before the chute opened . . ."[29] But "Airborne Divisions" were given that designation rather than "Paratroop Divisions" for a reason: by no means all of their units went into battle under parachutes.

An important component of the first American airborne divisions was their glider regiments. As noted above, each division contained one parachute infantry regiment but two of glider-borne infantry. Other parachute and glider sub-units were assigned artillery, medical, engineer, ordnance and signal responsibilities, bringing each division to a total of 8,825 officers and men.[30] All paratroopers, officers and men alike, were carefully selected volunteers, and trained to an elite status. In the case of gliders, however, a distinction must be made between glider pilots and glider infantry.

American gliders were generally small and carried a pilot and co-pilot when possible. As a result, the pilots represented about 7 percent of each glider regiment. Such pilots were supposed to be volunteers as well, though it did not always come about quite that way. John Lowden flunked out of power pilot training, and was assigned to a quartermaster company where the executive officer suggested the glider pilot program to him; Lowden turned the idea down, and was assigned to take inventory of a warehouse full of GI blankets. "There were hundreds stacked in a warehouse with a corrugated-steel roof, where the temperature was in the 90s by mid-morning. I spent five days taking inventory, and the morning of the sixth found me standing in front of the executive officer's desk," ready to volunteer for glider training.[31] However motivated or persuaded to volunteer, these pilots were officers only if they already had officer rank. The Air Corps ruled that "only power pilots could be commissioned officers and that only commissioned officers could command an aircraft in flight!"[32] According to a compromise of November, 1942, all glider pilots were at least "flight officers," a new rank created especially for this purpose, equivalent to today's "warrant officer." Most of the pilots—unlike the glider infantrymen—were actually volunteers, however, for a variety of reasons: they wanted to fly but had failed in one program or another, or were too old, or did not pass the physical tests, or wanted to escape the infantry or another apparently undesirable outfit, or, in the case of a few men, had enjoyed civilian glider experience. Though in general glider pilots were given only minimal combat training, they went into harm's way since they took their unarmored and fragile craft into often dangerous landing zones, and their losses were considerable.

Glider pilots were trained first in a civilian elementary flying school under contract to the Army Air Corps, learning the basics of aircraft control in a Piper Cub or other light plane, practicing particularly in simulated glider flight with the engine off (at first there were very few gliders with which to train). After roughly forty hours of this, they moved on to basic glider school, using such civilian gliders as were available, or, by mid-1943 anyway, the Waco CG-4A glider which was to be the principal American combat glider. The transition from Piper Cubs or delicate civilian gliders was substantial: the CG-4A had an eighty-four-foot wingspan for a forty-eight-foot fuselage, nearly as big, in other words, as the C-47s generally used to tow the gliders, but without the engines which gave it power and effective controls. Once this beast was mastered, the pilots were assigned to Troop Carrier Command elements, mainly at Fort Bragg, North Carolina, to practice such demanding skills as formation flying behind towplanes and night landings, before being sent on to Europe.[33]

Glider pilots were in a sort of limbo, denied the respect given to power pilots, but clearly faced with demanding choices and much responsibility for the thirteen men the Waco could carry (the glider itself was recognized as basically expendable, though it would be recovered for further use if this proved possible). But glider infantry clearly were not elite troops, or at least they were not so considered by American military authorities. Glider infantry were simply infantry who had been assigned to glider duty, without any element of volunteering. Their status was made very clear by the fact that all glidermen, pilots and infantrymen alike, were denied both the flight pay given the pilots of the planes which towed the gliders into battle or the hazardous pay given paratroopers. They wore no special insignia aside from the glider wings given the pilots, nor were they issued the parachutes given to aircrew (and, obviously, to paratroopers). Nor—a most symbolic point—were they initially allowed to wear the distinctive paratroop "jump boots." Though by late 1943 the Army had activated eleven glider infantry regiments along with another ten glider artillery battalions (and set out to train six thousand glider pilots), it was only in mid-1944 that glider troops were given the extra $50 per month for enlisted men and $100 for officers which the paratroopers were paid for hazardous duty. At the same time, glider troops were permitted a special silver badge similar to that of paratroopers but which replaced the parachute symbol with a CG-4A glider (pilots had silver wings with a "G" in the center—standing for "guts," they always claimed). Even then, glidermen seemed to be very much on the low end of combat decorations. In Gerard Devlin's opinion, "For some undisclosed reason there seemed to be a belief in most higher headquarters that glider pilots were incapable of personal heroics on the battlefield."[34] Glider pilot Lowden's conclusion: "We were expendable, so why bother with overseas training in ground combat?"[35]

The first serious action seen by American glider forces was at Sicily, and the result was even more disastrous than that experienced by the paratroops. "Because of strong winds, inexperienced pilots, and faulty calculations of the lead tow planes' navigators, sixty-nine gliders ended up in the windswept, white-capped sea. Forty-nine were never seen again. Sixty-eight of the 137 gliders made it to solid ground, but only thirteen of those reached their assigned landing zone."[36] So extensive was the failure of both gliders and paratroops to perform their assigned missions that after the invasion General Eisenhower wrote to Army Chief of Staff Marshall to argue that the airborne regiments should be broken into self-contained units no larger than augmented regiments (i.e., regimental combat teams). Had his advice been taken, the five airborne divisions then in existence (11th, 13th, 17th, 82d, and 101st) would very probably have lost their glider components, and the programs then in place for the glider construction and the training of glider pilots would have disappeared. Instead, Marshall ordered a new focus on training and combat procedures, and by the end of 1943, glider-parachute maneuvers in North Carolina had won the approval of key witnesses, including Lieutenant General McNair. The glider forces would go on to further glory—and losses—in Normandy, southern France, Holland, Germany, New Guinea, and the Philippines. Volunteer glider pilots took badly needed doctors and supplies into the American pocket at Bastogne in the Battle of the Bulge, for example, in an extraordinary if little-noted mission.[37] When the war ended, the United States had constructed nearly fifteen thousand gliders for its more than six thousand pilots; by the end of 1945, only one glider regiment, the 82d Airborne's 325th Glider Infantry, remained on active duty, and by 1953, the U.S. Army no longer had a glider capability.[38]

One elite glider unit of World War II deserves special notice. This was the 5318th Air Unit, a secret formation which was activated in mid-1943 in order to give support to the operations in Burma conducted behind Japanese lines by the British "Chindit" force commanded by Maj. Gen. Orde Wingate. The initiative for this support formation had come from President Roosevelt himself, who had been most impressed by Wingate's own account of what could be done in Burma, which he delivered in person to Roosevelt, Churchill and their top commanders at the Quebec Conference of mid-August, 1943. Army Air Force commander Gen. Hap Arnold gave command of the unit, code-named "Project Nine" for security reasons, to Col. Philip C. Cochran, a colorful character well-known to the American public in the form of "Colonel Flip Corkin," hero of Milton Caniff's popular comic strip, "Terry and the Pirates."[39]

Cochran's multi-purpose unit included 175 gliders, a number of C-47 and C-54 transports, and one hundred light planes of various types. But Cochran also had a powerful strike force that included thirty P-51A Mustangs and twenty B-25H (Mitchell) fast medium bombers which could at least in some ways approximate the artillery support that Allied forces in Burma lacked in contrast to their Japanese opponents. Cochran's command even incorporated six prototype Sikorsky helicopters, the first American military helicopters to be used operationally. Wingate's Chindits much appreciated the new force, believing, with some justification, that their own independent-minded Royal Air Force would have been less likely to subordinate their strategic goals to Chindit tactical needs as did Cochran's unit.[40]

For Cochran's glider force, one hundred glider pilots were selected from among two hundred trained volunteers (already volunteers in the first place, at least in theory); they were told only that they were being organized for a dangerous overseas combat mission, with no idea of the locale. The chosen pilots were given special training in a six-week commando course at Goldsboro, North Carolina. When their training was concluded, they proceeded to India. At Pangarah, north of Calcutta, with one hundred glider mechanics, all now formed into the "1st Air Commando Group," they assembled the gliders they would use to support Wingate from two bases in the Imphal Valley in Assam near the Burma frontier.

Their operations over the next few months were as harrowing as those of the men they supported, for their gliders had to be landed in remote jungle locations and then whenever possible "snatched" back into the air, often loaded with wounded Chindits, by a special cable retrieval method, and thus to be used again if still serviceable. By the time the Chindits were finally withdrawn from Burma for rest and recovery in India, the Air Commando's glider detachment had flown ninety-six sorties, mostly at night. Their record, and that of a later arrived 2d Air Commando Group which supported British General Slim's operations in Burma, deserves to be noted as an elite group.

Like commandos and paratroopers, gliders seemed a weapon of the future, and every American branch of service tried its hand at establishing such a force. The Marines began their quest shortly after German gliders seemed to have had such success in taking the island of Crete.[41] In July 1941, Marine Corps Commandant Maj. Gen. Thomas Holcomb issued a call for fifty officers and one hundred NCOs to volunteer to be glider pilots, and a training program was soon initiated. The initial plan was to establish a glider battalion in each regiment, but progress, particularly in obtaining gliders, was slow, and the program was soon reduced to a total of two battalions, one on each American coast. In May 1943, however, the entire program was terminated; the officers and men, who did not yet total three hundred in all, were more urgently needed for operations against the Japanese, where glider operations "would be about as useful on the Pacific islands as pogo sticks."[42] A separate Navy program in the end actually flew the largest American glider made during the war (109 feet in length, designed to carry eighty men), but none were ever used in combat.

On the whole, it seems fair to state that the glidermen, pilots and passengers alike, fell into a sort of limbo, given special, very dangerous responsibilities to be carried out in conjunction with recognized elites, but themselves denied that same elite status for too long—and even then acknowledged rather grudgingly. It is certainly true that an individual gliderman did not have that final responsibility to jump out an aircraft door and control his own fate with his parachute risers on the way down (assuming he was not what was known as a "streamer"), and perhaps if his glider made it safely to the landing zone and did not crash into forest or rock or hedgerow or (in Normandy) "Rommel's asparagus," stout poles set in likely landing fields, he might even go into action as part of a functioning squad or platoon. Still, the odds were not favorable for combat landings in the face of such obstacles as bad weather, night conditions, anti-aircraft fire, aroused enemy opposition on the ground, even friendly fire, and it seems fair to say that the glidermen deserved more credit than they have generally received. Perhaps had they all been volunteers from the start, their reputation would be better known, but that was not to be.

The same August 1943 Quebec Conference which authorized the 1st Air Commando unit to supply Wingate's Chindits also approved the formation of an American ground combat force of three battalions, totalling roughly 2,830 officers and men, which would join the fighting in the China-Burma-India Theater in a manner similar to, but separate from, Wingate's operation. The operation was given the intriguing codename Galahad; the unit itself, on the other hand, was designated rather unromantically as the "5307th Composite Unit (Provisional)." A formation of this size would normally have been a regiment, but as will be seen it was soon to be commanded by a general, and generals do not command regiments—hence the provisional "unit." Recruitment was of volunteers from jungle-trained and jungle-experienced troops, hence "composite"; the force was "provisional" since it was only expected to exist for the few months in which Wingate would be conducting his operations. All in all they were a tough crew, and some knew well what jungle fighting was like.

About a third of the men were veterans of Guadalcanal and other operations in the South and Southwest Pacific commands. Another third came from the Caribbean Defense Command with service on Trinidad and Puerto Rico, and the final element came from trained ground force units in the United States. Initial training and organization were in the hands of Lt. Col. Charles N. Hunter (USMA 1929), the senior volunteer officer and a former combat and weapons instructor at Fort Benning's Infantry School; with three years in the Philippines with the 45th Infantry Philippine Scout Regiment and two and a half years in the Canal Zone with the 14th Infantry, he was well qualified for this job. The original two battalions ("Casual Detachments 1688 A and B") sailed from San Francisco in September 1943 on the converted luxury liner *Lurline,* picking up the Pacific volunteers at Noumea, New Caledonia (670 combat veterans) and at Brisbane (270 more men, of whom only about fifty-five had actually been in combat), before proceeding to Bombay, arriving at the end of October. The South Pacific and Southwest Pacific Theater veterans at first were formed into the unit's rather cocky 3d Battalion; later, to their disgust, the jungle veterans were distributed throughout the command.[43]

Once in India, the unit came under the overall command of Gen. Joseph W. Stilwell, commander of American forces, such as they were, in CBI (China-Burma-India), Mountbatten's deputy supreme commander of the theater, commander in chief of Chinese forces in India and, finally, Chinese leader Chiang Kai-shek's chief of staff: quite enough in total to make him "the best symbol of the fundamental disharmony of Anglo-American aims in South-East Asia."[44] Stilwell was at once determined to remove these newly arrived American troops from the hands of the British, meaning Wingate, under whose immediate command they had first been placed, and after some difficulty finally persuaded Mountbatten to turn them over to his control. The unit had proven to be rather unruly, hardly an unknown result of creating a volunteer formation, earning a notorious reputation with the Indian Military Police for various wondrous deeds, including flagging down and commandeering an express train on the Great Indian Peninsula Railway for unauthorized leave to Bombay. Mountbatten is supposed to have said, "For God's sake, take them off my hands!" Or, as a unit ditty put it:

> The Five-Three-Oh-Seventh Com Unit, Provisional,
> Sinned on a scale that was super-Divisional.[45]

In January 1944 Lieutenant General Stilwell appointed to command of the 5307th one of his favorite staff officers, Brig. Gen. Frank D. Merrill (USMA, also 1929). Merrill was a genial cavalry officer who had specialized in the study of the Japanese language but had little experience of infantry command or active operations in general; his position at the time was Stilwell's G-3 or assistant chief of staff for Plans and Operations. Though initially popular, he was not a great choice, not least because of persistent heart trouble (of which Stilwell was well aware) and, at least in Hunter's view, "a rather subservient attitude toward his superiors." The nickname given the unit by *Time* and *Life* correspondent James Shapley, "Merrill's Marauders," indeed proved rather inappropriate. Merrill was not lacking in courage and did his best to withstand the strain of jungle operations, but for most of the brief history of the 5307th Merrill had to leave the field command to Colonel Hunter (Hunter was promoted to full colonel in early 1944), a fine commander but a man who was decidedly not in Stilwell's favor. The feeling was mutual; indeed Hunter found that both Stilwell and Merrill with their long experience of the East and its languages "had a discouraging way of thinking with an Oriental slant . . ."[46]

The interaction of the Allied high command in the Far East is not an appealing story, but it has been well delineated by others and may be avoided here except to note that it certainly did not make operations in Burma any easier. In particular, the Marauders had no love for Stilwell, who seemed to take little interest in the unit once it was under his control. As one Marauder put it, "[Stilwell] avoided the Marauders before, during, and after the great victories [of the Marauders against the Japanese], even though our efforts had won him a fourth star."[47] Hunter in his own rather bitter post-war memoirs made it clear that in his mind the unit in the end was "expanded to bolster the ego of an erstwhile Theater Commander such as 'Vinegar Joe' Stilwell."[48] Stilwell's defenders may claim, as does Gary Bjorge, that the 5307th was the victim not of Stilwell's ego, "but that both the 5307th and Stilwell were affected by the exigencies and requirements of coalition warfare and combined operations," but this seems an inadequate explanation for the unnecessarily high losses which the unit took in the end from causes other than combat.[49]

After a demoralizing three-week stay at a transit camp at Deolali, north of Bombay, in November 1943 the three battalions at last moved to Deogarh to spend nine weeks in a searing, dry, rugged, thorn-covered landscape, little resembling Burma, about three hundred miles south of New Delhi. Here, still technically under the command of Wingate, who chose the location but never visited it during the Marauders' stay, they began serious training in long-range penetration tactics, stressing marksmanship, patrolling, map reading, celestial navigation for night movements, radio and cipher procedures, all in addition to increasingly demanding route marches. Each battalion was divided into two "combat teams" which could operate independently; each team was broken down into three rifle platoons, a heavy weapons platoon, a pioneer and demolition platoon, a reconnaissance platoon, and a medical detachment—sixteen officers and 456 enlisted men in all. Each team was equipped with 81mm and 60mm mortars, 2.56-inch rocket launchers, and heavy and light machine guns in addition to the normal infantry weapons. Rifle platoon tactics were at a premium, since it was expected that most operations would be particularly demanding at that level; the men had also to become familiar with the mules and horses which would be their basic means of supply transport. But the unit's ultimate purpose was not explained to the men. "The British made no effort to teach us anything about the proposed operation in Burma. No books or maps were available, and no instruction was given about the political situation in China, India, Burma, or any Asian country. To most of the infantrymen, Burma was a total mystery." At least in the new year, with the arrival of General Merrill, food, clothing, and conditions generally improved.[50]

Within the unit as a whole, there was an inner elite: the intelligence and reconnaissance (I&R) platoons, one of about fifty men for each battalion, which were expected to roam up to twenty-four hours' marching time ahead of the parent unit, to find the enemy in the first instance, preferably without becoming engaged. James Hopkins, the 3d Battalion's surgeon, describes the process: "The men were carefully selected by their respective platoon leaders. Intelligence, strength, endurance, enthusiasm, leadership, loyalty, common sense, health, and past record all played a part in the selection process. Above all, the men had to volunteer to become members of these important units."[51] The battalions trained separately, and rather desperately sought some symbol which could give them a shared identity. Hopkins's 3d Battalion, for example, proved expert at finding extra food and thus won the sobriquet "Chow Raiders," adopting as a badge the small collapsible can opener which came with "10-in-1" field rations. "For the group—with no logical name, no flag, no colors, no history, no chaplain, no dentist, no recreational facilities, no post exchange, no leave, inadequate transportation, inadequate facilities for personal hygiene, poor general health, and many months without female companionship—this small can opener provided a prized insignia. It was worn with pride, pinned to the lapel of our fatigue jackets."[52]

By early February 1944, the entire unit assembled at Ledo in Assam's Brahmaputra Valley. Ledo would be their principle base in the coming attempt to reopen communications through to China from

Bhamo on the Burma Road; the "Ledo Road" was expected to replace the Rangoon-China route now severed by the Japanese. Ledo was some three hundred air miles from Bhamo, across most difficult terrain, memorable for such features as six-foot-high razor-edged elephant grass, malaria, dysentery, "Naga sores" induced by leeches, dengue fever, and mite-borne typhus; meanwhile the men lived mainly on air-dropped "K-rations" (never had K-rations been intended for a sustained diet), all of which meant very high casualty rates from non-combat causes. Not surprisingly, Merrill himself became seriously ill and was evacuated at the end of March, recovered sufficiently to return to his base camp in April, but had to be evacuated once again a few weeks later.[53]

The end goal of the campaign over the next four months (February–May 1944) was Myitkyina in North Burma's Hukawng valley, the nearest railhead connecting to Rangoon and the head of navigation on the Irrawaddy River. The airfield here served as the main Japanese base for attacking American planes as they carried supplies for China over the "Hump," and its loss would be a definite blow to Japanese efforts in North Burma. Not surprisingly, once the purpose of the attack was evident, the Japanese concentrated substantial forces to defend this hamlet and its nearby strategic airstrip; the official American history estimates that at least 4,600 Japanese fought in this battle, the peak strength at any one time being about 3,500 men.[54] The mission of the Marauders, together with some Kachin guerrilla units, was to guide and assist the 88th and 150th Chinese Infantry Regiments in making the attack, and in particular to seize the airfield, after which they were told they would be evacuated by air in the same transports designated to bring in Chinese reinforcements.

This final battle for the Marauders was not well planned or executed. Stilwell had given complete control over the "Myitkyina Task Force" to Merrill, briefly (and, considering the state of his health, inexplicably) back in the field, relegating Colonel Hunter to the command of one of the attacking columns.[55] The airfield was captured soon enough (May 17) in a surprise attack, but then the two hundred Marauders considered still fit for battle were left in place to continue operations against the town. Stilwell, who had kept the operation secret from Mountbatten, had Col. John E. McCammon flown in on May 18 and (rather irregularly) promoted him to brigadier to take command of all Chinese (at the time, four infantry regiments) and American units in the area, bypassing Colonel Hunter, who was left in command of the three now-reunited battalions of Merrill's Marauders, still the "5307th Composite Unit (Provisional)." McCammon, technically Merrill's second in command and executive officer, had just been released from a hospital, was suffering from pleurisy, and had little current knowledge of either the operation or the troops he was supposed to command. He lasted one week, and then was replaced by Brig. Gen. Hayden Boatner, Stilwell's deputy and chief of staff. "Galahad is just shot . . . put Boatner in command, he took hold at once," recorded Stilwell on May 30, but on June 15, "Either our officers are all rotten, or else Boatner is getting hysterical. I'll have to go down." When Stilwell did drop in, he was most fortunate not to have been shot by his own men, who clearly hated him. Boatner lasted only until malaria felled him in late June, when, finally, Hunter was placed in command of what was left of the U.S. forces at Myitkyina.[56]

The Allied forces found the Japanese to be tenacious indeed, and every pocket had to be cleaned out by intense fighting. It did not help that two battalions of the 150th Chinese Regiment mistook each other for Japanese and inflicted disastrous casualties. Rain poured down, Myitkyina became a quagmire, and the remaining Marauders were decimated by disease. Some 1,300 of the original force of 3,000 had reached the airfield (about 2,500 had actually set out on the march), after having fought through roughly five hundred miles of Burma. By the time the town of Myitkyina was taken on August 3, only about two hundred of those who began the march were there to see it. Hopkins, who had first-hand knowledge of the medical history of the Marauders, estimates that over the course of their existence, the Marauders had suffered over 80 percent casualties and was finished as a fighting unit.[57]

British historian Shelford Bidwell, writing nearly four decades later, pointed out one reason for the breakdown: "The treatment of the sick and wounded, many of whom Stilwell's staff had attempted to hustle back into action half-healed or half-cured, became a scandal. The administration and the welfare of the men was a disgrace and conditions at the convalescent depot so bad that the men rioted. . . . The scandal of Galahad's treatment was hushed up, conditions improved, medals were distributed . . ." Bidwell was only echoing the official history, which in turn relied on after-action investigation by the inspector general: "Extremely heavy moral pressure, just short of outright orders, was placed on medical officers to return to duty or keep in the line every American who could pull a trigger." The end result, by

June 1, was "almost complete breakdown of morale in the major por-
tion of the unit."[58] Bjorge offers what must be the only explanation
which holds plausibility: "As the only American combat unit within
the combined force, Galahad could not avoid being given the special
burdens that came from being Americans. . . . Their participation in
operations was necessary to encourage the units of other nations to
stay in the struggle and to fight hard. The 5307th was the means by
which the American field commander, General Stilwell, showed that
he was not asking more of his coalition partners than he was asking of
American soldiers. What was especially damaging to the 5307th was
that . . . it was the only U.S. combat unit under Stilwell's command. It
had to bear America's fighting burden alone. Eventually, and perhaps
inevitably, it collapsed under the weight of its combined load."[59]

Decorations were indeed distributed. No Marauder was awarded
the Medal of Honor, but six received the Distinguished Service Cross,
and a number of officers and men received other decorations, including the Legion of Merit, the Silver Star, and the Bronze Star.[60] The unit
as a whole, which with considerable dispatch was disbanded on August 10 after an abortive attempt to replace its diminished numbers
with raw replacements (New Galahad), was awarded the Distinguished
Unit Citation and the battle-honor "Myitkyina." No effort was made
by Stilwell to express his thanks or congratulations to the unit.[61] The
5307th's veterans were transferred into the 475th Infantry Regiment,
which preserved Marauder battle honors. The 475th was deactivated
in China in mid-1945, but activated again in 1954–56. In 1969, the
adjutant general recognized the 5307th as the parent organization of
the 75th Ranger Regiment, which incorporated Marauder insignia as
their distinctive uniform emblem and on their organizational flag.[62]

The actual contribution which the Chindits and Marauders made
to the Burma war will no doubt long remain a subject of debate. There
can be little question, however, that despite their rather casual origins,
the Marauders were formed into an effective unit (mostly by Colonel
Hunter), and fought the veteran Japanese forces operating in Northern
Burma on an equal basis. It is certainly the case that for six months the
Marauders were the only American infantry forces fighting on the Asian
mainland, indeed, the first to do so since the days of the Boxers. Given
the nature of their accomplishments under very trying conditions, to
which were added the complications of inter-allied squabbling and poor
decision-making in higher leadership echelons, by the time the Ma-

rauders passed into history, they surely deserved the title of "elite." Perhaps Colonel Hunter, who, though awarded the Silver Star by Stilwell, was packed off to duty in Washington D.C., and retired—still a colonel—in 1959, should have the last word: "Galahad force was the most beat upon, most misunderstood, most mishandled, most written about, most heroic and yet most unrewarded regimental sized unit that participated in World War II."[63]

The special demands of jungle fighting produced another American elite which demonstrated an interesting point: such a unit might be established through little more than the accidents of time and place— and then find that its specially honed skills were put to little or no use. One such was the 158th Infantry Regiment, an Arizona National Guard formation whose patrimony reached back to the 1st Infantry Regiment, Arizona Volunteers, formed in late 1865. Three-quarters of a century later, the unit contained not only many Mexican-Americans, but also members of more than twenty Indian tribes. Early in World War II, the 158th, about 1,900 men in all, was sent for training to the Panama Canal Zone, where it was brought up to strength with about three hundred men drawn from other Guard units and some three hundred others from the 5th and 14th regular infantry regiments. Regulars and guardsmen did not meld easily, and the tension was considerable, providing the unit's commander, Col. J. Prugh Herndon—a man noted for iron discipline who had commanded the 158th since 1932—with a considerable challenge. Herndon had another important attribute: his understanding and appreciation of Indian life, for it seems that he had been the first to see the possibility of Indians of the various tribes communicating with fellow members in their own languages, and thus thoroughly confounding enemy intelligence efforts. In pre-war Arizona training camps, and in maneuvers in Louisiana in 1940, he had demonstrated the effectiveness of the scheme using Papagos and Pimas (who spoke the same language), Apaches, and Navajos. The exclusive use of such "code-talkers" has long been claimed by the Marines, but in fact that was not the case.[64]

Until Pearl Harbor, units serving in Panama made little use of the difficult jungle surrounding them; they trained according to accepted schedules for direct assaults as practiced in World War I and thought little of jungle combat, and meanwhile "did their fighting in the scurvy bars of Panama City, Balboa, and Cristobal Colon."[65] Now, however, the regiment was selected for training in jungle warfare on the basis of reports returned from Malaya and the Philippines on Japanese capabilities in such combat. At first a single platoon was chosen and placed under Capt. Cresson Kearny (Rhodes Scholar, reserve captain, and great grandson of Gen. Philip Kearny of Mexican and Civil War fame). The intention was to train this force in infiltration techniques for individuals and small units for penetration in rugged jungle conditions, and indeed Panama furnished all that was required in that respect. Kearny required initiative, independence, superior physical fitness, and aggressiveness from his men, in addition, as he explained in a summary report of March 1943 just as the regiment was sent to Australia, to "the ability to make long marches, the ability to advance, attack, defend and maneuver in the jungle . . . perfection in scouting and patrolling, and in use of cover and concealment; and the ability to operate in the jungle for considerable periods of time, conserving and using only his initial supplies and rations."[66] Nat Burrows, a reporter from the *Chicago Daily News*, coined the phrase "Bushmasters" in reports from Panama to his paper, and the name stuck with the men themselves. By the time they left Panama, the 158th, now expanded to around five thousand men, were all trained in the same procedures, expecting to serve as typical commandos in a jungle setting.

As it turned out, the 158th served in the New Guinea area, experiencing its first combat in early 1944 at Arawe, New Britain Island. After enlargement in March to the 158th Regimental Combat Team, the unit saw considerable action at Wadke-Sarmi, New Guinea and in the Luzon campaign in the Philippines where it lost nearly 25 percent of its men by death or injury, finally being deactivated in January 1946. Little of its combat time actually took the form of behind-the-lines, commando-style infiltration, aside from reconnaissance patrols. The main reason for this was the different tactical approaches used by Japanese and Americans. Anthony Arthur explains: "The Americans attacked in force during the day and hunkered down at night within their defensive perimeters. The Japanese, outnumbered and outgunned, fought delaying actions when they had to in daytime and attacked at night. The Americans shot at anything that moved after dark, including not only the enemy but water buffalo and GIs outside the perimeter. Extended fighting patrols such as those envisioned in Panama were consequently not common . . ."[67]

There is little doubt that the 158th RCT fought well in their several campaigns, aided by their unique communication abilities, though these seem to have attracted little historical attention. Similarly, the service of nisei (second-generation Japanese-Americans) soldiers in Europe with the 442d Regiment (discussed below) may be well known, but that is less true of a small detachment trained not in Panama but in several language schools in the United States, which served with the 158th as translators of documents and in prisoner interrogation—not an easy assignment, given the fact that nisei looked like enemy soldiers to virtually every GI serving in the Pacific. Overall, the 158th appears to have been rather unique. Trained in commando-style tactics, it never made maximum use of its skills, though through no fault of its own; nevertheless, the lesson is clear again that American World War II elites, intended or actual, were formed of men expected to demonstrate individual expertise and initiative in the continuing Ranger tradition.

Before departing the Far Eastern/Pacific Theaters, note should be taken of two relatively small formations which were part of the war in the air. The first demonstrates again that military elites were not always what they have been made to appear through media attention and popular history. This was the unit known popularly as the "Flying Tigers," but more officially as the 1st American Volunteer Group, a collection of some 300–350 pilots, ground crew, and assorted staff who fought the Japanese on behalf of China from early 1941 to mid-1942, at which time the unit was absorbed into the United States Army Air three hundred Japanese aircraft destroyed, usually in the face of very superior odds and at a time when few other Americans were in successful combat with any enemy. As a result the "Flying Tigers" not surprisingly became the stuff of military myth.[68] There is little question that the "AVG," as its members preferred to call themselves until after their experience was over, were significantly better at what they did than their Japanese Army Air Force opponents. The question is why that was so.

The AVG had its origin in China's desperate need for foreign expertise to aid in the development of the Chinese Air Force (CAF), which as a rule fared very badly against the Japanese. In early 1941, a request was made to the United States for assistance, and a positive response was approved by President Roosevelt himself. However, since the United States was not yet at war, any personnel would by necessity be private citizens on individual contracts, and all volunteers who came from various branches of the United States military would have to resign their official positions (in theory, they would be entitled to reinstatement without loss of precedence when the contract expired or the United States went to war).[69] This procedure was only possible when orders came from on high to permit and facilitate the process. Moreover, the several American military veterans who worked as recruiters for the CAF were allowed to visit continental military bases and speak with active military personnel. Their offer to pilots was for pay of $600 per month with a bonus of $500 for every Japanese plane destroyed—in 1941, exceedingly good wages by any standard, and money was certainly a strong incentive.

Eventually just over one hundred pilots and two hundred ground crew were recruited and sent off to the China-India-Burma theater. Not all lasted out their year's contract: twenty-two pilots and forty-three ground crew dropped out for various reasons (a 25 percent failure rate), while only about half of the one hundred planes were still flyable, often in very poor repair.[70] The volunteers were not necessarily chosen because they were elite, but rather because they were willing to volunteer. Some joined out of a spirit of adventure, but at least as many believed that Asian duty was likely to be less dangerous than the war in Europe, which America was expected to join in the very near future. Still others doubted the likelihood of fighting the Germans, and wished to see action against Japan, and in the process fly the state-of-the-art Curtiss P-40 fighters which had been promised to China. Greg Boyington, a Marine Corps regular first lieutenant who later would return to the Corps and become famous as a fighter ace, joined because his penchant for alcohol and trouble-making had landed him in serious debt. Finally, some joined out of boredom (one flying boat pilot, for example, had washed out of flying the fighters he yearned for), others simply to escape the discipline of an army or navy uniform.

The AVG's leader was Claire Lee Chennault, a colorful man to head a colorful outfit. A tough and difficult Louisiana Cajun, Chennault remains hard to fathom despite more than two dozen biographies of this well-known war hero. He was a pre-war fighter pilot of considerable fame who organized the Air Corps' aerobatic team and thought out new tactical methods, but who saw few prospects as a captain with health problems in the interwar service. In 1937 he retired, and through connections made in his barnstorming years took a job as chief advisor to the Chinese Air Force at the incredible salary for that time of $,1000 per month (plus expenses). The Chinese promoted him to colonel, and, after an abortive effort to form a mercenary International Squadron, placed him in charge of recruiting American pilots and ground crew to man the one hundred P-40C fighters which the United States sold to China. This was in the spring of 1941, and the first recruits arrived in Rangoon at the end of July. Most of the pilots were Navy-trained, and six came from the Marines; the Army provided fewer than half.[71] Chennault constructed a "kindergarten" for his men at Keydaw Aerodrome in Burma, with training on the P-40s and in such essential subjects as the geography of China-Burma and Japanese tactics and equipment.[72] When the Pearl Harbor attack occurred, Chennault's small force was thus in a very unique position, already taking the battle directly to the Japanese—though they were still in the employ of China and remained so until mid-1942 when the group was disbanded.[73]

There is no question that the AVG was badly outnumbered as it fought off the Japanese first in Burma and then in China. What it did have in its favor, however, was Chennault's tactical understanding (Chennault himself did not lead his men in battle), and the P-40. The Tomahawk was not much use above twenty thousand feet, which is why it was not desired in Europe where much combat would occur above that height, but it was sturdy, heavily armed, and adequately protected with both self-sealing fuel tanks and armor plate behind the pilot. Japanese planes had greater mobility and faster speed in level flight, so it was inadvisable to duel with them in "dogfights," but as Chennault realized, the P-40 could outdive Japanese fighters while attacking them and then survive high-stress pullouts to return quickly to altitude for another pass at the enemy. Individual combat, the stuff of the Battle of Britain, was discouraged; Chennault's men fought in pairs, a lead plane which attacked and a wingman who protected his tail: the two hands of a boxer, Chennault liked to explain. His tactics were disdained by Royal Air Force pilots who disapproved of refusing a challenge to a "dogfight," to their severe cost over Burma, but properly executed, Chennault's tactics worked for the AVG. As Jerome Klinkowitz remarks, while such tactics did not even the odds, they "did account for the wildly disproportionate number of Flying Tiger kills to losses." The weight of the armor and other modifications added to the original production model P-40 did give the P-40C an unfortunate habit of spinning end over end on occasion, and unless a pilot had enough altitude to get out of a spin the result was likely to be unfortunate. With a tendency to groundloop and a "hot" landing speed, for the time, of 100 mph, it was easy enough to pile up the plane on the ground, and there were far too few of them—and too few spare parts or pilots—for that luxury. Once in action, the AVG's P-40s were decorated with shark's teeth after AVG pilot Charles Bond saw a magazine picture of a similarly decorated Australian fighter in North Africa. The name "Flying Tigers" (*fei-hu* in Chinese) had nothing to do with the decoration; it was contributed by the Chinese press and only later after Walt Disney's illustrators had developed an appropriate leaping tiger insignia did it become popular with the unit itself.[74]

The unit's end in mid-1942 was less than epic. Chennault wanted all his men to join the USAAF (which had given him the rank of brigadier general), and applied much pressure to achieve this end—and considerable harassment of those who declined. But the unit was credited with 296 kills (historian Daniel Ford considers that figure to be nearly 300 percent too high), to which may be added another two hundred which the unit estimated it had destroyed on the ground. Three AVG pilots died in training, and twenty-two were lost in combat.[75] Compared to statistics from other theaters, the numbers were quite small, but the AVG's role was not inconsiderable. While it can be argued that the AVG aided the British in their retreat from Burma and the Chinese in their defense against the Japanese onslaught, above all they were Americans fighting Japanese when few others could—and, most important, they made clear that Japan's vaunted flyers were by no means invincible. Chennault and his men were deemed heroes, "aerial Sergeant Yorks," as *Newsweek* put it.[76] Many of the AVG's men received Chinese decorations, and eight pilots earned British medals for their heroism over Rangoon. Chennault himself stayed on in China, was promoted to major general, and given command of the 14th American Air Force until, after extensive conflict with his superior, Lt. Gen. Joseph Stilwell, he was recalled to Washington. After further adventures with flying in China, he died of cancer in 1958.[77] Chennault had never been easy to deal with, and he certainly was lacking in "interpersonal communication skills," but he had treated his men with respect, and under his guidance they had developed a fierce unit pride which clearly had inspired each man to do his best though they were "in some respects outcasts of their own government, doing a job their government wanted done but was not willing to do publicly," as Martha Byrd has explained.[78] Pearl Harbor changed all that—in time.

At times an elite force is created in the popular mind by a single event when in fact it is questionable whether the definition of elite fits at all. One such was the unit known as "Special Bombing Project No. 1," which in mid-April 1942 used its carrier-launched B-25 medium bombers to bomb Japan, and Tokyo in particular. The goal of taking the war home to the Japanese capital existed from December 7, 1941; the problem was how to deliver the attack. Japanese security patrols made an assault by Navy dive bombers impractical; the carriers would be discovered long before they reached a launch position within range from Japan. It fell to Navy Capt. Francis Low, chief operations officer for Adm. Ernest J. King, Chief of Naval Operations, to suggest the possibility of launching longer-range Army bombers from the deck of a carrier. Admiral King was taken with the idea and personally obtained the cooperation of Lieutenant General Arnold, and after a trial flight of two B-25s from the deck of the carrier *Hornet* to see if the scheme was practical, orders were issued in early 1942 to prepare the mission.[79]

Arnold picked as the project's commander Lt. Col. James H. Doolittle. Doolittle, a former stunt man and airplane racer, was known as a skilled airman, but he also had the intelligence and leadership abilities to carry out such a mission. Doolittle was responsible for recruiting the group, and at Arnold's suggestion approached the 17th Bombardment Group and the 17th Reconnaissance Squadron, two units which were undergoing combat training in B-25 bombers in South Carolina at the time. Doolittle had no trouble in finding volunteers from the two groups for the twenty-four crews (each B-25 required a crew of five) he wanted. The problem, however, was that the volunteers had no combat experience whatsoever and very little time to work together. Doolittle's crews, picked rather haphazardly from the pool of volunteers, were sent off to Eglin Field in Florida for a cram training course. As author James Merrill remarks, "They were not the cream of the Air Corps, not the chosen, but brave men who chose."[80]

At Eglin Field, the crews were given intensive training, most notably in taking off from a 500-foot runway, but also in cross-country flying (especially at low levels), navigation, and night flying techniques. They had one month to prepare before the final selection of sixteen crews and their planes were moved to San Francisco and loaded aboard the *Hornet*. The *Hornet* with her escorts (Task Group 16.2) departed the Golden Gate on April 2, 1942, launching their attack on

April 18. The subsequent fate of the mission need not be discussed here; it is sufficient to say that some planes hit their scheduled targets, and some did not. Only one landed safely—in Vladivostok, Russia—while the others all crashed. Some crewmen were killed, others captured (and executed) by the Japanese, others escaped through China. The physical damage dealt to Japan was minimal, but the psychological effect was substantial, not least because it forced the Japanese to devote more resources to defense of the home islands. At the same time, the effect on American morale was very positive—once enough details of the mission were known in Washington and released to the public. Each of the aviators received the Distinguished Flying Cross. Doolittle, who parachuted to safety in China, was promoted to brigadier general and later given the Congressional Medal of Honor for organizing and leading the mission. These were ironic rewards, in a sense, because Doolittle had led just one raid in which he had lost his entire force for minimal results; on the other hand, it must be said they were well-deserved for turning a group of one hundred volunteers with minimal skills at best into a group who performed the sort of feat of which elitist legends are made.

8 World War II: The Later War

To return to the ground wars, the U.S. Army's Rangers owed their origin to the same impulse which motivated the formation of similar Marine units previously discussed. According to orders from the highest American command echelons, the Army would also emulate the British commandos, the main attraction of which was an ability to take the war to the enemy in Europe, if only in small doses. In the spring of 1942, Army Chief of Staff Marshall sent Brig. Gen. Lucien K. Truscott, Jr. to England to make arrangements for some selected American troops to take part in British commando raids against the continent. Organization of an American unit, structured along British commando lines and intended to be trained by British commandos and to operate alongside of them, soon followed. The original concept was to take men from a substantial number of units, and once their training and field experience was completed, to return them to their original formations, meanwhile rotating others through the commando structure, and thus spreading the knowledge gained as widely as possible among units which would be likely to participate in a cross-channel invasion of German-occupied territory, originally anticipated for the spring of 1943.[1]

The men to be selected were, not surprisingly, to possess outstanding physical and mental qualities, with preference going to soldiers

193

skilled in self-defense, scouting, seamanship, or demolition, and who
were familiar with radio, engineering, power plants, and the like. Bat-
talion-sized, the new force was to be trained in Northern Ireland by the
British Special Services Brigade, but administered through the newly
formed 34th Infantry Division and using American equipment (especially the new Garand M-1 rifle) and tactical doctrine wherever possible. Also, whenever possible, the unit subsisted on American rations:
breakfast of fish and tea was never popular with the Rangers.

The commander selected for the new force was Artillery Capt.
William Orlando Darby, at the time serving as aide-de-camp to Maj.
Gen. Russell Hartle who commanded American army forces in Northern Ireland; Darby was soon promoted to Major and after another ten
weeks to lieutenant colonel. Darby (USMA 1933), a well-liked and
competent officer, had served mainly in the field artillery, but he was
experienced in pack, motorized, and horse artillery units and was one
of the few officers to have participated in joint Army-Navy exercises,
including amphibious landings, in both Puerto Rico and North Carolina.[2] Truscott claimed responsibility for choosing the name "Rangers," in honor of the early American units discussed in a previous chapter, after the War Department's Chief of Operations, Brig. Gen. Dwight
D. Eisenhower, made it clear that the term "commandos" was a term
too closely associated with the British.[3]

In early June, all American units in Northern Ireland were informed of the formation of the 1st Ranger Battalion, and commanders
informed of the demanding criteria for volunteers. "Each major unit or
command was required to furnish a specified number of men of each
rank, private through captain; division and separate unit commanders
were directed to establish boards of officers to interview all volunteers
and selected personnel to determine their suitability," though Darby
himself retained a final veto, rejecting about 20 percent of the volunteers who came to his headquarters at Carrickfergus outside Belfast.[4]
Darby and the volunteer officers who passed his scrutiny interviewed
some two thousand men from the Army's V Corps. "There was no
intention of selecting a six-foot 'Guards' unit," Darby explained. "Physical condition, natural athletic ability, and stamina were sought without
regard to a man's height. . . . Looking beyond the physical, we attempted to determine whether a volunteer had good judgment and if
his desire to be a Ranger was genuine. Our interviews had the object of
weeding out the braggart and the volunteer looking for excitement but

who, in return, expected to be a swashbuckling hero who could live as he pleased if only he exhibited courage and daring in battle."[5]

As originally formed, the 1st Ranger Battalion included 488 enlisted men from thirty-four different units of a wide variety of types: infantry, field artillery, coast artillery, combat engineers, quartermasters, even a few cavalrymen. Most (60 percent) came from V Corps' two divisions: the 34th ("Red Bull") Infantry Division, a National Guard formation recruited mainly from Iowa, Nebraska, and Minnesota, and the 1st Armored Division (30 percent).[6] Actual training was done at the Commando depot at Achnacarry, in Scotland's bleak Hebrides, and it was demanding indeed, including extensive speed marches, a Ranger specialty, and live ammunition exercises (by mid-July, one Ranger had drowned and another three had been wounded by bullets or grenades). In July, a further month of training followed at Argyle with the Royal Navy to practice amphibious landings in the rugged western islands, and then on for several weeks at Dundee to practice with the Commandos in attacking coastal defenses. Meanwhile, six officers and forty-five men participated with British Commandos in support of the 2d Canadian Division's disastrous raid on Dieppe (the Canadians lost nearly 70 percent of the attacking force; from the Rangers, two officers and four enlisted men were killed and four enlisted men taken prisoner).[7]

Contrary to the original concept, Dieppe was the only operation in which the Rangers fought in association with Commandos; the need for specially trained American units in Torch, the landings in North Africa, meant that the Rangers were soon on their own. In any case there was some resistance from the Commandos themselves to including Americans in their limited-scale raids, if only because Britain had some 4,500 trained Commandos, but relatively few operations with which to keep them gainfully employed, meaning that whatever the degree of cooperation, only a small number of Americans would be able to gain commando-style battle experience. In theory, the number of operations might be increased, but here another obstacle arose in the form of British army resistance to Commandos in general, as the only soldiers actually seeing action, and garnering too much publicity in the process, for doing what many commanders thought any well-trained units could do—much the same view, in other words, that United States Marine commanders felt about the formation of raider battalions. For U.S. Army Rangers, Torch came at a good time.[8]

For Torch, the force which now was attached to the 1st Infantry Division numbered twenty-six officers and 452 enlisted men, lightly armed with BARs (Browning Automatic Rifles), M-1 rifles, some submachine guns and 30-caliber machine guns, 60mm mortars, and anti-tank rifles (soon replaced with "bazookas," hand-held anti-tank rocket-firing tubes). In North African operations, experience demonstrated that the Rangers needed greater firepower, particularly since, once their first invasion assignments were fulfilled, they tended to be used as regular infantry. Paradoxically, the addition of more firepower (heavier 81mm and 4.2-inch mortars, more and heavier machine guns, and so on) lessened mobility and tended to bring the Rangers to resemble regular infantry all the more, and, when that happened, the temptation to commanders on the ground to use them as such was often too great to resist. As Matthew King, the historian of the Rangers' North African operations puts it, "With that use came the heavier casualties that, when replaced, diluted the effectiveness of the remaining Rangers and, in turn, weakened the cohesion and effectiveness of Ranger Force," meaning all Ranger Battalions and not just Darby's Rangers.[9]

In North Africa, the 1st Ranger Battalion took part in several actions in Algeria and Tunisia, sometimes on missions appropriate to their training, but sometimes functioning as conventional infantry, including the battle of Kasserine Pass in February 1943. The Rangers moved on to Sicily on Darby's recommendation, enlarged by another two battalions (3d and 4th Rangers; the 2d and 5th Ranger Battalions were soon to be activated at Camp Forrest, Tennessee, while the 6th would be formed later in the Pacific Theater), an additional fifty officers and one thousand enlisted volunteers, the whole organized into "Ranger Force." The new Rangers were found in various replacement depots in the North African Theater, particularly Oran, again subject to Darby's veto.

Recruitment this time was a bit tougher. Darby and his officers had to tour various installations and off-duty hangouts, making numerous speeches, stressing, according to Darby, "the exacting discipline and the less glamorous sides of Ranger life" in order to attract the sort of men he wanted.[10] Though the new men were not required to have had infantry training, they did need to be in top condition and possess excellent character records. The leadership cadre of the new battalions was formed of 1st Ranger veterans who had trained in Britain and served with the Rangers in combat. Darby technically remained in command only of 1st Ranger Battalion, though the new units were attached to his own—making him, in effect, a regimental commander, though without the appropriate headquarters organization (Darby's repeated requests for such an organization, which incidentally would have had the effect of making him a full colonel, despite strong endorsement from Seventh Army Commander Maj. Gen. George S. Patton, Jr., had been repeatedly turned down by General Eisenhower).[11]

After Sicily, where the Rangers were mainly responsible for effective assaults on Porto Empedocle, Gela, and Butera, Darby added still more firepower in a cannon company (four 75mm guns on halftracks), which found a use in the Salerno and Anzio landings. The 83d Chemical Battalion was also now regularly attached to the Rangers; this unit featured heavy 4.2-inch mortars. In the Anzio campaign, the Rangers, now designated the "6615th Ranger Force (Provisional)," met disaster. In late January 1944, leading an attack made by the 3d Infantry Division at Cisterna di Littoria, all but a half-dozen of "Ranger Force," 767 men in all, were captured or killed in action against German forces that included elements from the Hermann Goering Panzer Division and the 2d Parachute *Lehr* Battalion. Though they fought most bravely, some for several weeks, in the end the 1st and 3d Ranger Battalions were overrun and annihilated.

Several reasons can be offered to explain the defeat, including serious casualties among leaders in the fighting leading up to Cisterna, the replacements for which had nothing like the same training and battlefield experience; the lack until it was too late of a headquarters to acquire intelligence, plan, and direct missions in a coherent manner; and indeed the very establishment of that headquarters which required Darby to shuffle his top officers at the last minute to create the necessary staff (both the 1st and 3d Battalions thus had brand-new commanders). To these explanations must be added shrewd German prediction of American intentions.[12] Darby himself, as a long time artilleryman, did not attempt in his memoirs to look beyond firepower for a cause: "All my soldiers were rugged raiders, but we lacked enough artillery for a fullscale defense. We were equipped to hit and run but not to stick it out in a slugging match against forces armed with medium and heavy artillery and outnumbering us at least eight to one." The problem was that the steady increase of Ranger firepower had made it even more likely that the Rangers would continue on in precisely such a conventional infantry role.[13]

"Ranger Force" did not long outlive Cisterna. Those Rangers still surviving, which included the 4th Ranger Battalion, were attached for the time being to the Canadian-American First Special Service Force (discussed below), and saw some service in the Naples area. Recent recruits to the Rangers remained with 1st SSF, but veterans returned to the United States, where in October 1944 the 1st, 3d, and 4th Rangers were deactivated at Camp Butner, North Carolina. Darby counted nineteen officers and 137 enlisted men who were sent home; at that time, eighty-seven Rangers remained in these units of the five hundred who had survived training in Scotland.[14] Darby himself, promoted to colonel after Anzio (he and his headquarters had not been lost at Cisterna), went on to other assignments, but in April 1945, as ADC (assistant division commander) of the 10th Mountain Division he was killed by German artillery fire, only two days before German forces in Italy surrendered. In May, he was promoted posthumously to brigadier general, the only Army officer to be so promoted to star rank during World War II.

The remaining Ranger battalions continued to fight on. The 2d and 5th Battalions, originally formed in Tennessee respectively in April and September 1943, landed at Normandy on D-Day, where, attached to the 116th Infantry, they were tasked with capturing the feared Pointe du Hoc (in Norman usage, Pointe du Hoe) 155mm coastal battery atop a one hundred-foot cliff in the center of Omaha Beach; they had trained extensively for this operation on the cliffs of the Isle of Wight (the Germany heavy guns, in fact, had not yet been installed). After Normandy, both battalions fought throughout the rest of the European war as conventional infantry, only occasionally being used for infiltration and other assignments more suited to their original mission, such as 2d Battalion's important establishment of a salient in German lines in the Heurtgen Forest in December 1944, and the 5th Battalion's operations in the Saar River basin in early 1945.[15]

The 6th Ranger Battalion, on the other hand, fought in the Pacific. Its origins relate to the creation, in late 1943, of an elite force known as the "Alamo Scouts" by Lt. Gen. Walter Krueger, commanding general of Sixth Army. Krueger admired the navy's underwater assault teams ("frogmen") and believed that small units composed of one officer and six enlisted men, carefully selected and trained to probe behind enemy lines, would be most useful. So it proved, and Krueger decided to create a larger force with the same mission, using the 98th Field Artillery Battalion, then serving in New Guinea, as the nucleus of his new units. In April 1944, the battalion, commanded by Lt. Col. Henry A. Mucci, was redesignated the 6th Ranger Infantry Battalion. The Rangers of this battalion were thus volunteers only to the point that Mucci encouraged all who did not wish to be Rangers to put in for transfer.[16]

Mucci's battalion saw its first combat in the Philippines, making a number of landings on Luzon and elsewhere (and also from time to time serving as Krueger's headquarters guard). The unit earned particular fame from its efforts, and performed in conjunction with two Alamo Scout teams and an eighty-man Philippine guerrilla force to liberate American and Allied prisoners from a Japanese compound and reinforcement center near Cabanatuan, Luzon, well behind enemy lines at the time. At a cost of twenty-seven Ranger and guerrilla dead, more than five hundred POWs were freed (and several hundred Japanese killed). Mucci was awarded the Distinguished Service Cross; all American officers who took part received the Silver Star; and all enlisted men, Philippine officers, and Philippine enlisted men received the Bronze Star at Gen. Douglas A. MacArthur's orders. After Cabanatuan,

TWO DAYS AFTER D-DAY, U. S. ARMY RANGERS ON THE BEACH AT NORMANDY MOVE GERMAN PRISONERS AFTER THEIR CAPTURE BY RELIEVING FORCES. THE AMERICAN FLAG SPREAD OUT BEHIND THEM WAS TO STOP THE FIRE OF FRIENDLY TANKS COMING FROM INLAND. *U.S. CENTER FOR MILITARY HISTORY.*

the 6th Rangers did not take part in combat, serving instead as Sixth Army headquarters security forces.[17]

There can be little question that the Rangers were formed as elite units, and were sometimes used as such. No Ranger was awarded the Medal of Honor, but many received other medals, and twenty-seven Rangers received battlefield commissions; the 1st Battalion was twice the recipient of a Presidential Citation for gallantry, and the 3d once. While six battalions served in the war, the Rangers never had any central organization or command structure, meaning that their missions, and the use to which they were put, depended entirely upon the commanders of the larger units to which they were severally attached. As historian Michael King points out, "The commanders and headquarters that controlled the Rangers were usually too busy fighting their own conventional battles to exert themselves developing special missions for the Rangers,"[18] hence their frequent use as conventional infantry. At times losses were high—disastrously so for the 1st and 3d Rangers—but no centralized recruiting process or replacement training center existed to support the continued effective existence of these units. It is hard not to conclude that, some notable successes aside, the Rangers were dribbled out in penny packets and not developed to their full potential. Most significantly, though in four occasions in North Africa and Europe the Rangers spearheaded an invasion, each time they were then used as conventional infantry rather than being withdrawn for further special operations. Always, of course, commanders on the spot were eager to make continued use of skilled troops, but as King concludes, for example, on the fighting in central Italy, "It is difficult to believe . . . that the Rangers' participation in conventional combat was so important to the outcome of the fighting on the Winter Line that they could not be used in a role which was commensurate with their skills."[19] Indeed, it was not until 1984 that the lineal descendants of World War II Rangers, the 1st, 2d, and 3d Battalions of the 75th Infantry (Ranger), were given their own single regimental commander and regimental headquarters, four decades after their original formation.[20]

One interesting and rather unusual unit in the Ranger/Commando mode—unusual certainly for its joint Army/Navy composition—was known as the "Amphibious Scouts and Raiders (Joint)," formed in August 1942 and used first for amphibious operations in the European Theater. The origin of the unit lay in the clear need for more expertise in joint landing operations on the part of both the Army and Navy/ Marines. In mid-1941 joint maneuvers of the 1st Marine Brigade and the 1st Infantry Division, combined in a provisional corps precisely for such operations, at New River, North Carolina, revealed numerous problems, not least of which was the need for corps reconnaissance capability, including the ability to conduct small-scale diversional raids, land special groups for special purposes by night or day, and generally facilitate landing on a hostile shore.[21]

The "S&R" unit which was actually established, however, and entered into serious training at the Navy's amphibious base at Little Creek, Virginia, included no Marines, for the Marines had been ordered to the Pacific, and the S&Rs were intended for Europe. Instead, the unit's first members included primarily Navy men—ten volunteer chiefs and forty sailors simply selected for the assignment—from the Boat Pool at the Naval Amphibious Training Base, Solomons Island, Maryland, an establishment which trained sailors and chief specialists in the operation and maintenance of different small types of landing craft. Many of these men, in turn, had come from the Navy's Physical Training Program: athletes, sometimes on a professional level, under the orders of heavyweight boxer Commander Gene Tunney. Another ten Army volunteers were only added to the unit when the S&Rs were already in convoy on their way to their first assignment in Operation Torch, the landings in North Africa. The S&Rs were never numerous, but their training was notoriously difficult, as befitting their general water-borne assignments along enemy-held beaches. In that regard, the S&Rs were the lineal ancestor formation of the modern Navy's SEAL (sea-air-land) Teams.

The S&Rs proved most useful during Torch. As a result, the S&R school, now including six officers and seventy-five enlisted men, was moved to the warmer waters of Florida at "United States Naval Amphibious Training Base Ft. Pierce." Both Navy and Army men were trained here, though the Army men received one month's training and the Navy men double that. Many of the first Army members came from a similar establishment run by the Army, but now closed, at the Army Amphibious Training Center in Carrabelle, Florida. Men of both services now trained in all the necessary skills and abilities for the type of operation for which they were intended, and indeed were joined from time to time by other elements, for example the 2d and 5th Army Ranger Battalions and Free French and Norwegian units.

The next duty assigned to the S&Rs was Operation Husky in Sicily. Not enough trained men were available, however, so more volunteers were recruited from American units spread throughout North Africa, either drawn by the appeal of hazardous duty or dissatisfaction with the job they currently held (or both). One group that volunteered, for example, included sixteen men from a reconnaissance troop in the 3d Infantry Division, already trained in swimming and kayak scout techniques. From Sicily, the S&Rs moved on to assignments at Salerno, Anzio, Elba, the Yugoslav Coast, and southern France—and, above all, Normandy, all of which activities have been chronicled elsewhere.

S&Rs also took an active part in the Pacific War. An Amphibious Training Command was established in Australia in early 1943, preparing underwater demolition teams (UDTs), beach parties, and a unit known as the "Amphibious Scouts," alike in every way to the S&Rs and over time replaced by Ft. Pierce graduates. The first recruits for the Pacific element included graduates of San Diego's Landing Craft Schools, Australian veterans of North Africa, Australian coastwatchers, 1st Marine Division volunteers, even twenty New Guinea natives. Eventually the resulting unit, offically designated "7th Amphibious Force Special Service Unit #1," successfully conducted assignments along the New Guinea coast, the Philippines, Okinawa, even Korea (after the Japanese surrender) and China, training Chinese guerrillas, intelligence, and raiding elements. The S&Rs were disbanded after the war, but their memory is preserved in the historical records. In 1987, the Naval Amphibious Base in Coronado, where Navy SEAL Teams are trained, was dedicated in honor of Capt. Phil Bucklew, USNR Ret., former Cleveland Rams football player, and one of the first ten volunteers, S&R commander during Avalanche (Salerno) as an ensign, and subsequent revered S&R leader from Normandy to China. Virtually unknown until after World War II, the S&Rs "pioneered the tactics and techniques of amphibious reconnaissance and intelligence gathering," displaying outstanding perseverance in the most difficult of circumstances, and they certainly deserve their place in any catalog of American elite units.[22]

A special force similar to, and indeed intimately connected with, the "scouts and raiders" was the Navy's underwater Demolition Teams. Their origin is simply explained: the attack on Tarawa, America's first on a heavily defended coral reef, showed the need for considerably more intelligence about nearshore conditions than had been available for this battle, in which of the 16,800 Marines who participated, a shocking toll of over three thousand deaths was incurred. The first direct response in this special area was the formation of Combat Demolition Teams (by the end of the war, the Navy had thirty such teams) of picked sailors, at first men with Pearl Harbor salvage and other underwater experience, for training at Little Creek, Virginia. After a quick cram course in combat techniques, explosives, and the like, the first team, seventeen men in all, was employed to attack the barrier across the Sebou River near Port Lyautey in North Africa as a part of Operation Torch (November 1942). One ad hoc team was hardly enough, however, and its members were returned to the United States to aid in the formation of more successor units. In the spring of 1943 orders went out for the creation of more permanent beach clearance elements (defining a "beach" as wherever American troops were scheduled to land against hostile opposition).[23]

The new units were drawn mainly from the Dynamiting and Demolition School at Camp Perry, Virginia, and the Navy Construction Battalions ("Seabees"), and trained at the Naval Amphibious Training Base at Solomons Island, Maryland. The first assignment for the new Amphibious Forces, Atlantic Fleet team was to aid in the invasion of Sicily, but although they were present during the operation (July 1943) they were never called upon to use their skills. Once again, the unit was sent back to the United States to serve as instructors. More progress was made under the leadership of Lt. Cmdr. Draper L. Kauffman, founder and head of the Navy Bomb Disposal School, to take charge of the new program. Kauffman chose Ft. Pierce, where the Naval Amphibious Training Base was under construction. Most of his early recruits, thirty-five officers and men, were men of strength, endurance, and swimming ability (and no fear of explosives) drawn from the Seabees, and were required to volunteer for "'hazardous, prolonged, distant duty.'"[24]

The training program began with "Hell Week," which incorporated many highlights borrowed from the Scouts and Raiders, who trained at the same base and were eager to hel Physical conditioning and intensive work with boats, swamps, beaches, and explosives dominated a schedule which "washed out" 30 to 40 percent of the volunteers. Those who survived were certainly an elite force, and their survival chances were enhanced by the pairing off team members in a "buddy system" which came to typify the six-man Naval Combat Demolition Units, above all when in the water. Eleven teams graduated in the first Ft. Pierce class. Two went to the South Pacific, where they served with the Seventh Amphibious Force under General MacArthur.

The remaining teams were scattered about the world, including Hawaii, England, and North Africa. The three units which proceeded to Hawaii became the nucleus of Underwater Demolition Teams 1 and 2 (UDT 1 and 2), larger formations which each included one hundred officers and men, divided into a headquarters and four platoons for operations, all trained at Waimanolo Amphibious Base according to an urgent schedule for the forthcoming invasion of Kwajalein and Roi-Namur. Some of the additional men came from Marines with Tarawa experience, but the UDTs drew on any manpower source with the right kind of experience. The training was completed in time for Kwajalein, and the UDTs did good work there; though American casualties were high (nearly two thousand at Kwajalein, Roi, and Namur), the techniques of assault reconnaissance and demolition had made a considerable advance over Tarawa. Similar responsibilities followed at Eniwetok Atoll before the UDTs returned to Hawaii for further training.

The one six-man Combat Demolition Team which was sent to England was joined in subsequent weeks by a total of twenty-six more units from later Ft. Pierce classes. They were there of course to aid in the invasion of Normandy, and they trained in destroying the sort of obstacles which were to be expected on Utah and Omaha Beaches, to which they would be assigned (though neither officers nor men knew this very secret fact until shortly before D-Day), and to work in conjunction with Army Combat Engineers and the special "Beach Battalions" which would organize near-shore operations once the invasion was underway. When the day came, all worked successfully together to clear passages through the German defenses, but at high cost, calculated by historian (and UDT veteran) Francis Fane at 52 percent of the Navy roster of 175 CDT officers and men. Many received decorations, and the entire Navy Combat Demolition Unit of the Omaha force received one of three Presidential Unit Citations awarded to the Navy for the Normandy operation. The men assigned to Utah Beach performed the same functions, but found the opposition to be far less challenging.[25] Subsequent UDT operations during the invasion of southern France concluded their European assignments, but much remained to be done in the Pacific.

For subsequent operations against Japan, the newly formed UDTs

1 and 2 were joined by three more (3, 4, and 5), and all worked to establish a new "Naval Combat Demolition Training and Experimental Base" at the Kamaole Amphibious Training Base on the Hawaiian island of Maui (teams 6 and 7 soon followed). Here the UDTs were molded into coherent units, using some veterans from the earlier UDT operations together with newly recruited Navy volunteers and new graduates from Ft. Pierce. Their competitive spirit was fierce, and included not only the predictable battles with Marines, but occasionally with each other, to the point that two UDTs were not given leave in the same port at the same time. The "demolitioneers" (they did not regularly call themselves "frogmen") had plenty of work to do at Saipan, Guam (where in a famous incident at Agat beach men from UDT 4 left a prominent welcoming sign of plywood for the Marines), Tinian, Peleliu, Leyte, the Lingayan Gulf, Iwo Jima, Okinawa, and Balikpapan (Borneo). As the war came to an end, three thousand trained demolition experts in thirty UDT teams were preparing for the final assault on the Japanese home islands.[26] As with many small elite units, the UDTs were soon decommissioned, and by 1948 had been reduced to four skeleton teams, two each in the Pacific and Atlantic, with a total complement of seven officers and forty-five men. They would be needed again in Korea.

Members of the several American elite units of World War II will no doubt continue to argue over the merits of their respective training programs as long as there are survivors (and historians to continue the discussion), but certainly one candidate for "most demanding" is the First Special Service Force, known at times as the "Black Devils" for reasons which will be explained, but distinguished in their uniforms by a red spearhead patch with gold lettering reading "USA" and "Canada," together with a red, white, and blue braided *aiguillette* (shoulder-cord). The scheme for this force seems to have originated with Geoffrey Pyke, an English civilian scientific adviser to the British Commander of Combined Operations, Adm. Lord Louis Mountbatten. Pyke reasoned that a unit specially trained for winter operations, outfitted with lightly armored special snow vehicles, would be most useful to attack certain continental targets such as Norwegian or Italian alpine hydroelectric plants or the Romanian oilfields at Ploesti. Mountbatten was intrigued, as was Winston Churchill, with the result that the scheme was ordered into operation in April 1942 with the codename Project Plough.[27]

Presumably because the British army already had all the special commando-type formations it required, the Americans were to take on Plough, and implementation was placed in the hands of American Lt. Col. Robert T. Frederick (USMA 1928), a coast artilleryman then on Eisenhower's staff in the War Plans Division, who was first given the assignment of examining the plans for Plough in detail. Frederick, who concluded that of all the various ideas put forward, only Norway might be feasible (and even at that, he saw no practical way to withdraw the unit once its mission was fulfilled), now set about organization of the force, a task which was further complicated by Mountbatten's proposal that the formation should include Canadians as well as Americans. Frederick's unit was quite unique. Not only did it include tactical command elements which would normally be defined as infantry, engineers, parachutists, mountain troops, even armored troops for the versatile "Weasels" (an all-terrain snow vehicle developed by Studebaker) with which it was originally to be equipped, but also Frederick separated out his supply echelon of cooks, clerks, and medical support so that the combat echelons could concentrate entirely on training. These echelons were broken down into three regiments, each of two battalions divided into three companies, each of which contained three platoons, each of which in turn contained two nine-man "sections" (a Canadian term; "rifle squad" was the American equivalent), but each of Frederick's regiments, though commanded by a full colonel, only numbered about four hundred men. The combat echelon, when filled out with headquarters, medical and other detachments, made up 108 officers and 1,167 men; the service battalion brought the Force total to 133 officers and 1,688 enlisted men.[28]

The unit as a whole was formally commissioned in mid-July 1942. Frederick had selected the vague title of "First Special Service Force" to replace Plough, largely because the mission was highly secret and it was most undesirable to give anything away by the name—and in any case, "Commando" and "Ranger" were already taken. Since the British Commandos at the time were organized within the "Special Service Brigade," the designation was hardly revolutionary. One unforeseen result, however, was that as long as it remained in being, 1st SSF was confused with the U.S. Army's Special Services branch, the function of which was to bring entertainment to the troops.[29]

A call now circulated throughout the American military establishment for "Single men between the ages of twenty-one and thirty-five who had completed three years or more grammar school with the occupational range of Lumberjacks, Forest Rangers, Hunters, Northwoodsmen, Game Wardens, Prospectors, and Explorers." Officers already found for the force by Frederick from various sources, including the Parachute School and the Officer Candidate program at the Infantry School, Fort Benning, Georgia, now set out in search of volunteers, who not surprisingly came from a variety of sources, including a number of military stockades, where "hard-case troublemakers . . . were given the option of continuing their sentences or 'volunteering' for Frederick's Force."[30]

At the same time, recruitment was undertaken in Canada of a somewhat different sort for a contingent to number forty-seven officers and 650 enlisted men (all were destined for the combat echelon). Here Special Service "forcemen" volunteers were required to be "non-commissioned-officer" material; since they were recruited and remained technically under the designation "2d Canadian Parachute Battalion," many were unaware of their ultimate destination. Some of the Canadian volunteers came from the 1st Canadian Parachute Battalion and had qualified in parachutes already, some even having passed through British parachute training in England as well; now they were to do it again for their American parachute wings.[31]

Initial force training was done at Fort William Henry Harrison, a remote, derelict National Guard post near Helena, Montana, where the Canadian and American recruits were thoroughly mixed down to the section level. Officer assignments were made as much as possible in proportion to that of American to Canadian troops. Though there was inevitably some measuring up of each other, national rivalry was not a general feature of this unit—though there was always inevitable resentment at the fact that Canadians and Americans were each paid at their regular rates (meaning that Canadian sergeants were paid the same as American privates). As one bonus, combat echelon troops were designated as on parachute duty, which meant parachute pay, though here again American rates were higher than Canadian. "You couldn't afford to get into a craps game with the Americans, I remember that much," reported one Canadian private.[32]

Frederick, with orders to have his men ready for a projected Norwegian operation by the end of the year, set out upon "the most challenging and rigorous training program known to any infantry unit in World War II," according to Joseph A. Springer, who has collected an oral history of the unit. An abbreviated parachute training (one week and two jumps to qualify, versus the Army's usual four weeks and five jumps) came first, and was part of the weeding out process. To facilitate this part of the preparation, the 1st SSF was given its own organic element of six C-47 transport planes from the Army Troop Carrier Command; unlike standard paratroop training routines, the "Forcemen" were given no tower jumps, since there were no towers at Fort Harrison. Dawn calisthenics and obstacle runs were interlarded with long marches with full combat loads of thirty miles or more at a special quick pace (140 paces to the minute, versus the American Army standard "quick march" of 120; French Zouaves, it will be recalled, were really jogging at 150), mountain and rock climbs, ski instruction (from borrowed Norwegian instructors), a regular cycle of demolition training, map reading, first aid, vehicle operation and maintenance, and other classroom instruction, including lectures four nights each week in a day which ran from 4:45 AM to 9:30 PM. Not only were Forcemen qualified on the American weapons they would use, including machineguns, mortars, flamethrowers, and bazookas, but also in a wide range of German weapons they could expect to encounter, training which would prove very useful when the time came. Officers all underwent the same training as the men.[33]

After considerable thought, the Norwegian operation was canceled. There seemed to be no way to get the Weasels into operation in Norway; the likelihood of extraction of the unit was small; the effect of the destruction of Norway's hydroelectric capacity would be devastating to a friendly population; and finally, it became apparent that there had been a considerable security leak, and the Germans might well know of the plan.[34] The Brigade cancelled its winter training, and in April 1943, after a grand parade through downtown Helena, moved to Camp Bradford, Virginia (the Little Creek training center) for amphibious training (April–May, 1943)—standard for all combat units headed overseas at this time—and then on to Fort Ethan Allen in the Green Mountains near Burlington, Vermont, for further mountain training (May–June). In the light of possible new assault landing responsibilities, the unit underwent some basic reorganization, most notably the enlargement of individual sections to at least a dozen men by the addition of more support weapons and the men to operate them. The change was of considerable import, demonstrating that the Force's mission was now deemed more likely to be combat rather than infiltration and sabotage.[35] Throughout this long process, the attrition rate was high; it is estimated that "the Force, during the weeding out process [up to the spring of 1943] went through twice as many men as it eventually kept," and all those men initially had been volunteers.[36] At the end, the result, as described by the Force's intelligence officer, was "a singular unit made up of what has best been described as 'the leaders of gangs.' The individual soldier, almost to a man, had resourcefulness, mental and physical toughness, and an initiative that surmounted all obstacles."[37] John Schuetz, who fought in the 3d Regiment, put it a bit differently. "We had an awful lot of courage; that was the main thing on the Force. It cost a lot of people their lives because they were overactive, overcouraged. Men would rush in where they should have thrown a few grenades first. There was a real close comradeship, and I think any man would throw his life on the line for another one. You never thought about that, you'd just do it; you were trained to do it and that was that."[38]

Only in the early summer of 1943 did the Force receive orders to leave the continental United States, but, to the surprise of many of its men, it now headed west, not east. The First Special Service Force was in fact assigned to Task Force 9 which had the mission of retaking the Aleutians from the Japanese. The Force, now 2,640 in all, including 604 Canadians, did indeed take part in the landing on the island of Kiska (Operation Cottage), but the Japanese had already withdrawn in late July. After what was clearly an anticlimax, the question arose of what to do with the force, and the decision was made to send it to Europe, with the result that the First Special Service Force was one of only two Allied combat units to fight in both the Pacific and European theaters (the other was the 10th Mountain Division's 87th Regiment, discussed below).[39]

As the Forcemen were soon to find, the bulk of their war effort was to be expended in Italy. Arriving in Naples in November after a brief stop in North Africa, the Force became attached to the 36th Infantry Division, II Corps, in Gen. Mark Clark's Fifth Army. Now, really for the first time, their special training was put to practical use, for the Force was sent to break a long-standing stalemate along Field Marshal Albert Kesselring's *Winterstellungen* ("Winter Line"), blocking control of the Liri Valley and a final approach to Rome. In a most difficult campaign for Monte la Difensa and Monte la Remetanea, the Force used all its skills of rockclimbing and mountain operation techniques. The Force did take Monte la Difensa, where other American units had failed, but at a cost of one-third of the entire combat echelon killed, wounded, or missing (over six hundred men). The American public was given some taste of the nature of the landscape, at least, after the unit was visited by Robert Capa, who would prove to be one of the foremost photographers of the war; some of his shots appeared in *Life* magazine (January 31, 1944).[40]

As with every Force combat experience, wounded Forcemen, because of their special skills, were sent back to the unit as soon as possible, rather than to general replacement depots as was the custom for most American soldiers. Returnees were not enough, however, and the unit found itself with many replacements. Some were former Rangers from units which had been chewed up in battle; the Forcemen did not consider them as equals. Other replacements required even more on-the-spot training; inevitably, the quality of the unit, while still high, began to deteriorate as a result.[41]

After further fighting in the mountains, the Force found itself drawn into the cauldron of Anzio (Operation Shingle), where the landings had not gone as planned. The Force, now reduced in numbers to sixty-eight officers and 1,165 men in all, was given the difficult task of holding nearly eight miles of perimeter on the right flank of the American position, in particular the "Mussolini Canal," a useful barrier some 170 feet wide and 12–20 feet dee Badly outnumbered by opposing enemy units that included the Luftwaffe's prestige ground unit, the Hermann Goering Division, Frederick (by now a brigadier general), unhappy with orders to remain in a static defensive position, concluded that the only way to succeed was to take the battle to the Germans, with nightly patrols and deep reconnaissance penetrations. The result was successful enough to keep the Germans believing that they faced at least a full American division—and a particularly vicious division at that, composed of men who sought out ambushes and other adventures by night in their baggy black mountain uniforms and darkened faces: "The Black Devil Brigade." Certainly the unit deserved its special reputation among the Germans, not least by its habit of placing various stickers on the foreheads of the men they killed with unit insignia or disheartening slogans (for example, "Das dicke Ende kommt noch," or "The worst is yet to come!").[42] But one can still ask, as so often with the relatively small elite units of World War II, whether this was the best use to which the Special Force should have been put. General Clark, it appears, had hoped to use Frederick's unit in more appropriate missions, but as Allied planners focused more on the future Normandy landings and shifted resources to England, Clark was increasingly desperate for men of any sort for his lines in Italy.[43]

After Anzio, the Special Force led Clark's advance into Rome. Later it was assigned to Operation Anvil, the landing in southern France, where the Force was given the task of seizing the Hyeres Islands (Port Cros and Levant) on the allied left flank; heavy German guns were thought to be located there, though these proved to be fake installations for the most part. After Anvil, the Force continued in combat as part of the 1st Airborne Task Force, but in December 1944 both that parent unit and the Force itself were deactivated, since there seemed little further need for its special qualifications.[44]

The final ceremony was bittersweet, as the remaining Canadian contingent of 620 officers and men was simply told to fall out of parade formation, and marched off, leaving the Americans in place. The Canadians went to various Canadian units, above all the 1st Canadian Parachute Battalion, from which quite a few had volunteered in the first place. Those Americans who wished were transferred into American airborne divisions, while the rest were joined with other elements, including over four hundred officers and men from the 1st, 3d, and 4th Ranger Battalions, and in January 1945 became part of a new "474th Infantry Regiment (Separate)," which fought on to the end of the war under Gen. George S. Patton's Third Army. The 474th's last assignment was to aid in the disarming and repatriation of the three hundred thousand German troops who had surrendered in Norway; in October, 1945, the unit returned to the United States. In all, some five hundred Forcemen had died in the war, and another 2,300 were wounded (many more than once): historian Springer estimates the turnover rate of the Force with returns and replacements to have been "an astonishing six hundred percent."[45]

Springer's epitaph makes clear the Force's contribution:

The success of the Force in the European war is beyond dispute; the Force never met defeat in battle, and its combat performance lived up to its reputation on both sides of the front lines. From December 1943 through November 1944, the First Special Service Force accounted for as many as seven thousand enemy prisoners of war and an estimated twelve thousand enemy dead. These astonishing figures correspond to the destruction of an entire German division, and more.[46]

To put it another way, the SSF, itself little more than the size of an infantry regiment, in the words of Maj. Scott R. McMichael, "consistently accepted tasks appropriate to a regular division. Moreover, the unit remained effective even after it had sustained casualties that would have incapacitated another force."[47]

Yet it is hard not to conclude that for most of its history, the unit's unique capabilities were at least misused, if not simply wasted. Robert Todd Ross, in his comprehensive study of First Special Service Force, puts it well:

> Squandered in the meat grinder that was the Winter Line, consumed in the costly daylight frontal attack that was the breakout of the Anzio Beachhead, and wasted in the advance across Southern France, each casualty the Force sustained represented the irreplaceable loss of not just a fighting-man, but that of a parachute jumper, a demolitionist, a saboteur, a ski-trooper, a mountain climber, and an amphibious raider.[48]

Certainly his conclusion is sustainable for those Forcemen who had experienced the full training regime, but is less accurate for many later replacements. In any case, the 1st SSF's contribution overall, though significant, was perhaps not commensurate with the efforts involved in its creation. Rather like the Kiska operation, the concept was worthwhile, but mismanagement at higher levels meant that the final record was not all it might have been.

Since racial desegregation did not come to the American armed forces until after World War II, and since African American units seldom went into combat, in this war minorities and military elites were anything but synonymous. One interesting exception was formed from nisei, Japanese Americans born in the United States. Two separate units were involved in this case, the 100th Infantry Battalion and the 442d Regimental Combat Team.

The first, the 100th, was formed mainly of National Guardsmen from the Hawaiian Islands who made up the 298th and 299th Regiments; some had volunteered, but most had been drafted. About half of the men in these units were Japanese Americans, and there were serious reservations in Washington and elsewhere about using these men in a war against Japan. A second source for the 100th was the Hawaiian Territorial Guard, the first unit which had in fact been called out after

Pearl Harbor and was actively doing guard duties wherever needed, and which contained many nisei officers and men. In late January 1942, the commanding general of the Hawaiian War Department, Lt. Gen. Delos Emmons, ordered all 317 Japanese Territorial Guardsmen dismissed. About half of these, mostly students from the University of Hawaii's ROTC element which had been incorporated into the Territorial Guard, to prove an important point voluntarily went to work with the local Army Engineers digging ditches and stringing barbed wire, calling themselves the "Varsity Victory Volunteers." On the other hand, the need for manpower, combined with anti-discriminatory clauses in the laws governing the National Guard, precluded a similar purge of the fourteen hundred Japanese Americans in the National Guard regiments, though for one night after Pearl Harbor their rifles and ammunition had been confiscated in a moment of panic on the part of the higher command.[49]

After considerable debate and reflection, the solution to this dilemma was to decree that the two regiments would form the "Hawaiian Provisional Infantry Battalion" (May 1942), later redesignated the "100th Infantry Battalion (Separate)," just over 1,400 officers and men in all. Since obvious problems of identification would arise in Pacific Theater combat, the battalion was sent to the mainland, to continue training at Camp McCoy near Sparta, Wisconsin, a National Guard base, where by a cruel irony one of the first assignments given to nisei soldiers was to mount guard duty over issei, first-generation Japanese immigrants from the west coast states, who had been interned in concentration camps (the term which was used at the time; "internment camps," was a post-war euphemism adopted to distinguish American methods from the horrors of German concentration camps) by presidential order in February 1942. In early 1943, the battalion, oversized in six rather than four companies, moved to Camp Shelby, Mississippi. At this point the only factors which distinguished the 100th from other army battalions were its racial composition and discriminatory regulations (including one that prohibited any Japanese from commanding a rifle company), its lack of divisional affiliation, and a general reluctance in higher command circles to commit the unit to battle.[50]

In the meantime, however, pressure had been placed upon the administration from the Japanese American community elements which had not been interned, along with civil libertarians, both arguing that loyal Japanese Americans should be allowed to volunteer. An army which found itself in increasing need of manpower agreed, not over-

looking the fact that such a unit might have what Army Chief of Staff
Gen. George C. Marshall called "a profound propaganda effect" on
those peoples who were exposed to the Japanese propaganda claim
that this was indeed a racial war.[51] In February 1943 the 442d Infantry
Regimental Combat Team (RCT) was established, to be formed of Japanese American volunteers under white officers down to company command level (this rule was later dropped when the unit had clearly proven
itself in combat). Many of the nearly ten thousand volunteers in fact
came from the Hawaiian Islands, to which the internment order had
not applied. The RCT was to include, in addition to the infantry battalion, artillery, engineer, cannon, anti-tank, service, medical, and band
detachments, to a total of over four thousand men.

After considerable winnowing, nearly 2,700 of these left for the
mainland in March (some were selected for training in the Military
Intelligence Service because of their knowledge of the Japanese language; in this role they served in teams of ten with 150 units around the
world). At Camp Shelby, they went into training, their numbers augmented by 1,500 volunteers from the mainland, including some from
ten "relocation camps" (though only some 5 percent of eligible men in
these camps had actually volunteered).[52] At Shelby, training went forward, but by no means did all relationships go smoothly: NCOs were
mostly mainland nisei draftees. A typical story was that of Jack
Wakamatsu, a 1940 draftee from Venice, California, who was a rifle
company sergeant in the 53rd Infantry Regiment. After America entered the war, Wakamatsu's unit was assigned to guard railway tracks
in Nevada. In early 1942 all Japanese American soldiers in his regiment were separated out and ordered, along with Japanese Americans
from other units, about three hundred men in all, to Camp Crowder,
Missouri, where they basically killed time. Only in February 1943 was
the group ordered to Camp Shelby to become cadre for the 442d. They
were not told what their assignment was until arrival. "No one asked
our opinion or asked us to volunteer for this duty," though none seemed
to object to their new assignment as far as Wakamatsu recalled.[53]

At Shelby, problems abounded. The camp was in a state of physical disrepair, and the men had to turn to with pick and shovel, hammer
and nails. When the islanders arrived, there was little love lost between them and the mainland recruits, with too many fights and other
disturbances, though these diminished as time passed, and, in particular, as the 100th and 442d got used to each other. No one had told the

islanders that an NCO cadre already existed, and many who expected to be NCOs were disappointed, but it was a matter of "lifestyles" as much as specific grievances: the mainland nisei were far more diversified in education, experience, and attitude than the mostly agricultural laborers from plantations of the islands. Ernest Uno from Los Angeles, for example, interned with his family in Colorado, found after arriving at Shelby "that I had to learn to listen [to] and speak pidgin English" in order to communicate with the islanders. The latter, on the other hand, felt that the mainlanders—*kontonks*, they were called dismissively by the islanders, supposedly from the sound made when heads were knocked together or on barrack room floors—"were aloof and standoffish, acted superior, and talked too much like the haoles [Caucasians]." *Buddhaheads*, on the other hand, was the mainlander term for islanders, supposedly a corruption of the Japanese word *buta* (pig) heads.[54] Finally, many of the officers assigned to the unit were inept: "I don't relish saying this," commented Wakamatsu, "but most of them were not suited for the job," and a number failed in combat.[55]

Just as the origins of the 100th and 442d differed, so too did their combat history differ, at least at first. In August 1943 the 100th Infantry Battalion left the United States for North Africa, where it became attached organizationally to the 34th Infantry Division. The Battalion moved on to Salerno, Anzio, Cassino, and Rome. At Salerno, the 100th included 1,300 men; after Cassino, where its Gustave Line opponents included the elite German 1st Parachute Division, it could call upon only fifty-one effectives. "This was the end of the original 100th Infantry Battalion . . .," remarked war correspondent and historian Lyn Crost, though some replacements arrived from the 442d, sent on while the rest of that unit continued to train in Mississippi.[56]

In April 1944 the bulk of the 442d RCT arrived, and the 100th was now formally attached to it when the two units combined in June at Civitavecchia near Rome, in all numbering roughly 4,300 officers and men including an engineer company and the 522d Artillery Battalion. After amassing a most successful combat record in Italy, including a Presidential Citation for destroying a German SS Battalion on Mount Belvedere in the tough fighting in the Apennines, in October the unit was sent to Marseilles and on up the Rhône Valley to the Vosges Mountains on the German frontier. Here they won considerable fame for taking the town of Bruyères and for rescuing the "Lost Battalion," a formation from the 141st Infantry Regiment which had been cut off and surrounded. The rescue was accomplished in the end by a famous bayonet charge by I and K Companies of the 442d along with the 100th against heavily entrenched and well-defended German positions. Some 211 Texans had been rescued of the 275 originally entrapped; the 442d took 814 casualties in the process, but their efforts won a well-deserved unit citation.[57]

Meanwhile General Clark successfully appealed to have the 442d returned to his command in March of 1945, where it remained until the end of the war, organizationally attached to the 92d Infantry Division. This association was not popular with the 442d, since the 92d Division was an entirely African American unit, the only such division in the American Army to see combat in World War II. (Only two others were composed of African Americans, the 93d and the 2d Cavalry Division; the former did mainly garrison work in the Pacific, while the latter, including both the 9th and 10th Cavalry, after extensive training was shipped to North Africa, only to be broken up into various service units.) Neither the implications of racial segregation nor the fact that the 92d's record was at best undistinguished appealed to the men of the 442d RCT. To digress for a moment, it should be realized that despite various promises to the contrary, little had been done to improve the position of blacks in the military over what had been experienced in World War I, and such concessions as had been made, as Jack Foner has pointed out, "were prompted more by the desire to silence the clamor against discrimination and to forestall black political reprisals than out of a genuine commitment to integration."[58] Ninety percent of black soldiers drafted or accepted as volunteers did labor work only, and of the remainder only half actually saw combat, mainly from the 92d and the 332d Fighter Group, particularly the latter's 99th Fighter Squadron. The 92d was the most prominent, fighting in Italy from July 1944 to the end of the war, receiving more than seven thousand individual awards, but its reputation as "The Luckless 92d" which melted under enemy pressure tended to prevail.[59] There would be no elite African American units in this war.

To return to the nisei, General Clark in his memoirs had special praise for the 100th, "one of the most valuable units in the Fifth Army" (rather strangely, he does not mention the 442d RCT), pointing out its heavy casualties and "fourteen Distinguished Service Crosses and seventy-five Silver Stars. . . . I was proud to have them in the Fifth Army."[60] According to historian Lawrence Fuchs, "Of the 7,500 men on its rolls at one time or another . . . seven hundred never came back; 700 were maimed; another 1,000 were seriously wounded. . . . Their slogan, 'Go for broke,' reflected the spirited determination of men anxious to vindicate themselves and their families."[61] The decorations awarded to the 100th/442d included seven Presidential Unit Citations; 9,486 Purple Hearts; one Congressional Medal of Honor; 52 DFCs; 560 silver stars (and 28 oak leaf clusters in lieu of second awards); and over 5,200 bronze stars and clusters.[62] Of those who earned such awards and did survive, many returned to be leaders of Hawaii, and some indeed of the United States, including United States Senators Daniel K. Inouye, a much decorated captain in the 442d, and Spark M. Matsunaga, twice wounded with the 100th before being transferred to the Military Intelligence Service. The 100th had already earned its elite status in Europe before the 442d arrived, hence its subsequent unusual semi-independent designation (normally, having become the 1st Battalion of the 442d, it would henceforth have been called exactly that; as it was, the 442d's three battalions were known as the 100th, 2d, and 3d), but there can be little question that the combined "100th/442d" in the end forged an enviable elite combat record.

Perhaps the last word, however, is best left to Frank Seto of the 442d's anti-tank company. "I think everybody set out to prove that we were good Americans and that we were going to show them. I think we all had that in mind because of everything we did. When we had to take a hill or something we were going to take it regardless of how many got killed. Our folks would always say, 'Don't fail, since that would bring a bad name on the rest of the community.' Everything we did we tried to do, we tried to do it right."[63]

We have in general restricted our consideration of elite American units to smaller formations, usually battalion level or smaller, created for special purposes. In World War II, however, the Army gave serious consideration to four different division-sized elements intended for particular assignments. Airborne divisions have already been discussed; the others were mountain, jungle, and "light" divisions. Not all top commanders believed in special-type units. General McNair, for example, pointed out that while the special purposes might not materialize, the need for standard forces was indeed likely; in any case, he was firmly convinced that every man in the army should be a competent all-round soldier first, and then receive special training when and where necessary.[64]

Between March and September, 1942, four special centers were established for airborne, amphibious, desert, and mountain training and testing of equipment; special airborne and mountain formations were indeed established, but no special units for amphibious or desert operations. Jungle training would be conducted in Panama. Another alternative to special task divisions, preferred by McNair, was to form "light" divisions, which could be used in any conditions and which would be expected to travel "light," that is, to be able to operate without organic integrated transport vehicles or even animals; mission flexibility was the real appeal to McNair, who worried about the danger of overspecialization. The light divisions had the added apparent advantage of being easier to move, supply, or maintain than a standard division; where transport was necessary, it would be developed locally. Such a unit would have about nine thousand men, and have no artillery heavier than three battalions of 75mm pack howitzers (these were given either pack mules or small trucks).

Debate over this concept was extensive, and included the possibility of converting the new airborne, or the old cavalry, to light division status. Eventually ten divisions were proposed through the conversion of six infantry and four airborne divisions, but a good many top generals, including Eisenhower and MacArthur, questioned the utility of these formations. Nevertheless, three such divisions were authorized in June 1943, out of a total of ninety divisions of all types called for in the organizational table then in force. The "89th Light Division (Truck)" was to be given the basis for mobility; it was to be created from the 89th Infantry Division. The "71st Light Division (Pack, Jungle)" was formed from the 5th Infantry and 14th Infantry, already jungle-trained in Panama; its fate, however, was to be converted back to regular infantry as the 71st Division and to fight in Europe where it was badly needed after the German breakthrough of December 1944. In any case, a light division simply was not wanted in the Pacific where any elements landing on defended hostile shores would require heavy artillery and vehicles at once. The 89th, as well, was converted back into a standard division, in which form it served mainly as a source of replacements; some three thousand men were withdrawn from it and sent to other divisions overseas, before the remainder was sent off to Europe in 1945.[65]

The 10th Mountain Division, however, did in due course enjoy a special role. The term "mountain" was a bit misleading; the unit was intended as ski troops, and snow is not only found in the mountains. Indeed, it is likely that the incentive for an American ski force was provided by the impact of ski troops in the Russo-Finnish War of 1939–40, and, more importantly, in the Russian response to the German invasion of 1941, which involved whole Russian ski divisions. For that reason, recruitment for the 10th in 1943 was originally conducted by the National Ski Patrol System (NSPS), a civilian organization, whose founder and head, Charles Minot "Minnie" Dole, was influential in the first place in persuading the Army that such a unit was desirable. The NSPS sought out skiers, aiming particularly for college students, on the theory that it would be easier to make soldiers out of skiers than vice versa.[66] Another important source was the American Alpine Club (AAC), which contacted such organizations as the Harvard Mountaineering Club; it surely did not hurt the unit's formation that Henry L. Stimson, secretary of war, was an AAC member, and could override the opposition of Lieutenant General McNair. In 1943 McNair was a fast-rising officer. Promoted to major general in September 1940 and lieutenant general in June 1941, in March of 1942 he was moved from his position as chief of staff to Army Headquarters, i.e., chief of staff to Army Chief of Staff Marshall, to head of the newly established "Army Ground Forces" command (McNair would be the highest ranking officer killed in the Normandy landings of 1944). McNair opposed elites in general including this particular elite, on the grounds that the army was being denied too many of the best recruits for ordinary ground combat units. As will be seen, however, McNair himself succumbed to a quite different scheme regarding tank destroyers.[67]

The nucleus of the 10th Division was the "1st Battalion (Reinforced) 87th Infantry Mountain Regiment," authorized in November, 1941, less than a month before Pearl Harbor. The army had actually foreseen the need for some ski-trained troops, and earlier in the year had ordered the commanders of the 1st, 3d, 5th, 6th, 41st, and 44th divisions—all based in areas with reasonable access to snow slopes—to form select ski-patrol elements, so it had already learned that soldiers could be taught to ski. These elements were now combined into the 87th Regiment, stationed at Fort Lewis, Washington, with much of its training taking place on Mount Rainier. The 87th was designed to serve as the nucleus of a proposed entire mountain division.[68]

To build up to divisional strength, originally only volunteers were accepted, and according to Robert Ellis, who served through the war as a machine gunner in the 10th, "Each applicant had to submit three letters of recommendation attesting to his skiing prowess and good character." (Ellis, an undergraduate at the University of Chicago, had skiing experience in Switzerland in addition to fluent French and the necessary physical qualifications.)[69] Recruits took the requirement seriously. William Putnam, a Harvard climber, had letters from top leaders of the AAC, including Kenneth Henderson, author of the "bible," *A Handbook of American Mountaineering*; he soon found himself assigned as a ski instructor.[70] Not all such letters were from notables: "My Dear Son: You ask for a recommend. I think you are fit for the mountain troops. You always were a good boy and a hard worker. And I also think you are a brave boy and willing to do the work that is set before you. Your Mother." This letter worked, however, for applicant Harold J. Loudon.[71]

The promise of extra pay probably attracted some men, though this proved to be no more than a hopeful rumor. A Warner Brothers short movie feature on "Mountain Fighters," filmed at the beautiful Sun Valley resort by Otto Lang, together with much media attention on an outfit which required its men "to carry a 75-pound pack 20 miles in 8 hours at 12,000 feet above sea level—this while on snowshoes," produced the necessary recruits to form a second regiment, the 86th. Roughly 60 percent of the division's men had some college education; twenty percent were foreign-born. Many of the latter were refugees from Nazi-controlled Europe. One battalion, the 99th, was made up entirely of Norwegians and men of Norwegian ancestry.[72] Hal Burton, who served as an officer with the 10th, adds up the result of combining an inner core of "one mammoth ski club," some three thousand men, with another three thousand eager recruits from the colleges, and a final contingent of three thousand draftees when the stream of volunteers ran dry to bring the 10th up to full strength: "Certainly there were infinitely more college graduates and college students, infinitely more men from moneyed families, and the only group of men in the Army who found common cause in a sport," just the sort of thing, in other words, to which McNair objected.[73]

The thirteen thousand–man unit was activated as the "10th Light Infantry Division (Pack, Alpine)" in mid-July; by that time it was already in training at Camp Hale, Colorado, a new facility some twenty miles from Leadville high in the Rockies near the Continental Divide. Training for all was similar, but the careers of the two regiments were rather different, since in mid-1943 the 87th was sent to the North Pacific to take part in the attack on Kiska, returning to Camp Hale only in early 1944, while the newer 86th stayed on in training.

At Camp Hale—"Camp Hell" to many—the training and conditioning were extraordinarily difficult whether in summer swamps or winter ice and snow, with temperatures falling to thirty degrees below zero. The altitude was simply too high at nine thousand feet, a good thousand feet higher than most alpine passes; altitude sickness was a common complaint for unacclimated men. A carrier pigeon detachment sent to work there was a complete failure, since the pigeons, unable to fly at ten thousand feet, preferred to walk to their destination. Nevertheless the men trained on skis and snowshoes, climbed rocky cliffs, and worked extensively with pack mules and more amenable M-29 cargo carriers, or "Weasels," in addition to the normal weapons and munitions training. Injuries were frequent. According to Roger Beaumont, "the most elite U.S. division in the twentieth century in terms of intelligence scores, fitness and training, suffered five times more casualties preparing for combat than any other American division in the Second World War."[74]

In June of 1944, the division moved to Camp Swift near Austin, Texas, for "flatland" training, which seemed to many men to be an unnecessary waste of time, over and above the sudden shock of mid-summer Texas. For a time, morale suffered; not only did the division temporarily lose its "Alpine" designation, but to those in the know it seemed that the division was lacking in purpose. Neither Pacific nor European theater commanders seemed to want a division which would fight on skis in mountain country, to say nothing of the accompanying 3,200 mules of the four 75mm pack artillery battalions, and yet came equipped with none of the 105mm and 155mm howitzers normally supplied to infantry divisions. Only when the division was given a new commander, the "Mountain" designation restored, and a curved patch issued with the word "Mountain" embroidered on it to sew above the divisional symbol—just as "Airborne" and "Rangers" had similar visual elite identification—did morale improve, just in time for the division to be ordered to Italy, where its talents would not go to waste. Lt. Gen. Mark Clark was more than glad to have them as he moved towards the mountains of northern Italy.[75]

The 10th Division did not go into combat until January 1945, but it was given a most challenging assignment opposite the Gothic Line in the Apennine Mountains, a line that the Germans had to hold if they were not to lose the entire Po River Valley. Not surprisingly, almost none of the top quality equipment the division had used at Camp Hale, such as high quality nylon rope, pitons, eiderdown zippered sleeping bags, pile-lined parkas, and alpine boots ever turned up for use in Italy.[76] The divisional record may be followed in official histories and memoirs, and cannot be considered here, but the 10th certainly justified its training in scaling the stark 1,500-foot cliff to Riva Ridge (Pizzo di Campiano-Monte Mancinello to the Italians). Very careful reconnaissance, along with training on the cliffs of a rock quarry, preceded the attack. It had been planned that the assault platoons would be specially chosen from the entire force, not least because by this point only 70 percent of the unit had been through the climbing training at Camp Hale. When morale flagged at this announcement, it was decided instead that each company commander would send one of his platoons to the final attack. A night assault up, using fixed ropes (placed in advance by men using hammers muffled in cloth), by the 1st and 2d Battalions of the 86th Regiment completely surprised the German defenders on the summit, and the 10th then moved on to take nearby Mt. Belvedere.[77]

"To my surprise," German commander Field Marshal Albert Kesselring wrote later, "in deep snow—the remarkably good American 10th Mountain Division launched an attack" which took the position from a "static" German Infantry division, the 232d; "excellent division," was the evaluation of Cassino's defender, Gen. Frido von Senger und Etterlin.[78] German counterattacks were ferocious, but the 10th refused to be pushed off the mountain, taking heavy casualties before being relieved. One very seriously wounded casualty was replacement 2d Lt. Robert Dole (no relation to Charles Minot Dole), sent to the 3d Battalion of the 85th Mountain Regiment. Dole had no special mountain training; such skills, along with letters of recommendation and other requirements, had all been waived in the need for manpower. Dole was indeed lucky to survive his mountain experience and go on to be a United States senator and presidential candidate in 1996. One who did not survive this battle was Technical Sgt. Torge Dahl Tokle, a Norwegian world champion ski jumper and hero to his unit.[79]

The 10th fought on in Italy to the end of the war, earning considerable further glory in the process, not least by taking a lead in crossing the Po River in rubber boats to establish a beachhead against German resistance. By May, when the Germans finally issued cease-fire orders in Italy, the 10th had experienced 114 days of combat, suffering 4,154 wounded and 992 killed. It is hard not to agree with machine gunner Ellis that in the end the division's establishment had proved worthwhile in the context of the Italian campaign, for in the mountains it certainly used its hard-earned skills. This was rather an unusual accomplishment as it happened, since most European mountain divisions found themselves thrown into battle wherever needed as ordinary combat infantry, seldom making use of their special abilities. Whether the 10th could have continued in mountain/ski conditions for very long is yet another issue, since, as Beaumont explains, "When they were committed to action in Italy against German mountain troops, the 10th suffered the heaviest casualties relative to time in combat of any U.S. division in the Italian campaign."[80]

The point remains that the replacements fed into the 10th did not have the same training and thus its special skills were quickly eroded, a common danger facing elite formations based upon unusual or unique weaponry or techniques. As it was, the 10th Division was lucky not to have been worn out through ordinary combat before reaching the Apennines, and thus was still in possession of its mountain-climbing skills when they were needed. In the larger historical context, it may still be asked whether the effort involved in this campaign was commensurate with the results, but that is an issue of strategy which may be left to others.

One commonly shared trend in twentieth-century military history was the ambition of new service arms, principally air and armored elements, to have the same sort of independent status as generally enjoyed by armies and navies. The Royal Air Force, for example, had earned its separate status before World War II, while the American Army Air Force would gain a similar position only after the war. An independent Armored Force, however, was a more complicated issue for most armies, since it was generally agreed that tanks needed to be coordinated with other arms to be successful in combat, a truism that did not always apply to an air force. The United States did in fact establish a separate Armored Force in July 1940, as a direct response to the success of relatively autonomous German armored formations in western Europe in the preceding months.[81]

The commander of this force, Brig. Gen. Adna R. Chaffee, was given control of all tank units, no matter whether their previous home had been with the infantry or the cavalry. The first two armored divi-

sions appeared in the summer of 1941, and two soon became five, as
the force developed its own training schemes and tactical doctrines.
The issue, however, was whether this force would evolve in an autonomous direction, a path which the Army Air Force was already taking.
In the end, a compromise decision was to keep armored units within
the existing larger organizational structure of the army as a whole, but
to leave them still in possession of their own distinct headquarters and
training commands. The debate was not simply a struggle for independent control; armored commanders, with some justification, feared that
without centralized control of armor higher commanders untrained in
its use would fail to exploit it to its maximum potential. The decision
made in mid-1940 nevertheless left armored divisions or corps under
the overall control of commanders of combined arms. By that time, the
United States had lost much ground indeed: "By 1936, while the Americans were still debating the horse, the Germans and Russians each had
raised an armored corps."[82]

But there were several questions involved in this matter. Aside
from the need perceived by some armor commanders to concentrate
armored forces to deal with the German threat, there was also the issue
of which weapons were best suited to stop German tanks: anti-tank
guns, or other tanks? And what sort of anti-tank guns, or anti-tank tanks,
using what tactics? What balance should be sought concerning speed,
firepower, and armor protection? And so on. These questions are relevant to the study of elites, because after 1940 an important policy was
initiated to develop special, new elite "tank destroyer" units. Much of
the initiative for this development came from General McNair, still
Marshall's chief of staff until the spring of 1942, who "refused to believe that tanks could be beaten only by other tanks," convinced that
they needed the support of antitank mines and antitank guns. McNair
concluded that special mobile tank destroyers were required, to be concentrated in groups of at least three battalions, preferably under the
aegis of a larger Tank Destroyer Force which would stand in rough
equality to the Armored Force (an innovation which McNair did not
happen to favor, and which in any case "perceived antitank defense to
be antithetical to its offensive philosophy and declined any interest in
assuming responsibility").[83] Before his appointment under Marshall,
McNair had run the Command and General Staff School which had
much influence in the evolution of doctrine, including supervision of
the *Field Service Regulations*; after becoming Marshall's chief of staff,

McNair was basically in charge of training. It is little wonder therefore that his viewpoint had much influence.[84]

The first step in mid-1941 was to create provisional anti-tank battalions in each division, with the further object of building a large Antitank Force of some sort by the end of the year. The success of German anti-aircraft 88mm and other artillery in stopping British tanks in North Africa only lent urgency to the plan, which seemed to go well at least in maneuvers. McNair lost his fight to establish an independent Antitank Force, however; the new battalions would be subordinated to the Armored Force. Nevertheless, in December 1941, a Tank Destroyer Tactical and Firing Center was established at Fort Meade, Maryland, with the expectation that here details on equipment and tactics would be worked out. In early January, 1942, however, a new base was built at Camp Hood, in Killeen, Texas, and the TD Center moved there to oversee all training. For this purpose it was agreed that tank destroyers would be "removed from organic assignment to divisions, corps, and armies and concentrated under the commanding general of the field forces in order to allow quick massing of mobile antitank power, preferably for offensive action."[85] That such offensive action was not easily reconciled with lying in ambush was a problem which would have to be faced in the future.

Two requirements now had to be met. One was for new and more effective weaponry, since one basic flaw in McNair's plan was the army's lack of any modern antitank weapon. Since weaponry had much to do with the ultimate fate of the tank destroyers, some technical discussion is required here. Until 1940, the principle antitank weapon was the .50 caliber machine gun, which indeed had stopped early model light tanks of World War I, but was hopelessly inadequate in the late 1930s. The first attempts to remedy this situation were not promising. The M-6 tank destroyer was a 37mm gun mounted on a Dodge 3/4 ton truck. It had really been intended for training only, not combat, and therefore it was not really surprising that when it was introduced into combat in North Africa in 1942, it proved ineffective, not least because the gun though quite new was already obsolete. The M-6 was soon abandoned. The M-3 carried a more powerful but low-velocity World War I vintage 75mm gun mounted on a lightly armored personnel carrier ("half-track"). Some 2,200 were built, but the M-3 too was judged unsuccessful in Tunisia, and was phased out after Sicily, though some were used to good purpose with the Marines in the Pacific, where each division had a dozen in a special weapons battalion.[86]

The M-10 was more successful. In essence it was an M-4 "Sherman tank" chassis equipped with a different, unroofed turret with a lightweight, high velocity anti-aircraft three-inch gun with a rapid rate of fire (a most useful attribute). The use of diesel fuel rather than the gasoline needed by the Sherman made it a considerably quieter vehicle. After overcoming numerous teething troubles, it went into production, and nearly five thousand were completed. Introduced in 1943, it proved useful against German tanks up to the PzKpfw IV, but could not deal with either the Panther or the Tiger tank, and its open turret created serious dangers, since it was very vulnerable to shell splinters, small arms, and grenades. Many tankers responded by building up sandbag protection, improvising overhead armor, and at a minimum, trading the tanker's leather helmet for the more sturdy metal pot of the infantry.

The M-18 "Hellcat," used from 1944 onward, was a speedy (forty-five m.p.h. or better) purpose-built vehicle weighing under twenty tons, with an improved high-velocity 76mm gun, but it too did not measure up to the Panther or Tiger, most notably the Mark VI Tiger which incorporated a version of the much feared 88mm gun. The M-18 was favored among available American choices by tank destroyer personnel for its speed and its lower silhouette, but it remained vulnerable due to its thin armor and open turret. About 2,500 were built before production was ended in October 1944. By the end of the war, while the majority of units still used M-10s, 40 percent had been re-equipped with the M-18.[87]

One cost of this focus on the development of anti-tank tanks, at least in Army historian Lido Mayo's view, was to delay the development of a main battle tank more powerful than the well-known Sherman. "This was one example," concludes Mayo, "of a tendency among U.S. Army planners to apply the earlier experience of the Allies without enough imagination or flexibility," though others have argued that the United States had no effective heavier tank even in the beginning stages of development at the time.[88] Roman Jarymowycz adds further details: in 1942 army plans included sixty armored divisions, but only sixteen were actually raised, in part because of the expenditure of resources on the tank destroyers. Only five armored divisions were on hand for a breakout after the Normandy landings (Operation Cobra); had another five or six been available, Jarymowycz speculates, "the Rhine may well have been crossed by the fall of 1944," but instead the operations commander, Maj. Gen. Omar Bradley, had forty-five tank destroyer battalions, "equivalent to fifteen armored divisions except for the drawback of their being incapable of offensive operations." It was, in his opinion, a classic case of "powerful lobbyists pushing a wrong doctrine into an inappropriately powerful position," basically a matter of "tribal shortsightedness." Ironically, McNair was killed by American bombs dropped short of their target in precisely that breakout of July 1944; the tank destroyers lost their leading advocate, and the United States the highest ranking officer killed in action in the war.[89]

Even when American units were equipped with the M-18, the top German tanks were quite willing to take on the U.S. tank destroyers. The need was always for more firepower. One short-term answer was to mount a 105mm howitzer on an M-3 "Stuart" tank chassis to create a self-propelled howitzer, known as the "Priest" because of a machine-gun platform which resembled a pulpit; General Montgomery had some of these at El Alamein, though no American personnel were present. With a fixed forward-firing gun, however, it was an artillery piece, not a tank. At least it could be said that when American armor came to fight in Europe, many lessons had been learned. For example, the Sherman's 75mm gun had in many cases been replaced with a new 76mm gun which fired a much more powerful tungsten-carbide-core shell, capable in the right conditions of disabling a German Panther. The second-generation turreted, thin-skinned M-36 tank destroyers—

PAINTED WHITE TO BLEND WITH SNOW-COVERED TERRAIN, AN M-36 TANK DESTROYER CROSSES A FIELD NEAR DUDELANGE, LUXEMBOURG ON JANUARY 3, 1945. *U.S. CENTER FOR MILITARY HISTORY.*

"can openers" the tankers called them—introduced in October 1944, carried a 90mm anti-aircraft weapon in a larger turret on the M-10 chassis, but even the shell from a 90mm had to hit perfectly to penetrate the 100mm frontal armor of a Tiger tank at one thousand yards. Though it was impressive against the Panther and performed very well in support roles, it was still inadvisable for the M-36 to try "fire-and-movement" duels with good German tanks.[90] By the end of the war, a definitive answer had yet to be found—one strong reason why a separate tank destroyer force was disbanded in 1946.

The second issue was recruitment of the men for the tank destroyers—the reason for listing these units as "elites." As the official 1942 manual put it, only the best men would do. "Tanks and armored cars can be destroyed only by tough and determined fighting men who are masters of their weapons. Tank destroyer soldiers are taught that they must be superior soldiers. The moral qualities of aggressiveness, group spirit, and pride in an arduous and dangerous combat mission must pervade each tank destroyer unit. All ranks must possess a high sense of duty, an outstanding degree of discipline, a feeling of mutual loyalty and confidence with regard to their comrades and leaders, and a conscious pride in their organization."[91]

Despite the hyperbole, for the most part manpower for the tank destroyers was selected by a process little different from that which sent men to infantry, armor, or artillery, that is, mainly the luck of the draw. In the light of European events, in the fall of 1940 each Army regiment was authorized to include an anti-tank company, though few of the men assigned within each regiment had any experience with tanks in any form whatsoever. Nevertheless, the original anti-tank battalions (renamed "tank destroyer battalions" in November 1941 for psychological reasons)[92] were simply those 1940 companies withdrawn from their parent infantry, armored, or field artillery units, formed into battalions, and given new battalion numbers based on original branch of service respectively in the 600s, 700s, or 800s, and now detached for special, separate training. Though subsequent training was expected to develop tactical doctrines and instill a special esprit de corps, it also meant that the anti-tank force ran the risk of insufficient day-to-day association with the other arms.

Some men volunteered for the Tank Destroyers, but most did not. The recruitment process is typified at the top by the account of Col. Paul Bell, who commanded the 45th Division's 189th Field Artillery

Battalion. Bell was simply told (July 1941) by his divisional chief of staff to form an anti-tank battalion from the individual anti-tank platoons already established in each of the division's four artillery battalions. Having nothing but towed 75mm guns with which to train, in lieu of any self-propelled weapons Bell's new unit improvised by fixing trees and telephone poles on one-and-a-half ton trucks shortly before they moved off to Louisiana for maneuvers (here they were judged by McNair to have been most successful). Milton Blair's experience was at a less august level: At his induction center, ". . . the guy there asked me what I wanted to do. They always asked you what you wanted to do. So, I told him I wanted to be in the Medical Corps. He says, 'Fine, we'll put you in the Tank Destroyers as a driver.'"[93]

But perhaps an elite could be fashioned anyway. Training at Camp Hood, reports Combat Studies Institute historian Christopher Gabel, "was in large measure driven by the extraordinary emphasis that FM 18-5 [the *Tank Destroyer Field Manual*] placed on the élan and spirit of tank destroyer personnel." Not only did the men undergo the expected courses of vehicle operation, range firing, and other predictable subjects, but also out of two to three months here they spent a week on a "Tank Hunting Course," later called "Battle Conditioning," learning how to destroy enemy tanks when their own tank destroyer had been disabled, making use of the methods used by commandos and other special forces. For the first time in U.S. Army history, according to Gabel, live fire overhead was a feature of this course, on which the men spent a week. At its peak, Camp Hood had twenty-eight battalions and assorted battle groups under training at one time: "By World War II standards, the training program at Camp Hood ranked with the best." Unfortunately, some of the first battalions did not go through the entire program, but were shipped out to North Africa after only as little as seven weeks of training. "In addition, the deliberate cultivation of élan was not equally successful in all individuals, and some trainees questioned the value of such melodramatic and dangerous aspects of tank destroyer doctrine as dismounted tank hunting."[94]

The point was well made by Lt. Col. Barney of the 776th TD Battalion, writing back to friends at Camp Hood from Tunisia: "The next idea that MUST be taught the Bns [Battalions] is that all that stuff about TANK HUNTING and chasing tanks is . . . [left blank in original]. YOU MUST SELECT POSITIONS, DIG INTO THEM, LEAVE THEM FOR OTHERS AND ONLY OCCUPY THEM WHEN YOU

ARE READY TO SHOOT OR YOU GET DESTROYED JUST BE-
FORE THE ATTACK COMES. . . . If you try any shooting it out with
an 88 or a souped up 75 or a 50mm you are a dead goose unless you hit
him with the first round." The Tank Destroyer, in other words, was a
defensive weapon, a point which was fully recognized in a rewritten
version of the manual (July 1944): "Tank destroyers ambush hostile
tanks, but do not charge nor chase them."[95]

At least from the standpoint of numbers, the effort to create a
tank destroyer elite initially was more extensive than that concerning
any other American elite formations of World War II. McNair originally visualized some 222 battalions (more than 5,500 tank destroyers,
and with 800 men to a battalion, nearly 178,000 soldiers). The War
Department, however, was prepared to authorize only 144 battalions.
When the first units arrived in North Africa, the initial reports were
less than positive; indeed the official conclusion was that "the separate
tank destroyer arm is not a practical concept on the battlefield." The
problem was that the tank destroyers really needed to lie in ambush for
advancing tanks, but the conditions of North Africa had dictated that
concealment was not that easy, and the destroyers had to take the fight
to the enemy, though they themselves were protected by very little
armor, and even in concealment the self-propelled 75mm was too often revealed by its high silhouette. Field commanders, not surprisingly,
favored the towed 3-inch gun for defense against tanks, mainly because it could be dug in and concealed much more readily. McNair
continued to believe that it was the misapplication of tactical principles, not the basic concept, which was flawed, but in late 1943 the
decision was made to convert half the battalions to towed artillery.[96]

Even at that, there was apparently no need for even 144 battalions, since the American forces did not really experience the massed
German armor attacks, at least in North Africa, which had been anticipated. Tank destroyers were simply not in demand, compared to tanks
and field artillery. They would not be in demand in the Pacific either,
though some did appear there in the role of support artillery. Even
McNair understood the situation, "and assumed the initiative in check-
ing the growth of an enterprise which was in many ways his own child."[97]
In April 1943, the 144 was cut to 106; by 1944, only seventy-eight
battalions were left. In 1944, the War Department ordered the Tank
Destroyer School consolidated with the Armored School. The Tank
Destroyer Force was at that point on its way to extinction, not because

of the men, certainly, or even in the end the equipment, but rather the realization that the basic doctrine had been flawed from the start.[98] Nevertheless, Camp Hood (later Fort Hood) by war's end, according to the National TD Association, "had trained two brigades, 21 groups and 100 battalions, totaling between 85-87,000 men," at a vast camp including over 5,600 buildings and thirty–five firing ranges.[99]

Though never quite fulfilling their planned role, the surviving battalions, of the 106 activated, remained important, not least because they were heavily mechanized and largely self-sufficient in terms of maintenance. By now each battalion had been increased to three dozen 3-inch or 76mm guns, either towed or self-propelled, and were quite effective in the role of supporting artillery. Once they were used in that role, or assigned to attack antitank positions, or reconnaissance, or covering withdrawals, they had moved beyond the limited, specialized role once planned for them. Roger Beaumont notes that the Tank Destroyer Corps stands as a good example of "the gap between the role for which elite forces were created and the role that the actual conditions of war forced them into by the time they were raised and trained." In this case, the Corps "had drifted so far from their original mission that they were disbanded in 1946," which, while accurate enough, somewhat misses the point that had the tank destroyer force not been flexible enough to change its mission, its last battalions might well have been disbanded well before 1946.[100]

Even in their original role, the tank destroyers still could prove very useful. In November 1944 on the Roer plain, for example, the 6th Armored Regiment (three battalions of Shermans) claimed five Panther tanks killed; the single 702d Tank Destroyer Battalion, equipped with 90mm M-36s, ran up a tally of fifteen.[101] In the Battle of the Ardennes, interestingly, the original tank destroyer doctrine should have come into its own, with massed battalions in groups laying in wait for the massed attacking panzers. "But, of course, the tank destroyers were dispersed beyond recall, and with hundreds of panzers on the loose, their host divisions were most unlikely to release them. . . . By and large, the two dozen tank destroyer battalions that participated significantly in the Ardennes campaign fought in small units and in relatively static, defensive roles."[102] Most famous in this regard were the determined defensive stands of several tank destroyer battalions at Saint-Vith and in support of the 101st Airborne Division at Bastogne, which won well-deserved fame for the men with the famous tank destroyer patch of a black panther crushing a tank in its mouth.[103]

It is indicative of the flawed design of the intended elite tank destroyer corps that this was a scheme adopted by no other country. While the Germans did have formations of light tanks and self-propelled guns used in an anti-tank role, it was because heavy tanks were always in short supply, and it seemed better to use the light tanks they did have in some role rather than leave them idle. In short, the American Tank Destroyer Force turned out to be one quite substantial force designed to be an elite, but which for multiple reasons never quite fulfilled its purpose.

World War II in the Pacific came to an end, not with the feared invasion of the Japanese home islands, but with the dropping of the atomic bombs on Hiroshima and Nagasaki. To deliver these weapons, in mid-December 1944 the Army Air Force created a special elite unit, the 509th Composite Group: 225 officers and 1,542 enlisted men, equipped with the best, most up-to-date model B-29 heavy bombers, armor, and guns (except for tail turret) removed for extra height and speed. The unit was commanded in person by "Hap" Arnold, now a leiutenant general and in effect the Air Force's commander in chief. Of them all, only Arnold, Navy Capt. William S. ("Deak") Parsons, the unit's tactical commander who would actually decide upon the use (or emergency disposal) of the bomb, and the lead pilot who would fly the plane to drop the bomb, Lt. Col. Paul Tibbets, were aware of the actual mission contemplated.[104]

Arnold gave Tibbets a free hand to select the men for his unit, which would include both a bomb squadron and enough support elements to be virtually self-sufficient. The group originated in September 1944 in the 393d Heavy Bombardment Squadron, then in training for Europe at Fairmont, Nebraska, "because of the fine reputation it had gained during its training," according to Manhattan project director Maj. Gen. Leslie R. Groves.[105] The squadron had been ordered overseas with the 504th Bombardment Group, but now found itself assigned to train with fifteen specially modified aircraft (in the spring of 1945, the original fifteen were replaced with even more improved planes) at Wendover Field in northwestern Utah under the codename Silverplate to deliver atomic bombs over Germany and Japan. Tibbets was one of the Air Force's top pilots, who among other accomplishments had flown the first B-17 on a bombing mission over Europe, led the first Air Force raid on North Africa, and supervised the flight-testing of the new B-29 bomber.[106]

The squadron now trained for months through the winter and spring of 1944–45 over the deserts of Utah and Nevada, practicing especially the techniques needed for a visual bomb drop (radar was deemed not accurate enough for this task), and then a rapid escape to avoid the danger zone—though they were not told what the danger was. In December, the unit shifted to Batista Field in Cuba, for two months of practicing long solo oceanic flights and the requisite navigational challenges.[107]

By December Tibbets's command had become the 509th Group, including his original 393d, the 320th Troop Carrier Squadron, the 390th Air Service Group, the 603d Air Engineering squadron, and the 1027th Air Material Squadron, with various technical detachments and a military police unit for security.[108] In the spring the group moved to Tinian Island in the Marianas to join the 21st Bomber Command, though always they were kept under rigid security, physically separate from all other units. Tibbets had now cut his original squadron to the best fifteen crews; each bombardier had fifty or more missions, practice or otherwise, behind him. In small three-plane groups, they practiced raids on Japan, dropping single "Pumpkin" bombs of the size and characteristics of "Little Boy," the first uranium bomb which would be dropped, obtaining more experience while the scientists analyzed blast results.

It was necessary to name a precise target. Groves selected Japan's ancient capital, Kyoto, as his first choice, not least because it was so historically important, but this suggestion was opposed by Secretary of War Stimson, who persuaded President Truman to veto the plan. Stimson had visited the city, and was well aware of both its historical significance and the likely worldwide criticism which would follow its destruction. "After the sudden ending of the war I was very glad that I had been overruled . . . ," Groves would later write.[109]

Hiroshima, the largest city (aside from Kyoto) still undamaged by bombs, was chosen instead. Maj. Thomas Ferebee, the lead bombardier and a veteran of sixty-three combat missions over Europe, selected the target point of impact near the center of the city on August 2. On August 4, Parsons explained the mission, and the general nature of the bomb, to the seven crews selected for the final run to three target cities, Hiroshima and the alternates of Kokura and Nagasaki. One plane would proceed in advance to each city to monitor weather conditions; one plane was a spare held at Iwo Jima in case of the need to shift the bomb to another plane. Of the three remaining planes destined for

Hiroshima, two had observation duties and carried cameras, scientific instruments, and observers. Tibbets's own Enola Gay, named for his mother, carried the bomb. At 2:27 a.m. (Tinian time) on August 6, the Enola Gay departed Tinian; at 8:15 (Hiroshima time; it was 9:15 in Tinian), from 31,600 feet, Little Boy was released. It exploded at a height of 1,850 feet fifty-one seconds later, by which time Enola Gay was fifteen miles distant. At 2:58 P.M., Enola Gay touched down at Tinian. Tibbets was at once presented with the Distinguished Service Cross by Gen. Carl A. Spaatz, commander of the Strategic Air Forces, on hand to await the mission's results. A new era was born, and the 509th Composite Group had assisted importantly at its birth.[110]

9 Conclusion

Gen. George C. Marshall, with all the weight of his five-star rank, ended his last report on World War II to the War Department in 1945 with a notable statement: "We have tried since the birth of our nation to promote our love of peace by a display of weakness. This course has failed us utterly."[1] It is an apt comment. Certainly an unwillingness to pay for the preparation for war which, as the old adage has it, is the best prescription for peace, has been a common theme in American military history. But there are other themes. The belief in the nation's ability to respond effectively to any serious military challenge with its citizen army is one such, and of course it is a belief that has long been the stalwart pillar of military economy. Finally, an unwillingness to spend for peacetime preparedness has gone hand in hand with a suspicion of standing armies, and not simply large standing armies. The often minuscule armies which resulted were hard put to respond to immediate demands, let alone train reserves of whatever sort. The formation, training, and permanent establishment of military elites for all these reasons has generally been low on the list of American military priorities.

Such a trend is directly linked to America's populist distaste for socio-economic elites in general. Though we have always had them, since independence they have never been marked off by hereditary titles and, more important for this study, guaranteed military elite roles in regime-defending guards regiments. Nothing, indeed, better shows America's distrust of anything resembling such an elite than the constant attacks made upon the elitist institution which West Point was seen to be. But even in the question of social elites, American military history has its exceptions in the militia units so popular in the nineteenth century, often closed to the lower classes if only through the expenses of membership: as has been seen in the preceding chapters, some such units managed not only to persevere over time but to do well in combat, most notably in the Civil War.

On the other hand, ethnicity has only rarely played a role in the history of military units, most notably, but not exclusively, in the Civil War—and in such cases a particular ethnic identity cannot really be said to have had any direct correlation to elite status or the lack thereof, though certainly a shared culture could be an important ingredient in unit pride. Race is another matter, and some readers will be surprised, perhaps angered, that no African American unit is termed elite in this study. The main reason for that fact, of course, is quite simple: black Americans were only encouraged to participate in America's struggles up through World War II when manpower needs were desperate. When they were used in segregated units, inevitably black Americans faced numerous racially-inspired difficulties which other units did not encounter, including the desire among many white officers in positions of command that the black units fail.

This book has mentioned some fine black units: a few regiments in the Civil War, black infantry and cavalry in the Indian Wars, the 92d division in World War I, the four squadrons of the 332d Fighter Group (particularly the 99th Fighter Squadron) in World War II. Yet none of these few units really was regarded as exceptional enough to warrant the title of "elite." The 99th Squadron, for example, won a rare accolade from an Air Force study in 1944 as a "superb tactical fighter unit" (this was for Mediterranean operations in P-40s; the unit's main reputation was earned in the last months of the war flying P-51s), finding "no significant general difference" between it and other similar white combat squadrons, much the same conclusion reached by William Dobak and Thomas Phillips in their study of the post-Civil War black regulars.[2]

But the suspicion of elites is only one side of the coin. The historical record shows clearly a countervailing trend, at least in wartime, of the emergence of such elites, whether established as purpose-driven forces or evolving more by accident or chance than design, and this study has discussed both general categories. Examples of the first are found from colonial-era rangers through the many case studies from World War II. Fewer cases of "accidental" elites have been included in this work mainly because it was not really possible to deal with that large subject in the context of World War II aside from a few elements, such as the pilots of the Flying Tigers or the 10th/442d nisei units, but examples have been seen in the Civil War's Iron and Stonewall Brigades, or World War I's 1st and 2d Divisions.

Recruitment methods varied for both categories. In general, most pre-designated elites were formed on the basis of physical and mental qualifications rather than special skills; paratroopers needed no paratrooper training to join. To volunteer was often enough, provided certain basic qualifications were met and the recruit survived his basic training and indoctrination, as in the Marines. Some units did require special skills as well, of course: the original skiers of the 10th Mountain Division or the pilots of any of the flying units discussed in the context of both world wars.

Duration and replacement methods clearly are key factors in the definition of an elite. Some elite units discussed in the preceding pages were only intended for short-term service, such as General Washington's light units which were regularly broken up after each campaign. More often, elites designated as such in advance were intended for longer-term service; after all, the investment in training and perhaps outfitting could be considerable. In such cases, elite quality, once proven on the battlefield, was likely to be sustained only by replacing casualties with men selected and trained according to the same qualifications, and this was not a common experience in American military history. Particularly when an elite unit was used in a generally non-elite role, the tendency was to funnel replacements with none of the requisite skills into the unit, even in a specialist formation like the 10th Mountain Division. In such circumstances, elite status may be visualized as a graphable curve, sometimes quite sharp, designating a falloff from elite status. The option was to withdraw the unit from combat, bring replacements up to the necessary standard, and recommit the unit when and where appropriate, but as this study has shown, such theoretically ideal procedures were not always possible in practice.

The question of how such elites have been used is a large issue, and there is no simple conclusion. Some earned heroic records over a considerable time period, such as the Marines in the Pacific in World War II. The Airborne Divisions won similar praise, but it is hard to point to a particular instance of their employment and conclude definitely that there was a turning point, and that without the Airborne—or other elite—the tide would not have turned. Some general themes again emerge, for example a tendency to employ men trained in special skills in ways that might not use them to the best advantage. This is particularly the case given the natural inclination, as has been seen, of every general once he has command of skilled elite units to keep control of them. Such units are costly to form and difficult to replace in any era, and not to be used wastefully if at all possible—but often there seemed no alternative: the "fortunes of war." American commanders never quite reacted in the way Hitler did after Crete, deciding not to use his airborne forces in an airborne role again, but the United States did have special cases, such as the 13th Airborne Division, which trained for more than three years and was sent to Europe, but never saw combat (it was scheduled to take part in operations against the German "National Redoubt" in the Bavarian Alps, but this never became necessary).[3]

One can ask, of course, whether elites, particularly when they are small and the army from which they are drawn is large, may not form an interesting escape valve for the wilder elements of the armed forces, indeed, perhaps for society as a whole. To this there really can be no one answer: much depends on the process of recruitment and evaluation. Some units as noted in this volume have been famous, or infamous, for their indiscipline, at least off the battlefield, a fame which, it may be postulated, is likely to be acquired in a direct ratio to such factors as the degree to which the unit is encouraged to regard itself as better than any other, or the feeling that once specially trained and selected the unit was mis- or under-used. In that sense, of course, it was to be hoped that undisciplined behavior could be transformed into individual battlefield initiative. It seems inappropriate, however, to draw conclusions on this issue beyond the obvious: units that expect to draw upon individual initiative are likely to contain individualists who strain against disciplined behavior. The successful unit will find the proper balance.

But what of the influence of elites on larger formations? Is an army likely to respond better to the challenge of combat because it contains elites to be emulated? Certainly the Emperor Napoleon was of this mind, continuing as he did to evolve formations of his Guard until virtually the end of his career. On the other hand, there was an inevitable cost to removing the best veterans from line units; obviously they were no longer available to provide role models and inspiration—and more than once Napoleon was heavily criticized by commentators both contemporary and after the fact for not committing his guards when the time had come to commit them. Elites, moreover, tend to run to exclusiveness, which arouses quite legitimate suspicions: Rome's Praetorian Guard, after all, was composed (at least some of the time) of experienced veterans. America had no Praetorians, but the word was familiar, particularly to the founding fathers who had studied their classical history, and were determined to have no emperor-making military elites. But as this book has demonstrated, we had elites anyway, in nearly every major military conflict in our history. To put it another way, it was no accident that "Rangers" in one form or another have persistently formed part of America's military heritage. This has been true for better or worse, and this volume includes examples of both circumstances. Whether in peace or in war, America's love of the fabled hunter/rifleman has seldom dwindled, and never died, even though in the twenty-first century he may wear a green beret rather than a coonskin cap.

Notes

Preface

1. Thomas Wentworth Higginson, *Army Life in a Black Regiment* (1870; repr., East Lansing, MI: Michigan State University Press, 1960), 190.

Chapter 1: The Colonial Tradition

1. John Shy, "A New Look at the Colonial Militia," in *A People Numerous and Armed: Reflections on the Military Struggle for American Independence* (New York: Oxford University Press, 1976), 24–25.

2. T. H. Breen, "The Covenanted Militia of Massachusetts Bay: English Background and New World Development," in Breen, *Puritans and Adventurers: Change and Persistence in Early America* (New York: Oxford University Press, 1976), 24–25.

3. Quoted in Breen, "Covenanted Militia," 38.

4. John K. Mahon, *History of the Militia and National Guard* (New York: Macmillan, 1983), 18.

5. Maj. John R. Galvin, *The Minute Men: A Compact History of the Defenders of the American Colonies 1645–1775* (New York: Hawthorne Books, 1967; repr., Washington, D.C.: Brassey's, Inc., 1996), 22; on the war, Alfred A. Cave, *The Pequot War* (Amherst: University of Massachusetts Press, 1996); Harold E. Selesky, *War and Society in Colonial Connecticut* (New Haven: Yale University Press, 1990), 6–9; Harry M. Ward, *The United Colonies of New England, 1643–90* (New York: Vantage Press, 1961), ch. 13. An interesting study of the general context is John E. Ferling, *A Wilderness of Miseries: War and Warriors in Early America* (Westport, CT: Greenwood, 1980), and the same author's "The New England Soldier: A Study in Changing Perceptions," *American Quarterly* 33 (1981): 26–45; see also on these and other studies, Don Higginbotham, "The Early American Way of War: Reconnais-

sance and Appraisal," in *The William & Mary Quarterly*, 3rd ser. 44 (1987): 230–73.

6. Quoted in Galvin, *Minute Men*, 24.

7. Douglas Edward Leach, *The Northern Colonial Frontier, 1607–1763* (New York: Holt, Rinehart, Winston, 1966), 57–8, both quotes.

8. Galvin, *Minute Men*, 29; Douglas Edward Leach, *Flintlock and Tomahawk: New England in King Philip's War* (New York: Macmillan, 1958), 103–4, 185.

9. Douglas Edward Leach, *Roots of Conflict: British Armed Forces and Colonial Americans, 1677–1763* (Chapel Hill: University of North Carolina Press, 1986), is the main source of this paragraph; Allan R. Millett and Peter Maslowski, *For the Common Defense: A Military History of the United States of America* (New York: Free Press, 1984), 41–4. Important studies on the subject include John Shy, *Toward Lexington: The Role of the British Army in the Coming of the American Revolution* (Princeton: Princeton University Press, 1965), and Sylvia R. Frey, *The British Soldier in America: A Social History of Military Life in the Revolutionary Period* (Austin: University of Texas Press, 1981).

10. Paul E. Kopperman, *Braddock at the Monongahela* (Pittsburgh: University of Pittsburgh Press, 1977), 15.

11. Kopperman, *Braddock*, 45.

12. Journal of a British Officer, quoted in Charles Hamilton, ed., *Braddock's Defeat* (Norman: University of Oklahoma Press, 1959), 50.

13. Kopperman, *Braddock*, 79; Hamilton, *Braddock's Defeat*, 29.

14. Kopperman, *Braddock*, 131, quoted; Fred Anderson, *Crucible of War: The Seven Years' War and the Fate of Empire in British North America, 1754–1766* (New York: Knopf, 2000), ch. 9; Stanley Pargellis, "Braddock's Defeat," *American Historical Review* 4 (1936), 253–69: "Braddock inexcusably neglected the fundamentals of the European art of War," (265). Still lively and most readable is Francis Parkman, *Montcalm and Wolfe* (1884; repr., New York: Collier, 1962), ch. 7. Parkman and Anderson, writing well over a century apart, both give the French and Indians a total of nine hundred men at the battle.

15. Fred Anderson, *A People's Army: Massachusetts Soldiers and Society in the Seven Years' War* (Chapel Hill: University of North Carolina Press, 1984), 61.

16. Galvin, *Minute Men*, 34.

17. Stephen Brumwell, *Redcoats: The British Soldier and War in the Americas, 1755–1763* (Cambridge: Cambridge University Press, 2002), 213.

18. Galvin, *Minute Men*, ch. 2; G. A. Rawlyk, *Yankees at Louisbourg* (Orono, ME: University of Maine Press, 1967); Selesky, *War and Society*, 27, 44.

19. Lawrence Delbert Cress, *Citizens in Arms: The Army and the Militia*

in American Society to the War of 1812 (Chapel Hill: University of North Carolina Press, 1982), 4–7.

20. Mahon, *Militia,* 21; Millett and Maslowski, *For the Common Defense*; Douglas Edward Leach, *Arms for Empire: A Military History of the British Colonies in North America, 1607–1763* (New York: Macmillan, 1973), 171.

21. Robert Rogers, *Reminiscences of the French War with Robert Rogers' "Journal" and a Memoir of General Stark* (Freedom, NH: Freedom Historical Society, 1988 reprint of 1831 edition, itself reprinting Rogers' 1765 Journal), Appendix, "General Rules for the Ranging Service," 149–154 (149 quoted); Rogers on writing the rules, 41. A recent edition is Timothy J. Todish, ed., *The Annotated and Illustrated Journals of Major Robert Rogers* (Fleischmanns, N.Y.: Purple Mountain Press, 2002). The most detailed history is by Burt Garfield Loescher, *The History of Rogers' Rangers* (Bowie, MD: Heritage, 2002), 4 vols., 2002.

22. John R. Cuneo, *Robert Rogers of the Rangers* (New York: Oxford University Press, 1959); Anderson, *Crucible of War*, 186–89; Russell Bellico, *Chronicles of Lake George* (Fleischmanns, New York: Purple Mountain Press, 1995), ch. 5.

23. Rogers, *Reminiscences*, 41–6.

24. Capt. John Knox, *The Siege of Quebec and the Campaigns in North America, 1757–1760*, ed. Brian Connell (Mississauga, Ontario: Pendragon House, 1980), 22 (quoted), 99.

25. William R. Nester, *The First Global War: Britain, France, and the Fate of North America, 1756–1775* (Westport: Praeger, 2000), 5–6, 51, 101; Oliver W. B. Peabody, "Life of Israel Putnam," in Jared Sparks, ed., *American Biography, vol. 3* (New York: Harper, 1902), 1–116.

26. Daniel Justin Herman, *Hunting and the American Imagination* (Washington, D.C.: Smithsonian Institution, 2001), 23.

27. Randolph Roth, "Guns, Gun Culture, and Homicide: The Relationship between Firearms, the Uses of Firearms, and Interpersonal Violence," in *The William and Mary Quarterly*, 3rd, 59 (2002): 231.

28. Herman, *Hunting*, 35.

29. Newcomer, *Embattled Farmers*, 51.

30. Leach, *Flintlock*, 13 (quoted), 67, 91–2, 106, 133–4, 152–3; somewhat similar remarks on guns are made in Leach, *Northern Frontier,* 77; Jill Lepore, *The Name of War: King Philip's War and the Origins of American Identity* (New York: Knopf, 1998), 173–174.

31. Selesky, *War and Society*, 91.

32. Jeremy Black, *America as a Military Power: From the American Revolution to the Civil War* (Westport: Praeger, 2002), 183.

33. Numbers are drawn from my study of A. Merwyn Carey, *American Firearms Makers: When, Where and What They Made from the Colonial Period*

to the End of the 19th Century (New York: Crowell, 1953), and L. D. Satterlee and Arcadi Gluckman, *American Gun Makers* (Buffalo: O. Ulbrich, 1940).

34. Satterlee and Gluckman, *American Gun Makers*, 10, 182. On the strategic position of Valley Forge—and the myths of the winter encampment—see Wayne Bodle, *The Valley Forge Winter* (University Park, PA: Pennsylvania State University Press, 2002), ch. 1.

35. The Pennsylvania State Gun Factory was dismantled in 1778.

36. Satterlee and Gluckman, *American Gun Makers*, 126.

37. Satterlee and Gluckman, *American Gun Makers*, 49, 83.

38. Loudoun to Cumberland, 22 November–26 December 1756, in Stanley Pargellis, ed., *Military Affairs in North America, 1748–1756: Selected Documents from the Cumberland Papers in Windsor Castle* (New York: Appleton-Century, 1936), 269, 279 (both quotes).

39. Hugh Hastings, ed., *Orderly Book and Journal of Major John Hawks on the Ticonderoga-Crown Point Campaign, under General Jeffrey Amherst 1759–1760* (New York: Society of Colonial Wars in the State of New York, 1911), 36.

40. Galvin, *Minute Men*, ch 4.

41. Galvin, *Minute Men*, 43; at the last moment the name "Picket Guards" was replaced by "Province Guards" in the legislative proposal.

42. Anderson, *Crucible of War*, 181.

43. Peter Way, "The Cutting Edge of Culture: British Soldiers Encounter Native Americans in the French and Indian War," in M. Daunton and R. Halpern, eds., *Empire and Others: British Encounters with Indigenous Peoples, 1600–1850* (Philadelphia: University of Pennsylvania Press, 1999), 139 (first two quotations); Brumwell, *Redcoats*, n. 10, 229.

44. Loudoun to Commanding Officers of the 62nd or Royal American Regiment, 28 December 1756, in Stanley M. Pargellis, *Lord Loudoun in North America* (New Haven: Yale University Press, 1933), 299–300 (quoted); Germans, Brumwell, *Redcoats*, 74. On the British response, Richard Holmes, *Redcoat: The British Soldier in the Age of Horse and Musket* (London: Harper Collins, 2001), 41–2, 112, and in general, David Gates, *The British Light Infantry Arm, c. 1790–1815: Its Creation, Training, and Operational Role (London: Batsford, 1987)*.

45. Holmes, *Redcoats*, 42 (both quotes).

46. Brumwell, *Redcoats*, 230, 249 (both quotes).

47. Russell F. Weigley, *History of the United States Army* (New York: Macmillan, 1967), 25–8.

48. Brumwell, *Redcoats*, 51–3. The issue of how much the evolution of light infantry formations and tactics were influenced by continental European warfare can be left to others.

49. Don Higginbotham, "The Military Institutions of Colonial America:

The Rhetoric and the Reality," in *War and Society in Revolutionary America: The Wider Dimensions of Conflict* (Columbia, S.C.: University of South Carolina Press, 1988), 20.

50. Brumwell, *Redcoats*, 99.

51. Parkman, *Montcalm and Wolfe*, 302.

Chapter 2: The Revolutionary War

1. Robert A. Gross, *The Minutemen and Their World* (1976; repr., New York: Hill & Wang, 2001), 59–70 (59 quoted).

2. Don Higginbotham, *The War of American Independence: Military Attitudes, Policies, and Practice, 1763–1789* (New York: Macmillan, 1971), 68–78; Christopher Ward, The War of the Revolution (New York: Macmillan, 1952), I:35, 84–5; Richard M. Ketchum, *The Battle for Bunker Hill* (New York: Doubleday, 1962), 123 (Howe) quoted.

3. In a letter to Giovanni Fabbroni, June 8, 1778, *The Portable Thomas Jefferson*, Merrill D. Peterson, ed. (New York: Penguin, 1975), 359.

4. Quoted in Richard M. Ketchum, *Saratoga: Turning Point of America's Revolutionary War* (New York: Henry Holt, 1997), 126.

5. Willard M. Wallace, *Appeal to Arms: A Military History of the American Revolution* (New York: Harper & Bros., 1951), 46.

6. Gross, *Minutemen*, 135, 152 (quoted).

7. Washington to President of Congress, 24 September 1776, *The Writings of George Washington from the Original Manuscript Sources 1745–1799*, John C. Fitzpatrick, ed. (Washington: USGPO, 1932), Vol. 6, 107 [hereafter *WGW* 6:107].

8. Wallace, *Appeal to Arms*, 52–3; Lloyd Kramer, *Lafayette in Two Worlds: Public Cultures and Personal Identities in an Age of Revolutions* (Chapel Hill: University of North Carolina Press, 1996), 26; Robert K. Wright, Jr., "'Nor is Their Standing Army to be Despised': The Emergence of the Continental Army as a Military Institution," in R. Hoffman and P. J. Albert, eds., *Arms and Independence: The Military Character of the American Revolution* (Charlotte: University Press of Virginia, 1984), 50–74.

9. Washington to President of Congress, 24 September 1776, *WGW* 6:110–1 (quoted); Mark V. Kwasny, *Washington's Partisan War, 1775–1783* (Kent, OH: Kent State University Press, 1996), 273; Don Higginbotham, "The American Militia: a Traditional Institition with Revolutionary Responsibilities," in *Reconsiderations on the Revolutionary War: Selected Essays* (Westport, CT: Greenwood, 1978), ch. 6; Mahon, Militia, ch. 2.

10. "Sentiments," 2 May 1783, *WGW* 26:374ff.

11. Washington to Committee of Congress, 21 August 1781, *WGW* 23:30.

12. Washington to John Augustus Washington, 6 July 1780, *WGW* 19:134

(quoted); Charles Knowles Bolton, *The Private Soldier under Washington* (New York: Scribners, 1902), 96–7, 173.

13. Allen Bowman, *The Morale of the American Revolutionary Army* (Washington, D.C.: American Council on Public Affairs, 1943), 32 (quoted), 59, 72–74; James Kirby Martin, "A 'Most Undisciplined Profligate Crew': Protest and Defiance in the Continental Ranks, 1776–1783," in Hoffman and Albert, *Arms and Independence*, 119–40.

14. Washington to Committee of Congress with the Army, 29 January 1778, WGW 10:379.

15. General Order, 7 August 1782, *WGW* 23:488 (quoted); boards, 25:181–2; sample certificate, 25:373–4; Arthur E. Du Bois, "The Heraldry of Heroism," *National Geographic* 83 (1943): 411.

16. General Order, 7 August 1782, *WGW* 23:487.

17. Charles Patrick Neimeyer, *America Goes to War: A Social History of the Continental Army* (New York: New York University Press, 1996), is a useful general study. Mark Edward Lender, "The Social Structure of the New Jersey Brigade: The Continental Line as an American Standing Army," in Peter Kersten, ed., *The Military in America from the Colonial Era to the Present* (New York: Free Press, 1980), 27–44, adds interesting detail. On the Army as a whole, see Robert K. Wright, Jr., *The Continental Army* (Washington, D.C.: Center of Military History, 1983). German legion: Washington to Baron Steuben, 12 April 1782, *WGW* 24:112.

18. Washington to Commanding Officer of 14th Virginia Regiment, 4 June 1877, *WGW* 8:178.

19. Ibid. (quoted); General Orders, 11 March 1776, *WGW* 4:386–7.

20. Washington to Capt. Caleb Gates, 22 April 1777, *WGW* 7:452–3.

21. Washington to Col. Alexander Spotswood, 30 April 1877, *WGW* 7:495.

22. Remarks on the Guard in this and following two paragraphs are based upon Carlos E. Godfrey, *The Commander-in-Chief's Guard, Revolutionary War* (Baltimore: Genealogical Publishing Co., 1972).

23. On Steuben, see John McAuley Palmer, *General von Steuben* (New Haven: Yale University Press, 1937), ch. 21–25; Friedrich Kapp, *The Life of Frederick William von Steuben, Major General in the Revolutionary Army* (New York: Mason Bros., 1859), ch. 6 and 10; and Rudolf Cronau, *The Army of the American Revolution and Its Organizer* (New York: Privately printed, 1923), 19–47.

24. James Kirby Martin, *Benedict Arnold: Revolutionary Hero, An American Warrior Reconsidered* (New York: New York University Press, 1997), provides a dramatic account of the events of September 1780, 1–10; Williard Sterne Randall, *Benedict Arnold: Patriot and Traitor* (New York: Morrow, 1990), 438–9, 480–1, 519, 538; Louis Gottschalk, *Lafayette and*

the Close of the American Revolution (Chicago: University of Chicago Press, 1942), 135–7.

25. Washington, notes for letter to Congress, 11 July 1775, *The Papers of George Washington: Revolutionary War Series*, D. Chase, etc., eds. (Charlottesville: University Press of Virginia, 1986–1991), vol. 1, 85–91, 85 quoted; hereafter *PGW* 1:85; Don Higginbotham, *George Washington and the American Military Tradition* (Athens, GA: University of Georgia Press, 1985), 18–22.

26. Washington to Samuel Washington, 30 September 1775, *PGW* I:73.

27. General Orders, 1 June 1777, *WGW* 8:156.

28. Weigley, *History*, 66–7; Wright, *Continental Army*, 149.

29. Quoted in David Nelson, *Anthony Wayne: Soldier of the Early Republic* (Bloomington: Indiana University Press, 1985), 72.

30. Quoted in Charles Royster, *A Revolutionary People at War: The Continental Army and American Character, 1775–1783* (Chapel Hill: University of North Carolina Press, 1980), 34.

31. Gen. C. Lee to Col. Thompson, 21 June 1776, in Jared Sparks, *Correspondence of the American Revolution* (Boston: Little, Brown, 1853), vol. 2, 501–2; this was clearly Washington's view: Washington to Maj. Gen. Horatio Gates, 20 August 1777, *WGW* 9:102.

32. Washington to Capt. Daniel Morgan, 4 October 1775, *WGW* 4:2.

33. Washington to Brig. Gen. Charles Scott, and General Orders, both 14 August 1778, *WGW* 12:323–4, and to Committee of Congress, 28 January 1778, *WGW* 10:368 (quoted).

34. John W. Wright, "The Corps of Light Infantry in the Continental Army," *American Historical Review* 31 (1926): 455.

35. Royster, *Revolutionary People at War*, 46–7, 213–22.

36. Wright, "Corps of Light Infantry," 456; Charles J. Stillé, *Major-General Anthony Wayne and the Pennsylvania Line in the Continental Army* (Philadelphia: Lippincott, 1893), 180–1 (light corps) and ch. 5 (Stony Point); Armstrong Starkey, "Paoli to Stony Point: Military Ethics and Weaponry During the American Revolution," *Journal of Military History* 58 (1994): 7–28; Nelson, Wayne, ch. 5; Glenn Tucker, *Mad Anthony Wayne and the New Nation* (Harrisburg: Stackpole, 1973), ch. 12; William H. Guthman, *March to Massacre: A History of the First Seven Years of the United States Army, 1774–1781* (New York: McGraw-Hill, 1975), ch. 2.

37. Washington to Wayne, 10 July 1779, *WGW* 15:397.

38. Washington to Wayne, 14 September 1779, *WGW* 16:288.

39. Washington to Steuben, 18, 22, and 24 July 1780, *WGW* 19:202–3, 231–2, 239–40.

40. Wright, "Corps of Light Infantry," 457, quoting Steuben to Washington, 28 July 1780.

41. Washington, General Orders, 26 November 1780, *WGW* 20:402, and 1 February 1781, 21:169–70 (quoted).

42. Wright, "Corps of Light Infantry," 460 (Lafayette quoted), and 461 (quoted); Olivier Bernier, *Lafayette: Hero of Two Worlds* (New York: Dutton, 1983), 96, and Gottschalk, Lafayette and Close, 121–3 (feathers).

43. Don Higginbotham, *Daniel Morgan, Revolutionary Rifleman* (Chapel Hill: University of North Carolina Press, 1961), 22–77; North Callahan, *Daniel Morgan: Ranger of the Revolution* (New York: Holt, Rinehart, Winston, 1961), ch. 3; Richard B. LaCross, Jr., *Revolutionary Rangers: Daniel Morgan's Riflemen and Their Role in the Northern Frontier* (Bowie, MD: Heritage, 2002), includes many individual biographies; Wright, *Continental Army*, 116–7. Rifle exchange: General Orders, 13 June 1777, WGW 8:246.

44. Washington to Maj. Gen. Israel Putnam, 16 August 1777, *WGW* 9:70.

45. Washington to Gov. George Linton, 16 August 1777, *WGW* 9:78.

46. Washington to Maj. Gen. Horatio Gates, 20 August 1777, *WGW* 9:102.

47. Quoted in Eric Robson, *The American Revolution in Its Political and Military Aspects, 1763–1783* (New York: Oxford University Press, 1955), 130–1.

48. Ketchum, Saratoga, 132–9, 352–60; Martin, *Benedict Arnold*, ch. 16.

49. Quoted in Paul David Nelson, *General Horatio Gates: A Biography* (Baton Rouge: Louisiana State University Press, 1976), 134.

50. Thomas G. Frothingham, *Washington: Commander in Chief* (Boston: Houghton Mifflin, 1930), 230. Gates had taken control of Morgan's unit from General Arnold; in the resulting shouting match, Gates told Arnold he would be glad to give him a pass to leave the army; Randall, *Benedict Arnold*, 360.

51. George Washington to James McHenry, 13 December 1788, in H. C. Syrett, ed., *The Papers of Alexander Hamilton* (New York: Columbia University Press, 1975), vol. 22, 364.

52. Higginbotham, *Morgan*, 80–109. Wayne had asked for the light corps: Nelson, *Anthony Wayne*, 91; Tucker, *Mad Anthony Wayne*, 141.

53. Higginbotham, *War of American Independence*, 402 (quoted), but see 102. On Cowpens, Lawrence E. Babits, *A Devil of a Whipping: The Battle of Cowpens* (Chapel Hill: University of North Carolina Press, 1998); Weigley, *History of the American Army*, 70–72, and Weigley, *The Partisan War: The South Carolina Campaign of 1780–1782* (Columbia, S.C.: University of South Carolina Press, 1970).

54. Washington to Reed, 24 June 1781, *WGW* 22:257.

55. Washington to Maj. Thomas Parr, 28 July 1781, *WGW* 22:427.

56. General Orders, 8 June 1782, *WGW* 24:322.

57. George Athan Billias, *General John Glover and his Marblehead Mariners* (New York: Holt, 1960), brawl, 68; Wright, *Continental Army*, 218; Ward, *War of Revolution*, 234, 257–9, 293–4; Higginbotham, *War of Ameri-*

can Independence, 99, 161, 166–7; A. E. Zuker, *General De Kalb, Lafayette's Mentor* (Chapel Hill: University of North Carolina Press, 1966), 42–3; Mark Thistlewaite, "'Washington Crossing the Delaware': Navigating the Image(s) of the Hero," in Kevin L. Cope, ed., *George Washington In and As Culture* (New York: AMS Press, 2001), 39–63.

58. Robert D. Bass, *Swamp Fox: The Life and Campaigns of General Francis Marion* (New York: Holt, 1959), 4 quoted. An interpretative work on Lee is Charles Royster, *Light-Horse Harry Lee and the Legacy of the American Revolution* (New York: Knopf, 1981).

59. Wallace, *Appeal to Arms*, 70.

60. Charles A. Jellison, *Ethan Allen, Frontier Rebel* (Syracuse: Syracuse University Press, 1969), ch. 3–5.

61. Ibid., 105.

62. Edward Hamilton, *Fort Ticonderoga: Key to a Continent* (Ticonderoga, NY: Fort Ticonderoga, 1964; repr., 1995, ch. 8; John J. Duffy, ed., Ethan Allen and His Kin: Correspondence, 1772–1819 (Hanover, N.H.: University Press of New England, 1998), vol. 1, 20–1.

63. Barnet Schecter, *The Battle for New York: The City at the Heart of the American Revolution* (New York: Walker, 2002), 196–7, 213–4; Henry Johnston, *The Battle of Harlem Heights, September 16, 1776* (New York: Macmillan, 1897), 53, 79, 96–7, 178, 189–92; Bruce Bliven, Jr., Battle for Manhattan (New York: Holt, 1956), 84; Henry Phelps Johnston, *Nathan Hale, 1776: Biography and Memorials* (New Haven: Yale University Press, 1914), 103–111.

64. Fred Anderson Berg, *Encyclopedia of Continental Army Units* (Harrisburg, PA: Stackpole, 1972), 48, 57, 78.

65. John C. Dann, ed., *The Revolution Remembered: Eyewitness Accounts of the War for Independence* (Chicago: University of Chicago Press, 1980), 253 (spies), 258 (worthless set), 259 (Roush); see also 95–100.

Chapter 3: The Early Republic

1. C. Joseph Bernardo and Eugene H. Bacon, *American Military Policy: Its Development Since 1775* (Harrisburg, PA: Military Service Publishing, 1955), 61.

2. James Kirby Martin and Mark Edward Lender, *A Respectable Army: The Military Origins of the Republic, 1763–1789* (Arlington Heights, IL: Harlan Davidson, 1982), 95; Don Higginbotham, "The Federalized Militia Debate: A Neglected Aspect of Second Amendment Scholarship," *William and Mary Quarterly* 3rd 55 (1998): 39–58; E. Wayne Carp, "The Problem of National Defense in the Early American Republic," in Jack Greene, ed., *The American Revolution: Its Character and Limits* (New York: New York University Press, 1987), 14–50.

3. Allan R. Millett and Peter Maslowski, *For the Common Defense: A Military History of the United States of America* (New York: Free Press, 1984), 83–4; Lawrence Delbert Cress, *Citizens in Arms: The Army and the Militia in American Society to the War of 1812* (Chapel Hill: University of North Carolina Press, 1982), ch. 4.

4. Remarks on the Cincinnati in this and following paragraphs are based upon Minor Myers, Jr., *Liberty Without Anarchy: A History of the Society of the Cincinnati* (Charlottesville: University Press of Virginia, 1983), 19 quoted.

5. Willard Sterne Randall, *Alexander Hamilton: A Life* (New York: HarperCollins, 2003), 309; on Knox's role, North Callahan, *Henry Knox: General Washington's General* (New York: Rinehart, 1958), ch. 11.

6. Nathaniel Greene to Washington, 29 August 1784, Lt.-Col. Edgar E. Hume, ed., *General Washington's Correspondence Concerning the Society of the Cincinnati* (Baltimore: Johns Hopkins Press, 1941), 205.

7. Jefferson to James Madison, 28 December 1784, in Hume, *Correspondence*, 34.

8. Quoted in Myers, *Liberty*, 54.

9. Quoted in Myers, *Liberty*, 99; Charles Royster, *A Revolutionary People at War: The Continental Army and American Character, 1775–1783* (Chapel Hill: University of North Carolina Press, 1979), 349–359.

10. Remarks on West Point are based upon Theodore Joseph Crackel, "The Founding of West Point: Jefferson and the Politics of Security," *Armed Forces and Society* 7 (1981): 529–543; Stephen E. Ambrose, *Duty, Honor, Country: a History of West Point* (Baltimore: Johns Hopkins University Press, 1966); James L. Morrison, Jr., *"The Best School in the World": West Point, the Pre-Civil War Years, 1833–1866* (Kent, OH: Kent State University Press, 1986); Thomas J. Fleming, *The Men and Times of the United States Military Academy* (New York: William Morrow, 1969); Sidney Forman, *West Point: A History of the United States Military Academy* (New York: Columbia University Press, 1950); James L. Morrison, Jr., "Military Education and Strategic thought, 1846–1861," in Kenneth J. Hagan and William R. Roberts, eds., *Against All Enemies: Interpretations of American Military History from Colonial Times to the Present* (New York: Greenwood, 1986), 113–132.

11. Ambrose, *Duty, Honor, Country*, 107.

12. William B. Skelton, "The Army in the Age of the Common Man, 1815–1845," in Kenneth J. Hagan and William R. Roberts, eds., *Against All Enemies*, 97, 98, 99 (quoted in that order).

13. Wiley Sword, *President Washington's Indian War: The Struggle for the Old Northwest, 1790–1795* (Norman: University of Oklahoma Press, 1985); James Ripley Jacobs, *The Beginning of the U.S. Army, 1783–1812* (Princeton: Princeton University Press, 1947), 127–55; Bernado and Bacon, *American Military Policy*, ch. 3, especially 74–84; Black, America as a Military Power, 84–5.

14. Bernardo and Bacon, *American Military Policy*, ch. 4; John K. Mahon, *History of the Militia and the National Guard* (New York: Macmillan, 1983), ch. 4.

15. Weed is quoted in Clayton Mau, *The Development of Central and Western New York, from the arrival of the white man to the eve of the Civil War, as portrayed chronologically in contemporary accounts . . .* (Dansville, N.Y.: F.A. Owen, 1958), 154.

16. Bernardo and Bacon, *American Military Policy*, 109.

17. J. C. A. Stagg, *Mr. Madison's War: Politics, Diplomacy, and Warfare in the Early American Republic, 1793–1830* (Princeton: Princeton University Press, 1983), 176.

18. Russell F. Weigley, *History of the United States Army* (New York: Macmillan, 1967), 121.

19. Leland Winfield Meyer, *The Life and Times of Col. Richard M. Johnson of Kentucky* (New York: Columbia University Press, 1932), ch. 3; John K. Mahon, *The War of 1812* (Gainesville: University of Florida Press, 1972), 182–5; C. Edward Skeen, *Citizen Soldiers in the War of 1812* (Lexington: University Press of Kentucky, 1999), 90–3; Donald R. Hickey, *The War of 1812: A Forgotten Conflict* (Urbana: University of Illinois Press, 1989), 137–9; Stagg, *Mr. Madison's War*, 324–30.

20. Wilburt S. Brown, *The Amphibious Campaign for West Florida and Louisiana, 1814–1815* (University, AL: Tuscaloosa of Alabama Press, 1969), is a critical review of strategy and tactics at New Orleans; Robin Reilly, *The British at the Gates: The New Orleans Campaign in the War of 1812* (New York: Putnams, 1974). On the size of the Army, Weigley, *History of the United States Army*, 141–142.

21. Daniel Justin Herman, *Hunting and the American Imagination* (Washington, D.C.: Smithsonian Institution, 2001), 63 (quoted), 114–117.

22. Randy Roberts and James S. Olson, *A Line in the Sand: The Alamo in Blood and Memory* (New York: Simon Schuster, 2001).

23. Roberts and Olson, *Line in the Sand*, 180.

24. Russell F. Weigley, *Towards an American Army: Military Thought from Washington to Marshall* (New York: Columbia University Press, 1962), 39 (quoted); Marcus Cunliffe, *Soldiers and Civilians: The Martial Spirit in America, 1775–1865* (Boston: Little, Brown, 1968),155–6; Edward M. Coffman, *The Old Army: A Portrait of the American Army in Peacetime, 1784–1898* (Oxford: Oxford University Press, 1986), 46.

25. Richard M. McMurray, *Two Great Rebel Armies: an Essay in Confederate Military History* (Chapel Hill: University of North Carolina Press, 1989.

26. Cunliffe, *Soldiers and Civilians*, 75–7, 216–36 for this and the following two paragraphs.

27. Rod Andrew, Jr., *Long Gray Lines: The Southern Military School Tradition, 1839–1915* (Chapel Hill: University of North Carolina Press, 2001), 3, 19; Bruce Allardice, "West Points of the Confederacy: Southern Military Schools and the Confederate Army," *Civil War History*, 43 (1997): 310–31.

28. Weigley, *History of the United States Army*, 158–187; Oliver Knight, *Life and Manners in the Frontier Army* (Norman: University of Oklahoma Press, 1978), 93. On the frontier, see Francis Paul Prucha, *Broadax and Bayonet: The Role of the United States Army in the Development of the Northwest, 1815–1860* (Lincoln: University of Nebraska Press, 1953; repr., 1995).

29. Richard Bruce Winders, *Polk's Army: The American Military Experience in the Mexican War* (College Station, TX: Texas A&M University Press, 1997), 24–5, 54–7 (57 quoted).

30. Winders, *Polk's Army*, 68–9.

31. James M. McCaffrey, *Army of Manifest Destiny: The American Soldier in the Mexican War, 1846–1848* (New York: New York University Press, 1992), 117–29.

32. Jefferson Davis, Speech at Vicksburg, 10 November 1846, James T. McIntosh, et. al., eds., *The Papers of Jefferson Davis* (Baton Rouge: Louisiana State University Press, vol. 3, 1981), 82–3 (quoted); Joseph E. Chance, *Jefferson Davis's Mexican War Regiment* (Jackson: University Press of Mississippi, 1991).

33. Walter Prescott Webb, *The Texas Rangers: A Century of Frontier Defense* (Austin: University of Texas Press, 2nd. ed., 1965), 14. See also, Charles M. Robinson, III, *The Men who Wear the Star: The Story of the Texas Rangers* (New York: Random House, 2000), Part I: Samuel C. Reid, Jr., *The Scouting Expeditions of McCulloch's Texas Rangers* (Philadelphia: J. W. Bradley, 1860); David Lavender, *Climax at Buena Vista: The American Campaigns in Northeastern Mexico 1846–47* (Philadelphia: Lippincott, 1966), 33–5.

34. Quoted in Webb, *Texas Rangers*, 119.

35. "Lawless set": letter of 7 July 1846, quoted in Webb, *Texas Rangers*, 99; Robinson, *Men Who Wear the Star*, ch. 6; "licentious vandals": Stephen B. Oates, "Los Diablos Tejanos: The Texas Rangers in the Mexican War," *Journal of the West*, 9 (1970): 488; Justin H. Smith, *The War with Mexico* (New York: Macmillan, 1919), vol. 2, 212–3, 450; Charles Spurlin, "Ranger Walker in the Mexican War," *Military History of Texas and the Southwest* 9 (1971), 259–80.

36. L. Giddings, *Sketches of the Campaign in N. Mexico*, 221–2, quoted in Webb, *Texas Rangers*, 110.

37. Robert M. Utley, *Lone Star Justice: The First Century of the Texas Rangers* (New York: Oxford University Press, 2002), 74.

38. K. Jack Bauer, *The Mexican War, 1846–1848* (New York: Macmillan, 1974), 158 (quoted); Joseph G. Dawson, III, *Doniphan's Epic March: The 1st Missouri Volunteers in the Mexican War* (Lawrence, KS: University of Kansas

Press, 1999); Roger D. Launius, *Alexander William Doniphan, Portrait of a Missouri Moderate* (Columbia, MO: University of Missouri Press, 1997), ch. 4–9; George Winston Smith and Charles Judah, *Chronicles of the Gringos: The U.S. Army in the Mexican War, 1846–1848: Accounts of Eyewitnesses and Combatants* (Albuquerque: University of New Mexico Press, 1968), 31–3, 142–3; Smith, *The War with Mexico*, vol. 1, ch. 15.

39. Robert W. Johannsen, *To the Halls of the Montezumas: The Mexican War in the American Imagination* (New York: Oxford University Press, 1985), 123; William B. Green, *Letters from a Sharpshooter: The Civil War Letters of Private William of Greene Co., G., 2d United States Sharpshooters (Berdan's Army of the Potomac, 1861–1865)*, ed. W. H. Hastings (Belville, WI: Historical Publications, 1993), introduction and 192–3, 294–5, 298.

40. Smith, *War with Mexico*, vol. 2, 154–7.

41. Grady McWhiney and Perry D. Jamieson, *Attack and Die: Civil War Military Tactics and the Southern Heritage* (Tuscaloosa, AL: University of Alabama Press, 1982), 29.

42. Maj. Gen. Ethan Allen Hitchcock, *Fifty Years in Camp and Field* (New York: Putnam's, 1909), 298; Smith, *War with Mexico, vol. 2*, 143–5; Robert Selph Henry, *The War with Mexico* (Indianapolis: Bobbs-Merrill, 1950), 353–6.

43. Durwood Ball, *Army Regulars on the Western Frontier, 1848–1861* (Norman: University of Oklahoma Press, 2001), xx.

44. Ball, *Army Regulars*, xxi.

45. Ball, *Army Regulars*, ch. 2.

46. Ball, *Army Regulars*, 30 and 32, quoted in order.

47. Frederick S. Daniel, *Richmond Howitzers in the War* (Gaithersburg, MD: Butternett Press, 1891; repr. n.d.).

48. This and the following four paragraphs are based upon H. E. Aumale, *Les Zouaves et les Chasseurs à pied* (Paris: M. Legy, 1855); General Paul Azan, *L'Armée d'Afrique de 1830 à 1852* (Paris: Plon, 1936); Gen. R. Hure, ed., *L'Armée d'Afrique, 1830–1862* (Paris: Charles Lavauzelle, 1977), ch. 1; Gen. Jean J. G. Cler, *Reminiscences of an Officer of Zouaves* (New York: Appleton, 1860).

49. George B. McClellan, *The Armies of Europe* (Philadelphia: Lippincott, 1861), 61.

50. George N. Vourlojianis, *The Cleveland Grays: an Urban Military Company, 1837–1919* (Kent, OH: Kent State University Press, 2002), 20–1.

51. On American Zouaves: Col. E. E. Ellsworth, *The Zouave Drill* (Philadelphia: T. B. Peterson, 1861); Michael J. McAfee, *Zouaves: The First and the Bravest* (Gettysburg: Thomas Publications, 1991); Robin Smith, *American Civil War Zouaves* (London: Osprey, 1996), 6–10, 21; Cunliffe, Soldiers and Civilians, 241–7; Paddy Griffith, *Battle Tactics of the Civil War* (New Haven: Yale University Press, 1989), 101–2.

Chapter 4: The Civil War

1. General William T. Sherman, *Memoirs* (New York: Appleton, 1875), II, 384, is one of the few to comment on flank companies.

2. Captain Ujanirtus Allen, *Campaigning with 'Old Stonewall': Confederate Captain Ujanirtus Allen's Letters to His Wife*, ed. R. Allen and K. S. Bohannon (Baton Rouge: Louisiana State University Press, 1998), 289.

3. Charles B. Haydon, *For Country, Cause and Leader: The Civil War Journal of Charles B. Haydon*, ed. Stephen W. Sears (New York: Ticknor & Fields, 1993), November 1862, 1862.

4. Paddy Griffith, *Battle Tactics of the Civil War* (New Haven: Yale University Press, 1989), 148, 127, quoted in that order.

5. Quoted in John Hope Franklin, *The Militant South, 1800–1861* (Cambridge, MA: Harvard University Press, 1956), 2.

6. Lt. Col. James A. L. Fremantle, *The Fremantle Diary*, ed. Walter Lord (Boston: Little, Brown, 1954), 246–7.

7. Franklin, *Militant South*, 2–3, quoted; ch. 8 is entitled, "West Points of the South". Percentages: James M. McPherson, *Drawn with the Sword: Reflections on the American Civil War* (New York: Oxford University Press, 1996), ch. 1. The counter-argument notes that the South was closer to the scene of the Mexican War fighting, and it was simply easier to use Southern militia units. For further discussion, see Michael Barton, *Goodmen: The Character of Civil War Soldiers* (University Park: Pennsylvania State University Press, 1981), ch. 1, and, from the perspective of myths, literary and otherwise, William R. Taylor, *Cavalier and Yankee: The Old South and American National Character* (New York: George Braziller, 1961); Richard E. Nisbett and Dov Cohen, *Culture of Honor: The Psychology of Violence in the South* (Boulder, CO: Westview, 1996); Jack K. Williams, *Duelling in the Old South: Vignettes of Social History* (College Station, TX: Texas A&M University Press, 1980); Herman Hattaway and Archer Jones, *How the North Won: A Military History of the Civil War* (Urbana: University of Illinois Press, 1991), 172–3; Michael C. C. Adams, *Fighting for Defeat: Union Military Failure in the East, 1861–1865* (Lincoln: University of Nebraska Press, 1978, reprinted 1992), ch. 1–2; and Randall C. Jimerson, *The Private Civil War: Popular Thought During the Sectional Conflict* (Baton Rouge: Louisiana State University Press, 1988), particularly ch. 5 on perceptions of the enemy.

8. Marcus Cunliffe, *Soldiers and Civilians: The Martial Spirit in America, 1775–1865* (Boston: Little, Brown, 1968), especially ch. 10.

9. Dudley Taylor Cornish, *The Sable Arm: Black Troops in the Union Army, 1861–1865* (Lawrence, KS: University Press of Kansas, 1956, reprint 1987), 200.

10. Richard M. McMurry, *Two Great Rebel Armies: An Essay in Confederate Military History* (Chapel Hill: University of North Carolina Press,

1989), 5; Gary W. Gallagher, *The Confederate War* (Cambridge, MA: Harvard University Press, 1997), 95. This theme is further explored in Gallagher's *Lee and His Army in Confederate History* (Chapel Hill: University of North Carolina Press, 2001).

11. John Beatty, *Memoirs of a Volunteer, 1861–1863*, Harvey S. Ford, ed. (New York: Norton, 1946), 14.

12. Reid Mitchell, *Civil War Soldiers* (New York: Viking, 1988), 183; Gallagher, Confederate War, ch. 3. An argument similar to Mitchell's is H. Hattaway, A. Jones, and W. N. Still, Jr., *Why the South Lost the Civil War* (Athens, GA: University of Georgia Press, 1986), 64: "We contend that lack of will constituted the decisive deficiency in the Confederate arsenal."

13. Bell Irvin Wiley, *The Life of Johnny Reb: The Common Soldier of the Confederacy* (Baton Rouge: Louisiana State University Press, 1943), and *The Life of Billy Yank: The Common Soldier of the Union* (Baton Rouge: Louisiana State University Press, 1952). (Both have been reprinted.)

14. John M. Schofield, *Forty-Six Years in the Army* (Norman: University of Oklahoma Press, 1897; repr., 1998), 248.

15. Weigley, *History of the United States Army*, 199, 232.

16. Larry J. Daniel, *Soldiering in the Army of the Tennessee* (Chapel Hill: University of North Carolina Press, 1991), 24, 26; Earl J. Hess, *The Union Soldier in Battle: Enduring the Ordeal of Combat* (Lawrence, KS: University Press of Kansas, 1997), 55–6.

17. Weigley, *History of the United States Army*, 238.

18. J. Tracy Power, *Lee's Miserables: Life in the Army of Northern Virginia from the Wilderness to Appomattox* (Chapel Hill: University of North Carolina Press, 1998), 114–5 (both quotations); Hess, *Union Soldier in Battle*, 107.

19. Quoted in Ernest B. Furgurson, *Not War But Murder: Cold Harbor 1864* (New York: Knopf, 2001), 173.

20. Frank Wilkeson, *Turned Inside Out: Recollections of a Private Soldier in the Army of the Potomac* (Lincoln: University of Nebraska Press, 1886; repr; 1997), 120–1.

21. Haydon, *Country, Cause*, 13 April 1862, 220.

22. William Rhadamanthus Montgomery, *Georgia Sharpshooter: The Civil War Diary and Letters of . . .*, George Montgomery, ed. (Macon, GA: Mercer University Press, 1997), 82 (May 1863); see also 98 (27 November 1863).

23. Sgt. Edwin H. Fay, *"This Infernal War": The Confederate Letters of . . .*, Bell Irvin Wiley, ed. (Austin: University of Texas Press, 1958), 20 May 1862, 55.

24. John Walters, *Norfolk Blues: The Civil War Diary of the Norfolk Light Artillery Blues*, Kenneth Wiley, ed. (Shippensburg, PA: Burd Street Press, 1997), 161.

25. Roy M. Marcot, *Civil War Chief of Sharpshooters Hiram Berdan, Military Commander and Firearms Inventor* (Irvine, CA: Northwood Heritage Press, 1989), ch. 2 (22 quoted). The essential official history is Capt. C. A. Stevens, *Berdan's United States Sharpshooters in the Army of the Potomac, 1861–1865* (Dayton, OH: Morningside Bookshop, 1892; repr., 1984).

26. Wiley Sword, *Sharpshooter: Hiram Berdan, His Famous Sharpshooters and their Sharps Rifles* (Lincoln, R.I.: Andrew Mowbray, 1988), 10–11; Wyman S. White, *The Civil War Diary of . . . First Sergeant of Company F, 2nd United States Sharpshooter Regiment, 1861–1865*, Russell C. White, ed. (Baltimore: Butternut and Blue, 1993), 7–8.

27. William J. Miller, *The Training of an Army: Camp Curtain and the North's Civil War* (Shippensburg, PA: White Mane, 1990), 51; Raymond J. Herek, *These Men Have Seen Hard Service: The First Michigan Sharpshooters in the Civil War* (Detroit: Wayne State University Press, 1998), 9, 440 (n. 39), 456 (n. 140); Augustus Meyers, *Ten Years in the Ranks: U. S. Army* (New York: Arno Press, 1979 reprint of 1914 edition), 208. Marcot, *Berdan*, 46 (Colts).

28. White, *Diary*, 323–4.

29. White, *Diary*, 119; Marcot, Berdan is the best source on the unit's early history.

30. Wyman White, *Diary*, 119 ("high toned"); Sword, *Sharpshooter*, 45 ("somebody killed").

31. Sword, *Sharpshooter*, 42, 44–45, 61.

32. William F. Fox, *Regimental Losses in the American Civil War 1861–1865* (Dayton, OH: Morningside Bookshop, 1898; repr., 1985), 419 (quoted); Sword, *Sharpshooter*, 61 (Gettysburg veteran).

33. Furguson, *Not War but Murder*, 20, quoted; see also Warren Lee Goss, *Recollections of a Private: A Story of the Army of the Potomac* (New York: Crowell, 1890), 284.

34. Griffith, *Tactics*, 74; Sword, Sharpshooter, 61 (Green berets).

35. This and following three paragraphs based on Maj. W. S. Dunlop, *Lee's Sharpshooters: or, the Forefront of Battle* (Dayton, OH: Morningside House, 1988, reprint).

36. Dunlop, *Lee's Sharpshooters*, 18.

37. Quoted in Dunlop, *Lee's Sharpshooters*, 425–6.

38. Quoted in Dunlop, *Lee's Sharpshooters*, 361.

39. Paddy Griffith, "Civil War Cavalry: Missed Opportunities," *Military History Quarterly*, 1:3 (1989): 60–71 (65 quoted).

40. Griffith, "Civil War Cavalry," 65; McWhiney and Jamieson, *Attack and Die*, 133–4; Weigley, *History of the United States Army*, 239–40; William Woods Averell, *Ten Years in the Saddle: The Memoir of . . . 1851–1862* (San Rafael: Presidio Press, 1978), 333 (quoted). The most extensive study of cav-

alry—North or South—is Stephen Z. Starr, *The Union Cavalry in the Civil War*, 3 vols. (Baton Rouge: Louisiana State University Press, 1979–85); the introductory chapter to volume I is a detailed account of the Selma campaign.

41. Philip Katcher, *Union Cavalryman 1861–1865* (London: Osprey, 1995), 18.

42. Quoted in Griffith, *Battle Tactics*, 121.

43. Albert E. Castel, *William Clarke Quantrill: His Life and Times* (New York: Fell, 1962); Richard S. Brownlee, *Grey Ghosts of the Confederacy: Guerrilla Warfare in the West, 1861–1865* (Baton Rouge: Louisiana State University Press, 1958); Jeffry D. Wert, *Mosby's Rangers* (New York: Simon & Schuster, 1990); James A. Ramage, *Rebel Raider: The Life of General John Hunt Morgan* (Lexington: University Press of Kentucky, 1986); Jack Hurst, *Nathan Bedford Forrest: A Biography* (New York: Knopf, 1993); Stephen Z. Starr, *Jennison's Jayhawkers: A Civil War Cavalry Regiment and Its Commander* (Baton Rouge: Louisiana State University Press, 1973).

44. Darl L. Stephenson, *Headquarters in the Brush: Blazer's Independent Union Scouts* (Athens: Ohio University Press, 2001), 7 (Lee), 37 (quoted).

45. Powell A. Casey, "Early History of the Washington Artillery of New Orleans," *Louisiana History Quarterly* 23 (1940), 471–84; Peggy Robbins, "New Orleans' Finest: The Skillful and Stylish Washington Artillery," *Civil War Times Illustrated* 34 (1996):42–9; Robert C. Reinders, "Militia in New Orleans, 1853–1861," *Louisiana History* 3 (1962): 33–42; William Miller Owen, *In Camp and Battle with the Washington Artillery of New Orleans* (Boston: Ticknor, 1885), remains a very readable memoir. The fifth company: Nathaniel C. Hughes, Jr., *The Pride of the Confederate Artillery: The Washington Artillery in the Army of Tennessee* (Baton Rouge: Louisiana State University Press, 1997); Rice C. Bull, *Soldiering: The Civil War Diary of . . .*, K. Jack Bauer, ed. (San Rafael, CA: Presidio Press, 1977), 61.

46. John Walters, *Norfolk Blues: The Civil War Diary of the Norfolk Light Artillery Blues*, Kenneth Wiley, ed. (Shippensburg, PA: Burd Street Press, 1997), especially 2–14; Judith N. McArthur and O.V. Burton, *A Gentleman and an Officer: A Military and Social History of James B. Griffin's Civil War* (New York: Oxford University Press, 1996), 49–71; "kid glove": Larry J. Daniel, *Shiloh: The Battle that Changed the Civil War* (New York: Simon & Schuster, 1997), 93.

47. George N. Vourlojianis, *The Cleveland Grays: An Urban Military Company, 1837–1919* (Kent, OH: Kent State University Press, 2002), ch. 3 (41 quoted).

48. Wiley, *Life of Johnny Reb*, 246.

49. The background of the medical side is explored in Paul E. Seiner, *Disease in the Civil War: Natural Biological Warfare in 1861–1865* (Spring, IL: Charles C. Thomas, 1968), especially ch. 1. Healthier urban types were

notable in the cavalry as well: Starr, *Union Cavalry*, I:169.

50. This and the following two paragraphs are based on William L. Burton, *Melting Pot Soldiers: The Union's Ethnic Regiments* (New York: Fordham University Press, 1998).

51. Carl Schurz, *Reminiscences*, 3 vols. (New York: McClure, 1908), III:340.

52. Burton, *Melting Pot Soldiers*, 84.

53. Fox, *Regimental Losses*, 210; W. Mark McKnight, *Blue Bonnets O'er the Border: The 79th New York Cameron Highlanders* (Shippensburg, PA: White Mane Books, 1998).

54. Michael Bacarella, *Lincoln's Foreign Legion: The 39th New York Infantry—The Garibaldi Guard* (Shippensburg, PA: White Mane, 1996); Webb Garrison, *Mutiny in the Civil War* (Shippensburg, PA: White Mane, 2001), 178–9.

55. This and the following three paragraphs are based upon Michael J. McAfee, *Zouaves: The First and the Bravest* (Gettsyburg: Thomas Publications, 1991), and Robin Smith, *American Civil War Zouaves* (London: Osprey, 1996). Avengo Zouaves: Daniel, *Shiloh*, 93.

56. William C. Davis, *Battle at Bull Run* (Garden City, N.Y.: Doubleday, 1977), 207–8.

57. Meyers, *Ten Years in the Ranks*, 202 (quoted); Col. Charles S. Wainwright, *A Diary of Battle: The Personal Journals of . . . 1861–1865*, ed. Allan Nevin (Gettysburg: S. Clark Military Books, 1962), 36; Alfred Davenport, *Camp and Field Life of the Fifth New York Volunteer Infantry* (Duryee Zouaves) (New York: Dick and Fitzgerald, 1879), 93 ('Zoo-Zoo'), 110, 388, 423–4; Patrick A. Schroeder, *We Came to Fight: The History of the 5th New York Veteran Volunteer Infantry, Duryee's Zouaves (1863–1865)* (Brookneal, VA: Schroeder Productions, 1998, 30 (highest fatalities quoted).

58. Edward J. Hagerty, *Collis' Zouaves: The 114th Pennsylvania Volunteers in the Civil War* (Baton Rouge: Louisiana State University Press, 1997).

59. McAfee, *Zouaves*, 42.

60. Smith, *Zouaves*, 30.

61. John Beatty, *Memoirs of a Volunteer, 1861–1863*, H. S. Ford, ed. (New York: Norton, 1946), 81.

62. Gordon C. Rhea, *Cold Harbor: Grant and Lee, May 26–June 3, 1864* (Baton Rouge: Louisiana University Press, 2002), 302–3.

63. Ella Lonn, *Foreigners in the Union Army and Navy* (Baton Rouge: Louisiana State University Press, 1951), 140–2.

64. The brigade was not allowed to recruit after the battle, over Meagher's protests; Lonn, *Foreigners*, 598–9. A general account is D. Conyngham, *The Irish Brigade and Its Campaigns*, L. F. Kohl, ed. (New York: Fordham University Press, 1994); Captain Conyngham was a staff officer in the brigade. On the brigade's origins, 119–21.

65. William McCarter, *My Life in the Irish Brigade*, Kevin E. O'Birne, ed. (Campbell, CA: Savas Publications, reprint, c. 1996), 167 quoted (Sgt. McCarter was Meagher's clerk); McCleland's remarks are appended to the same volume, 225–6 (quoted). For Fredericksburg: Peter Welsh, *Irish Green and Union Blue: The Civil War Letters of . . ., Color Sergeant 28th Regiment Massachusetts Volunteers*, L. F. Kohl, ed. (New York: Fordham University Press, 1986).

66. St. Clair A. Mulholland, *The Story of the 116th Regiment Pennsylvania Volunteers in the War of the Rebellion*, L. F. Kohl, ed. (New York: Fordham University Press, 1996), introduction.

67. Cornish, *The Sable Arm*, especially 105, 154, and Joseph T. Glatthaar, *Forged in Battle: The Civil War Alliance of Black Soldiers and White Officers* (New York: Meridian, 1991), are standard references; William H. Leckie, *The Buffalo Soldiers: A Narrative of the Negro Cavalry in the West* (Norman: University of Oklahoma Press, 1967), 5 (180,000).

68. On the 54th, Luis F. Emilio, *A Brave Black Regiment: The History of the 54th Massachusetts, 1863–1865* (New York: Da Capo, 1995 reprint of 1894 1st edition); James M. McPherson, "The Glory Story," in his *Drawn with the Sword: Reflections on the American Civil War* (New York: Oxford University Press, 1996), ch. 7.

69. Gerald F. Linderman, *Embattled Courage: The Experience of Combat in the American Civil War* (New York: Free Press, 1987), 248; Hess, *Union Soldier in Battle*, 149; Warren Lee Goss, *Recollections of a Private: A Story of the Army of the Potomac* (New York: Crowell, 1890), 249 (quoted). On morale in general, see Peter Maslowski, "A Study of morale in Civil War Soldiers," in Peter Karsten, ed., *The Military in America from the Colonial Era to the Present* (New York: Free Press, 1980), 133–144.

70. Basic data in this and the following three paragraphs are from Fox, *Regimental Losses*, especially 5–6, 15.

71. Charles Winslow Elliott, *Winfield Scott: The Soldier and the Man* (New York: Macmillan, 1937), 719 (quote); Herman M. Hattaway, "The Civil War Armies: Creation, Mobilization, and Development," in Stig Forster and Jorg Nagler, On the Road to Civil War: The American Civil War and the German Wars of Unification, 1861–1871 (Cambridge: Cambridge University Press, 1997), 177.

72. Hattaway, "Civil War Armies," 178–9.

73. Letter of 3 August 1861, Gen. William T. Sherman, *Home Letters*, M. A. D. Howe, ed. (New York: Scribners, 1909), 211. T. W. Higginson, an amateur soldier who became colonel of the North's 1st South Carolina Regiment made a classic analysis of the value of trained officers; the essay is reprinted in Commager, *The Blue and the Gray*, vol. I, 482–7.

74. Fox, *Regimental Losses*, 420.

75. Armin Rappaport, "The Replacement System During the Civil War," in editors of Military Affairs, *Military Analysis of the Civil War* (Millwood, N.Y.: KTO Press, 1977), 115.

76. 15 December 1861, Haydon, *Country, Cause*, 148.

77. Maj. Abner R. Small, *The Road to Richmond: Civil War Memoirs . . . 16th Maine Volunteers* (Berkeley: University of California Press, 1939), 14.

78. Richard Weinert, Jr., *The Confederate Regular Army* (Shippensburg: White Mane, 1991).

79. Joseph T. Glatthaar, *The March to the Sea and Beyond: Sherman's Troops in the Savannah and Carolinas Campaigns* (New York: New York University Press, 1985), 20 and 15 quoted in that order.

80. Except where noted, remarks on the Stonewall and Iron Brigades are based on Jeffry D. Wert, *A Brotherhood of Valor: The Common Soldiers of the Stonewall Brigade, C.S.A.*, and the Iron Brigade, U.S.A. (New York: Simon & Schuster, 1999), 16 quoted. On the Stonewall Brigade, see also James I. Robertson, Jr., *The Stonewall Brigade* (Baton Rouge: Louisiana State University Press, 1963).

81. Wert, *Brotherhood of Valor*, 16.

82. Wert, *Brotherhood of Valor*, 38, 48 (both quoted).

83. Wert, *Brotherhood of Valor*, 234.

84. John Selby, *Stonewall Jackson as Military Commander* (London: Batsford, 1968), 27.

85. Martin Schenck, *Up Came Hill: The Story of the Light Division and Its Leaders* (Harrisburg, PA: Stackpole Books, 1958), 46; see also Gary W. Gallagher, "Confederate Corps Leadership on the First Day at Gettysburg: A. Hill and Richard S. Ewell in a Difficult Debut," in Gallagher, ed., *Three Days at Gettysburg: Essays on Confederate and Union Leadership* (Kent, OH: Kent State University Press, 1999), 25–43.

86. Allen, *Campaigning with 'Old Stonewall'*, 131 (27 July 1862); see also 140 (15 August 1862).

87. William Thomas Poague, *Gunner with Stonewall: Reminiscences*, M. F. Cockrell, ed. (Jackson, TN: McCowart-Merce, 1957), 30 and 50 (both quoted).

88. John Esten Cooke, *Stonewall Jackson and the Old Stonewall Brigade* (Charlottesville: University of Virginia Press, 1954), 51. (The quotation reads "Army of the Potomac," which is clearly in error.)

89. Robert K. Krick, "An Insurmountable Barrier between the Army and Ruin: The Confederate Experience at Spotsylvania's Bloody Angle," and Carol Reardon, "A Hard Road to Travel: The Impact of Continuous Operations in the Army of the Potomac and the Army of Northern Virginia in May, 1864," both in Gary W. Gallagher, ed., *The Spotsylvania Campaign* (Chapel Hill: University of North Carolina Press, 1998), 80–125, 170–201.

90. Robertson, *Stonewall Brigade*, viii; Wert, *Brotherhood of Valor*, 216. A detailed study is Gordon C. Rhea, *The Battles for Spotsylvania and the Road to Yellow Tavern, May 7–12, 1864* (Baton Rouge: Louisiana State University Press, 1997).

91. Power, *Lee's Miserables*, 37.

92. Steven J. Wright, "John Gibbon and the Black Hat Brigade," in Alan T. Nolan and Sharon Eggleston Vipond, eds., *Giants in Their Tall Black Hats: Essays on the Iron Brigade* (Bloomington: Indiana University Press, 1998), 53–66.

93. Wright, "John Gibbon," 55 and 57 (both quoted).

94. Dennis S. Lavery and Mark H. Jordan, *Iron Brigade General: John Gibbon, a Rebel in Blue* (Westport: Greenwood, 1993), 44 (quoted) 47.

95. John Gibbon, *Personal Recollections of the Civil War* (New York: Putnam's, 1928), 40.

96. Meyers, *Ten Years in the Ranks*, 130 (quoted). Hardee had spent 1841 at the Royal French Cavalry School; his hat was probably based on continental designs. Nathaniel Cheairs Hughes, Jr., *General William J. Hardee: Old Reliable* (Baton Rouge: Louisiana State University Press, 1992), 21, 52.

97. Wert, *Brotherhood of Valor*, 193–5, 242.

98. Quoted in Gaff, *Brave Men's Tears*, 39–40.

99. Wert, *Brotherhood of Valor*, 249–50.

100. Wright, "John Gibbon," 62; Sharon Eggleston Vipond, "'A New Kind of Murder': The Iron Brigade in the Wilderness," in Nolan and Vipond, *Giants in the Their Tall Black Hats*, 113–141.

101. Bragg quoted in Wright, "John Gibbon," 66. On this battle, Gaff, *Brave Men's Tears* (casualties, 190).

102. Schenck, *Up Came Hill*; James I. Robertson, Jr., *General A. Hill: The Story of a Confederate Warrior* (New York: Random House, 1987); Gallagher, "Confederate Corps Leadership on the First Day at Gettysburg," 25–43.

103. Webb Garrison, *Mutiny in the Civil War* (Shippensburg, PA: White Mane, 2001), 54–5.

104. Edward Cunningham, *The Port Hudson Campaign, 1862–1863* (Baton Rouge: Louisiana State University Press, 1963), 94–5 (quoted); John William DeForest, *A Volunteer's Adventures: A Union Captain's Record of the Civil War* (New Haven: Yale University Press, 1946), ch. 7–9; Brevet Brigadier General Willoughby Babcock, *Selections from the Letters and Diaries of* . . . (Albany: University of the State of New York, Division of Archives and History, 1922), 13, 31 (pride of place); St. Clair A. Mulholland, *The Story of the 116th Regiment Pennsylvania Volunteers in the War of the Rebellion*, L. F. Kohl, ed. (New York: Fordham University Press, 1996), 322–3 (Petersburg).

105. John Beatty, *Memoirs of a Volunteer, 1861–1863*, H. S. Ford, ed. (New York: Norton, 1946), October 1862, 140.

106. Peter Welsh, *Irish Green and Union Blue: The Civil War Letters of* . . . , L. F. Kohl and M. Richards, eds. (New York: Fordham University Press, 1986), 31 March 1863, 81.

107. Haydon, *Country, Cause*, 23 July 1862, 266; James I. Robertson, Jr., *Soldiers Blue and Gray* (Columbia, SC: University of South Carolina Press, 1989), 222–3; Linderman, *Embattled Courage*, 157–64.

108. The regiment's commander saw to it that only those who stayed actually received the medal. In 1916, the names of the 864 men were stricken from the rolls of Medal of Honor winners. The whole incident is discussed in detail in John J. Pullen, *A Shower of Stars: The Medal of Honor and the 27th Maine* (Philadelphia: Lippincott, 1966); see also U.S. Department of the Army, Public Information Division, *The Medal of Honor of the U.S. Army* (Washington: USGPO, 1948), ch. 1.

109. Charles Wellington Reed, *'A Grand Terrible Dramma [sic]': From Gettysburg to Petersburg: The Civil War Letters of* . . . . , E. A. Campbell, ed. (New York: Fordham University Press, 2000), 323–4, 375 (Meade presentation).

110. Col. Charles S. Wainwright, *A Diary of Battle: The Personal Journals of* . . . *1861–1865*, A. Nevin, ed. (Gettysburg: Swan Clark Military Books, 1962), 14 May 1863, 208; Adams, *Fighting for Defeat*, 139; John D. Billings, *Hardtack & Coffee: The Unwritten Story of Army Life* (Chicago: R. R. Donnelley, 1887; repr., 1960), 278–91. Veteran volunteers: Linderman, *Embattled Courage*, 262.

111. Walter H. Hebert, *Fighting Joe Hooker* (Indianapolis: Bobbs-Merrill, 1944), 178–9.

112. Lavery and Jordan, *Iron Brigade General*, 130–4; James I. Robertson, Jr., *Soldiers Blue and Gray* (Columbia, S.C.: University of South Carolina Press, 1989), 222–3; Linderman, *Embattled Courage*, 157–64; Meyers, *Ten Years in the Ranks*, 308 ("brevet horses").

113. Wert, *Mosby's Rangers*, 76.

114. Linderman, *Embattled Courage*, 174.

115. Griffith, *Battle Tactics*, 49–50 quoted; Carlton McCarthy, *Detailed Minutiae of Soldier Life in the Army of Northern Virginia, 1861–1865* (Lincoln: University of Nebraska Press, 1882; repr., 1993); Frank E. Vandiver, *Their Tattered Flags: The Epic of the Confederacy* (New York: Harper & Row, 1970), 305 (quoted). A valuable study of how that "simmering" process worked is Joseph Allan Frank and George A. Reaves, *"Seeing the Elephant": Raw Recruits at the Battle of Shiloh* (Westport, CT: Greenwood, 1989). Some interesting conclusions on training are drawn by Mark A. Weitz, "Drill, Training, and the Combat Performance of the Civil War Soldier: Dispelling the Myth of the Poor Soldier, Great Fighter," *Journal of Military History* 62 (1998), 263–89.

Chapter 5: From the Civil War to World War II

1. Russell F. Weigley, *History of the United States Army* (New York: Macmillan, 1967), ch. 12–13 (313 quoted); Jack D. Foner, *The United States Soldier Between Two Wars, 1865–1898: Army Life and Reforms* (New York: Humanities Press, 1970) (pensions, 6; desertions, 84); Robert M. Utley, *Frontier Regulars: The United States Army and the Indian, 1866–1891* (New York: Macmillan, 1973), ch. 1; Clarence C. Clendenen, *Blood on the Border: The United States Army and the Mexican Irregulars* (New York: Macmillan, 1969), and Michael L. Tate, *The Frontier Army in the Settlement of the West* (Norman: University of Oklahoma Press, 1999), are valuable surveys.

2. Russell F. Weigley, *Towards an American Army: Military Thought from Washington to Marshall* (New York: Columbia University Press, 1962), 85 quoted (on Mahan, ch. 4).

3. Weigley, *Towards an American Army*, ch. 7; Stephen E. Ambrose, *Upton and the Army* (Baton Rouge: Louisiana State University Press, 1964).

4. Michael S. Nieberg, *Making Citizen Soldiers: ROTC and the Ideology of American Military Service* (Cambridge: Harvard University Press, 2000), 20 (quoted)–21.

5. Weigley, *Towards an American Army*, ch. 8.

6. Weigley, *Towards an American Army*, 161.

7. Cited in Foner, *United States Soldier*, 112.

8. This paragraph based on William A. Dobak and Thomas D. Phillips, *The Black Regulars, 1866–1898* (Norman: University of Oklahoma Press, 2000), quote xvii.

9. Gerald F. Linderman, *Embattled Courage: The Experience of Combat in the American Civil War* (New York: Free Press, 1987), 273 (quoted); Weigley, *History*, 267 (engagements). On post-war reforms, see James L. Abrahamson, *America Arms for a New Century: The Making of a Great Military Power* (New York: Free Press, 1981); Jerry Cooper, *The Rise of the National Guard: The Evolution of the American Militia, 1865–1920* (Lincoln: University of Nebraska Press, 1997); and Timothy K. Nenniger, *The Leavenworth Schools and the Old Army: Education, Professionalism, and the Officer Corps of the United States Army, 1881–1918* (Westport, CT: Greenwood, 1978); Peter Karsten, "Armed Progressives: The Military Reorganizes for the American Century," in Karsten, ed., *The Military in America from the Colonial Era to the Present* (New York: Free Press, 1980), 229–271.

10. William R. Roberts, "Reform and Revitalization, 1890–1903," in Kenneth J. Hagan and William R. Roberts, eds., *Against All Enemies: Interpretations of American Military History from Colonial Times to the Present* (New York: Greenwood, 1986), 198–9, and in the same volume, Timothy K. Nenninger, "The Army Enters the Twentieth Century, 1904–1917," 226–8.

11. Utley, *Frontier Regulars*, 25. Remarks on Wagner are based upon

T. R. Brereton, *Educating the U.S. Army: Arthur L. Wagner and Reform, 1875–1905* (Lincoln: University of Nebraska Press, 2000).

12. Brereton, *Educating the U.S. Army*, 33.

13. Brereton, *Educating the U.S. Army*, 37.

14. Brereton, *Educating the U.S. Army*, 44.

15. Edward M. Coffman, *The War to End All Wars: The American Military Experience in World War I* (Lexington: University Press of Kentucky, 1968; repr., 1986, 264 (quoted); John S. D. Eisenhower, *Yanks: The Epic Story of the American Army in World War I* (New York: Free Press, 2001), 22; Clendenen, *Blood on the Border*, 142, 285–8.

16. Clendennen, *Blood on the Border*, 140.

17. Weigley, *History*, ch. 13; Walter Millis, *The Martial Spirit* (Cambridge, MA: Literary Guild of America, 1931), 215–8; Graham A. Cosmas, *An Army for Empire: The United States Army in the Spanish-American War* (Shippensburg, PA: White Mane, 2nd edition, 1994).

18. Roosevelt to Cabot Lodge, quoted in G. J. A. O'Toole, *The Spanish War: An American Epic—1898* (New York: Norton, 1984), 225. This and following paragraph: Peggy Samuels and Harold Samuels, *Teddy Roosevelt at San Juan: The Making of a President* (College Station: Texas A & M University Press, 1997).

19. There is much on Roosevelt and the image of the Rough Riders in Gerald F. Linderman, *The Mirror of War: American Society and the Spanish-American War* (Ann Arbor: University of Michigan Press, 1974).

20. Smythe, *Guerilla Warrior*, 57.

21. Joy S. Kasson, *Buffalo Bill's Wild West: Celebrity, Memory, and Popular History* (New York: Hill and Wang, 2000), 241, 269 (both quoted).

22. Richard Slotkin, *Gunfighter Nation: The Myth of the Frontier in Twentieth-Century America* (New York: Atheneum, 1992), 79–87 (83 quoted); Robert A Carter, *Buffalo Bill Cody: The Man Behind the Legend* (New York: John Wiley, 2000), ch. 7 (1899 program: 388).

23. Brian McAllister Linn, *The U.S. Army and Counterinsurgency in the Philippine War, 1899–1902* (Chapel Hill: University of North Carolina Press, 1989), 14.

24. Thomas W. Dunlay, *Wolves for the Blue Soldiers: Indian Scouts and Auxiliaries with the United States Army, 1860–90* (Lincoln: University of Nebraska Press, 1982), 8.

25. Dunlay, *Wolves*, ch. 2; Pershing: Frank E. Vandiver, *Black Jack: The Life and Times of John J. Pershing* (College Station: Texas A&M University Press, 1977) I, 99–104; Donald Smythe, *Guerilla Warrior: The Early Life of John J. Pershing* (New York: Scribner's, 1973), 23–4.

26. Col. H. B. Wharfield, *Apache Indian Scouts* (El Cahon, CA: privately printed, 1964), 1.

27. Herbert Molloy Mason, Jr., *The Great Pursuit* (New York: Random House, 1970), 68 quoting press release; Smythe, *Guerilla Warrior*, ch. 15. Mexican background: Joseph A. Stout, Jr. *Border Conflict: Villistas, Carrancistas, and the Punitive Expedition, 1915–1920* (Fort Worth: Texas Christian University Press, 1999).

28. 10th in Cuba: Herschel V. Cashin, *Under Fire with the Tenth U.S. Cavalry* (New York: Arno Press, 1969 reprint of 1899 1st ed.), and T. G. Steward, *The Colored Regulars in the United States Army* (New York: Arno Press, 1904; repr., 1969), especially ch. 11. Pershing was appointed to the 10th in 1893; he attempted to stay with the 6th, his old regiment. Vandivar, *Pershing*, vol. I, 125.

29. Smythe, *Guerilla War*, 227 (both quotes), and 232 (airplanes); Col. Frank Tompkins, *Chasing Villa: The Story Behind the Story of Pershing's Expedition into Mexico* (Harrisburg, PA: Military Service Pub. Co., 1934), appendices B-C, 236–54.

30. Tompkins, *Chasing Villa*, 209; Mason, *Great Pursuit*, 206–212; Stout, Border Conflict, 84–88; Haldeen Braddy, *Pershing's Mission in Mexico* (El Paso: Texas Western Press, 1966), 48–57.

31. Mason, *Great Pursuit*, 202.

32. Meirion and Susie Harries, *The Last Days of Innocence: America at War, 1917–1918* (New York: Random House, 1997), ch. 7; Gary Mead, The *Doughboys: America and the First World War* (Woodstock, NY: Overlook Press, 2000), 66–71; on conscription, see John Whiteclay Chambers, II, *To Raise an Army: The Draft Comes to Modern America* (New York: Free Press, 1987).

33. Major General Hunter Liggett, A.E.F.: *Ten Years Ago in France* (New York: Dodd, Mead, 1928), 55.

34. Harries, *Last Days*, ch. 8 (100 quoted).

35. Mead, *Doughboys*, 10–11; John S. D. Eisenhower, *Yanks: The Epic Story of the American Army in Work War I* (New York: Free Press, 2001), 54.

36. Eisenhower, *Yanks*, 28 quoted; Edward M. Coffman, *The War to End All Wars: The American Military Experience in World War I* (Oxford: Oxford University Press, 1968), 127, 179, 227, 363; "mythology": Frank E. Vandiver, *Black Jack: The Life and Times of John J. Pershing* (College Station, TX: Texas A&M University Press, 1977), II:687.

37. Arthur E. Barbeau and Florette Henri Barbeau, *The Unknown Soldiers: African-American Troops in World War I* (New York: Da Capo Press, 1974; repr., 1996, ch. 2.

38. Barbeau, *Unknown Soldiers*, 20 (quoted), 77–8.

39. Jennifer D. Keene, *Doughboys, the Great War, and the Remaking of America* (Baltimore: Johns Hopkins University Press, 2001), ch. 4; Barbeau, *Unknown Soldiers*, ch. 7; Bernard C. Nalty, *Strength for the Fight: A History*

of Black Americans in the Military (New York: Macmillan, 1986), ch. 7–8; Jack D. Foner, *Blacks and the Military in American History: New Perspectives* (New York: Praeger, 1974), ch. 6. Much information on the 371st is in Chester D. Heywood, *Negro Combat Troops in the World War: The Story of the 371st Infantry* (New York: Negro Universities Press, 1928; repr., 1969).

40. Barbeau, *Unknown Soldiers*, ch. 7; Coffman, *War to End All Wars*, 72–3, 231–2, 317–20, 355; Robert Lee Bullard, *Personalities and Reminiscences of the War* (Garden City, N.Y.: Doubleday, Page, 1925), 298; John J. Pershing, *My Experiences in the World War* (New York: Frederick A. Stokes, 1931), vol. 2, 228. In general, see Barbeau, *Unknown Soldiers*, ch. 4–5.

41. Harries, *Last Days*, 123.

42. Bullard, *Reminiscences*, 102–3.

43. Bullard, *Reminiscences*, ch. 7; Vandiver, *Black Jack*, II, 770–1.

44. Harries, *Last Days*, 234,239; Eisenhower, *Yanks*, 82, 84 (quoted); Coffman, *War to End Wars*, 234–7.

45. Harries, *Last Days*, ch. 21 (240 quoted); Coffman, *War to End Wars*, 148–9.

46. Eisenhower, *Yanks*, 89; Laurence Stallings, The Doughboys: *The Story of the AEF, 1917–1918* (New York: Harper, 1963), 63–71.

47. Stallings, *Doughboys*, 75 ("wart"); Harries, *Last Days*, ch. 21; Coffman, *War to End All Wars*, 156–8; Eisenhower, *Yanks*, ch. 3; Mead, *Doughboys*, ch. 12.

48. Quoted in Liggett, *Ten Years*, 57.

49. Allen R. Millett and Peter Maslowski, *For the Common Defense: a Military History of the United States of America* (New York: Free Press, 1984), 349.

50. Pershing, *My Experiences*, vol. I, 181. The standard account remains Robert B. Asprey, *At Belleau Wood* (Denton, TX: University of North Texas Press, 1965; repr., 1996n).

51. Ross quoted in Hames H. Hallas, *Doughboy War: The American Expeditionary Force in World War I* (Boulder: Lynn Rienner, 2000), 143.

52. Liggett, *Ten Years*, 130 quoted.

53. Robert H. Zieger, *America's Great War: World War I and the American Experience* (Boston: Rowman & Littlefield, 2000), 86 quoted.

54. Kenneth Finlayson, *An Uncertain Trumpet: The Evolution of U.S. Army Infantry Doctrine, 1919–1941* (Westport, Ct: Greenwood, 2001), 28–31. See Stefan T. Possony and Etienne Mantoux, "Du Picq and Foch: The French School," and Crane Brinton, Gordon A. Craig, and Felix Gilbert, "Jomini," both in Edward Meade Earle, ed., *Makers of Modern Strategy* (New York: Atheneum, 1941; repr., 1969), chapters 4 and 9, and John Shy, "Jomini," and Michael Howard, "Men Against Fire: The Doctrine of the Offensive in 1914," in Paret, ed., *Makers of Modern Strategy* (Princeton: Princeton University Press, 1986), ch. 6 and 18.

55. Mead, *Doughboys*, 242 quoted; Stallings, Doughboys, ch. 6.

56. Harries, *Last Days*, 254 quoted.

57. Liggett, *Ten Years*, 155 quoted; Harries, *Last Days*, 259.

58. Translation of captured letter quoted by Sgt. H. L. Fisher, 77th Division, in Hallas, *Doughboy War*, 302.

59. Harries, *Last Days*, 259.

60. Harries, *Last Days*, 261.

61. Coffman, *War to End All Wars*, 221–2 quoted.

62. Quoted in Floyd Gibbons, *"And They Thought We Wouldn't Fight"* (New York: Doran, 1918), 25, and in Hallas, *Doughboy War*, 98.

63. 1st Army document, 29 September 1918, quoted in Hallas, *Doughboy War*, 257.

64. Quoted in Mead, *Doughboys*, 189.

65. Stallings, *Doughboys*, 171 quoted (première classe).

66. Quoted in Coffman, *War to End All Wars*, 246.

67. Marin Marix Evans, ed., *American Voices of World War I: Primary Source Documents, 1917–1920* (London: Fitzroy Dearborn, 2001), 91.

68. Harries, *Last Days*, 320 quoted; Stallings, *Doughboys*, ch. 8.

69. Eisenhower, *Yanks*, ch. 15–16; Harries, *Last Days*, ch. 30.

70. Mead, *Doughboys*, 288 quoted; Harries, *Last Days*, 389.

71. Harries, *Last Days*, ch. 31–2; Eisenhower, *Yanks*, 251 quoted; Coffman, *War to End Wars*, ch. 10.

72. Harries, *Last Days*, 371–8; Coffman, *War to End Wars*, 324–5; Stallings, *Doughboys*, 195; Eisenhower, *Yanks*, 237.

73. Griffin quoted in Hallas, *Doughboy War*, 263.

74. Harries, *Last Days*, 312.

75. Stallings, *Doughboys*, 346–50; Harries, *Last Days*, 318–33.

76. Coffman, *War to End All Wars*, 297.

77. Department of the Army, *The Medal of Honor of the United States Army* (Washington, D.C.: USGPO 1948), 469.

78. United States Senate, Committee on Veterans' Affairs, *Medal of Honor Recipients 1863–1978*, Senate Doc. 96 Congress 1st Session 1979, part 1; Gilbert Grosvenor, "Insignia of the United States Armed Forces," *National Geographic Magazine* 83 (1943):433–9; no figures on DSC DSM, but rough calc. over 4,000 DSC and ca. 1,000 DSM.

79. Jennifer D. Keene, *Doughboys, the Great War, and the Remaking of America* (Baltimore: Johns Hopkins University Press, 2001), 58–9, 59 quoted.

80. Kyler quoted in Evans, *American Voices*, 106.

81. Herbert Molloy Mason, Jr., *The Lafayette Escadrille* (New York: Random House, 1964), 6–7.

82. Mason, *Lafayette Escadrille*, 51; Philip M. Flammer, *The Vivid Air: The Lafayette Escadrille* (Athens, GA: University of Georgia Press, 1981),

ch. 1. Thenault's role: Capt. Georges Thenault, *The Story of the Lafayette Escadrille* (Nashville: Battery Press, reprint ed. 1990), 14–16.

83. Mason, *Lafayette Escadrille*, 72, 225; James Norman Hall and Charles Bernard Nordhoff, *The Lafayette Flying Corps* (Port Washington, N.Y.: Kenikat Press, 1920; repr., 1948), vol. 1, 38–9. Hotel Chatham: Thenault, *Story of the Lafayette Escadrille*, 70 quoted.

84. Mason, *Lafayette Escadrille*, 148. The original Cigognes were only Escadrille N. 3, but the name had been adopted by the entire group, and indeed a stork in one form or another was a popular emblem with many French squadrons; Hall and Nordhoff, *Lafayette Flying Corps*, II, 73, quoting Charles J. Bittle, *The Way of the Eagle*; the same volume's plate 3 shows six separate stork squadron ensignia.

85. Flammer, *Lafayette Escadrille*, 97, 159.

86. Mason, *Lafayette Escadrille*, 154, and Flammer, *Lafayette Escadrille*, 122, have slightly different accounts of the logo's history. Thenault credits himself: *Story of the Lafayette Escadrille*, 103.

87. Mason, *Lafayette Escadrille*, 180–1. The Lafayette Escadrille should not be confused with the "Lafayette Flying Corps," which was originally a civilian American support group for the squadron, but became the umbrella organization for all Americans flying for France. Hall and Nordhoff, *Lafayette Flying Corps*, vol. I, is essentially a compendium of all such pilots' biographies.

88. Lufbury: Hall and Nordhoff, *Lafayette Flying Corps*, I, 328–9; Mason, *Lafayette Escadrille*, 289–90 (roster of squadron, victories, etc., 295–308); Flammer, *Lafayette Escadrille*, ch. 7 discusses transfer.

89. Flammer, *Lafayette Escadrille*, 22 and 91, quoted in that order.

90. Denis Winter, *The First of the Few: Fighter Pilots of the First World War* (Athens: University of Georgia Press, 1983), ch. 11 (Rickenbacker, 123). On the 94th, rather an elite unit in its own right, see Charles Woolley, *The Hat in the Ring Gang: The Combat History of the 94th Aero Squadron in World War I* (Atglen, PA: Schipper, 2001).

91. Kennett, *First Air War*, ch. 9 ("kreuzsmerz", 167). For a list of eighty-one recorded American aces (five or more confirmed kills), see James J. Hudson, *Hostile Skies: A Combat History of the American Air Service in World War I* (Syracuse: Syracuse University Press, 1968), 308–11.

92. Winter, *First of the Few*, using figures from Ira Jones, 45.

93. Capt. Edward V. Rickenbacker, *Fighting the Flying Circus* (Philadelphia: J. B. Lippincott, 1919), 43 and 245–6 quoted in that order.

94. Coffman, *The War to End All Wars*, 357–8; Robert K. Griffith, Jr., *Men Wanted for the U.S. Army: America's Experience with an All-Volunteer Army Between the World Wars* (Westport, CT: Greenwood, 1982), ch. 1–2. Siberia: Carol Willcox Melton, *Between War and Peace: Woodrow Wilson*

and the American Expeditionary Force in Siberia, 1918–1921 (Macon, GA: Mercer University Press, 2001).

95. William O. Odom, *After the Trenches: The Transformation of U.S. Army Doctrine, 1918–1919* (College Station, TX: Texas A&M University Press, 1999), ch. 1.

96. Odom, *After the Trenches*, ch. 6; Frank E. Vandiver, *Black Jack: The Life and Times of John J. Pershing* (College Station, TX: Texas A&M University Press, 1977), vol. 2, 1045–6.

97. Odom, *After the Trenches*, 42–3 (quoted), 76.

98. Finlayson, *An Uncertain Trumpet*, ch. 1 and 5–6, 78 and 107 (Fuqua) quoted, and 161 (Lynch quoted). On German methods, see Ibid., ch. 1, and Bruce I. Gudmundsson, *Stormtroop Tactics: Innovation in the German Army, 1914–1918* (New York: Praeger, 1989).

99. Odom, *After the Trenches*, 56–7.

100. Millett and Maslowski, *For the Common Defense*, 381–2.

101. Odom, *After the Trenches*, 63–5; Millett and Maslowski, *For the Common Defense*, 382 (blitz and krieg).

102. Griffith, *Men Wanted*, 59.

103. Griffith, *Men Wanted*, 66–7.

104. Odom, *After the Trenches*, 93.

105. Victor Vogel, *Soldiers of the Old Army* (College Station, TX: Texas A&M University Press, 1980), 28 (quoted), 55; V. R. Cardozier, *The Mobilization of the United States in World War II: How the Government, Military and Industry Prepared for War* (Jefferson, NC: McFarland, 1995), 73.

107. Vogel, *Soldiers*, 28, 104.

108. Odom, *After the Trenches*, ch. 6 (87 quoted).

109. Griffith, *Men Wanted*, ch. 2.

110. Vogel, *Soldiers*, 3, 98–9.

111. Odom, *After the Trenches*, ch. 6 and 11; 116 (quoted), 201.

112. Millett and Maslowski, *For the Common Defense*, 395; Cardozier, *Mobilization*, ch. 4; Griffith, *Men Wanted*, ch. 14; John K. Mahon, *History of the Militia and the National Guard* (New York: Macmillan, 1983), ch. 12.

Chapter 6: The United States Marine Corps

1. Basic sources on the Marines used here are Allan R. Millett, *Semper Fidelis: The History of the United States Marine Corps* (New York: Macmillan, 1980); Edwin Howard Simmons, *The United States Marines: A History* (Annapolis: Naval Institute Press, 3rd edition, 1998); Robert Debs Heinl, *Soldiers of the Sea: The U.S. Marine Corps, 1775–1962* (Annapolis: U.S. Naval Institute, 1962); and Clyde H. Metcalf, *A History of the United States Marine Corps* (New York: Putnam, 1939).

2. Charles R. Smith, *Marines in the Revolution: A History of the Conti-*

nental Marines in the American Revolution, 1775–1783 (Washington, D.C.: History and Museums Division, Headquarters, U.S. Marine Corps, 1975), 228.

3. Millett, *Semper Fidelis*, 24.

4. Heinl, *Soldiers of the Sea*, 5.

5. Heinl, *Soldiers of the Sea*, ch. 2; Millett, *Semper Fidelis*, ch. 2–3; Metcalf, *History*, ch. 2–6; Gabrielle M. Neufeld Santelli, *Marines in the Mexican War* (Washington, D.C.: History and Museums Division, Headquarters, USMC, 1991).

6. Heinl, *Soldiers of the Sea*, 73 (quoting the 15th Commandant, Maj. Gen. Ben H. Fuller), and 86 (numbers); Metcalf, *History*, ch. 8. On the south, Ralph W. Donnelly, *The Confederate States Marine Corps* (Shippensburg, PA: White Mane, 1989).

7. Simmons, *United States Marines*, 63–4.

8. Simmons, *United States Marines*, 59. For a picture of life in the Corps: Col. Frederick M. Wise and M. O. Frost, *A Marine Tells It to You* (Quantico: Marine Corps Association, 1921; repr., 1981), ch. 1–14.

9. Heinl, *Soldiers of the Sea*, 104 (the phrase comes from Lieut. H. S. Knapp).

10. Millett, *Semper Fidelis*, 133 (quoted); Jack Shulimson, The Marine Corps' *Search for a Mission, 1880–1898* (Lawrence, KS: University Press of Kansas, 1993); Metcalf, *History*, ch. 10.

11. Simmons, *History*, 77–8.

12. Quoted in Heinl, *Soldiers of the Sea*, 155; Simmons, History, 82.

13. Millett, *Semper Fidelis*, 144.

14. Simmons, *History*, 84; Heinl, *Soldiers of the Sea*, 151.

15. Heinl, *Soldiers of the Sea*, ch. 4; Millett, *Semper Fidelis*, ch. 5–6; Simmons, *History*, 6; Lt. Col. Kenneth J. Clifford (USMCR), *Progress and Purpose: A Developmental History of the United States Marine Corps, 1900–1970* (Washington, D.C.: History and Museums Division, Headquarters, USMC, 1973), ch. 1.

16. Heinl, *Soldiers of the Sea*, 191.

17. Quoted in Allan R. Millett, *In Many a Strife: General Gerald C. Thomas and the U.S. Marine Corps, 1917–1956* (Annapolis: Naval Institute Press, 1993), 20.

18. Heinl, *Soldiers of the Sea*, ch. 5 (207 quoted); Millett, *Semper Fidelis*, ch. 10–11. Much detail is to be found in the official history, Edwin N. McClellan, *The United States Marine Corps in the World War* (Nashville: Battery Press, 1920; repr., 1997).

19. Millett, *Semper Fidelis*, 291 and 290, quoted in that order.

20. Simmons, *History*, 97.

21. Meirion and Sussie Harries, *The Last Days of Innocence: America at War, 1917–1918* (New York: Random House, 1997), 251; Gary Mead, *The*

Doughboys: America and the First World War (Woodstock, N.Y.: Overlook Press, 2000), 245; Simmons, *History*, 98; Laurence Stallings, *The Doughboys: The Story of the AEF, 1917–1918* (New York: Harper, 1963), 88, all give slightly varying versions of this incident.

22. Heinl, *Soldiers of the Sea*, 203.

23. Eisenhower, *Yanks*, 144.

24. Heinl, *Soldiers of the Sea*, 203 (quoted)-204.

25. Harries, *Last Days of Innocence*, 257; Mead, *Doughboys*, 246–7.

26. This paragraph is based upon Robert Lindsay, *This High Name: Public Relations and the U.S. Marine Corps* (Madison: University of Wisconsin Press, 1956), ch. 2–6.

27. Millett, *Semper Fidelis*, 311 ("centerpiece"); Heinl, Soldiers of the Sea, 206–216.

28. Warren R. Jackson, *His Time in Hell: a Texas Marine in France* (Novato, CA: Presidio, 2001), 212.

29. Heinl, *Soldiers of the Sea*, 209.

30. Millett, *In Many a Strife*, 26–9.

31. Clifford, *Progress and Purpose*, ch. 2–3; Millett, *Semper Fidelis*, 252.

32. Major General John A. Lejeune, *The Reminiscences of a Marine* (Philadelphia: Dorrance, 1930), 115; on Lejeune, see Merril L. Bartlett, *Lejeune: A Marine's Life, 1867–1942* (Columbia, SC: University of South Carolina Press, 1991).

33. See George B. Clark, *Treading Softly: U.S. Marines in China, 1819–1949* (Westport, CT: Praeger, 2001). For a view of the interwar Corps, Brig. Gen. Robert Hugh Williams, *The Old Corps: A Portrait of the U.S. Marine Corps Between the Wars* (Annapolis: Naval Institute Press, 1982); Lt. Col. Jon T. Hoffman, *Chesty: The Story of Lieutenant General Lewis B. Puller, USMC* (New York: Random House, 2001), ch. 2–7.

34. Millett, *Semper Fidelis*, 440.

35. Foner, *Blacks and the Military*, 173.

36. Millett, *Semper Fidelis*, 373–4, 390–1, 439.

37. Charles L. Updegraph, Jr., *U.S. Marine Corps Special Units of World War II* (Washington, D.C.: History and Museums Division, Headquarters, USMC, 1972), 1–35; James Ladd, *Commandos and Rangers of World War II* (New York: St. Martins, 1978), ch. 6.

38. Both leaders have received considerable attention, with the edge to Edson: see Joseph H. Alexander, *Edson's Raiders: The 1st Marine Raider Battalion in World War II* (Annapolis: Naval Institute Press, 2001), and John T. Hoffman, *Once a Legend: "Red Mike" Edson of the Marine Raiders* (Novato, CA: Presidio, 1994).

39. General A. A. Vandergrift, *Once a Marine* (New York: Norton, 1964), 100.

40. General Holland M. Smith, *Coral and Brass* (New York: Scribners, 1949), 231.

41. Simmons, *History*, 131–2; Patrick K. O'Donnell, "Raid on Makin," *MHQ: Quarterly Journal of Military History*, 14:3 (Spring 2002), 56–9.

42. Updegraph, *Special Units*, 34, quoting December 1943 memo, Pacific Section, War Plans Division, Office of Chief of Navy Operations; Vandergrift, *Once a Marine*, 183, 241 (quoted)-2.

43. Updegraph, *Special Units*, 36–46.

44. Updegraph, *Special Units*, 38.

45. Updegraph, *Special Units*, 75.

46. Smith, *Coral and Brass*, 118.

Chapter 7: World War II: The Early Formation

1. Roger A. Beaumont, *Military Elites* (Indianapolis: Bobbs-Merrill, 1974), 44–6.

2. Beaumont, *Military Elites*, 2–3.

3. Beaumont, *Military Elites*, 4.

4. Beaumont, *Military Elites*, 6.

5. Beaumont, *Military Elites*, 7.

6. John Ellis, *The Sharp End: The Fighting Man in World War II* (New York: Scribners, 1980), 156 and 335 (quoted).

7. S. L. A. Marshall, *Men Against Fire: The Problem of Battle Command* (Norman: University of Oklahoma, 1947; repr., 2000), 56 quoted. An introduction to this edition by R. W. Glenn puts Marshall's book in a larger historiographical perspective. See, in particular, F. D. G. Williams, *SLAM: The Influence of S. L .A. Marshall on the United States Army* (Fort Monroe, VA: Office of the Command Historian, U.S.A. Training and Doctrine Command, 1990).

8. Clay Blair, *Ridgway's Paratroopers: The American Airborne in World War II* (New York: William Morrow, 1985), 26–27.

9. Leroy Thompson, *The All Americans: The 82nd Airborne* (Newton Abbott: David & Charles, 1988), ch. 2 for this and next paragraph.

10. Quoted in Patrick K. O'Donnell, *Beyond Valor: World War II's Ranger and Airborne Veterans Reveal the Heart of Combat* (New York: Free Press, 2001), 25.

11. Blair, *Ridgway's Paratroopers*, ch. 5; William B. Breuer, *Geronimo! American Paratroopers in World War II* (New York: St. Martin's, 1989), introduction; Thompson, *All Americans*, ch. 2.

12. Kurt Gabel, *The Making of a Paratrooper: Airborne Training and Combat in World War II* (Lawrence, KS: University Press of Kansas, 2nd edition 1990), 32, 49 (quoted), 54 (quoted, 56); Donald R. Burgett, *Currahee! A Screaming Eagle at Normandy* (New York: Dell, 1967; repr., 2000), chapter 1.

13. Thompson, *All Americans*, 19.

14. Breuer, *Geronimo!*, 7.

15. Gabel, *Making of a Paratrooper*, 127.

16. Breuer, *Geronimo!*, 9; Breuer believes that McNair's remark was one of "concealed admiration"; perhaps this was so, but as will be seen, McNair was not generally a supporter of elite units.

17. Thompson, *All Americans*, ch. 2; Blair, *Ridgway's Paratroopers*, ch. 4–5.

18. Blair, *Ridgway's Paratroopers*, 33, 304 (1944).

19. Blair, *Ridgway's Paratroopers*, 102 (27 percent), 197; Breuer, *Geronimo!*, ch. 6–8.

20. Blair, *Ridgway's Paratroopers*, 236.

21. Blair, *Ridgway's Paratroopers*, 295.

22. Blair, *Ridgway's Paratroopers*, ch. 34.

23. Blair, *Ridgway's Paratroopers*, part VI.

24. Blair, *Ridgway's Paratroopers*, parts VI-VII; O'Donnell, *Beyond Valor*, 271 (509th).

25. David Kenyon Webster, *Parachute Infantry: An American Paratrooper's Memoir of D-Day and the Fall of the Third Reich* (Baton Rouge: Louisiana State University Press, 1994), 155.

26. Blair, *Ridgway's Paratroopers*, ch. 47–48.

27. Robert Ross Smith, *Triumph in the Philippines* (Washington, D.C.: Center of Military History, 1963; repr., 1991), 44–8, 425, 570–1, 607.

28. Bradley Biggs, *The Triple Nickles* (North Haven, CT: Archon, 1986); Biggs was one of the unit's first officers. See also Charles E. Francis, *Tuskegee Airmen: The Story of the Negro in the U.S. Air Force* (Brookline Village, ME: Braden Press, 1948); Blair, Ridgway's Paratroopers, ch. 38.

29. Webster, *Parachute Infantry*, 260.

30. Gerard M. Devlin, *Silent Wings: The Saga of the U.S. Army and Marine Combat Glider Pilots During World War II* (New York: St. Martins, 1978), 48–9; on early glider developments, James E. Mrazek, *The Glider War* (New York: St. Martins, 1975), ch. 3; Milton Dank, *The Glider Gang: An Eyewitness History of World War II Glider Combat* (Philadelphia: Lippincott, 1977), ch. 2.

31. John L. Lowden, *Silent Wings at War: Combat Gliders in World War II* (Washington: Smithsonian Institution, 1992), 7.

32. Dank, *Glider Gang*, 52.

33. Dank, *Glider Gang*, ch. 2.

34. Devlin, *Silent Wings*, 107. Jump boots: C. Riddle, 325th Glider Infantry Regiment (82nd Airborne), testimony in Patrick K. O'Donnell, *Beyond Valor: World War II's Ranger and Airborne Veterans Reveal the Heart of Combat* (New York: Free Press, 2001), 157. On lack of infantry training, see Mrazek, *Glider War*, ch. 8. Dank, *Glider Gang*, 53, notes that some glider pilots were

attracted by flight pay, but this did not apply until mid-1944; "guts," 61.

35. Lowden, *Silent Wings at War*, 113.

36. Lowden, *Silent Wings at War*, 50 quoted. Dank, *Glider Gang*, 78, notes that only 54 of 144 gliders which set off landed in Sicily, and only four in the landing zones.

37. Devlin, *Silent Wings*, ch. 7–11 (Ike: 110–1); for more on Normandy, see Charles J. Masters, *Glidermen of NEPTUNE: The American D-Day Glider Attack* (Carbondale: Southern Illinois University Press, 1995).

38. Devlin, *Silent Wings*, 372–3.

39. Devlin, *Silent Wings*, ch. 6.

40. Shelford Bidwell, *The Chindit War: Stilwell, Wingate, and the Campaign in Burma, 1944* (New York: Macmillan, 1979), 64–5.

41. Devlin, *Silent Wings*, 67–72.

42. Devlin, *Silent Wings*, ch. 6.

43. James E. T. Hopkins, *Spearhead: A Complete History of Merrill's Marauder Rangers* (Baltimore: Galahad Press, 1999), 1–12; Charlton Ogburn, Jr., *The Marauders* (Greenwich, CT: Crest Books, 1964), 36–56.

44. Raymond Callahan, *Burma, 1942–1945* (London: Davids-Poynter, 1978), 151.

45. Hopkins, *Spearhead*, 66; ditty: Ogburn, *Marauders*, 66; train, 67.

46. Col. Charles N. Hunter, *Galahad* (San Antonio: Naylor, 1953), 4 (both quotes).

47. On the higher politics, Shelford Bidwell, *The Chindit War: Stilwell, Wingate, and the Campaign in Burma, 1944* (New York: Macmillan, 1979), especially ch. 5; Louis Allen, *Burma: The Longest War, 1941–45* (New York: St. Martin's, 1984), ch. 5; Shapley: Hopkins, *Spearhead*, caption, plate 3; Ogburn, *Marauders*, 73–4.

48. Hunter, *Galahad*, 1–2.

49. Gary J. Bjorge, *Merrill's Marauders: Combined Operations in Northern Burma in 1944* (Fort Leavenworth, KS: Combat Studies, U.S. Army Command and General Staff College, 1996), 9.

50. Hopkins, *Spearhead*, 82–3; Charles F. Romanus and R. Sunderland, *Stilwell's Command Problems* (Washington, D.C.: Office of Chief of Military History, Dept. of the Army, 1956), 34–5.

51. Hopkins, *Spearhead*, ch. 4 (quote, 61); Ogburn, *Merrill's Marauders*, 61–2.

52. Hopkins, *Spearhead*, 60. For a useful discussion of "10-in-1" and the difference between it and "K rations," see John Ellis, *The Sharp End: The Fighting Men in World War II* (New York: Scribners, 1980), 280–4.

53. Hopkins, *Spearhead*, ch. 35. On the Ledo Road, Leslie Anders, *The Ledo Road: General Joseph W. Stilwell's Highway to China* (Norman: University of Oklahoma Press, 1965).

54. Romulus, *Stilwell's Command Problems*, 233.

55. Bidwell, *Chindit War*, ch. 15; Hopkins, *Spearhead*, ch. 18.

56. Joseph W. Stilwell, *The Stilwell Papers*, ed. Theodore H. White (New York: William Sloane, 1948), 30 May and 15 June 1944 (p 301, 304); Hunter, *Galahad*, 124–7; Ogburn, *Marauders*, 279, had Stilwell in his sights, but did not fire; Allen, *Longest War*, 366–7. Stilwell did tell Lieutenant General Slim, but swore him to secrecy; Field Marshal the Viscount Slim, *Defeat into Victory* (New York: David McKay, 1961), 220. Boatner: Romanus, *Stilwell's Command Problems*, 248–9.

57. Hopkins, *Spearhead*, 68; Bjorge, *Merrill's Marauders*, 2; United States, War Department, Historical Division, *Merrill's Marauders (February–May 1944)* (Washington, D.C.: U.S. Government Printing Office, 1945), 23, 94.

58. Romanus, *Stilwell's Command Problems*, 240, quoting GALAHAD investigation by the Inspector General; Bidwell, Chindit War, 284 quoted; Hopkins, *Spearhead*, ch. 22 and 25, gives detailed medical evidence, especially on the failure to supply a mobile hospital, 619.

59. Bjorge, *Merrill's Marauders*, 45–6.

60. List in U.S. War Dept., *Merrill's Marauders*, 115–17 and Hopkins, *Spearhead*, 739–43.

61. Hopkins, *Spearhead*, 681.

62. Hopkins, *Spearhead*, 733; the badge is described in Ogburn, *Merrill's Marauders*, 262.

63. Hunter, *Galahad*, 1; his career: 198–9.

64. Anthony Arthur, *Bushmasters: America's Jungle Warriors of World War II* (New York: St. Martin's, 1987), is the source for this section.

65. Arthur, *Bushmasters*, 21.

66. Arthur, *Bushmasters*, 38.

67. Arthur, *Bushmasters*, 24 (25 percent: 187).

68. Daniel Ford, *Flying Tigers: Claire Chennault and the American Volunteer Group* (Washington, D.C.: Smithsonian Institution Press, 1991), 389–97.

69. Colonel Gregory "Pappy" Boyington, *Baa Baa Black Sheep* (Blue Ridge Summit, PA: TAB Books, 1958; repr., 1989), 16.

70. Jerome Klinkowitz, *With the Tigers over China, 1941–1942* (Lexington: University Press of Kentucky, 1999), 57–62.

71. Charles R. Bond, Jr., and Terry H. Anderson, *A Flying Tiger's Diary* (College Station, TX: Texas A&M University Press, 1984), 18–19; Major-General Claire Lee Chennault, *Way of a Fighter: Memoirs* (New York: Putnams, 1949), ch. 7.

72. Chennault, *Way of a Fighter*, ch. 8; Martha Byrd, *Chennault: Giving Wings to the Tiger* (Tuscaloosa, AL: University of Alabama Press, 1987), ch. 8.

73. Bond, *Diary*, Introduction; Klinkowitz, *With the Tigers*, ch. 1.

74. Chennault, Way of a Fighter, 112–6; Robert Lee Scott, Jr., *Flying Tiger: Chennault of China* (New York: Doubleday, 1959), 62–9; Boyington, *Baa Baa*, 41; Bond, *Diary*, 12–14; Klinkowitz, *With the Tigers*, 36 (quoted).

75. Ford, *Flying Tigers*, 270; Klinkowitz, With the Tigers, 94.

76. Bond, *Diary*, 214.

77. Bond, *Diary*, Epilogue.

78. Byrd, *Chennault*, 129.

79. James M. Merrill, *Target Tokyo* (Chicago: Rand McNally, 1964), ch. 1.

80. Merrill, *Target Tokyo,* 25.

Chapter 8: World War II: The Later War

1. Robert W. Black, *Rangers in World War II* (New York: Ivy Books, 1992), ch. 7; Michael J. King, *William Orlando Darby, a Military Biography* (Hamden, CT: Archon, 1981), 28; James Ladd, *Commandos and Rangers of World War II* (New York: St. Martins, 1978), ch. 7.

2. William O. Darby and William H. Baumer, *We Led the Way: Darby's Rangers* (San Rafael, CA: Presidio, 1980), 2–3; King, *Darby*, ch. 1.

3. Lieutenant General L. K. Truscott, *Command Mission: A Personal Story* (New York: Dutton, 1954), 40. Several other commanders have been credited with the name, including both Eisenhower, in Richard Garrett, *The Raiders* (New York: Van Nostrand, 1980), 154, and Mountbatten (Black notes the claim in Rangers, 16).

4. Michael J. King, *Rangers: Selected Combat Operations in World War II* (Fort Leavenworth, KS: Combat Studies Institute, U.S. Army Command and General Staff College, 1985), Leavenworth Papers, vol. 11, 7.

5. Darby, *We Led*, 26.

6. Darby, *We Led*, 27; Truscott, *Command Mission,* 39; 10 percent additional manpower was included in the original complement to allow for rejections, injuries, and dismissals.

7. Black, *Rangers*, chapters 2 (training) and 3 (a detailed account of the Rangers at Dieppe); King, *Rangers*, 8–9; King, *Darby*, 40.

8. Truscott, *Command Mission*, 37–8; Black, *Rangers*, ch. 4.

9. King, *Rangers*, 3.

10. Darby, *We Led*, 84.

11. King, *Darby*, ch. 3–7; Black, *Rangers*, ch. 4–5.

12. King, *Darby*, ch. 4; Black, *Rangers*, ch. 6–7; Darby, We Led, ch. 11.

13. Darby, *We Led*, 116; for further criticism, King, *Darby*, 144–5.

14. Darby, *We Led*, 174.

15. Ladd, *Commandos and Rangers*, ch. 11; Black, *Rangers*, ch. 8–12; Darby, *We Led*, Appendix B.

16. King, *Rangers*, ch. 6; Black, Rangers, ch. 14–15.

17. Ladd, *Commandos and Rangers*, ch. 13; Black, *Rangers*, ch. 13.

18. King, *Rangers*, 74.

19. King, *Darby*, 185.

20. King, *Rangers*, 75.

21. Discussion of the S&Rs is based upon John B. Dwyer, *Scouts and Raiders: The Navy's First Special Warfare Commandos* (Westport, CT: Praeger, 1993).

22. Dwyer, *Scouts and Raiders*, 171.

23. Cdr. Francis D. Fane and Don Moore, *Naked Warriors: The Story of the U.S. Navy's Frogmen* (New York: Appleton, 1956; repr., St. Martin's, 1996), is the principle source for this section; also useful is James Douglas O'Dell, *The Water is Never Cold: The Origins of the U.S. Navy's Combat Demolition Units, UDTs, and Seals* (Washington, D.C.: Brassey's, 2000), and Kevin Dockery, *Navy Seals: A History of the Early Years* (New York: Berkeley Books, 2001).

24. Fane, *Naked Warriors*, 18.

25. Fane, *Naked Warriors*, 66; ch. 6–7 on UTAH and the south of France.

26. Fane, *Naked Warriors*, ch. 8–17. "Red" Fane was designated to command UDT 13 in that operation; *Naked Warriors*, 230.

27. Joseph A. Springer, *The Black Devil Brigade: The True Story of the First Special Service Force, an Oral History* (Pacifica, CA: Pacifica Military History, 2001); Robert Todd Ross, *The Supercommandos: First Special Service Force, 1942–1944: An Illustrated History* (Atglen, PA: Schiffer Military History, 2000), ch. 1; Robert H. Adelman and Col. George Walton, *The Devil's Brigade* (Philadelphia: Chilton Books, 1966), ch. 1; Lt. Col. Robert D. Burhans, *The First Special Service Force: A War History of the North Americans, 1942–1944* (Washington, D.C.: Infantry Journal Press, 1947), ch. 1. Berhans, then a captain, was the 1st SSF Intelligence officer.

28. Ross, *Supercommandos*, 14–15; Adleman and Walton note that Churchill wanted the Canadians, *Devil's Brigade*, 53.

29. Burhans, *First Special Service Force*, 15–16; Ross, *Supercommandos*, ch. 2.

30. Adleman and Walton, *Devil's Brigade*, 49 quoted.

31. Ross, *Supercommandos*, 16 (quoted); Springer, Black Devil Brigade, 9; Brian Nolan, *Airborne: The Heroic Story of the 1st Canadian Parachute Battalion in the Second World War* (Toronto: Lester Publication Co., 1995), 36–7.

32. Burhans, *First Special Service Force*, 15–17; Springer, *Black Devil Brigade*, 19, quoted; Adleman and Walton, Devil's Brigade, ch. 3–4.

33. Springer, *Black Devil Brigade*, Introduction, quoted; Ross, *Supercommandos*, ch. 2; Burhans, First Special Service Force, ch. 2–3.

34. Burhans, *First Special Service Force*, 28–38; Springer, *Black Devil Brigade*, 46–8.

35. Burhans, *First Special Service Force*, 42; Springer, *Black Devil Brigade*, 48–52.

36. Burhans, *First Special Service Force*, 42; compare Ross, *Super-commandos*, 33 (15–16 men per section).

37. Burhans, *First Special Service Force*, 47.

38. Quoted in O'Donnell, *Beyond Valor*, 102.

39. Adleman and Walton, *Devil's Brigade*, ch. 5, makes the common claim that the 1st SSF was the only such unit. See also Ross, *Supercommandos*, ch. 3; Burhans, *First Special Service Force*, ch. 4.

40. Ross, *Supercommandos*, ch. 4–6 (p 128–136 includes a selection of Capa photos); Burhans, *First Special Service Force*, ch. 5–9.

41. Springer, *Black Devil Brigade*, 171.

42. Springer, *Black Devil Brigade*, 165; for illustration, Ross, *Supercommandos*, 188.

43. Ross, *Supercommandos*, 92; ch. 7–8 for Italy.

44. Ross, *Supercommandos*, ch. 9.

45. Springer, *Black Devil Brigade*, 255 quoted; Ross, *Supercommandos*, Epilogue.

46. Springer, *Black Devil Brigade*, 256.

47. Quoted in Ross, *Supercommandos*, 277; Burhans, *First Special Service Force*, ch. 10–12 cover the last months (p 322–376 includes a roster of all officers and men).

48. Ross, *Supercommandos*, 277–8.

49. Gavan Daws, *Shoal of Time: A History of the Hawaiian Islands* (Honolulu: University of Hawaii Press, 1968), 348–9; Masayo Umezawa Duus, *Unlikely Liberators: The Men of the 100th and 442nd* (Honolulu: University of Hawaii Press, 1987), 18; Hawaii Nikkei History Editorial Board (HNHEB), *Japanese Eyes, American Heart: Personal Reflections of Hawaii's World War II Nisei Soldiers* (Honolulu: Tenda Educational Foundation, 1998), testimony of Mike N. Tokunaga, 373.

50. Lyn Crost, *Honor by Fire: Japanese Americans at War in Europe and the Pacific* (Novato, CA: Presidio, 1994), 37; Duus, *Unlikely Liberators*, ch. 3.

51. Daws, *Shoal of Time*, 350 quoted.

52. Crost, *Honor by Fire*, 21; Duus, Unlikely Liberators, 58–70; Edward Joesting, *Hawaii: An Uncommon History* (New York: Norton, 1972), 321.

53. Jack K. Wakamatsu, *Silent Warriors: a Memoir of America's 442nd Regimental Combat Team* (New York: Vantage Press, 1995), ch. 4 (56 quoted); Edwin M. Nakasone, *The Nisei Soldier: Historical Essays on World War II and the Korean War* (White Bear Lake, MN: J-Press, 1999), 38; Orville C. Shirley, *Americans: The Story of the 442nd Combat Team* (Nashville: Battery Press, 1948; repr., 1998), ch. 1.

54. Uno is quoted in HNHEB, *Japanese Eyes*, 141 (Buddhaheads, 201).

55. Wakamatsu, *Silent Warriors*, ch. 5 (59 quoted).

56. HNHEB, Japanese Eyes, 75 quotes comment by Crost; Duus, *Unlikely Liberators*, ch. 5; Crost, *Honor by Fire*, ch. 8.

57. Wakamatsu, *Silent Warriors*, ch. 12; Chester Tanaka, *Go for Broke: A Pictorial History of the Japanese American 100th Infantry Battalion and the 442nd Regimental Combat Team* (Novato, CA: Presidio, 1982), 84–101; Crost, *Honor by Fire*, ch. 12; Joesting, Hawaii, 321; Duus, Unlikely Liberators, ch. 7; Nakasone, *Nisei Soldiers*, 41–2.

58. Jack D. Foner, *Blacks and the Military in American History: A New Perspective* (New York: Praeger, 1974), ch. 7 (p 132, 158 quoted).

59. Foner, *Blacks and the Military,* 160; Bernard C. Nalty, *Strength for the Fight: A History of Black Americans in the Military* (New York: Macmillan, 1986), ch. 11. A detailed history is Hondon B. Hargrove, *Buffalo Soldiers in Italy: Black Americans in World War II* (Jefferson, N.C.: McFarland, 1985).

60. General Mark C. Clark, *Calculated Risk* (New York: Harper, 1950), 220.

61. Lawrence Fuchs, *Hawaii Pono: A Social History* (New York: Harcourt, Brace, Jovanich, 1961), 306.

62. Crost, *Honor by Fire*, 331–2; Tanaka, *Go for Broke*, 146.

63. Seto is quoted in O'Donnell, *Beyond Valor*, 193.

64. Kent Roberts Greenfield, Robert R. Palmer, and Bell I. Wiley, *The Organization of Ground Combat Troops* (United States Army in World War II) (Washington, D.C.: Historical Division, Department of the Army, 1947), 339–50 for this and next paragraph.

65. Robert R. Palmer, Bell I. Wiley, and William R. Keast, *The Procurement and Training of Ground Combat Troops* (United States Army in World War II) (Washington, D.C.: Historical Division, Department of the Army, 1948), 441, 471n; Greenfield, *Organization*, 346–9.

66. Kenneth S. Templeton, 10th Mountain Division: America's Ski Troops (Chicago: privately printed, 1945), 15–16; Robert B. Ellis, *See Naples and Die: A World War II Memoir of a United States Army Ski Trooper in the Mountains of Italy* (Jefferson, N.C.: McFarland, 1996), ch. 1. On "Minnie" Dole, Hal Burton, *The Ski Troops* (New York: Simon & Schuster, 1971), ch. 4 (Burton had been skiing correspondent for the New York Daily News before enlisting in the 10th).

67. William Lowell Putnam, *Green Cognac: The Education of a Mountain Fighter* (New York: AAC Press, 1991), 8–9; Palmer, *Procurement*, 3–4; Greenfield, *Organization*, 38–40; Burton, *Ski Troops*, 93.

68. Burston, *Ski Troops*, ch. 7.

69. Ellis, *See Naples*, 9.

70. Putnam, *Green Cognac*, 10–11.

71. Letter quoted in Burton, *Ski Troops*, 98.

72. Ellis, See Naples, 9 (quoted), 23–32; Templeton, *10th Mountain Division*, 17.

73. Burton, *Ski Troops*, 143 quoted.

74. Roger A. Beaumont, *Military Elites* (Indianapolis: Bobbs-Merrill, 1974), 117; Burton, Ski Troops, ch. 8 ("Camp Hell," 124; pigeons, 125).

75. Ellis, *See Naples*, 80, 90; Clark, *Calculated Risk*, 417.

76. Putnam, *Green Cognac*, 90.

77. See official report on Riva Ridge of Lt. Col. Henry J. Hampton, reprinted in Harris Dusenbery, *The North Apennines and Beyond with the 10th Mountain Division* (Portland, OR: Binford & Mort, 1998), 177–200; Putnam, *Green Cognac*, ch. 11. A popular but still informative account by a participant is Frank Harper, *Night-Climb: The Story of the Skiing 10th* (New York: Longmans, 1946).

78. Field-Marshal Albert Kesselring, *Memoirs* (Novato, CA: Presidio, 1989), 221; Ellis, *See Naples*, 153; General Frido von Senger und Etterlin, *Neither Fear nor Hope* (New York: Dutton, 1964), 299.

79. Jake H. Thompson, *Bob Dole: The Republicans' Man for All Seasons* (New York: Donald Fine, 1996), ch. 2; Ellis, *See Naples*, ch. 6.

80. Ellis, *See Naples*, ch. 9, especially 254; Beaumont, *Military Elites*, 177 quoted. The later Italian operations may be followed in Ernest F. Fisher, Jr., *Cassino to the Alps* (US Army in World War II) (Washington, D.C.: Center of Military History, 1977).

81. K. R. Greenfield, et. al., eds., *The Organization of Ground Combat Troops (Army Ground Forces, vol. I)* (Washington, D.C.: Historical Division, Department of the Army, 1947), ch. 3. On the study of and response to the German model, see Thomas C. Mahnken, *Uncovering Ways of War: U.S. Intelligence and Military Innovation, 1918–1941* (Ithaca: Cornell University Press, 2002), ch. 2.

82. Roman Johann Jarymowycz, *Tank Tactics: From Normandy to Lorraine* (Boulder: Lynne Rienner, 2001), 27–31 (30 quoted).

83. Christopher R. Gabel, *Seek, Strike, and Destroy: U. S. Army Tank Destroyer Doctrine in World War II* (Fort Leavenworth, KS: Combat Studies Institute, U.S. Army Command and General Staff College, 1985), 11.

84. Greenfield, *Organization*, ch. 7 (74 quoted); Jarymowycz, Tank Tactics, 73–4; William O. Odom, *After the Trenches: The Transformation of U.S. Army Doctrine, 1918–1939* (College Station, TX: Texas A&M University Press, 1999), 151–2.

85. Greenfield, *Organization*, 84.

86. Odom, After the Trenches, 152–3; details on tanks from National Tank Destroyer Association (NTDA), *Tank Destroyer Forces, World War II* (Paducah, KY: Turner Publishing, 1992), 16–18, and Stephen J. Zaloga, U.S.

Tank Destroyers of World War II (New York: Arms and Armor Press, 1985).

87. NTDA, *Tank Destroyer Forces*, 38–9; Macksey, 124, 133; Zaloga.

88. Lido Mayo, *The Ordnance Department on Beachhead and Battle-front (U.S. Army in World War II: The Technical Services)* (Washington, D.C.: Center of Military History, 1968; repr., 1991), 37 quoted; Robert M. Citino, *Armored Forces: History and Sourcebook* (Westport, CT: Greenwood, 1994), 257, notes that the M1A1 was a good solution, but did not appear until after the war.

89. Jarymowycz, *Tank Tactics*, 74, 149, and 73 quoted in that order.

90. Mayo, *Ordnance*, 322, 325, 327; Gabel, *Seek*, 535; NTDA, *Tank Destroyers*, 40–1 (details on armor from appendices 3–4).

91. *Tank Destroyer Field Manual, 5-26-42* (Washington, D.C.: U.S. G.P.O., 1944), 7; part quoted in NTDA, *Tank Destroyers*, 16.

92. Gabel, *Seek*, 17.

93. NTDA, *Tank Destroyers*, 10–15 (14 quoted); Gabel, Seek, 17.

94. Gabel, *Seek*, 30–1 quoted.

95. Barney quoted in NTDA, *Tank Destroyers*, 34–5, *Manual*, 37.

96. Greenfield, *Organization*, 426–7.

97. Greenfield, *Organization*, 428 quoted.

98. Gabel, *Seek*, 46.

99. NTDA, *Tank Destroyers*, 44.

100. Roger A. Beaumont, *Military Elites* (Indianapolis: Bobbs-Merrill, 1974), 182–3.

101. Mayo, *Ordnance*, 327.

102. Gabel, *Seek*, 61 quoted.

103. NTDA, *Tank Destroyers*, 88–103; Gabel, Seek, 61–3.

104. Dennis D. Wainstock, *The Decision to Drop the Atomic Bomb* (Westport, CT: Praeger, 1996), 82–3; Gordon Thomas and Max M. Witts, *ENOLA GAY* (New York: Stein & Day, 1977), 52.

105. Leslie R. Groves, *Now It Can be Told: The Story of the Manhattan Project* (New York: Harper, 1962), 259.

106. Thomas and Witts, *ENOLA GAY*, 13–14; Vincent C. Jones, *Manhattan: The Army and the Atomic Bomb* (Washington, D.C.: Center of Military History, 1985), 621–3; Richard Rhodes, *The Making of the Atomic Bomb* (New York: Simon & Schuster, 1986), 582–3.

107. Peter Wyden, *Day One: Before Hiroshima and After* (New York: Simon & Schuster, 1984), 192.

108. Thomas and Witts, *ENOLA GAY*, 56; Jones, *Manhattan*, 521; Groves, *Now It Can Be Told*, 259–62.

109. Wyden, *Day One*, 198; Groves, *Now It Can Be Told*, 273–6 (275 quoted).

110. Wesley Frank Craven and James Lee Cate, eds., *The Army Air Forces*

in World War II (Washington, D.C.: Office of Air Force History, 1983 reprint of 1953 1st edition), vol. V, 713–15; Wainstock, *Decision*, 83–6; Rhodes, *Making of the Atomic Bomb*, Part III.

Chapter 9: Conclusion

1. Laurence Stallings, The *Doughboys*, (New York: Harper & Row, 1963), 273 quoted.

2. Lynn M. Homan and Thomas Reilly, *Black Knights: The Story of the Tuskegee Airmen* (Gretna, LA: Pelican Publishing, 2001), 118 quoted. See also Benjamin O. Davis, Jr., *Benjamin O. Davis, Jr.: American* (Washington, D.C.: Smithsonian Press, 1991); Lt. Col. Charles W. Dryden, *A-Train: Memoirs of a Tuskegee Airman* (Tuscaloosa: University of Alabama Press, 1997); and, in general, Ulysses Lee, *United States Army in World War II: The Employment of Negro Troops* (Washington, D.C.: Office of the Chief of Military History, United States Army, 1966). The one black bomber group, the 477th, which flew B-25s, never actually saw combat. (*Black Knights*, ch. 13). Black regulars: William A. Dobak and Thomas D. Phillips, *The Black Regulars, 1866–1898* (Norman: University of Oklahoma Press, 2000).

3. O'Donnell, *Beyond Valor*, 321.

Bibliography

This bibliography is intended primarily as a guide to further reading. Memoirs, diaries, biographies, official histories and document collections, together with studies of individual battles and single unit histories, are all excluded from this list, but titles of those I have used are given in the chapter notes. Titles of some published article collections are listed below, but individual contributions are cited only in the notes.

Adams, Michael, C. *Our Masters the Rebels: A Speculation on Union Military Failure in the East, 1861–1865*. Cambridge, MA: Harvard University Press, 1978.

———. *Fighting for Defeat: Military Failure in the East 1861–1865*. 1978. Reprint, Lincoln: University of Nebraska Press, 1992.

Allardice, Bruce. "West Points of the Confederacy: Southern Military Schools and the Confederate Army," *Civil War History,* 43 (1997): 310–31.

Ambrose, Stephen E. *Duty, Honor, Country: A History of West Point*, Baltimore: Johns Hopkins University Press, 1966.

———. *Upton and the Army*. Baton Rouge: Louisiana State University Press, 1964.

Anders, Leslie. *The Ledo Road: General Joseph W. Stillwell's Highway to China*. Norman: University of Oklahoma Press, 1965.

Anderson, Fred. *Crucible of War: The Seven Years' War and the Fate of Empire in British North America, 1754–1766*. New York: Knopf, 2000.

———. *A People 's Army: Massachusetts Soldiers and Society in the Seven Years' War*. Chapel Hill: University of North Carolina Press, 1984.

———. "Why did Colonial New Englanders Make Bad Soldiers?" *William & Mary Quarterly,* 31 vol. 38 (1981):395–417.

Andrew, Rod. J. *Long Grey Lines: The Southern Military School Tradition, 1839–1915*. Chapel Hill: University of North Carolina Press, 2001.

Armstrong, David A. *Bullets and Bureaucrats: The Machine Gun and the United States Army, 1861–1916.* Westport, CT: Greenwood, 1982.

Axtell, James. *The Invasion Within: The Contest of Cultures in Colonial North America.* New York: Oxford University Press, 1985.

Ball, Durwood. *Army Regulars on the Western Frontier, 1848–1861.* Norman: University of Oklahoma Press, 2001.

Barbeau, Arthur E., and Florette Henri. *The Unknown Soldiers: African-American Troops in World War I.* 1874. Reprint, New York: Da Capo Press, 1996.

Barton, Michael. *Goodmen: The Character of Civil War Soldiers.* University Park: Pennsylvania State University Press, 1981.

Bauer, K. Jack. *The Mexican War, 1846–1848.* New York: MacMillan, 1974.

Beaumont, Roger A. *Military Elites.* Indianapolis: Bobbs-Merrill, 1974.

Berg, Fred A. *Encyclopedia of Continental Army Units.* Harrisburg, PA: Stackpole, 1972.

Beringer, Richard E., Herman Hattaway, Archer Jones, and William N. Still, Jr. *Why the South Lost the Civil War.* Athens, GA: University of Georgia Press, 1986.

Bidwell, Shelford. *The Chindit War: Stillwell, Wingate, and the Campaign in Burma, 1944.* New York: Macmillan, 1979.

Billias, George A., ed. *George Washington's Generals.* New York: Morrow, 1964.

Billings, John D. *Hardtack and Coffee: The Unwritten Story of Army Life.* 1888. Reprint, Chicago: Lakeside Press, 1960.

Billington, Monroe L. *New Mexico's Buffalo Soldiers, 1866–1900.* Boulder: University Press of Colorado, 1991.

Black, Jeremy. *America as a Military Power: From the American Revolution to the Civil War.* Westport: Praeger, 2002.

Black, Robert W. *Rangers in World War II.* New York: Ivy Books, 1992.

Blair, Clay. *Ridgway's Paratroopers: The American Airborne in World War II.* New York: Morrow, 1985.

Bodle, Wayne. *The Valley Forge Winter: Civilians and Soldiers in War.* University Park: Pennsylvania State University Press, 2002.

Bolton, Charles K. *The Private Soldier Under Washington.* 1902. Reprint, Williamstown, MA: Corner House, 1976.

Boritt, Gabor. *Why the Confederacy Lost.* New York: Oxford University Press, 1992.

Bowman, Allen. *The Morale of the American Revolutionary Army.* Washington, D.C.: American Council on Public Affairs, 1953.

Braddy, Haldeen. *Pershing's Mission in Mexico.* El Paso: Texas Western Press, 1966.

Bradford, James C., ed. *Crucible of Empire: The Spanish American War and Its Aftermath.* Annapolis: Naval Institute Press, 1993.

Brandes, Ray, ed. *Troopers West: Military and Indian Affairs on the American Frontier.* San Diego: Frontier Heritage Press, 1970.

Breen, T. H., ed. *Partisans and Adventurers: Change and Persistence in Early America.* New York: Oxford University Press, 1980.

Brereton, T. R. *Educating the U.S. Army: Arthur L. Wagner and Reform, 1875–1905.* Lincoln: University of Nebraska Press, 2000.

Breuer, William B. *Geronimo! American Paratroopers in World War II.* New York: St. Martins, 1989.

Brown, M. L. *Firearms in Colonial America: The Impact on History and Technology, 1492–1792.* Washington, D.C.: Smithsonian Institute Press, 1980.

Brown, Richard M. *No Duty to Retreat: Violence and Values in American History and Society.* Norman: University of Oklahoma Press, 1991.

Brownlee, Richard S. *Gray Ghosts of the Confederacy: Guerilla Warfare in the West, 1861–1865.* Baton Rouge: Louisiana State University Press, 1958.

Brumwell, Stephen. *Redcoats: The British Soldier and War in the Americas, 1755–1763.* Cambridge: Cambridge University Press, 2002.

Buel, Richard, Jr. *Dear Liberty: Connecticut's Mobilization for the Revolutionary War.* Middleton, CT: Wesleyan University Press, 1980.

Burton, Art T. *Black, Buckskin, and Blue: African American Scouts and Soldiers on the Western Frontier.* Austin, TX: Eakin Press, 1999.

Burton, William L. *Melting Pot Soldiers: The Union's Ethnic Regiments.* New York: Fordham University Press, 1998.

Cardozier, V. R. *The Mobilization of the United States in World War II.* Jefferson, N.C.: McFarland, 1995.

Carey, A. Merwyn. *American Firearms Makers.* New York: Crowell, 1953.

Carroll, John M., and Colin F. Baxter, eds. *The American Military Tradition from Colonial Times to the Present.* Wilmington, DE: Scholarly Resources, 1993.

Carter, Robert A. *Buffalo Bill Cody: The Man Behind the Legend.* New York: Wiley, 2000.

Carter, Samuel, III. *The Last Cavaliers: Confederate and Union Cavalry in the Civil War.* New York: St. Martins, 1979.

Catton, Bruce. *Mr. Lincoln's Army.* Garden City: Doubleday, 1951.

———. *U. S. Grant and the American Military Tradition.* Boston: Little, Brown, 1954.

Chambers, John Whiteclay, II. *To Raise an Army: The Draft Comes to Modern America.* New York: Free Press, 1987.

Christian, Garna L. *Black Soldiers in Jim Crow Texas, 1889–1917.* College Station, TX: Texas A&M University Press, 1995.

Clark, George B. *Treading Softly: U.S. Marines in China, 1819–1949.* Westport: Praeger, 2001.

Clendennen, Clarence C. *Blood on the Border: The United States Army and the Mexican Irregulars.* New York: Macmillan, 1969.

Clifford, Kenneth J. *Progress and Purpose: A Developmental History of the U.S. Marine Corps, 1900–1970.* Washington, D.C.: USMC, History and Museums Division, 1973.

Coakley, Robert W. *The Role of Federal Military Forces in Domestic Disorders, 1788–1878.* Washington, D.C.: U.S. Army, Center of Military History, 1988.

Coffman, Edward M. "The American Regular Army Officer Corps Between the World Wars," *Armed Forces and Society*, 4 (1977): 55–73.

———. *The Old Army: A Portrait of the American Army in Peacetime, 1784–1898.* New York: Oxford University Press, 1986.

———. *The War to End All Wars: The American Military Experience in World War I.* New York: Oxford University Press, 1968.

Conway, Stephen. "To Subdue America: British Army Officers and the Conduct of the Revolutionary War," *William & Mary Quarterly*, 43 (1986): 381–407.

Cooper, Jerry. *The Rise of the National Guard: The Evolution of the American Militia, 1865–1920.* Lincoln: University of Nebraska Press, 1997.

Cope, Kevin L., ed. *George Washington in and as Culture.* New York: AMS Press, 2001.

Cornish, Dudley T. *The Sable Arm: Black Troops in the Union Army, 1861–1865.* Lawrence, KS: University Press of Kansas, 1956.

Cosmas, Graham A. *An Army for Empire: The United States Army in the Spanish-American War.* Columbus: University of Missouri Press, 1979.

Crackel, Theodore J. "The Founding of West Point: Jefferson and the Politics of Security," *Armed Forces and Society*, 7 (1981): 529–43

Cress, Lawrence D. *Citizens in Arms: The Army and the Militia in American Society to the War of 1812.* Chapel Hill: University of North Carolina Press, 1982.

Crost, Lyn. *Honor by Fire: Japanese Americans at War in Europe and the Pacific.* Novato, CA: Presidio, 1994.

Cunliffe, Marcus. *Soldiers and Civilians: The Martial Spirit in America, 1775–1865.* Boston: Little, Brown, 1968

Dederer, John M. *War in America to 1775: Before Yankee Doodle.* New York: New York University Press, 1990.

Devlin, Gerard M. *Silent Wings: The Saga of the U.S. Army and Marine Combat Glider Pilots During World War II.* New York: St. Martins, 1978.

Dobak, William A. and Thomas D. Phillips. *The Black Regulars, 1866–1898.* Norman: University of Oklahoma Press, 2001.

Dunlay, Thomas W. *Wolves of the Blue Soldiers: Indian Scouts with the United States Army, 1860–90.* Lincoln: University of Nebraska Press, 1982.

Dwyer, John B. *Scouts and Raiders: The Navy's First Special Warfare Commandos*. Westport: Praeger, 1993.

Eisenhower, John S. D. *Yanks: The Epic Story of the American Army in World War I*. New York: Free Press, 2001.

Eliot, Ellsworth, *West Point in the Confederacy*. New York: G. A. Baker, 1941.

Ferling, John E. "The New England Soldier: A Study in Changing Perceptions," *American Quarterly* 33 (1981): 26–4.

———. *A Wilderness of Miseries: War and Warriors in Early America*. Westport, CT: Greenwood, 1980.

Finlayson, Kenneth. *An Uncertain Trumpet: The Evolution of U.S. Army Infantry Doctrine, 1919–1941*. Westport: Greenwood, 2001.

Fitzpatrick, David J. "Emory Upton and the Citizen Soldier," *Journal of Military History* 65 (2001): 355–90.

Fleming, Thomas J. *West Point: The Men and Times of the United States Military Academy*. New York: Morrow, 1969.

Fletcher, Marvin. *The Black Soldier and Officer in the United States Army, 1891–1917*. Columbia: University of Missouri Press, 1974.

Foner, Jack D. *Blacks and the Military in American History: A New Perspective*. New York: Praeger, 1974.

———. *The United States Soldier Between Wars, 1865–1898*: *Army Life and Reforms*. New York: Humanities Press, 1970.

Forman, Sidney. *West Point: A History of the United States Military Academy*. New York: Columbia University Press, 1950.

Fowler, Arlen L. *The Black Infantry in the West, 1869–1891*. Norman: University of Oklahoma Press, 1996.

Fox, William F. *Regimental Losses in the American Civil War, 1861–1865*. 1898. Reprint, Dayton, OH: Morningside Bookshop, 1984.

Franco, Jere B. *Crossing the Pond: The Native American Effort in World War II*. Denton, TX: University of North Texas Press, 1999.

Franklin, John H. *The Militant South, 1800–1861*. Cambridge, MA: Harvard University Press, 1956.

Frey, Sylvia R. *The British Soldier in America: A Social History of Military Life in the Revolutionary Period*. Austin: University of Texas Press, 1981.

Gallagher, Gary W. *The Confederate War*. Cambridge: Harvard University Press, 1997.

———. *Lee and His Army in Confederate History*. Chapel Hill: University of North Carolina Press, 2001.

Galvin, John R. *The Minute Men: A Compact History of the Defenders of the American Colonies, 1645–1775*. New York: Hawthorne Books, 1967.

Ganoe, William Addleman. *The History of the United States Army*. New York: Appleton-Century, 1942.

Garrison, Webb. *Mutiny in the Civil War*. Shippensburg, PA: White Mane, 2001.

Geary, James W. *We Need Men: The Union Draft in the Civil War*. DeKalb: Northern Illinois University Press, 1991.

Glatthaar, Joseph T. *Forged in Battle: The Civil War Alliance of Black Soldiers and White Officers*. New York: Meridian, 1991.

Greene, Jack P., ed. *The American Revolution: Its Character and Limits*. New York: New York University Press, 1987.

Griffith, Paddy. *Battle Tactics of the Civil War*. New Haven: Yale University Press, 1989.

Griffith, Robert K., Jr. *Men Wanted for the U.S. Army: America's Experience with an All-Volunteer Army Between the World Wars*. Westport: Greenwood, 1982.

Gross, Robert A. *The Minutemen and Their World*. 1976. Reprint, New York: Hill & Wang, 2001.

Guthman, William H. *March to Massacre: A History of the First Seven Years of the United States Army, 1784–1791*. New York: McGraw-Hill, 1975.

Hagen, Kenneth J., and William R. Roberts, eds. *Against All Enemies: Interpretations of American Military History to the Present*. Westport: Greenwood, 1986.

Hagerman, Edward. *The American Civil War and the Origins of Modern Warfare: Ideas, Organization, and Field Command*. Bloomington: Indiana University Press, 1988.

Hallas, James H., ed. *Doughboy War: The American Expeditionary Force in World War I*. Boulder, CO: Lynne Rienner, 2000.

Hamilton, Edward *The French and Indian Wars*. New York: Doubleday, 1962.

———. *Fort Ticonderoga: Key to a Continent*. 1974. Reprint, New York: Fort Ticonderoga, 1995.

Hargreaves, Reginald. *The Bloodybacks: The British Serviceman in North America and the Caribbean, 1655–1783*. New York: Walder, 1968.

Harries, Meirion and Susie Harries. *The Last Days of Innocence: America at War, 1917–1918*. New York: Random House, 1997.

Harvey, Robert. *"A Few Bloody Noses": The Realities and Mythologies of the American Revolution*. Woodstock: Overlook, 2001.

Hattaway, Hennan, and Archer Jones. *How the North Won: A Military History of the Civil War*. Urbana: University of Illinois Press, 1991.

Heinl, Robert Debs, Jr. *Soldiers of the Sea: The U.S. Marine Corps, 1775–1962*. Annapolis: U.S. Naval Institute Press, 1962.

Heller, Charles E., and William A. Stofft, eds. *America's First Battles, 1776–1965*. Lawrence, KS: University Press of Kansas, 1986.

Herman, Daniel J. *Hunting and the American Imagination*. Washington, D.C.: Smithsonian Institute Press, 2001.

Hickey, Donald R. *The War of 1812: A Forgotten Conflict.* Urbana: University of Illinois Press, 1989.

Higginbotham, Don. "The Early American Way of War: Reconnaissance and Appraisal," *William & Mary Quarterly,* 44 (1987): 230–73.

———. *George Washington and the American Military Tradition.* Athens: University of Georgia Press, 1985.

———, ed. *Reconsiderations on the Revolutionary War: Selected Essays.* Westport, CT: Greenwood, 1978.

———. *War and Society in Revolutionary America: The Wider Dimensions of Conflict.* Columbia: University of South Carolina Press, 1988.

———. *The War of American Independence.* New York: Macmillan, 1971.

Higgins, W. Robert, ed. *The Revolutionary War in the South: Power, Conflict, and Leadershi* Durham, N.C.: Duke University Press, 1979.

Higham, Robin, ed. *Bayonets in the Streets: The Use of Troops in Civil Disturbances.* Lawrence, KS: University Press of Kansas, 1969.

Hoffman, Ronald, and Peter J. Albert, eds. *Arms and Independence: The Military Character of the American Revolution.* Charlottesville: University Press of Virginia, 1984.

Holl, Jim D. *The Minute Man in Peace and War: A History of the National Guard.* Harrisburg, PA: Stackpole, 1964.

Jacobs, James Ripley. *The Beginning of the U.S. Army, 1783–1812.* Princeton, N.J.: Princeton University Press, 1947.

Jamieson, Perry D. *Crossing the Deadly Ground: United States Army Tactics, 1865–1899.* Tuscaloosa: University of Alabama Press, 1994.

Jarymowycz, Roman R. *Tank Tactics: From Normandy to Lorraine.* Boulder, CO: Lynne Rienner, 2001.

Johannsen, Robert W. *To the Halls of the Montezumas: The Mexican War in the American Imagination.* New York: Oxford University Press, 1985.

Johnson, Herbert A. *Wingless Eagle: U.S. Army Aviation Through World War I.* Chapel Hill: University of North Carolina Press, 2001.

Jones, Archer. *Civil War Command and Strategy: The Process of Victory and Defeat.* New York: Free Press, 1992.

Kammen, Michael. *A Season of Youth: The America Revolution and the Historical Imagination.* New York: Knopf, 1978.

Karsten, Peter, ed. *The Military in American from the Colonial Era to the Present.* New York: Free Press, 1980.

Kasson, Joy S. *Buffalo Bill's Wild West.* New York: Hill and Wang, 2000.

Keefer, Louis E. *Scholars in Foxholes: The Story of the Army Specialized Training Program in World War II.* Jefferson, N.C.: McFarland, 1998.

Keene, Jennifer D. *Doughboys, the Great War, and the Remaking of America.* Baltimore: Johns Hopkins University Press, 2001.

Knollenberg, Bernhard. *Washington and the Revolution: A Reappraisal.* New York: Macmillan, 1940.

Kohn, Richard H. *Eagle and Sword: The Federalists and the Creation of the Military Establishment in America, 1783–1802.* New York: Free Press, 1975.

Krulak, Victor H. *First to Fight: An Inside View of the U.S. Marine Corps.* Annapolis: Naval Institute Press, 1984.

Kwasny, Mark V. *Washington's Partisan War, 1775–1783.* Kent, OH: Kent State University Press, 1996.

Ladd, James. *Commandos and Rangers of World War II.* New York: St. Martins, 1978.

Leach, Douglas Edward. *Arms for Empire: A Military History of the British Colonies in North America, 1607–1763.* New York: Macmillan, 1973.

———. *Flintlock and Tomahawk: New England in King Philip's War.* New York: Macmillan, 1958.

———. *The Northern Colonial Frontier, 1607–1763.* New York: Holt, Rinehart and Winston, 1966.

———. *Roots of Conflict: British Armed Forces and Colonial Americans, 1677–1763.* Chapel Hill: University of North Carolina Press, 1986.

Leckie, William H. *The Buffalo Soldiers.* Norman: University of Oklahoma Press, 1967.

Leonard, Thomas C. *Above the Battle: War-Making in America from Appomattox to Versailles.* New York: Oxford University Press, 1978.

Lepore, Jill. *The Name of War: King Philip's War and the Origins of American Identity.* New York: Knopf, 1998.

Linderman, Gerald F. *Embattled Courage: The Experience of Combat in the American Civil War.* New York: Macmillan, 1987.

———. *The Mirror of War: American Society and the Spanish-American War.* Ann Arbor: University of Michigan Press, 1974.

Lindsay, Robert. *This High Name: Public Relations and the U.S. Marine Corps.* Madison: University of Wisconsin Press, 1956.

Linn, Brian M. *Guardians of Empire: The U.S. Army and the Pacific, 1902–1940.* Chapel Hill: University of North Carolina Press, 1997.

———. *The Philippine War, 1899–1902.* Lawrence, KS: University Press of Kansas, 2000.

———. *The U.S. Army and Counterinsurgency in the Philippine War, 1899–1902.* Chapel Hill: University of North Carolina Press, 1989.

Lohn, Ella. *Desertion During the Civil War.* 1928. Reprint, Lincoln: University of Nebraska Press, 1998.

———. *Foreigners in the Union Army and Navy.* Baton Rouge: Louisiana State University Press, 1951.

Mackesy, Piers. *The War for America, 1775–1783.* Cambridge, MA: Harvard University Press, 1965.

Mahnken, Thomas G. *Uncovering Ways of War: U.S. Intelligence and Foreign*

Military Innovation, 1918–1941. Ithaca, N.Y.: Cornell University Press, 2002.

Mahon, John K. "Anglo-American Methods of Indian Warfare, 1676–1794," *Mississippi Valley Historical Review,* 45 (1958): 254–75.

———. *History of the Militia and National Guard.* New York: Macmillan, 1983.

———. *The War of 1812.* Gainesville: University of Florida Press, 1972.

Malone, Patrick M. *The Skulking Way of War: Technology and Tactics Among the New England Indians.* Lanham, MD: Madison Books, 1991.

Martin, James K., and Mark E. Lender. *A Respectable Army: The Military Origins of the Republic, 1763–1789.* Arlington Heights, IL: Harlan Davidson, 1982.

Martin, Joseph *Private Yankee Doodle.* Boston: Little, Brown, 1962.

McCaffrey, James M. *Army of Manifest Destiny: The American Soldier in the Mexican War, 1846–1848.* New York: New York University Press, 1992.

McClellan, Edwin N. *The United States Marine Corps in the World War.* 1920. Reprint, Nashville: Battery Press, 1997.

McPherson, James M. *Drawn with the Sword: Reflections on the American Civil War.* New York: Oxford University Press, 1996.

McWhiney, Grady, and Perry D. Jamieson. *Attack and Die: Civil War Military Tactics and the Southern Heritage.* Tuscaloosa, AL: University of Alabama Press, 1982.

Mead, Gary. *The Doughboys: America and the First World War.* Woodstock, N.Y.: Overlook Press, 2000.

Metcalf, Clyde H. *A History of the United States Marine Corps.* New York: Putnam, 1939.

Miller, Stuart. *"Benevolent Assimilation": The American Conquest of the Philippines, 1899–1903.* New Haven: Yale University Press, 1982.

Millett, Allan R. *The General: Robert L. Bullard and Officership in the United States Army, 1881–1925.* Westport, CT: Greenwood, 1975.

———. *In Many a Strife: General Gerald C. Thomas and the U.S. Marine Corps, 1917- 1956.* Annapolis: Naval Institute Press, 1993.

———. *Semper Fiedlis: The History of the United States Marine Corps.* New York: Macmillan, 1980.

———. and Peter Maslowski. *For the Common Defense: A Military History of the United States of America.* New York: Free Press, 1984.

Mitchell, Reid. *Civil War Soldiers.* New York: Viking, 1988.

Montross, Lynn. *Rag, Tag and Bobtail: The Story of the Continental Army, 1775–1783.* New York: Harper, 1952.

Morris, James M. *America's Armed Forces: A History.* New York: Prentice Hall, 2nd ed., 1996.

Morrison, James L., Jr. *"The Best School in the World": West Point, the Pre-*

Civil War Years, 1833–1866. Kent, OH: Kent State University Press, 1986.

Musicant, Ivan. *The Banana Wars: A History of United States Military Intervention in Latin America from the Spanish-American War to the Invasion of Panama.* New York: Macmillan, 1990.

Myers, Minor, Jr. *Liberty Without Anarchy: A History of the Society of the Cincinnati.* Charlottesville: University Press of Virginia, 1983.

Nalty, Bernhard C. *Strength for the Fight: A History of Black Americans in the Military.* New York: Macmillan, 1986.

Neiberg, Michael S. *Making Citizen-Soldiers: ROTC and the Ideology of American Military Service.* Cambridge, MA: Harvard University Press, 2000.

Neimeyer, Charles *America Goes to War: A Social History of the Continental Army.* New York: New York University Press, 1996.

Nenninger, Timothy K. *The Leavenworth Schools and the Old Army: Education, Professionalism and the Officer Corps of the United States Army, 1881–1918.* Westport, CT: Greenwood, 1978.

Nester, William R. *The First Global War: Britain, France and the Fate of North America, 1756–1775.* Westport, CT: Praeger, 2000.

Newcomer, Lee N. *The Embattled Farmers: A Massachusetts Countryside in the American Revolution.* New York: King's Crown Press, 1953.

Nisbett, Richard E. and Dov Cohen. *Culture of Honor: The Psychology of Violence in the South.* Boulder, CO: Westview, 1996.

Odom, William O. *After the Trenches: The Transformation of U.S. Army Doctrine, 1918- 1919.* College Station: Texas A&M University Press, 1999.

O'Leary, Cecilia E. *To Die For: The Paradox of American Patriotism.* Princeton, N.J.: Princeton University Press, 1999.

O'Toole, G. J. A. *The Spanish War: An American Epic, 1898.* New York: Norton, 1984.

Palmer, John M. *America in Arms: The Experience of the United States with Military Organization.* New Haven, CT: Yale University Press, 1941.

Pappas, George S. *Prudens Futuri: The U.S. Army War College, 1901–1967.* Carlisle Barracks, PA: Alumni Association of the U.S. Army War College, 1967.

Parkman, Francis. *Montcalm and Wolfe.* New York: Collier, 1962.

Pearlman, Michael D. *Warmaking and American Democracy: The Struggle over Military Strategy, 1700 to the Present.* Lawrence: University Press of Kansas, 1999.

Peckham, Howard H. *The Colonial Wars, 1689–1762.* Chicago: University of Chicago Press, 1964.

Peterson, Harold L. *Arms and Armor in Colonial America, 1526–1783.*

Harrisburg, PA: Stackpole, 1956.

Purcha, Francis Paul. *Broadax and Bayonet: The Role of the United States Army in the Development of the Northwest, 1815–1860.* Lincoln: University Nebraska Press, 1953.

———. *The Sword of the Republic: The United States Army on the Frontier, 1783–1846.* Lincoln: University of Nebraska Press, 1969.

Reardon, Carol. *Soldiers and Scholars: The U.S. Army and the Uses of Military History, 1865–1920.* Lawrence: University Press of Kansas, 1990.

Reid, John *In Defiance of the Law: The Standing Army Controversy, the Two Constitutions, and the Coming of the American Revolution.* Chapel Hill: University of North Carolina Press, 1981.

Rickey, Don, Jr. *Forty Miles a Day on Beans and Hay: The Enlisted Soldier Fighting the Indian Wars.* Norman: University of Oklahoma Press, 1963.

Robson, Eric. *The American Revolution in Its Political and Military Aspects, 1763–1783.* New York: Norton, 1966.

Rosa, Joseph G. *Wild Bill Hickok: The Man and the Myth.* Lawrence: University Press of Kansas, 1996.

Ross, Steven. *From Flintlock to Rifle: Infantry Tactics, 1740–1866.* Cranberry, NJ: Associated University Press, 1979.

Rossie, Jonathan G. *The Politics of Command in the American Revolution.* Syracuse: Syracuse University Press, 1975.

Royster, Charles. *The Destructive War: William Tecumseh Sherman, Stonewall Jackson, and the Americans.* New York: Knopf, 1991.

———. *Light-Horse Harry Lee and the Legacy of the American Revolution.* New York: Knopf, 1981.

———. *A Revolutionary People at War: The Continental Army and American Character, 1775–1783.* Chapel Hill: University of North Carolina Press, 1979.

Russell, Carl *Guns on the Early Frontiers.* Lincoln: University of Nebraska Press, 1957.

Ryan, Garry D. and Timothy K. Nenninger, eds. *Soldiers and Civilians: The U.S. Army and the American People.* Washington, D.C.: National Archives and Records Administration, 1987.

Satterlee, L. D., and Arcadi Gluckman. *American Gun Makers.* Buffalo, N.Y.: Otto Ulbrich, 1940.

Schultz, Eric B., and Michael J. Tougias. *King Philip's War.* Woodstock, VT: Countryman Press, 1999.

Selesky, Harold E. *War and Society in Colonial Connecticut.* New Haven, CT: Yale University Press, 1990.

Shannon, Fred Albert. *The Organization and Administration of the Union Army, 1861–1869.* 2 vols. Cleveland: A. H. Clark, 1928.

Showalter, Dennis E. "Evolution of the U.S. Marine Corps as a Military Elite,"

Marine Corps Gazette 63 (1979): 44–57.

Shulimson, Jack. *The Marine Corps' Search for a Mission, 1880–1898.* Lawrence, KS: University Press of Kansas, 1993.

Shy, John. *A People Numerous and Armed: Reflections on the Military Struggle for American Independence.* New York: Oxford University Press, 1976.

Skeen, C. Edward. *Citizen Soldiers in the War of 1812.* Lexington: University Press of Kentucky, 1999.

Skelton, William B. *An American Profession of Arms: The Army Officer Corps, 1784- 1861.* Lawrence, KS: University Press of Kansas, 1992.

Smith, George W., and Charles Judah. *Chronicles of the Gringos: The U.S. Army in the Mexican War, 1846–1848.* Albuquerque: University of New Mexico Press, 1968.

Smith, Justin H. *The War with Mexico.* 2 vols. New York: Macmillan, 1919.

Stagg, J. C. A. *Mr. Madison's War: Politics, Diplomacy and Warfare in the Early American Republic, 1783–1830.* Princeton, N.J.: Princeton University Press, 1983.

Stallings, Laurence. *The Doughboys: The Story of the AEF, 1917–1918.* New York: Harper & Row, 1963.

Starkey, Armstrong. *European and Native American Warfare, 1675–1815.* Norman: University of Oklahoma Press, 1998.

Starr, Stephen Z. *The Union Cavalry in the Civil War.* 3 vols. Baton Rouge: Louisiana State University Press, 1979–85.

Steward, T. G. *The Colored Regulars in the United States Army.* 1904. Reprint, New York: Arno Press, 1969.

Stout, Joseph A., Jr. *Border Conflict: Villistas, Carrancistas and the Punitive Expedition, 1915–1920.* Fort Worth: Texas Christian University Press, 1999.

Sword, Wiley. *President Washington's Indian War: The Struggle for the Old Northwest, 1790–1795.* Norman: University of Oklahoma Press, 1985.

Taylor, William R. *Cavalier and Yankee: The Old South and American National Character.* 2nd ed. Cambridge, MA: Harvard University Press, 1979.

Titus, James. *The Old Dominion at War: Society, Politics and Warfare in Late Colonial Virginia.* Columbia: University of South Carolina Press, 1991.

Trask, David F. *The War with Spain in 1898.* Lincoln: University of Nebraska Press, 1981.

Upton, Emory. *The Military Policy of the United States.* 3rd ed. Washington, D.C.: Government Printing Office, 1910.

Utley, Robert M. *Frontier Regulars: The United States Army and the Indian, 1866–1891.* New York: Macmillan, 1973.

———. *Frontiersmen in Blue: The United States Army and the Indian, 1848–*

1865. New York: Macmillan, 1967.

———. *The Indian Frontier of the American West, 1846–1890*. Albuquerque: University of New Mexico Press, 1984.

———. *Lone Star Justice: The First Century of the Texas Rangers*. New York: Oxford University Press, 2002.

Wallace, Willard M. *Appeal to Arms: A Military History of the American Revolution*. New York: Harper, 1951.

Ward, Christopher. *The War of the Revolution*. 2 vols. New York: Macmillan, 1952.

Webb, Walter R. *The Texas Rangers: A Century of Frontier Defense*. 2nd ed. Austin: University of Texas Press, 1965.

Weems, John E. *To Conquer a Peace: The War Between the United States and Mexico*. New York: Doubleday, 1974.

Weigley, Russell F. *The American Way of War*. New York: Macmillan, 1973.

———. *History of the United States Army*. New York: Macmillan, 1967.

———. *Towards an American Army: Military Thought from Washington to Marshall*. New York: Columbia University Press, 1962.

Weitz, Mark A. "Drill, Training, and the Combat Performance of the Civil War Soldier." *Journal of Modern History,* 62 (1998): 263–289.

Wiley, Bell I. *The Life of Billy Yank: The Common Soldier of the Union*. Baton Rouge: Louisiana State University Press, 1952.

———. *The Life of Johnny Reb: The Common Soldier of the Confederacy*. Baton Rouge: Louisiana State University Press, 1943.

Williams, David. *Johnny Reb's War: Battlefield and Homefront*. Abilene, TX: McWhiney Foundation Press, 2000.

Williams, Jack K. *Duelling in the Old South: Vignettes of Social History*. College Station: Texas A&M University Press, 1980.

Winders, Richard Bruce. *Polk's Army: The American Military Experience in the Mexican War*. College Station: Texas A&M University Press, 1997.

Winton, Harold R., and David R. Mets, eds. *The Challenge of Change: Military Institutions and New Realities, 1918–1941*. Lincoln: University of Nebraska Press, 2000.

Wooster, Robert. *The Military and United States Indian Policy, 1865–1903*. Lincoln: University of Nebraska Press, 2000.

———. *Soldiers, Sutlers, and Settlers: Garrison Life on the Texas Frontier*. College Station: Texas A&M University Press, 1987.

Wright, John W. "The Rifle in the American Revolution." *American Historical Review* 29 (1924): 293–9.

Wright, Robert K., Jr. *The Continental Army*. Washington, D.C.: U.S. Army Center of Military History, 1983.

Wyatt-Brown, Bertram. *Southern Honor: Ethics and Behavior in the Old South*. New York: Oxford University Press, 1982.

Zedric, Lance Q., and M. F. Dilley. *Elite Warriors: 300 Years of America 's Best Fighting Troops.* Ventura, CA: Pathfinder, 1996.

Zieger, Robert J. *America's Great War: World War I and the American Experience.* Boston: Rowman and Littlefield, 2000.

Index

About The Author

Briton Cooper Busch, Ph.D., was William R. Kenan, Jr. professor of history at Colgate University in Hamilton, New York until his death in 2004.